Lecture Notes in Computer Science 7857

Commenced Publication in 1973
Founding and Former Series Editors:
Gerhard Goos, Juris Hartmanis, and Jan van Leeuwen

Armin Biere   Amir Nahir   Tanja Vos (Eds.)

Hardware and Software: Verification and Testing

8th International
Haifa Verification Conference, HVC 2012
Haifa, Israel, November 6-8, 2012
Revised Selected Papers

 Springer

Volume Editors

Armin Biere
Johannes Kepler University, 4040 Linz, Austria
E-mail: biere@jku.at

Amir Nahir
IBM Research Laboratory, 31905 Haifa, Israel
E-mail: nahir@il.ibm.com

Tanja Vos
Universidad Politecnica de Valencia, 46022 Valencia, Spain
E-mail: tvos@dsic.upv.es

ISSN 0302-9743   e-ISSN 1611-3349
ISBN 978-3-642-39610-6   e-ISBN 978-3-642-39611-3
DOI 10.1007/978-3-642-39611-3
Springer Heidelberg Dordrecht London New York

Library of Congress Control Number: 2013943016

CR Subject Classification (1998): D.2.4-5, D.3.1, F.3.1-2, D.2.11, I.2.2-3

LNCS Sublibrary: SL 2 – Programming and Software Engineering

Typesetting: Camera-ready by author, data conversion by Scientific Publishing Services, Chennai, India

Printed on acid-free paper

Springer is part of Springer Science+Business Media (www.springer.com)

Preface

This volume contains the proceedings of the Haifa Verification Conference (HVC 2012). The conference was hosted by IBM Research Haifa and took place during November 6–8, in 2012. It was the eighth event in this series of annual conferences dedicated to advancing the state of the art and state of practice in verification and testing.

The conference provided a forum for researchers and practitioners from academia and industry to share their work, exchange ideas, and discuss the future directions of testing and verification for hardware, software, and complex hybrid systems. In 2012, HVC extended the traditional focus on hardware and software verification to include verification, validation, and testing (VVT) of complex hybrid systems as a part of the systems-engineering paradigm.

The Intel DTS Symposium and a meeting of the COST Action IC0901 Rich-Model Toolkit were co-located events. The conference itself started with a tutorial day including "Idiom-Based Verification of Highly Concurrent Data Structures Using Temporal Separation Logic" by Noam Rinetzky, "Three-Valued Abstraction-Refinement" by Sharon Shoham Buchbinder, "Simulating Cyber-Physical Systems Using SysML and Numerical Simulation Tools" by Eldad Palachi, and on "Improving Verification Productivity with the Dynamic Load and Reseed Methodology" by Marat Teplitsky.

The Program Committee accepted 18 regular papers out of 36 submissions, whose post-conference versions are published in this volume. The conference chairs further selected three poster presentations out of four poster submissions submitted after the notification for regular papers.

The conference featured a keynote with the title "On Behavioral Programming" by David Harel and another keynote talk on "Verifying Real-Time Software Is Not Reasonable (Today)" by Edward Lee. There were two invited talks on "Reducing Costs While Increasing Quality" by Orna Raz and on "SMT in Verification, Modeling, and Testing at Microsoft" by Nikolaj Bjorner. The last day contained a session on security verification with talks on "A Vulnerability or a Bug? What's the Difference Anyway? Security Software Verification as Part of the Development Lifecycle" by Ofer Maor, another talk on "Formal Analysis of Security Data Paths in RTL Design" by Jamil Mazzawi, and a third presentation on "Simultaneous Information Flow Security and Circuit Redundancy in Boolean Gates" by Ryan Kastner.

The HVC Award, granted since 2007, recognizes the most promising academic and industrial contribution to the fields of testing and software and hardware verification from the last five years. The HVC 2012 Award Committee, chaired by Daniel Kroening, decided to give the 2012 award to Aaron R. Bradley of CU Boulder for the invention of the IC3 algorithm. Aaron Bradley gave the award talk on the last day of the conference.

The Best Paper was selected by the Conference Chairs and awarded to Vasco Pessanha, Ricardo Dias, and João Lourenço for their paper with entitled "Precise Detection of Atomicity Violations."

The Conference Chairs would like to thank the members of the Program Committee for their hard work reading the papers and writing reviews under a very tight schedule during essentially one month in July and August 2012.

We are very grateful to IBM Research – Haifa for hosting and sponsoring HVC 2012.

April 2013   Armin Biere
                                                                Amir Nahir
                                                                Tanja Vos

Organization

Program Committee

Cyrille Valentin Artho	AIST, Japan
Armin Biere	Johannes Kepler University Linz, Austria
Roderick Bloem	Graz University of Technology, Austria
Radu Calinescu	Aston University, UK
Hana Chockler	IBM Research - Haifa, Israel
Kerstin Eder	University of Bristol, UK
Maria Jose Escalona	University of Seville, Spain
Eitan Farchi	IBM Research - Haifa, Israel
Harry Foster	Mentor Graphics, USA
Franco Fummi	University of Verona, Italy
Alex Goryachev	IBM Research - Haifa, Israel
Ziyad Hanna	University of Oxford, UK
Mark Harman	University College London, UK
Ian Harris	University of California Irvine, USA
Klaus Havelund	Jet Propulsion Laboratory, USA
Michael Hsiao	Virginia Tech, USA
Alan Hu	University of British Columbia, Canada
Zurab Khasidashvili	Intel, Israel
Mark Last	Ben-Gurion University, Israel
João Lourenço	CITI - Universidade Nova de Lisboa, Portugal
Ken Mcmillan	Cadence Berkeley Labs, USA
Thomas Melham	Oxford University, UK
Amir Nahir	IBM Research - Haifa, Israel
Martina Seidl	Johannes Kepler University Linz, Austria
Onn Shehory	IBM Research - Haifa, Israel
Armando Tacchella	Università di Genova, Italy
Helen Treharne	University of Surrey, UK
Shmuel Ur	Consultant, Israel
Helmut Veith	Vienna University of Technology, Austria
Tanja Vos	Researcher, Spain
Li-C Wang	University of California Santa Barbara, USA
Joachim Wegener	Berner & Mattner, Germany
Heike Wehrheim	University of Paderborn, Germany

Additional Reviewers

Baars, Arthur
Bustan, Doron
Chen, Wen
Egly, Uwe
Finkbeiner, Bernd
Heljanko, Keijo
Heule, Marijn
Hjort, Hakan
Hofferek, Georg
Ivrii, Alexander
Jacobs, Swen
Johnson, Kenneth

Kikuchi, Shinji
Koenighofer, Bettina
Koenighofer, Robert
Korchemny, Dmitry
Nadel, Alexander
Ryvchin, Vadim
Schremmer, Alexander
Sinn, Moritz
Steenken, Dominik
Timm, Nils
Vizel, Yakir
Wolfovitz, Guy

Table of Contents

On Behavioral Programming

David Harel

The Weizmann Institute

The talk starts from a dream/vision paper I published in 2008, whose title, *"Can Programming be Liberated, Period?"*, is a play on that of John Backus' famous Turing Award Lecture (and paper). I will propose that --- or rather ask whether --- programming can be made a lot closer to the way we humans think about dynamics, and the way we somehow manage to get others (e.g., our children, our employees, etc.) to do what we have in mind. Technically, the question is whether we can liberate programming from its three main straightjackets: (1) having to directly produce a precise artifact in some language; (2) having actually to produce two separate artifacts (the program and the requirements) and having then to pit one against the other; (3) having to program each piece/part/object of the system separately. The talk will then get a little more technical, providing some evidence of feasibility of the dream, via LSCs and the play-in/play-out approach to scenario-based programming, and its more recent Java variant. The entire body of work around these ideas can be framed as a paradigm, which we call *behavioral programming*.

A. Biere, A. Nahir, and T. Vos (Eds.): HVC 2012, LNCS 7857, p. 1, 2013.
© Springer-Verlag Berlin Heidelberg 2013

Verifying Real-Time Software
Is Not Reasonable (Today)*
Abstract of Invited Talk

Edward A. Lee

UC Berkeley

Abstract. Verification is about demonstrating that a formal system holds certain properties. It is particularly important to verify safety-critical real-time control software, such as aircraft or automotive control systems. Unfortunately, many of the properties that need to be verified for such systems are not actually part of the formal system defined by the software. It therefore makes no sense to verify the software. So what should be verified? It is glib to say that "the system" must be verified, because "the system" is not a formal system. It is a bundle of silicon and wires. Only a model of the system can be verified. What model?

If the semantics of software is extended to include temporal properties, then verifying real-time software becomes possible. In this talk, I will argue that such extensions are practical and effective, but that they require rethinking software abstractions at a rather fundamental level. Moreover, they require reengineering of many performance optimizations that computer architects, compiler designers, and operating system designers have instituted. I will show for some of these that such reengineering yields designs that have competitive performance and verifiable timing.

* The work reported in this talk was supported in part by the Center for Hybrid and Embedded Software Systems (CHESS) at UC Berkeley (supported by the National Science Foundation, NSF awards #0720882 (CSR-EHS: PRET) and #0931843 (ActionWebs), the Naval Research Laboratory (NRL #N0013-12-1-G015), and the following companies: Bosch, National Instruments, and Toyota).

A. Biere, A. Nahir, and T. Vos (Eds.): HVC 2012, LNCS 7857, p. 2, 2013.

SMT in Verification, Modeling, and Testing at Microsoft

Nikolaj Bjørner

Microsoft Research
nbjorner@microsoft.com

The Satisfiability Modulo Theories (SMT) solver, Z3 [1], from Microsoft Research is a state-of-the art theorem prover that integrates specialized solvers for domains that are of relevance for program analysis, testing and verification. Z3 has been used within and outside of Microsoft for the past few years including the Windows 7 static driver verifier, the SAGE white-box fuzzer for finding security vulnerabilities, Pex, in a Verifying C Compiler, the Verve verified operating system kernel and the Dafny safe programming language. This talk delves into some of the more recent efforts around Z3, in particular using Z3 in a firewall analysis engine, and adventures in using Z3 for points-to analysis in JavaScript malware detection, and finally emerging support for reachability queries by solving Satisfiability Modulo Theories for Horn clauses.

Z3 is joint work with Leonardo de Moura and Christoph Wintersteiger.

Reference

1. de Moura, L., Bjørner, N.: Z3: An Efficient SMT Solver. In: Ramakrishnan, C.R., Rehof, J. (eds.) TACAS 2008. LNCS, vol. 4963, pp. 337–340. Springer, Heidelberg (2008)

A. Biere, A. Nahir, and T. Vos (Eds.): HVC 2012, LNCS 7857, p. 3, 2013.

Reducing Costs While Increasing Quality

Orna Raz

IBM Research – Haifa

Abstract. Non mission critical software systems have been challenged with conflicting requirements. On the one hand, these systems are becoming more and more complex and their quality is of paramount importance. On the other hand, to maintain competitiveness, there is a constant pressure to reduce the cost associated with developing such systems.

In this talk, I will raise some of the research questions stemming from these conflicting requirements. I will also present promising approaches to addressing the challenges of reduced costs while increasing quality that were explored at IBM Research.

A. Biere, A. Nahir, and T. Vos (Eds.): HVC 2012, LNCS 7857, p. 4, 2013.
© Springer-Verlag Berlin Heidelberg 2013

Special Session on Security Verification

Alex Goryachev

IBM Research – Haifa

Abstract. Alongside functionality, performance, and power, security is a critical aspect of any system. All software or hardware systems, web applications, and engineered systems built today must comply with stringent requirements in each of these aspects. Security requirements might include that a server must withstand malicious attacks such as stealing or damaging the data or even denial of service. Each of these attacks can have disastrous effects. During the last year alone we saw several examples of such attacks in the media, including: stealing money from bank accounts and ATM machines, bringing down websites, and even breaking into a car computer system while it is driving.

In this session we address the challenges of verifying and validating that a system being built fulfills its security requirements.

This year is the centennial year for Alan Turing. There are many events taking place throughout the world to celebrate Turing's life and his scientific impact. HVC, and this session in particular, is part of these world-wide events.

During his relatively brief life, Turing had an enormous impact on many different fields within computer science: theory of computability, artificial intelligence, and of course cryptography and security. During World War II, Turing worked at the British codebreaking center at Bletchley Park. He stood at the head of the section responsible for decoding German naval ciphers. He also invented several methods for breaking codes, with the most famous associated with deciphering the Enigma machine.

We devote this session to honoring Alan Turing's leadership in breaking German ciphers during World War II and his contribution to cryptography in general.

We would like to thank several people who made this session possible: Hana Chockler, Ronny Morad, and Amir Nahir.

A. Biere, A. Nahir, and T. Vos (Eds.): HVC 2012, LNCS 7857, p. 5, 2013.

Circuit Primitives for Monitoring Information Flow and Enabling Redundancy

Ryan Kastner

University of California, San Diego

Abstract. Critical systems require strict guarantees on information flow security and fault tolerance. We present a novel Boolean circuit methodology that can both monitor information flow throughout the hardware and simultaneously act as a triple modular redundant circuit. This is done by modifying the encoding technique for gate level information flow tracking (GLIFT). This new encoding not only has the added benefit of allowing for redundancy, it also reduces the size of the logic required for information flow tracking compared to the previous GLIFT encodings. This enables the development of high assurance systems on top of hardware with provable integrity and confidentiality properties. The new encoding also allows for these systems to be created with smaller area, lower power, and faster design time.

A. Biere, A. Nahir, and T. Vos (Eds.): HVC 2012, LNCS 7857, p. 6, 2013.
© Springer-Verlag Berlin Heidelberg 2013

Formal Analysis of Security Data Paths in RTL Design

Jamil Mazzawi and Ziyad Hanna

Consulting Services Manager, Jasper Design Automation
PhD, Chief Architect, VP of Research, Jasper Design Automation

Abstract. Recently we have seen an increasing demand to have industrial hardware design verify security information. Complex systems-on-chip such as smart phones, game consoles, and advanced CPUs contain secure information. This likely leads to vulnerabilities and possibly unauthorized access to secure data. The potential for damage, whether direct or indirect, is huge. Checking if the secure information can be leaked is hard to achieve with conventional RTL validation methods. In this talk we present how formal methods can be used to detect unauthorized access to secure data, using a method called security path verification and analysis.

A. Biere, A. Nahir, and T. Vos (Eds.): HVC 2012, LNCS 7857, p. 7, 2013.
© Springer-Verlag Berlin Heidelberg 2013

Precise Detection of Atomicity Violations

Ricardo J. Dias, Vasco Pessanha, and João M. Lourenço*

Departamento de Informática and CITI
Universidade Nova de Lisboa, Portugal
{ricardo.dias,v.pessanha}@campus.fct.unl.pt, joao.lourenco@fct.unl.pt

Abstract. Concurrent programs that are free of unsynchronized accesses to shared data may still exhibit unpredictable concurrency errors, called *atomicity violations*, which include both high-level data races and *stale-value* errors. Atomicity violations occur when programmers make wrong assumptions about the atomicity scope of a code block, incorrectly splitting it in two or more atomic blocks and allowing them to be interleaved with other atomic blocks. In this paper we propose a novel static analysis algorithm that works on a dependency graph of program variables and detects both high-level data races and *stale-value* errors. The algorithm was implemented for a Java Bytecode analyzer and its effectiveness was evaluated with well known faulty programs. The results obtained show that our algorithm performs better than previous approaches, achieving higher precision for small and medium sized programs, making it a good basis for a practical tool.

1   Introduction

The absence or misspecification of the scope of atomic blocks in a concurrent program may trigger atomicity violations and lead to runtime misbehaviors.

Low-level data races occur when the program includes unsynchronized accesses to a shared variable, and at least one of those accesses is a write, i.e., it changes the value of the variable. Although low-level data races are still a common source of errors and malfunctions in concurrent programs, they have been addressed by others in the past and are out of the scope of this paper. We will consider herein that the concurrent programs under analysis are free from low-level data races.

High-level data races results from the misspecification of the scope of an atomic block, by splitting it in two or more atomic blocks with other (possibly empty) non-atomic block between them. This anomaly is often referred as a high-level data race, and is illustrated in Fig. 1(a). A thread uses the method areEqual() to check if the fields 'a' and 'b' are equal. This method reads both fields in separate atomic blocks, storing their values in local variables, which are then compared. However, due to an interleaving with another thread running

---

* This work was partially supported by the Euro-TM EU COST Action IC1001, and by the Portuguese National Science Foundation (FCT) in the research project Synergy-VM (PTDC/EIA-EIA/113613/2009) and the research grant SFRH/BD/41765/2007.

A. Biere, A. Nahir, and T. Vos (Eds.): HVC 2012, LNCS 7857, pp. 8–23, 2013.

the method setPair(), between lines 12 and 13 the value of the pair may have changed. In this scenario the first thread observes an inconsistent pair, composed by the old value of 'a' and the new value of 'b'.

```
1   atomic void getA () {
2     return pair.a;
3   }
4   atomic void getB () {
5     return pair.b;
6   }
7   atomic void setPair(int a, int b){
8     pair.a = a;
9     pair.b = b;
10  }
11  boolean areEqual(){
12    int a = getA ();
13    int b = getB ();
14    return a == b;
15  }
```

(a) A high-level data race.

```
1   atomic int getX () {
2     return x;
3   }
4   atomic void setX(int p0) {
5     x = p0;
6   }
7   void incX(int val) {
8     int tmp = getX ();
9     tmp = tmp + val;
10    setX (tmp);
11  }
```

(b) A stale value error.

Fig. 1. Example of atomicity violations

Figure 1(b) illustrates a stale value error, another source of atomicity violations in concurrent programs. The non-atomic method incX() is implemented by resorting to two atomic methods, getX() (at line 1) and setX() (at line 4). During the execution of line 9, if the current thread is suspended and another thread is scheduled to execute setX(), the value of 'x' changes, and when the execution of the initial thread is resumed it overwrites the value in 'x' at line 10, causing a lost update. This program fails due to a stale-value error, as at line 8 the value of 'x' escapes the scope of the atomic method getX() and is reused indirectly (by way of its private copy 'tmp') at line 10, when updating the value of 'x' in setX().

In this paper we propose a novel approach for the detection of high-level data races and stale-value errors in concurrent programs. As our proposal only depends on the concept of atomic regions and is neutral concerning the mechanisms used for their identification, the atomic regions are not delimited using locks but rather using an **@Atomic** annotation. Our approach is based on a novel notion of variable dependencies, which we designate as *causal* dependencies. There is a *causal* dependency between two variables if the value of one of them influences the writing of the other. We also extended previous work from Artho et al. [2] by reflecting the read/write nature of accesses to shared variables inside atomic regions and additionally use the dependencies information to detect both high-level data races and stale-value errors. We formally describe the static analysis algorithms to compute the set of *causal* dependencies of a program and define safety conditions for both high-level data races and stale-value errors.

Our approach can yield both false positives and false negatives. However, the experimental results demonstrate that it still achieves high precision when detecting atomicity violations in well know examples from the literature, suggesting its usefulness for software development tools.

In the next Section of this paper we introduce the previous relevant work on detections of high-level data races and stale-value errors; in Section 3 we define a core language and introduce some definitions that support the remainder of the paper, namely Sections 4 and 5, where we propose algorithms for defining *causal dependencies* between variables and for detecting atomicity violations (data races). In Section 6 we briefly describe a tool that applies the proposed algorithms with static analysis techniques for Java Bytecode programs, and compare and discuss the results obtained. We terminate in Section 7 with some final concluding remarks.

2   Background and Related Work

Several past works have addressed the detection of the same class of atomicity violations in concurrent programs as addressed in this paper.

The work from Artho et al. [2] introduces the concept of *view consistency*, to detect high-level data races. A *view* of an atomic block is a set containing all the shared variables accessed (both for reading and writing) within that block. The *maximal views* of a process are those views that are not a subset of any other view. Intuitively, a maximal view defines a set of variables that should always be accessed atomically (inside the same atomic block). A program is free from high-level data races if all the views of one thread that are a subset of the maximal views from another thread form an inclusion chain among themselves.

Our work builds on the proposal from Artho et al. [2], but we extend it by incorporating the type of memory access (read or write) into the views, and refine the rules for detecting high-level data races to consider this additional information and the information given by the *causal* dependencies, with considerable positive impact in the precision of the algorithm, as demonstrated in Section 6.

Praun and Gross [9] introduce *method consistency* as an extension of view consistency. Based on the intuition that the variables that should be accessed atomically in a given method are all the variables accessed inside a synchronized block, the authors define the concept of *method views* that relates to Artho et al's maximal views, which aggregates all the shared variables accessed in a method and also differentiates between read and write memory accesses. Similarly to ours, this approach is more precise than Artho et al's because it also detects stale-value errors. Our algorithm however has higher precision than Praun's and give less false positives, as we use *maximal views* rather than *method views*.

Wang and Stoller [10] use the concept of *thread atomicity* to detect and prevent data races, where thread atomicity guarantees that all concurrent executions of a set of threads is equivalent to a sequential execution of those threads. In an attempt to reduce the number of false positives yield by [10], Teixeira et al. [7] proposed a variant of this algorithm based in the intuition that the majority of the atomicity violations come from two consecutive atomic blocks that should be merged into a single one. The authors detect data races by defining and detecting some anomalous memory access patterns for both high-level data races and stale-value errors. Our approach may be seen as a generalization of this

$$e ::= \qquad\qquad (expression)$$
$$x \qquad\qquad (variables)$$
$$\mid\ \text{null} \qquad\qquad (null\ value)$$

$$A ::= \qquad\qquad (assignments)$$
$$x := e \qquad\qquad (local)$$
$$\mid\ x := y.f \qquad\qquad (heap\ read)$$
$$\mid\ x := meth(\vec{y}) \qquad (method\ call)$$
$$\mid\ x.f := e \qquad\qquad (heap\ write)$$
$$\mid\ x := \text{new}\ id \in C \quad (allocation)$$

$$S ::= \qquad\qquad (statements)$$
$$S\,;S \qquad\qquad (sequence)$$
$$\mid\ A \qquad\qquad (assignment)$$
$$\mid\ \text{if}\ e\ \text{then}\ S\ \text{else}\ S \quad (conditional)$$
$$\mid\ \text{while}\ e\ \text{do}\ S \qquad (loop)$$
$$\mid\ \text{return}\ e \qquad\qquad (return)$$
$$\mid\ \text{skip} \qquad\qquad (Skip)$$

$$M ::= meth(\vec{x})\ \{S\} \qquad (methods\ decl)$$

$$C ::= \text{class}\ id\ \{field^*\ (M\mid \text{atomic}\ M)^*\}\ (class\ decl) \qquad P ::= C^+\ (program)$$

Fig. 2. Core language syntax

concept of memory access patterns, but in our case supported by the notion of *causal* dependencies between variables, which allow to reduce considerably the number of both false negatives and false positives.

3 Core Language

We start by defining a core language that captures essential features of a subset of the Java programming language, namely class declaration (class $id\{...\}$), object creation (new), field dereferencing ($x.f$), assignment ($x := e$), and method invocation ($meth(\vec{x})$). The syntax of the language is defined by the grammar in Fig. 2.

A program in this language is composed by a set of class declarations. Atomic blocks correspond to methods that are declared using the atomic keyword. We require the restriction of not allowing nesting of atomic blocks i.e., we do not allow to call an atomic method inside another atomic method. Variables can hold integers or object references and boolean values are encoded as integers using the value 1 for true and value 0 for false. We also do not support exception handling as normally found in typical object-oriented languages.

We now define some sets that are necessary to the understanding of the following sections:

- Classes: is the set of all class identifiers of all classes declared in the program.
- Fields: is the set of all class fields defined in the program.
- Methods: is the the set of all methods defined in the program.
- Atomics ⊆ Methods: is the subset of methods that were declared as atomic.

We define a local (stack) variable as a pair of the form (x, m) where x is the variable identifier and $m \in$ Methods is the method where this variable is declared. For the sake of simplicity we write the pair (x, m) as only x whenever is not ambiguous to do so. The set of all local variables of a program is denoted as LocalVars.

We define a global variable as an object field and we represent it as the pair (c, f) where $c \in$ Classes represents the class where field $f \in$ Fields is declared. The set of all global variables is denoted as GlobalVars. These global variables appear in the code when dereferencing an object reference. For instance, in the statement $x.f := 4$, the expression $x.f$ represents a global variable of the form (c, f) where c is the class of the object reference pointed by local variable x. We define a function typeof : LocalVars $\rightarrow$ Classes, which given a local variable returns the class of the object reference that it holds. So, in the example above $c = \text{typeof}(x)$.

Please note that by deciding to represent an access to a field of an object as a pair with the class of the object reference and the field accessed, we are not able to differentiate between different object instances of the same class, and hence we may consider that there is always at most one object instance of each declared class in the program. This allows us to avoid pointer analysis at the cost of losing precision and becoming unsound in some cases but, as the results in Section 6 show, this design choice has proven to be very effective.

Finally we define the set Vars $\equiv$ LocalVars $+$ GlobalVars, which corresponds to all variables used in the program, both local and global variables.

4   Causal Dependencies

There is a *Causal* dependency, which we will designate herein only as dependency, between two program variables (local or global) if the value read from one variable influences the value written into the other. For instance, the following expression

$$y := x$$

generates a dependency between variable x and y because the value that is written into variable y was read from variable x. As another example, consider the following code:

$$\textbf{if } (x == 0) \ \{ \ y := 4 \ \}$$

In this example, the variable y is written only if the condition $x = 0$ is true, thus it depends on the current value of variable x and therefore there is also a dependency between variables x and y. We represent a dependency between two variables x and y as $x \hookrightarrow y$ where $x \in$ Vars is the variable read and $y \in$ Vars is the variable written.

For each program we can compute a directed graph of *causal* dependencies. The information provided by this graph plays an important role in finding correlations between variables, which can be used to detect atomicity violations. We can define two kinds of correlations between variables.

Definition 1 (Direct Correlation). *There is a* direct *correlation between a read variable x and a written variable y if there is a path from x to y, in a dependency graph $\mathcal{D}$.*

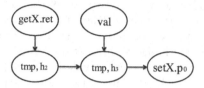

Fig. 3. Dependency graph example

Definition 2 (Common Correlation). *There is a common correlation between a read variable x and a read variable y if there is a written variable z, where $z \neq x$ and $z \neq y$, for which there is a path from x to z and another path from y to z, in a dependency graph $\mathcal{D}$.*

In the following section we describe how to compute the graph of dependencies using symbolic execution.

4.1 Dependency Analysis

The construction of the dependency graph is done in two steps. In the first step we only detect data dependencies between variables. In the second step we detect control dependencies between variables. In the end we merge all dependencies in a single graph.

Data Dependencies. The accurate detection of data dependencies relies on the precise localisation of where the variables are defined. SSA (Single Static Assignment) [1] could be used, because each variable would only have one definition site, but this only works for local variables, and we still need to track each definition site for global variables. Therefore we did not use SSA as internal representation and we solve the problem by defining a new variable version whenever the variable is updated.

A variable version is defined as a triple of the form (x, h, m) where $x \in$ Vars is a variable (local or global), h is a unique identifier, and $m \in$ Atomics $\cup \{\perp\}$ indicates if this variable is used inside an atomic method or not ($\perp$). The set of all variable versions is denoted as Versions.

The unique identifier h is a hash value based on the line of code of the respective definition site. If the version of the variable is not known in the current context, as in the case of method arguments, a special hash value is used. We denote this special hash value as $h_?$.

Figure 3 depicts the dependency graph for the method 'incX()' from Fig. 1(b). For the sake of simplicity, we omitted the method (m) part of the version representation. We denote $getX . ret$ as the return value of method getX(), and $setX . p0$ as the parameter of method setX(**int** p0). Both the return value and the parameter do not need to have an hash value associated, and thus we omitted it from their representation.

In method incX(**int** val), the value returned by the method getX() is written into a temporary variable tmp, which is then incremented using parameter val and is then used as a parameter on the invocation of method setX(**int** p0).

While analyzing this method, we first start by creating the dependency $getX.\,ret \hookrightarrow (tmp, h_2)$ between the return value of getX() method and variable tmp with an hash value h_2. In the next statement variable tmp is redefined with a value resulting from the sum of the previous tmp variable and the val parameter, and hence we create two dependencies $(tmp, h_2) \hookrightarrow (tmp, h_3)$ and $val \hookrightarrow (tmp, h_3)$, where the new version of tmp variable has the hash value h_3. Finally, we invoke method setX(**int** p0) with the value of tmp as parameter and therefore we create the dependency $(tmp, h_3) \hookrightarrow setX.\,p0$.

The symbolic execution rules are defined as a transition system ($\langle \mathcal{D}, \mathcal{H}, S \rangle \Longrightarrow \langle \mathcal{D}', \mathcal{H}' \rangle$) over a state composed by a dependency graph $\mathcal{D}$ and a set of versions, denoted has $\mathcal{H} \subseteq$ Versions, which holds the current versions of each program variable. In a single program point, we may find different versions of the same variable because our analysis over-approximates the run-time state of a program. The rules can be depicted in Figure 4, and we always omit the method (m) parameter from the representation of a variable version.

Function $\text{ver}_{\mathcal{H}}$ is used to retrieve the set of current versions of a variable, and is defined as follows:

Definition 3 (Version Retrieval). *Given a set of versions $\mathcal{H}$ and a variable $v \in$ Vars:*

$$\text{ver} : \mathcal{P}(\text{Versions}) \times \text{Vars} \to \mathcal{P}(\text{Versions})$$

$$\text{ver}_{\mathcal{H}}(v) \triangleq \begin{cases} \{(v, h, m) \mid (v, h, m) \in \mathcal{H}\} & \text{if } \exists (v, h, m) \in \mathcal{H} \\ \{(v, h_?, m)\} & \text{otherwise} \end{cases}$$

If a variable version cannot be found in $\mathcal{H}$, a version with the special hash value $h_?$ is returned.

Every time that a variable is written, it is created a new version for such variable and all other existing current versions are replaced by the new one. We define an helper function $\text{subs}_{\mathcal{H}}$ for this purpose as:

Definition 4 (Version Substitution). *Given a set of versions $\mathcal{H}$ and a variable version $(v, h, m) \in$ Versions:*

$$\text{subs} : \mathcal{P}(\text{Versions}) \times \text{Versions} \to \mathcal{P}(\text{Versions})$$

$$\text{subs}_{\mathcal{H}}((v, h, m)) \triangleq (\mathcal{H} \setminus \{(v, h', m') \mid (v, h', m') \in \mathcal{H}\}) \cup \{(v, h, m)\}$$

Each hash value is generated using the function nhash, which given a statement S generates a new and unique hash value based in the line number of that statement. This function is deterministic in the sense that for any statement S the same hash value is always returned.

At the beginning of the analysis, the sets $\mathcal{D}$ and $\mathcal{H}$ are empty. We represent the parameters of methods as $meth.\,p_i$, and the return value of a method as $meth.\,ret$.

$$\frac{\langle \mathcal{D}, \mathcal{H}, S_1 \rangle \Longrightarrow \langle \mathcal{D}', \mathcal{H}' \rangle \quad \langle \mathcal{D}', \mathcal{H}', S_2 \rangle \Longrightarrow \langle \mathcal{D}'', \mathcal{H}'' \rangle}{\langle \mathcal{D}, \mathcal{H}, S_1; S_2 \rangle \Longrightarrow \langle \mathcal{D}'', \mathcal{H}'' \rangle} (\text{SEQ})$$

$$\frac{\begin{array}{c} h = \mathsf{nhash}(x := y) \\ \mathcal{H}' = \mathsf{subs}_{\mathcal{H}}((x,h)) \quad \mathcal{D}' = \mathcal{D} \cup \{v \hookrightarrow (x,h) \mid v \in \mathsf{ver}_{\mathcal{H}}(y)\} \end{array}}{\langle \mathcal{D}, \mathcal{H}, x := y \rangle \Longrightarrow \langle \mathcal{D}', \mathcal{H}' \rangle} (\text{ASSIGN})$$

$$\frac{\begin{array}{c} c = \mathsf{typeof}(y) \quad h = \mathsf{nhash}(x := y.f) \quad \mathcal{H}' = \mathsf{subs}_{\mathcal{H}}((x,h)) \\ \mathcal{D}' = \mathcal{D} \cup \{v \hookrightarrow (x,h) \mid v \in \mathsf{ver}_{\mathcal{H}}((c,f))\} \end{array}}{\langle \mathcal{D}, \mathcal{H}, x := y.f \rangle \Longrightarrow \langle \mathcal{D}', \mathcal{H}' \rangle} (\text{HEAP READ})$$

$$\frac{\begin{array}{c} c = \mathsf{typeof}(x) \quad h = \mathsf{nhash}(x.f := y) \quad \mathcal{H}' = \mathsf{subs}_{\mathcal{H}}(((c,f),h)) \\ \mathcal{D}' = \mathcal{D} \cup \{v \hookrightarrow ((c,f),h) \mid v \in \mathsf{ver}_{\mathcal{H}}(y)\} \end{array}}{\langle \mathcal{D}, \mathcal{H}, x.f := y \rangle \Longrightarrow \langle \mathcal{D}', \mathcal{H}' \rangle} (\text{HEAP WRITE})$$

$$\frac{h = \mathsf{nhash}(x := \mathsf{new}\, C()) \quad \mathcal{H}' = \mathsf{subs}_{\mathcal{H}}((x,h))}{\langle \mathcal{D}, \mathcal{H}, x := \mathsf{new}\, C() \rangle \Longrightarrow \langle \mathcal{D}, \mathcal{H}' \rangle} (\text{ALLOCATION})$$

$$\frac{\begin{array}{c} h = \mathsf{nhash}(x := meth(\vec{y})) \quad \mathsf{spec}(meth) = \langle \mathcal{D}_f, \mathcal{H}_f \rangle \quad \mathcal{D}' = \mathcal{D}_f \cup \mathcal{D} \\ \mathcal{D}'' = \mathcal{D}' \cup \{v_i \hookrightarrow meth.\, p_i \mid y_i \in \vec{y} \wedge v_i \in \mathsf{ver}_{\mathcal{H}}(y_i)\} \cup \{meth.\, ret \hookrightarrow (x,h)\} \\ \mathcal{H}' = \{(v,h) \mid (v,h) \in \mathcal{H} \wedge ((v,h?) \in \mathcal{H}_f \vee (v,h) \notin \mathcal{H}_f)\} \\ \mathcal{H}'' = \{(v,h) \mid (v,h) \in \mathcal{H}_f \wedge h \neq h?\} \end{array}}{\langle \mathcal{D}, \mathcal{H}, x := meth(\vec{y}) \rangle \Longrightarrow \langle \mathcal{D}'', \mathcal{H}' \cup \mathcal{H}'' \rangle} (\text{METH CALL})$$

$$\frac{\begin{array}{c} \langle \mathcal{D}, \mathcal{H}, S_1 \rangle \Longrightarrow \langle \mathcal{D}', \mathcal{H}' \rangle \quad \langle \mathcal{D}, \mathcal{H}, S_2 \rangle \Longrightarrow \langle \mathcal{D}'', \mathcal{H}'' \rangle \\ \mathcal{H}''' = \mathcal{H}' \cup \mathcal{H}'' \cup \{(v,h?) \mid (v,h_1) \in \mathcal{H}' \wedge (v,h_2) \notin \mathcal{H}''\} \\ \cup \{(v,h?) \mid (v,h_1) \in \mathcal{H}'' \wedge (v,h_2) \notin \mathcal{H}'\} \end{array}}{\langle \mathcal{D}, \mathcal{H}, \mathsf{if}\, b\, \mathsf{then}\, S_1\, \mathsf{else}\, S_2 \rangle \Longrightarrow \langle \mathcal{D}' \cup \mathcal{D}'', \mathcal{H}''' \rangle} (\text{CONDITIONAL})$$

$$\frac{\begin{array}{c} \langle \mathcal{D}, \mathcal{H}, S \rangle \Longrightarrow \langle \mathcal{D}', \mathcal{H}' \rangle \quad \mathcal{H}'' = \mathcal{H} \cup \mathcal{H}' \cup \{(v,h?) \mid (v,h_1) \in \mathcal{H} \wedge (v,h_2) \notin \mathcal{H}'\} \\ \cup \{(v,h?) \mid (v,h_1) \in \mathcal{H}' \wedge (v,h_2) \notin \mathcal{H}\} \end{array}}{\langle \mathcal{D}, \mathcal{H}, \mathsf{while}\, b\, \mathsf{do}\, S \rangle \Longrightarrow \langle \mathcal{D} \cup \mathcal{D}', \mathcal{H}'' \rangle} (\text{LOOP})$$

$$\frac{\mathcal{D}' = \mathcal{D} \cup \{v \hookrightarrow \mathsf{retVar} \mid v \in \mathsf{ver}_{\mathcal{H}}(x)\}}{\langle \mathcal{D}, \mathcal{H}, \mathsf{return}\, x \rangle \Longrightarrow \langle \mathcal{D}', \mathcal{H} \rangle} (\text{RETURN}) \qquad \frac{}{\langle \mathcal{D}, \mathcal{H}, \mathsf{skip} \rangle \Longrightarrow \langle \mathcal{D}, \mathcal{H} \rangle} (\text{SKIP})$$

Fig. 4. Symbolic execution rules of data dependencies analysis

When evaluating the RETURN statement, the return value of the method is denoted as retVar.

All assignment operations, namely ASSIGN, HEAP READ, and HEAP WRITE, create dependencies between all versions of the variables used in the right side of the assignment and the new version of the assigned variable. The newly generated version is then used to replace all existing versions of that same variable.

In the rule METH CALL, the function spec returns the result, denoted as $\langle \mathcal{D}_p, \mathcal{H}_p \rangle$, of the analysis of method *meth*. The dependencies in $\mathcal{D}_p$ are merged with the current dependencies and we create a dependency between each value that is passed as an argument to *meth* and the respective declared parameter *meth.* p_i. We also need to update the variables' versions that are generated inside the method. If a variable was redefined ($h \neq h?$) inside *meth* then we replace the existing versions with the new version, otherwise we keep the current versions. Finally, we add one more dependency between the return value of method *meth* and the assigned value.

In the rule CONDITIONAL, the dependencies are generated in both branches and are merged with the initial $\mathcal{D}$. We also generate the versions for each branch, and if a variable x has a version $h \neq h_?$ in one branch but there is no version for the same variable in the other branch, then we generate a special version $h_?$ for variable x and we join it to all the other versions. The intuition behind this operation is that if a variable is written only in one of the branches then we also need to add the case that the variable might not have been written. The rule LOOP is similar to the CONDITIONAL rule. The remaining rules should be self-explanatory.

After analyzing all methods of the program we get a dependency graph for the whole program, based on data-flow information. Next, we have to add the remaining dependencies based on the control flow information.

Control Dependencies. If an assignment or return statement is guarded by some condition then that assignment or return statement depends on the variables used in the condition. This situation may occur with every conditional statement such as an if then else, or a while loop.

The analysis of control dependencies traverses the control flow graph and keeps the set of variables that the assignments may depend on. When an assignment or return statement is found we create a dependency between the current variables, that it may depend on, and the respective assigned variable.

The symbolic execution rules are shown in Figure 5 as a transition system $(\langle \mathcal{IS}, \mathcal{D}, S \rangle \Longrightarrow \langle \mathcal{IS}', \mathcal{D}' \rangle)$. The state is composed by a set of conditional variables $\mathcal{IS} \subseteq \mathsf{Versions}$, which correspond to the variable versions that the current statement depends on, and a dependency graph $\mathcal{D}$. In the beginning of the analysis the dependency graph is empty, and the set of conditional variables has the union of all conditional variables that are present at all calling contexts of the method that is going to be analyzed. For instance, given the program methods m_1, m_2 and m_3 where method m_1 calls method m_2 with the current conditional variables set $\mathcal{IS} = \{c_1, c_2\}$, and m_3 calls method m_2 with the current conditional variables set $\mathcal{IS} = \{c_3, c_4\}$, then the initial set of conditional variables when analyzing method m_2 is $\mathcal{IS} = \{c_1, c_2, c_3, c_4\}$.

In the end of this analysis the resulting graph of dependencies is merged with the one that resulted from the data dependencies analysis, described in the previous section, thus forming the complete graph of *causal* dependencies.

For every kind of assignment we create a dependency between the current conditional variables and the assigned variable. This situation may occur in the rules ASSIGN, HEAP READ, HEAP WRITE, ALLOCATION and METH CALL. In the case of a return statement, as in rule RETURN, we create a dependency with the special variable retVar.

In the rules CONDITIONAL and LOOP, we analyze each branch with a new set of conditional variables, which include the current conditional variables plus the variable of the condition. Each variable is actually a variable version with

$$\frac{\langle \mathcal{IS}, \mathcal{D}, S_1 \rangle \Longrightarrow \langle \mathcal{IS}', \mathcal{D}' \rangle \quad \langle \mathcal{IS}', \mathcal{D}', S_2 \rangle \Longrightarrow \langle \mathcal{IS}'', \mathcal{D}'' \rangle}{\langle \mathcal{IS}, \mathcal{D}, S_1; S_2 \rangle \Longrightarrow \langle \mathcal{IS}'', \mathcal{D}'' \rangle}(\text{Seq})$$

$$\frac{h = \mathsf{nhash}(x := y) \quad \mathcal{D}' = \mathcal{D} \cup \{v \hookrightarrow (x, h) \mid v \in \mathcal{IS}\}}{\langle \mathcal{IS}, \mathcal{D}, x := y \rangle \Longrightarrow \langle \mathcal{IS}, \mathcal{D}' \rangle}(\text{Assign})$$

$$\frac{h = \mathsf{nhash}(x := y.f) \quad \mathcal{D}' = \mathcal{D} \cup \{v \hookrightarrow (x, h) \mid v \in \mathcal{IS}\}}{\langle \mathcal{IS}, \mathcal{D}, x := y.f \rangle \Longrightarrow \langle \mathcal{IS}, \mathcal{D}' \rangle}(\text{Heap Read})$$

$$\frac{\begin{array}{c} c = \mathsf{typeof}(x) \\ h = \mathsf{nhash}(x.f := y) \quad \mathcal{D}' = \mathcal{D} \cup \{v \hookrightarrow ((c, f), h) \mid v \in \mathcal{IS}\} \end{array}}{\langle \mathcal{IS}, \mathcal{D}, x.f := y \rangle \Longrightarrow \langle \mathcal{IS}, \mathcal{D}' \rangle}(\text{Heap Write})$$

$$\frac{h = \mathsf{nhash}(x := \mathsf{new}\,C()) \quad \mathcal{D}' = \mathcal{D} \cup \{v \hookrightarrow (x, h) \mid v \in \mathcal{IS}\}}{\langle \mathcal{IS}, \mathcal{D}, x := \mathsf{new}\,C() \rangle \Longrightarrow \langle \mathcal{IS}, \mathcal{D}' \rangle}(\text{Allocation})$$

$$\frac{\begin{array}{c} h = \mathsf{nhash}(x := meth(\vec{y})) \\ \mathsf{spec}(meth) = \langle \mathcal{IS}_f, \mathcal{D}_f \rangle \quad \mathcal{D}' = \mathcal{D} \cup \mathcal{D}_f \cup \{v \hookrightarrow (x, h) \mid v \in \mathcal{IS}\} \end{array}}{\langle \mathcal{IS}, \mathcal{D}, x := meth(\vec{y}) \rangle \Longrightarrow \langle \mathcal{IS}, \mathcal{D}' \rangle}(\text{Meth Call})$$

$$\frac{\begin{array}{c} \mathcal{IS}' = \mathcal{IS} \cup \{b\} \\ \langle \mathcal{IS}', \mathcal{D}, S_1 \rangle \Longrightarrow \langle \mathcal{IS}', \mathcal{D}' \rangle \quad \langle \mathcal{IS}', \mathcal{D}, S_2 \rangle \Longrightarrow \langle \mathcal{IS}', \mathcal{D}'' \rangle \end{array}}{\langle \mathcal{IS}, \mathcal{D}, \mathsf{if}\,b\,\mathsf{then}\,S_1\,\mathsf{else}\,S_2 \rangle \Longrightarrow \langle \mathcal{IS}, \mathcal{D}' \cup \mathcal{D}'' \rangle}(\text{Conditional})$$

$$\frac{\mathcal{IS}' = \mathcal{IS} \cup \{b\} \quad \langle \mathcal{IS}', \mathcal{D}, S \rangle \Longrightarrow \langle \mathcal{IS}', \mathcal{D}' \rangle}{\langle \mathcal{IS}, \mathcal{D}, \mathsf{while}\,b\,\mathsf{do}\,S \rangle \Longrightarrow \langle \mathcal{IS}, \mathcal{D} \cup \mathcal{D}' \rangle}(\text{Loop})$$

$$\frac{\mathcal{D}' = \mathcal{D} \cup \{v \hookrightarrow \mathsf{retVar} \mid v \in \mathcal{IS}\}}{\langle \mathcal{IS}, \mathcal{D}, \mathsf{return}\,x \rangle \Longrightarrow \langle \mathcal{IS}, \mathcal{D}' \rangle}(\text{Return}) \qquad \frac{}{\langle \mathcal{IS}, \mathcal{D}, \mathsf{skip} \rangle \Longrightarrow \langle \mathcal{IS}, \mathcal{D} \rangle}(\text{Skip})$$

Fig. 5. Symbolic execution rules of control dependencies analysis

an unique hash value. When we exit the scope of the condition we remove the condition variable and proceed with the analysis. The remaining rules are self-explanatory.

The result of these two analysis generate the graph of *causal* dependencies that is used to detect the existence of atomicity violations in a concurrent program, as we will show in the following sections.

5   Atomicity Violations

The purpose of our work is to detect two kinds of atomicity errors, the high-level data race and the stale-value error, that may occur during the execution of concurrent programs that use atomic blocks to guarantee mutual exclusion in the access to shared data.

The definition of both errors assume that the concurrent program has no low-level data races, meaning that all accesses to shared variables are done inside atomic blocks.

5.1   High Level Data Races

A *view*, as described by Artho et al. in [2], expresses what variables are accessed inside a given atomic code block. We extend this definition by also keeping the kind of access (read or write) that was made for each variable in the *view*.

Please note that a *view* only stores global variables. Local variables are not shared between threads and thus do not require synchronized accesses.

We denote as Accesses the set of memory accesses made inside an atomic block. An access $a \in$ Accesses is a pair of the form (α, v) where $\alpha \in \{r, w\}$ represents the kind of access (r-read or w-write) and $v \in$ GlobalVars is a global variable[1]. A *view* is a subset of Accesses and the set of all views in a program is denoted as Views. A *view* is always associated with one atomic method, and we define the bijective function Γ that given a *view* returns the associated atomic method as:

$$\Gamma : \text{Views} \rightarrow \text{Atomics}$$

The inverse function, denoted as Γ^{-1}, returns the *view* associated with a given atomic method. The set of *generated views* of a process p, denoted as $V(p)$, corresponds to the atomic blocks executed by one process, and is defined as:

$$v \in V(p) \Leftrightarrow m = \Gamma(v) \wedge \text{executes}(p, m)$$

The predicate executes asserts if a method m may be executed by process p, and is defined by an auxiliary static analysis that computes the set of processes and the atomic methods that are called in each process.

We can refine the previous definition of $V(p)$ with a parameter α, where $\alpha \in \{r, w\}$, to get only the views of a process with read (V_r) or write accesses (V_w).

Definition 5 (Procedure Views)

$$V_\alpha(p) = \{v_2 \mid v_1 \in V(p) \wedge v_2 = \{(\alpha, x) \mid (\alpha, x) \in v_1\}\} \quad \text{where } \alpha \in \{r, w\}$$

We defined a static analysis to compute a *view* of an atomic method. Every time a global variable is read or written, the corresponding read or write access is created and added to the *view*. The *view* resulting from a method call is merged with the current *view* that is being computed. In the case of conditional and loop statements we perform an over-approximation union of the *views* of each branch. In the end of the analysis we have the set of *views* corresponding to the atomic methods present in the program code.

The *maximal views* of a process, denoted as M_α, are all the views of the process that are not a subset of any other view in that same process. A maximal view is defined as follows:

---

[1] Please remember that global variables are represented as a pair with a class identifier and the field accessed.

Definition 6 (Maximal Views). *Given a process p, a maximal view v_m is defined as:*

$$v_m \in M_\alpha(p) \Leftrightarrow v_m \in V_\alpha(p) \wedge (\forall v \in V_\alpha(p) : v_m \subseteq v \Rightarrow v = v_m) \quad \text{where } \alpha \in \{r, w\}$$

Each *maximal view* represent the set of variables that should be accessed atomically, i.e., should always be accessed in the same atomic block.

Given a set of views of a process p and a *maximal view* v_m of another process, we define the read or write *overlapping views* of process p with *view* v_m as all the non empty intersection views between v_m and the views of process p.

Definition 7 (Overlapping Views). *Given a process p and maximal view v_m:*

$$\text{overlap}_\alpha(p, v_m) \triangleq \{v_m \cap v \mid v \in V_\alpha(p) \wedge v_m \cap v \neq \emptyset\} \quad \text{where } \alpha \in \{r, w\}$$

The notion of compatibility between a process p and a *view* v_m, defined in [2], states that a process p and a *view* v_m are *compatible* if all their *overlapping views* form a chain. We extended this definition with the information given by the *causal* dependencies graph, and we additionally require that, even if the read overlapping views do not form a chain, there may not exist a *common correlation* (Definition 2) between the variables in the read overlapping views.

Definition 8 (Process Compatibility). *Given a process p and maximal view v_m:*

$$\text{comp}_w(p, v_m) \Leftrightarrow \forall v_1, v_2 \in \text{overlap}_w(p, v_m) : v_1 \subseteq v_2 \vee v_2 \subseteq v_1$$
$$\text{comp}_r(p, v_m) \Leftrightarrow \forall v_1, v_2 \in \text{overlap}_r(p, v_m) : v_1 \subseteq v_2 \vee v_2 \subseteq v_1$$
$$\vee \neg \text{CommonCorrelation}(v_1, v_2)$$

The intuition behind this additional condition is that, even if two shared variables that belong to a *maximal view* were read in different atomic blocks, we will only consider that there is an incompatibility if both variables are used in a common write operation.

We can now define the *view consistency* safety property in terms of the compatibility between all pairs of processes of a program. A process may only have *views* that are compatible with all *maximal views* of another process. A program is free from high-level data races if the following condition holds:

Definition 9 (View Consistency)

$$\forall p_1, p_2 \in \mathcal{P}_S, m_r \in M_r(p_1), m_w \in M_w(p_1) : \text{comp}_w(p_2, m_r) \wedge \text{comp}_r(p_2, m_w)$$

where $\mathcal{P}_S$ is the set of processes.

5.2   Stale-Value Error

Stale-value errors are a class of atomicity violations that are not detected by the *view consistency* property. Our approach to detect this kind of errors uses the graph of *causal* dependencies to detect values that escape the scope of an atomic block (e.g., by assigning a shared variable to a local variable) and are later used inside another atomic block (e.g., by assigning the previous local variable to a shared variable).

First we define the set IVersions $\subseteq$ Versions, which stores all global variable versions that were accessed inside an atomic block. Each variable version has a parameter m that indicates in which atomic method it was defined, or has the value $\perp$ if it was not used inside an atomic method.

Definition 10 (Atomic Variable Version). *A global variable version* (x, h, m) *is an atomic variable if:*

$$(x, h, m) \in \text{IVersions} \Leftrightarrow (x, h, m) \in \text{Versions} \wedge x \in \text{GlobalVars} \wedge m \neq \perp$$

Now we define a new graph, denoted as $\mathcal{D}_\mathcal{V}$, which represent the dependencies between views. A labeled edge of this graph $\mathcal{D}_\mathcal{V}$ is represented as (m_1, x, m_2) where $m_1, m_2 \in$ Atomics and $x \in$ GlobalVars, and can be interpreted as atomic method m_2 depends on atomic method m_1 through global variable x. Intuitively, this means that the value of variable x exited the scope of method m_1 and entered the scope of method m_2, and while it was out of the atomic scopes it might have become outdated.

Each edge (m_1, x_1, m_2) of a *view* dependency graph $\mathcal{D}_\mathcal{V}$, is created when, given two version variables $a_1 = (x_1, h_1, m_1) \in$ IVersions and $a_2 = (x_2, h_2, m_2) \in$ IVersions, and a *causal* dependency graph $\mathcal{D}$, the following conditions hold:

$(\text{DirectCorrelation}(\mathcal{D}, a_1, a_2) \wedge m_1 \neq m_2) \vee (m_1 = m_2$
$\wedge \text{DirectCorrelation}(\mathcal{D}, a_1, m_1. \, ret) \wedge \text{DirectCorrelation}(\mathcal{D}, m_1. \, ret, m_1. \, p_i)$
$\wedge \text{DirectCorrelation}(\mathcal{D}, m_1. \, p_i, a_2))$

The predicate DirectCorrelation asserts if two variables are *directly correlated* according to Definition 1. These conditions state that there is a dependency between m_1 and m_2 through variable x_1, if the variable version a_1 is directly correlated with a_2 when m_1 and m_2 are two different atomic methods, or if the two methods m_1 and m_2 are the same, then we must be sure that the value of x_1 left out the scope of the method and then entered it again.

A process p writes in a variable $x \in$ Vars if there is a write access on variable x in one of the views of process p:

$$\text{writes}(x, p) \Leftrightarrow \exists v \in V_w(p) : (w, x) \in v$$

The safety property for *stale-value* errors can be defined as the case where no process writes to a global variable that leaves, and then enters, the scope of an atomic method of another process.

Definition 11 (Stale-Value Safety)

$$\forall p \in \mathcal{P}_\mathcal{S}, (m_1, x, m_2) \in \mathcal{D}_\mathcal{V} : \neg \text{writes}(x, p) \text{ where } \mathcal{P}_\mathcal{S} \text{ is the set of processes}$$

If there is a *view* dependency for variable x and there is a process p that writes on that variable then a *stale-value* error is detected.

Table 1. Results for benchmarks — *Set 1*

Tests	AV	False Negatives			False Positives			Acc. Vars	LOC	Time (sec.)
		MoTH	Artho	Teix.	*MoTH*	Artho	Teix.			
Connection [4]	2	0	1	1	0	0	1	34	112	45
Coord03 [2]	1	0	0	0	0	0	3	13	170	43
Local [2]	1	0	1	0	0	0	1	3	33	42
NASA [2]	1	0	0	0	0	0	0	7	121	43
Coord04 [3]	1	0	0	0	0	0	3	7	47	40
Buffer [3]	0	0	0	0	1	0	7	8	64	41
DoubleCheck [3]	0	0	0	0	1	0	2	7	51	41
StringBuffer [5]	1	0	1	1	0	0	0	12	52	44
Account [9]	1	0	1	0	0	0	0	3	65	40
Jigsaw [9]	1	0	0	0	0	0	1	33	145	40
OverReporting [9]	0	0	0	0	0	0	2	6	52	42
UnderReporting [9]	1	0	1	0	0	0	0	3	31	39
Allocate Vector [6]	1	0	1	0	0	0	1	24	304	41
Knight [7]	1	0	1	0	0	0	2	10	223	41
Arithmetic Database [7]	3	0	3	1	1	0	0	24	416	54
Total	**15**	**0**	**10**	**3**	**3**	**0**	**23**	–	–	–

6   Evaluation

To evaluate the accuracy of our algorithms and techniques, we adapted and implemented the theoretical framework described in the previous sections to the Java Bytecode language, where the atomic methods are defined using the **@Atomic** method annotation. We used the data-flow analysis infrastructure of the Soot framework [8] to implement all the described analysis.

Our tool starts by parsing a Java bytecode program and computing a set of analysis, namely: *process analysis* to identify which threads may exist when executing the program; *instance type analysis* to handle Java interfaces and dynamic dispatching; *views analysis*, to compute the *views* of each atomic method; inter-procedural *causal dependency analysis*, to compute dependencies between variables used in assignments and conditional code blocks. Once all these analysis are concluded, the tool creates the *causal dependency graph*. Another analysis is then ran over this dependency graph to identify atomic blocks that break the atomicity violation safety properties.

Besides comparing our results with those reported on the literature for individual benchmarks, we did an exhaustive comparison with two other approaches: the work of Artho et al [2], because our approach is an extension of this work; and the work of Teixeira et al [7], because their results are currently a reference for the field. The results presented were obtained by running our tool with the algorithms described in this paper; by using Artho et al's algorithm implemented with static analysis techniques (rather than the dynamic analysis reported in [2]); and by running Teixeira's tool on the Java source (instead of the Bytecode).

Tables 1 and 2 summarize the results achieved by applying our tool to a set of benchmarking programs, most of them well known from related works and compares them with the two works cited above. Teixeira's tool was unable to

Table 2. Results for benchmarks — *Set 2*

Tests	AV	False Negatives		False Positives		Acc. Vars	LOC	Time (sec.)
		MoTH	Artho	MoTH	Artho			
Elevator [9]	16	0	16	6	4	39	558	46
Philo [9]	0	0	0	2	0	9/594	96	45/612
Tsp [9]	0	0	0	2	0	635	795	869
Store	2	0	1	0	1	44/608	901	149/1763
Total	**18**	**0**	**17**	**10**	**5**	–	–	–

process some of the benchmarks, so they are reported in a separate second set. Columns *AV* indicate the number of known atomicity violations, *false negatives* indicate the number of known program atomicity violations that were missed by the approach[2], *false positives* indicate the number of reported but non-existing atomicity violations, *Acc. Vars* indicate the number of variables accessed inside atomic regions and is an indication of the problem size, together with the number of *LOC*, and how long it took for our analysis to run.

In the case of Table 2, the benchmarks Philo and Store have two different values for *accessed variables* and *time*. The second values report on the original benchmarks, which includes some (non-essential) calls to I/O methods in the JDK library. The first values report on a tailored version of the benchmarks where those calls to the JDK library were commented.

For the benchmarks listed in Table 1, our approach revealed a very high accuracy by reporting no false negatives and only three false positives. The false positive in the Buffer benchmark is due to an assumption claim from its authors that is not implemented in the actual code. The information collected by the Causal Dependency Analysis is incomplete and imprecise and originates false positives in the Double Check and Arithmetic Database benchmarks while checking for stale-value errors, which are not detected by Artho et al's approach.

For the benchmarks listed in Table 2, our appropriate again reveled very high accuracy, as although it reported 10 false positives (vs. only 5 from Artho et al's), it reported zero false negatives (vs. 17 from Artho et al's). These benchmarks also indicate that our algorithms scale well with the the size of the problem, both in the number of accessed variables inside the atomic blocks and the number of lines of code.

7   Conclusions

In this paper we presented a novel approach to detect high-level data races and stale-value errors in concurrent programs. The proposed approach relies on the notion of *causal* dependencies to improve the precision of previous detection techniques. The high-level data races are detected using an algorithm based on

---

[2] The identification of false negative is only possible because the sets of atomicity violations in the benchmarking programs are well known.

a previous work by Artho et al. refined to distinguish between read and write accesses and extended with the information given by the *causal* dependencies. The stale-value errors are detected using the information given by the *causal* dependencies, which exposes the values of variables that escaped an atomic block and entered into another atomic block.

Our detection analysis still remains unsound mainly due to the absence of pointer analysis and to the way that *views* are computed. But these design decisions allowed us to maintain the scalability of our approach without incurring in a strong precision loss, as our experimental results confirm.

We evaluated our analysis techniques with well known examples from the literature and compared them to previous works. Our results show that we are able to detect all atomicity violations present in the examples, while reporting a low number of false positives.

References

1. Alpern, B., Wegman, M.N., Zadeck, F.K.: Detecting equality of variables in programs. In: Proc. of the 15th ACM SIGPLAN-SIGACT Symp. on Principles of Programming Languages, POPL 1988, pp. 1–11. ACM, San Diego (1988)
2. Artho, C., Havelund, K., Biere, A.: High-level data races. Software Testing, Verification and Reliability 13(4), 207–227 (2003)
3. Artho, C., Havelund, K., Biere, A.: Using block-local atomicity to detect stale-value concurrency errors. In: Wang, F. (ed.) ATVA 2004. LNCS, vol. 3299, pp. 150–164. Springer, Heidelberg (2004)
4. Beckman, N.E., Bierhoff, K., Aldrich, J.: Verifying correct usage of atomic blocks and typestate. SIGPLAN Not. 43(10), 227–244 (2008)
5. Flanagan, C., Freund, S.N.: Atomizer: a dynamic atomicity checker for multi-threaded programs. In: Proc. of the 31st ACM SIGPLAN-SIGACT Symp. on Principles of Programming Languages, POPL 2004, Venice, Italy, pp. 256–267 (2004)
6. IBM HRL — Concurrency Testing Repository
7. Teixeira, B., Lourenço, J.M., Farchi, E., Dias, R.J., Sousa, D.G.: Detection of transactional memory anomalies using static analysis. In: Proc. of the 8th Workshop on Parallel and Distributed Systems: Testing, Analysis, and Debugging, PADTAD 2010, pp. 26–36. ACM, New York (2010)
8. Vallée-Rai, R., Co, P., Gagnon, E., Hendren, L., Lam, P., Sundaresan, V.: Soot - a Java bytecode optimization framework. In: Proc. of the 1999 Conference of the Centre for Advanced Studies on Collaborative Research, CASCON 1999, pp. 125–135. IBM Press (1999)
9. von Praun, C., Gross, T.R.: Static detection of atomicity violations in object-oriented programs. Journal of Object Technology, 2004 (2003)
10. Wang, L., Stoller, S.: Run-Time Analysis for Atomicity. Electronic Notes in Theoretical Computer Science 89(2), 191–209 (2003)

Proving Mutual Termination of Programs

Dima Elenbogen[1], Shmuel Katz[1], and Ofer Strichman[2]

[1] CS, Technion, Haifa, Israel
{katz,edima}@cs.technion.ac.il
[2] Information Systems Engineering, IE, Technion, Haifa, Israel
ofers@ie.technion.ac.il

Abstract. Two programs are said to be *mutually terminating* if they terminate on exactly the same inputs. We suggest a proof rule that uses a mapping between the functions of the two programs for proving mutual termination of functions f, f'. The rule's premise requires proving that given the same arbitrary input in, $f(in)$ and $f'(in)$ call mapped functions with the same arguments. A variant of this rule with a weaker premise allows to prove termination of one of the programs if the other is known to terminate for all inputs. We present an algorithm for decomposing the verification problem of whole programs to that of proving mutual termination of individual functions, based on our suggested rules.

1 Introduction

Whereas termination of a single program has been widely studied (e.g., [9,6,4,7]) for several decades by now, with the focus being, especially in the last few years, on automating such proofs, little attention has been paid to the related problem of proving that two similar programs (e.g., two consecutive versions of the same program) terminate on exactly the same inputs. Ideally one should focus on the former problem, but this is not always possible either because the automatic techniques are inherently incomplete, or because *by design* the program does not terminate on all inputs. In such cases there is value in solving the latter problem, because developers may wish to know that none of their changes affect the termination behavior of their program. Moreover, the problem and solution thereof can be defined in the granularity of functions rather than whole programs; in this case the developer may benefit even more from a detailed list of pairs of functions that terminate on exactly the same set of inputs. Those pairs that are not on the list can help detecting termination errors.

Our focus is on successive, closely related versions of a program because it both reflects a realistic problem of developers, and offers opportunities for decomposition and abstraction that are not possible with the single-program termination problem. This problem, which was initially proposed in [11] and coined *mutual termination*, can easily be proven undecidable as can be seen via a simple reduction from the halting problem. We argue, however, that in many cases it is easier to solve automatically, because unlike termination proofs for a single program, it does not rely on proving that the sequence of states in the programs'

A. Biere, A. Nahir, and T. Vos (Eds.): HVC 2012, LNCS 7857, pp. 24–39, 2013.

computations can be mapped into a well-founded set. Rather it can be proven by showing that the loops and recursive functions have the same set of function calls given the same inputs, which is relatively easier to prove automatically. In Sec. 3, for example, we show how to prove mutual termination of two versions of the famous Collatz's $3x + 1$ problem [10]; whereas proving termination of this program is open for many decades, proving mutual termination with respect to another version is simple.

Our suggested method for decomposing the proof is most valuable when the two input programs P and P' are relatively similar in structure. In fact, its complexity is dominated by the *difference* between the programs, rather than by their absolute size. It begins by heuristically building a (possibly partial) map between the functions of P and P'. It then progresses bottom-up on the two call graphs, and each time proves the mutual termination of a pair of functions in the map, while abstracting their callees. The generated verification conditions are in the form of assertions about 'flat' programs (i.e., without loops and recursive calls), which are proportional in size to the two compared functions. It then discharges these verification conditions with a bounded model-checker (CBMC [5] in our case). Each such program has the same structure: it calls the two compared functions sequentially with the same nondeterministic input, records all subsequent function calls and their arguments, and asserts in the end that they have an equivalent set of function calls. According to our proof rule, the validity of this assertion is sufficient for establishing their mutual termination.

The algorithm is rather involved because it has to deal with cases in which the call graphs of P and P' are not isomorphic (this leads to unmapped functions), with mutually recursive functions, and with cases in which the proof of mutual termination for the callees has failed. It also improves completeness by utilizing extra knowledge that we may give to it on the *partial equivalence* of the callees, where two functions are said to be partially equivalent if given the same inputs they terminate with the same outputs, or at least one of them does not terminate. Partial equivalence was studied in [11,13] and is implemented in RVT [13] and Microsoft's SYMDIFF [14]. We also implemented our algorithm in RVT, which enables us to gain this information in a preprocessing step.

To summarize our contributions in this paper, we present a) a proof rule for inferring mutual termination of recursive (and mutually-recursive) functions at the leaves of their respective call graphs, b) an extension of the first rule that applies also to internal nodes in the call graphs, and c) a proof rule for inferring *termination* (not mutual termination) in case the other function is known to be terminating. More importantly, d) we show how these rules can be applied to whole programs via a bottom-up decomposition algorithm, and e) report on a prototype implementation of this algorithm – the first to deal with the mutual termination problem.

2   Preliminaries

Our goal is to prove mutual termination of pairs of functions in programs that are assumed to be deterministic (i.e., single threaded and no internal nondeterminism). Formally:

Definition 1 (Mutual termination of functions). *Two functions f and f' are* mutually terminating *if and only if they terminate upon exactly the same inputs.*

By *input* we mean both the function parameters and the global data it accesses, including the heap. Denote by $m\text{-}term(f, f')$ the fact that f and f' mutually terminate.

Preprocessing and Mapping. As a preprocessing step, all loops are extracted to external recursive functions. After this step nontermination can only arise from recursion. In addition, all global variables that are read by a function are added to the end of its formal parameter list, and the calling sites are changed accordingly. This is not essential for the proof, but simplifies the presentation. It should be noted that this step in itself is impossible in general programs that access the heap, because it is undecidable whether there exists an input to a function that causes the function to read a particular variable. Our only way out of this problem is to point out that it is easy to overapproximate this information (in the worst case just take the whole list of global variables) and to state that, based on our experience with a multitude of real programs, it is rather easy to compute this information precisely or slightly overapproximate it with static analysis techniques such as alias analysis. Indeed, the same exact problem exists in RVT and SYMDIFF for the case of partial equivalence, and there, as in our case, overapproximation can only hinder completeness, not soundness. In general we will not elaborate on issues arising from aliasing because these are not unique to mutual termination, and are dealt with in [13,14].

As a second step, a *bijective* map $map_{\mathcal{F}}$ between the functions of P and P' is derived. For functions $f \in P$ and $f' \in P'$ it is possible that $\langle f, f' \rangle \in map_{\mathcal{F}}$ only if f and f' have the same prototype, i.e., the same list of formal input parameter types. We emphasize that the output of the two functions need not be compatible (e.g., f can update more global variables than f'). The restriction to bijective maps seems detrimental for completeness, because the two compared programs are not likely to have such a map. In practice with inlining such a mapping is usually possible, as we describe later in Sect. 3.

Definitions and Notations

– *Function isolation.* With each function g, we associate an uninterpreted function UF_g such that g and UF_g have the same prototype and return type[1].

---

[1] This definition generalized naturally to cases in which g has multiple outputs owing to global data and arguments passed by reference.

The following definition will be used for specifying which functions are associated with the *same* uninterpreted function:

Definition 2 (Partial equivalence of functions). *Two functions f and f′ are partially equivalent if any two terminating executions of f and f′ starting from the same inputs, return the same value.*

Denote by $p\text{-}equiv(f, f')$ the fact that f and f' are partially equivalent. We enforce that

$$UF_g = UF_{g'} \Rightarrow (\langle g, g' \rangle \in map_{\mathcal{F}} \wedge p\text{-}equiv(g, g')) \quad \text{(enforce)} \qquad (1)$$

i.e., we associate g and g' with the same uninterpreted function only if $\langle g, g' \rangle \in map_{\mathcal{F}}$, and g, g' were proven to be partially equivalent. The list of pairs of functions that are proven to be partially equivalent is assumed to be an input to the mutual termination algorithm. We now define:

$$f^{UF} \doteq f[g(expr_{in}) \leftarrow UF_g(expr_{in}) \mid g \text{ is called in } f] , \qquad (2)$$

where $expr_{in}$ is the expression(s) denoting actual parameter(s) with which g is called. f^{UF} is called the *isolated* version of f. By construction it has no loops or function calls, except for calls to uninterpreted functions.

The definition of f^{UF} requires all function calls to be replaced with uninterpreted functions. A useful relaxation of this requirement, which we will later use, is that it can inline non-recursive functions. Clearly, the result is still nonrecursive. Therefore, we still refer to this as an isolated version of f.

– *Call equivalence.*

Let $calls(f(\boldsymbol{in}))$, where $\boldsymbol{in}$ is a vector of actual values, denote the set of function call instructions (i.e., a function name and the actual parameter values) invoked in the body of $f()$ during the execution of $f(\boldsymbol{in})$. Note that $calls(f(\boldsymbol{in}))$ does not include calls from descendant functions and hence also not from recursive calls.

We can now define:

Definition 3 (Call-equivalence of functions). *f and f′ are call-equivalent if and only if*

$$\forall \langle g, g' \rangle \in map_{\mathcal{F}}, in_f, in_g. \; g'(in_g) \in calls(f'(in_f)) \Leftrightarrow g(in_g) \in calls(f(in_f)) .$$

Denote by $call\text{-}equiv(f, f')$ the fact that f and f' are call-equivalent. Recall that this rule is applied in a context in which $map_{\mathcal{F}}$ is bijective. Note that it is decidable whether f^{UF} and f'^{UF} are call-equivalent, because these are functions without loops and function calls, as explained above.

3 Proof Rules

In an earlier publication by the 3rd author [11], there appears a rule for proving mutual termination of individual 'leaf' functions (i.e., that do not call functions other than themselves). Here we strengthen that rule by making its premise weaker, and consider the more general problem of proving mutual termination of any pair of functions (including mutually recursive), which enable us to consider whole programs.

Given a call graph of a general program, a corresponding DAG may be built by collapsing each maximal strongly connected component (MSCC) into a single node. Nodes that are not part of any cycle in the call graph (corresponding to non-recursive functions) are called *trivial* MSCCs in the DAG. Other MSCCs correspond to either simple or mutually recursive function(s).

Given the two compared programs P, P', let map_m be a map between the nodes of their respective MSCC DAGs, which is consistent with map_f. Namely, if $\langle m, m' \rangle \in map_m$, f is a function in m, and $\langle f, f' \rangle \in map_{\mathcal{F}}$, then f' is a function in m' (and vice-versa).

Consider, then, a pair $\langle m, m' \rangle \in map_m$ of *leaves* in their respective MSCC DAGs. Denote by

$$map_{\mathcal{F}}(m) = \{\langle f, f' \rangle \mid \langle f, f' \rangle \in map_{\mathcal{F}}, f \in m, f' \in m'\} \,.$$

Our goal is to prove mutual termination of each of the pairs in $map_{\mathcal{F}}(m)$. The following proof rule gives us a way to do it by proving call-equivalence of each of these pairs:

$$\frac{\forall \langle f, f' \rangle \in map_{\mathcal{F}}(m).\ \textit{call-equiv}(f^{UF}, f'^{UF})}{\forall \langle f, f' \rangle \in map_{\mathcal{F}}(m).\ \textit{m-term}(f, f')} \quad \text{(M-TERM)} \qquad (3)$$

The premise of (3) is weaker than (hence the rule itself is stronger than) the one suggested in [11], because the latter required the compared functions to be partially equivalent. Furthermore, whereas [11] refers to leaf MSCCs only, later on in this section we generalize (3) so it also applies to non-leaf MSCCs, and hence tackles the general case.

Incompleteness. The abstraction of calls with uninterpreted functions is the source of incompleteness. Two examples of incompleteness are:

- *call-equiv*(f^{UF}, f'^{UF}) fails, but the counterexample relies on values returned by an uninterpreted function that are different than what the corresponding concrete function would have returned if called with the same parameters.
- The concrete function and its counterpart on the other side do not terminate, but their abstractions terminate and are followed by different function calls on the two sides, which leads to call equivalence not being true.

3.1   Checking the Premise

We check the premise of (3) by building a loop- and recursion-free program for each pair of functions that we want to prove call equivalent. Here we describe the construction informally, and only for the case of simple recursion at the leaf functions. We will consider the general case in a more formal way in Sec. 4.

Let f, f' be simple recursive functions that only call themselves. We associate a set of call instructions with each called function (this set represents $calls(f(\boldsymbol{in}))$. For example, in f only f itself is called, and hence we maintain a set of call instructions to f. We then build a program with the following structure: **main** assigns equal nondeterministic values to the inputs of f and f'. It then calls an implementation of f^{UF} and f'^{UF}, and finally asserts that the sets of call instructions are equal. The example below (hopefully) clarifies this construction.

---

function $f(\textbf{int } a)$	**function** $f'(\textbf{int } a')$
int $even := 0, ret := 0;$	**int** $t', odd' := 0, ret' := 0;$
if $a > 1$ **then**	**if** $a' \leq 1$ **then return** $ret';$
if $\neg(a \% 2)$ **then** ▷ even	$t' := a'/2;$
$a := a/2;$	**if** $a'\%2$ **then** ▷ odd
$even = 1;$	$a' := 6t' + 4;$
else $a := 3a + 1;$	$odd' := 1;$
$ret := even + f(a);$	**else** $a' := t';$
return $ret;$	$ret' := odd' + f'(a');$
	return $ret';$

Fig. 1. Two variations on the Collatz ("$3x+1$") function that are mutually terminating. f (f') returns the total number of times the function was called with an even (odd) number. Note than when a' is odd, $a'/2 = (a' - 1)/2$, and hence $6(a'/2) + 4 = 3a' + 1$.

Example 1. Consider the two variants of the Collatz ("$3x + 1$") program [10] in Fig. 1[2], which return different values (see explanation in the caption of the figure). The Collatz program is a famous open problem in termination: no one knows whether it terminates for all (unbounded) integers. On the other hand proving mutual termination of the two variants given here is easy. The comparison is not fair, however, because our decision procedure assumes finite types: we target C programs. But as we show in the full version of this article [1], it is solvable even when the input parameter is an unbounded integer, using a decision procedure for linear arithmetic.

The definitions of f^{UF}, f'^{UF} appear at the top part of Fig. 2. The middle part of the same figure shows an implementation UF of the uninterpreted functions. It receives a function index (abusing notation for simplicity, we assume here that a function name represents also a unique index) and the actual parameters. Note that it records the set of call instructions in the array **params**.

In this case f, f' are not partially equivalent, and therefore according to (1) we replace the recursive calls with different uninterpreted functions. Indeed, we call UF above with two different function indices (f and f'), which means that

---

[2] In the pseudocode we use the convention by which % is the modulo operator.

---

function f^{UF}(int a)
   int $even := 0, ret := 0$;
   if $a > 1$ then
      if $\neg(a \% 2)$ then   ▷ even
         $a := a/2$;
         $even = 1$;
      else $a := 3a + 1$;
     $ret := even + \mathrm{UF}(f, a)$;
   return ret;

function f'^{UF}(int a')
   int $t', odd' := 0, ret' := 0$;
   if $a' \leq 1$ then return ret';
   $t' := a'/2$;
   if $a'\%2$ then   ▷ odd
      $a' := 6t' + 4$;
      $odd' := 1$;
   else $a' := t'$;
   $ret' := odd' + \mathrm{UF}(f', a')$;
   return ret';

function UF(function index g, input parameters $\boldsymbol{in}$)
   if $\boldsymbol{in} \in params[g]$ then return the output of the earlier call UF($g, \boldsymbol{in}$);
   $params[g] := params[g] \cup \boldsymbol{in}$;
   return a nondeterministic value;

function MAIN
   $\boldsymbol{in} = nondet()$; $f^{UF}(\boldsymbol{in})$; $f'^{UF}(\boldsymbol{in})$;
   assert($params[f] = params[f']$);   ▷ checks call equivalence

---

Fig. 2. The flat program that we generate and then verify its assertion, given the two functions of Fig. 1

on equal inputs they do not necessarily return the same nondeterministic value. We defer the presentation of the case in which the functions are known to be partially equivalent to Sec. 4.   □

What if there is no bijective map $map_{\mathcal{F}}$, or if some of the pairs of functions cannot be proven to be mutually terminating? It is not hard to see that it is sufficient to prove mutual termination of pairs of functions that together intersect all cycles in m, m', whereas the other functions are inlined. The same observation was made with regard to proving *partial equivalence* in a technical report [12]. This observation can be used to improve completeness: even when there is no bijective mapping or when it is impossible to prove mutual termination for all pairs in m, m', it is still sometimes possible to prove it for some of the pairs. The algorithm that we describe in Sec. 4 uses this observation.

3.2   Generalization

We now generalize (M-TERM) to the case that m, m' are not leaf MSCCs. This means that there is a set of functions $C(m)$ outside of m that are called by functions in m. $C(m')$ is defined similarly with respect to m'. The premise now requires that these functions are mutually-terminating:

$$\frac{\begin{array}{l}(\forall \langle g, g' \rangle \in map_{\mathcal{F}}. \ (g \in C(m) \wedge g' \in C(m')) \rightarrow m\text{-}term(g, g'))\wedge \\ (\forall \langle f, f' \rangle \in map_{\mathcal{F}}(m). \ call\text{-}equiv(f^{UF}, f'^{UF}))\end{array}}{\forall \langle f, f' \rangle \in map_{\mathcal{F}}(m). \ m\text{-}term(f, f')} \ (\text{M-TERM}^+) \ .$$

$$(4)$$

Recall that (2) prescribes that calls to functions in $C(m)$ and $C(m')$ are replaced with uninterpreted functions in f^{UF}, f'^{UF}.

A full soundness proof of the generalized rule appears in Appendix A of the full version of this article [1], whereas here we only sketch its steps. The proof begins by showing that the premise implies $\forall \langle f, f' \rangle \in map_{\mathcal{F}}(m). \ call\text{-}equiv(f, f')$. Now, falsely assume that there is a pair $\langle f, f' \rangle \in map_{\mathcal{F}}(m)$ that is not mutually terminating whereas the premise holds. For some value in, suppose that it is $f(in)$ that terminates, while $f'(in)$ does not. The infinite call stack of $f'(in)$ must contain a call, say from $h'(in_1)$ to $g'(in_2)$, whereas $h(in_1)$ does not call $g(in_2)$ in the call stack of $f(in)$ (assuming $\{\langle g, \ g' \rangle, \ \langle h, \ h' \rangle\} \subseteq map_{\mathcal{F}}$). This contradicts our premise that $\langle h, \ h' \rangle$ are call-equivalent. The argument is a little more involved when there are multiple calls to the same function, and when there are calls to functions in $C(m), C(m')$, but we leave such subtleties to Appendix A in [1].

4 A Decomposition Algorithm

In this section we present an algorithm for proving mutual termination of full programs. As mentioned in Sec. 3, the call graph of a program can be viewed as a DAG where the nodes correspond to MSCCs. After building a mapping between the MSCCs of the two call graphs, the algorithm traverses the DAG bottom-up. For each mapped pair of MSCCs m, m', it attempts to prove the mutual termination of their mapped functions, based on (M-TERM$^+$).

The algorithm is inspired by a similar algorithm for verification of *partial equivalence*, which is described in a technical report [12]. The algorithm here is more involved, however, because it handles differently cases in which the checked functions are also partially equivalent (recall that this information, i.e., which functions are known to be partially equivalent, is part of the input to the algorithm). Furthermore, the algorithm in [12] is described with a non-deterministic step, and here we suggest a method for determinizing it.

The preprocessing and mapping is as in Sec. 2. Hence the program is loop-free, globals accessed by a function are sent instead as additional inputs, and there is a (possibly partial) mapping $map_{\mathcal{F}}$ between the functions of P and P'.

4.1 The Algorithm

The input to Alg. 1 is P, P', a (possibly partial) mapping $map_{\mathcal{F}}$ between their functions, and (implicitly) those paired functions that are known to be partially equivalent. Its output is a set of function pairs that are marked as m_term, indicating it succeeded to prove their mutual termination based on (M-TERM^+). We now describe the three functions used by this algorithm.

PROVEMT. This entry function traverses the call graphs of P, P' bottom-up, each time focusing on a pair of MSCCs. In line 2 it inlines all nonrecursive functions that are not mapped in $map_{\mathcal{F}}$. In line 3 it uses renaming to resolve possible name collisions between the globals of the two input programs. The next line builds the MSCC DAGs MD and MD' from the call graphs, as explained in Sec.3. Line 5 attempts to build map_m (as defined in Sect. 3), only that it must be *bijective*. If such a bijective map does not exist, the algorithm aborts. In practice one may run the algorithm bottom-up until reaching nonmapped MSCCs, but we omit this option here for brevity.

The bottom-up traversal starts in line 6. Initially all MSCCs are unmarked. The algorithm searches for a next unmarked pair $\langle m, m' \rangle$ of MSCCs such that all its children pairs are marked. If m, m' are trivial (see Sec. 3 for a definition), then line 10 simply checks the call-equivalence of the function pair $\langle f, f' \rangle$ that constitutes $\langle m, m' \rangle$, and marks them accordingly in line 10. Note that even if the descendants of m, m' are mutually-terminating, m, m' are not necessarily so, because they may call their descendants with different parameters. Also note that if this check fails, we continue to check their ancestors (in contrast to the case of non-trivial MSCCs listed next). The reason is that even if $\langle f, f' \rangle$ are not mutually terminating for every input, their callers may still be, because they can be mutually terminating in the context of their callers. We can check this by inlining them, which is only possible because they are not recursive.

Next, consider the case that the selected m, m' in line 7 are not trivial. In line 11 the algorithm chooses non-deterministically a subset S of pairs from $map_{\mathcal{F}}(m)$ that intersects all the cycles in m and m'. This guarantees that we can always inline the functions in m, m' that are not in S. Determinization of this step will be considered in subsection 4.3. If CALLEQUIV returns TRUE for all the function pairs in S, then all those pairs are labeled as m_term in line 13. Otherwise it abandons the attempt to prove their ancestors in line 14: it cannot prove that mapped functions in $\langle m, m' \rangle$ are mutually terminating, nor can it inline these functions in their callers, so we cannot check all its ancestors.

Regardless of whether $\langle m, m' \rangle$ are trivial, they get marked as $mscc\_covered$ in line 7, and the loop in PROVEMT continues to another pair.

ISOLATE. The function ISOLATE receives as input a pair $\langle f, f' \rangle \in map_{\mathcal{F}}$ and a set S of paired functions which, by construction (see line 11), contains only pairs from the same MSCCs as f, f', i.e., if $f \in m$ and $f' \in m'$, then $(g, g') \in S$ implies that $g \in m$ and $g' \in m'$. As output, it generates f^{UF} and f'^{UF}, or rather a relaxation thereof as explained after Eq. (2). We will occasionally refer to them as *side 0* and *side 1*. These functions do not have function calls (other than to uninterpreted functions), but may include inlined (nonrecursive) callees that were not proven to be mutually terminating. ISOLATE should be thought of as working on a new copy of the original programs in each invocation.

Algorithm 1. Pseudo-code for a bottom-up decomposition algorithm for proving that pairs of functions mutually terminate

---

1: **function** PROVEMT(Programs P, P', map between functions $map_\mathcal{F}$)
2:     Inline non-recursive non-mapped functions;
3:     Solve name collisions in global identifiers of P, P' by renaming.
4:     Generate MSCC DAGs MD, MD' from the call graphs of P, P';
5:     If possible, generate a bijective map map_m between the nodes of MD
            and MD' that is consistent with $map_\mathcal{F}$; Otherwise **abort**.
6:     **while** $\exists\langle m, m'\rangle \in map_m$ not marked *covered* but its children are, **do**
7:         Choose such a pair $\langle m, m'\rangle \in map_m$ and mark it *covered*
8:         **if** m, m' are trivial **then**
9:             Let f, f' be the functions in m, m', respectively;
10:             **if** CALLEQUIV (ISOLATE($f, f', \emptyset$)) **then** mark f, f' as m_term;
11:         **else** Select non-deterministically $S \subseteq \{\langle f, f'\rangle \mid \langle f, f'\rangle \in map_\mathcal{F}(m)\}$
                that intersect every cycle in m and m';
12:             **if** $\forall\langle f, f'\rangle \in S$. CALLEQUIV (ISOLATE($f, f', S$)) **then**
13:                 **for** each $\langle f, f'\rangle \in S$ **do** mark f, f' as m_term;
14:             **else** mark ancestors of m, m' as *covered*;

15: **function** ISOLATE(functions f, f', function pairs S)   ▷ Builds f^{UF}, f'^{UF}
16:     **for** each $\{\langle g, g'\rangle \in map_\mathcal{F} \mid g, g'$ are reachable from $f, f'\}$ **do**
17:         **if** $\langle g, g'\rangle \in S$ or $\langle g, g'\rangle$ is marked m_term **then**
18:             Replace calls to $g(\boldsymbol{in})$, $g'(\boldsymbol{in'})$ with calls to UF(g, $\boldsymbol{in}$), UF'(g', $\boldsymbol{in'}$), resp.;
19:         **else** inline g, g' in their callers;
20:     **return** $\langle f, f'\rangle$;

21: **function** CALLEQUIV(A pair of isolated functions $\langle f^{UF}, f'^{UF}\rangle$)
22:     Let δ denote the program:

    ▷ here add the definitions of UF() and UF'() (see Fig. 3).
    $\boldsymbol{in} := nondet(); f^{UF}(\boldsymbol{in}); f'^{UF}(\boldsymbol{in});$
    $\forall\langle g, g'\rangle \in map_\mathcal{F}.$ if g (or g') is called[a] in f (or f') assert($params[g] \subseteq params[g']$);

23:     **return** CBMC(δ);

---

[a] By 'called' we mean that a call appears in the function. It does not mean that there is necessarily an input that invokes this call.

The implementations of UF and UF' appear in Fig. 3, and are rather self-explanatory. Their main role is to check call-equivalence. This is done by checking that they are called with the same set of inputs. When $\langle g, g'\rangle$ is marked *partially_equiv*, UF and UF' emulate the *same* uninterpreted function, i.e.,

$$\forall\boldsymbol{in}.\ \text{UF}(g, \boldsymbol{in}) = \text{UF'}(g', \boldsymbol{in}) .$$

When $\langle g, g'\rangle$ is not marked *partially_equiv*, UF and UF' emulate two *different* uninterpreted functions.

1: **function** UF(function index g, input parameters **in**)   ▷ Called in side 0
2:     **if** **in** $\in params[g]$ **then return** the output of the earlier call UF(g, **in**);
3:     $params[g] := params[g] \cup$ **in**;
4:     **return** a non-deterministic output;

5: **function** UF'(function index g', input parameters **in'**)   ▷ Called in side 1
6:     **if** **in'** $\in params[g']$ **then return** the output of the earlier call UF'(g', **in'**);
7:     $params[g'] := params[g'] \cup$ **in'**;
8:     **if** **in'** $\in params[g]$ **then**   ▷ $\langle g, g' \rangle \in map_\mathcal{F}$
9:         **if** $\langle g, g' \rangle$ is marked *partially_equiv* **then**
10:             **return** the output of the earlier call UF(g, **in'**);
11:         **return** a non-deterministic output;
12:     **assert**(0);   ▷ Not call-equivalent: $params[g'] \not\subseteq params[g]$

Fig. 3. Functions UF and UF' emulate uninterpreted functions if instantiated with functions that are mapped to one another. They are part of the generated program δ, as shown in CALLEQUIV of Alg. 1. These functions also contain code for recording the parameters with which they are called.

CALLEQUIV. Our implementation is based on the C model checker CBMC [5], which enables us to fully automate the check for call-equivalence. CBMC is complete for bounded programs (i.e., loops and recursions are bounded), and, indeed, the program δ we build in CALLEQUIV is of that nature. It simply calls f^{UF}, f'^{UF} (which, recall, have no loops or function calls by construction), with the same nondeterministic value, and asserts in the end that the set of calls in f is included in the set of calls in f' (the other direction is checked in lines 8, 12 of UF'). Examples of such generated programs that we checked with CBMC are available online in [2].

4.2   An Example

The following example demonstrates Alg. 1. Consider the call graphs in Fig. 4.
    Assume that $\langle f_i, f_i' \rangle \in map_\mathcal{F}$ for $i = 1, \ldots, 5$, and that the functions represented by gray nodes are known to be partially equivalent to their counterparts. Line 4 generates the following nodes of the MSCC DAGs: $MD = \{\{f_5\},$

Fig. 4. Call graphs of the input programs P, P'. Partially equivalent functions are gray.

Table 1. Applying Alg. 1 to the call graphs in Fig. 4. '$\checkmark$' means that the pair is marked m_term, '$\checkmark^c$' that it is marked conditionally (it becomes unconditional once all other pairs in S are marked as well), and '$\boldsymbol{X}$' that it is not marked. ($\overset{=}{}$) and ($\overset{\neq}{}$) denote that UF, UF' emulate the same, or, respectively, different, uninterpreted functions.

MSCCs	Pair	Description	Res.
$\{f_5\}, \{f_5'\}$	$\langle f_5, f_5'\rangle$	In line 11 the only possible S is $\langle f_5, f_5'\rangle$. ISOLATE replaces the recursive call to f_5, f_5' with UF, UF', respectively ($\overset{=}{}$). Assume CALLEQUIV returns TRUE. $\langle f_5, f_5'\rangle$ is marked m_term in line 13.	$\checkmark$
$\{f_3\}, \{f_3'\}$	$\langle f_3, f_3'\rangle$	This is a case of trivial MSCCs, which is handled in lines 8–10. ISOLATE replaces the calls to f_5, f_5' with UF, UF', respectively ($\overset{=}{}$). Assume CALLEQUIV returns FALSE.	$\boldsymbol{X}$
$\{f_2, f_4\},$ $\{f_2', f_4', f_6'\}$		In line 11 let $S = \{\langle f_2, f_2'\rangle, \langle f_4, f_4'\rangle\}$.	
	$\langle f_2, f_2'\rangle$	In f_2 calls to f_3 are inlined, and calls to f_4, f_5 are replaced with calls to UF. In f_2' calls to f_3', f_6' are inlined, and calls to f_4', f_5' are replaced with calls to UF' ($\overset{=}{}$). Assume CALLEQUIV returns TRUE.	$\checkmark^c$
	$\langle f_4, f_4'\rangle$	In f_4, f_4' calls to f_2, f_2' are respectively replaced with calls to UF, UF' ($\overset{\neq}{}$). Assume CALLEQUIV returns TRUE. Now $\langle f_2, f_2'\rangle$ and $\langle f_4, f_4'\rangle$ are marked m_term in line 13.	$\checkmark$
$\{f_1\}, \{f_1'\}$	$\langle f_1, f_1'\rangle$	Again, a case of a trivial MSCC. Calls to f_2, f_2' are respectively replaced with UF, UF' ($\overset{\neq}{}$), while calls to f_4, f_4' are replaced with UF, UF', respectively ($\overset{=}{}$). Assume CALLEQUIV returns TRUE. $\langle\{f_1\}, \{f_1'\}\rangle$ is marked m_term.	$\checkmark$

$\{f_3\}, \{f_2, f_4\}, \{f_1\}\}$; $MD' = \{\{f_5'\}, \{f_3'\}, \{f_2', f_4', f_6'\}, \{f_1'\}\}$. The MSCC mapping map_m in line 5 is naturally derived from $map_{\mathcal{F}}$.

The progress of the algorithm is listed in Table 1. The output in this case, based on assumptions about the results of the checks for call-equivalence that are mentioned in the table, is that the following pairs of functions are marked as m_term: $\langle f_1, f_1'\rangle$, $\langle f_2, f_2'\rangle$, $\langle f_4, f_4'\rangle$, and $\langle f_5, f_5'\rangle$.

4.3 Choosing a Vertex Feedback Set Deterministically

In line 7 the choice of the set S is nondeterministic. Our implementation determinizes it by solving a series of optimization problems. In the worst case this amounts to trying all sets, which is exponential in the size of the MSCC. Observe, however, that large MSCCs are rare in real programs and, indeed, this has never posed a computational problem in our experiments.

Our objective is to find a maximal set S of function pairs, because the larger the set is, the more functions are declared to be mutually terminating in case of success. Further, larger sets imply fewer functions to inline, and hence the burden on CALLEQUIV is expected to be smaller. Our implementation solves this optimization problem via a reduction to a pseudo-Boolean formula, which is then solved by MINISAT+ [8]. Each function node g in m (and m') is associated with a Boolean variable v_g, indicating whether it is part of S. The objective is thus to maximize the sum of these variables that are mapped (those that are unmapped cannot be in S anyway). In addition, there is a variable e_{ij} for each edge (i, j), which is set to true iff neither i nor j is in S. By enforcing a transitive closure, we guarantee that if there is a cycle of edges set to true (i.e., a cycle in which none of the nodes is in S), then the self edges (e.g., $e_{i,i}$) are set to TRUE as well. We then prevent such cycles by setting them to FALSE. Let *mapped(m)* denote the set of functions in m that are mapped. The problem formulation appears in Fig. 5, and is rather self-explanatory. In case the chosen set S fails (i.e., one of the pairs in S cannot be proven to be mutually terminating), we add its negation (see constraint #6) and repeat.

$$\text{maximize } S: \qquad \max \sum_{g \in mapped(m)} v_g$$

subject to the following constraints, for $M \in \{m, m'\}$:

1. Unmapped nodes are not in S: $\forall g \in (M \setminus mapped(M)). \; \neg v_g$
2. Defining the edges: $\forall \{i, j \mid (i, j) \text{ is an edge in } M\}. \; \neg v_i \wedge \neg v_j \rightarrow e_{ij}$
3. Transitive closure: $\forall 0 < i, j, k \leq |M|. \; e_{ij} \wedge e_{jk} \rightarrow e_{ik}$
4. Self loops are not allowed: $\forall 0 < i \leq |M|. \; \neg e_{ii}$
5. Enforce mapping: $\forall \langle g, g' \rangle \in map_{\mathcal{F}}, g \in m. \; v_g \leftrightarrow v'_g$
6. For each failed solution Sl: $\bigvee_{\langle g, g' \rangle \in Sl} \neg v_g$

Fig. 5. A pseudo-Boolean formulation of the optimization problem of finding the largest set of function pairs from m, m' that intersect all cycles in both m and m'

5 An Inference Rule for Proving Termination

We now consider a different variant of the mutual termination problem: *Given that a program P terminates, does P' terminate as well?* Clearly this problem can be reduced to that of mutual termination, but in fact it can also be solved with a weaker premise. We first define *term(f)* to denote that f terminates and

$$call\text{-}contains(f, f') \doteq$$
$$\forall \langle g, g' \rangle \in map_{\mathcal{F}}, in_f, in_g. \; g'(in_g) \in calls(f'(in_f)) \Rightarrow g(in_g) \in calls(f(in_f)) \, .$$

Using these predicates, we can now define the rule for leaf MSCCs m, m':

$$\frac{\forall \langle f, f' \rangle \in map_{\mathcal{F}}(m). \left(term(f) \wedge call\text{-}contains(f^{UF}, f'^{UF}) \right)}{\forall \langle f, f' \rangle \in map_{\mathcal{F}}(m). \; term(f')} \quad (\text{TERM}) \, . \quad (5)$$

Theorem 1. (TERM) *is sound.*

Proof. The proof follows similar lines to that of (M-TERM$^+$). We give a proof sketch. Falsely assume that there is a function f' in m' that does not terminate, whereas for all $\langle g, g' \rangle \in map_{\mathcal{F}}(m)$, *call-contains*$(g, g')$. There exists a value *in* such that $f'(in)$ does not terminate. The infinite call stack of $f'(in)$ must contain a call, say from $h'(in_1)$ to $g'(in_2)$, whereas $h(in_1)$ does not call $g(in_2)$ in the call stack of $f(in)$ (assuming $\{\langle g, g' \rangle, \langle h, h' \rangle\} \subseteq map_{\mathcal{F}}$). This contradicts our premise that *call-contains*(h, h') is true.   □

Note that call-equivalence (Def. 3) is simply bi-directional call-containment. A generalization to non-leaf MSCCs can be done in a similar way to (4):

$$\frac{(\forall \langle g, g' \rangle \in map_{\mathcal{F}}. \ (g \in C(m) \wedge g' \in C(m')) \rightarrow m\text{-}term(g, g')) \wedge}{\forall \langle f, f' \rangle \in map_{\mathcal{F}}(m). \left(term(f) \wedge call\text{-}contains(f^{UF}, f'^{UF}) \right)} \quad (\text{TERM}^+) ,$$

$$\tag{6}$$

where, recall, $C(m)$ denotes the functions that are outside of m and are called by functions in m. A proof appears in [1].

The decomposition algorithm of the previous section (Alg. 1) applies with the following change: the last statement of line 22 (asserting $params[g] \subseteq params[g']$) should be removed. The only assertion that should be verified is thus inside UF (line 12 in Fig. 3), which checks that every call on side 0 is matched by a call on side 1.

6   Experience and Conclusions

We implemented Alg. 1 in RVT [13,2], and tested it with many small programs and one real software project. Here we describe the latter.

We tested our tool on the open source project BETIK [3], which is an interpreter for a scripting language. The code has 2 – 2.5 KLOC (depending on the version). It has many loops and recursive functions, including mutual recursion forming an MSCC of size 14. We compared eight consecutive versions of this program from the code repository, i.e., seven comparisons. The amount of changes between the versions varied with an average of 3–4 (related) functions. Somewhat to our surprise, many of the changes do *not* preserve termination behavior in a free context, mostly because these functions traverse global data structures on the heap.

In five out of the seven comparisons, RVT discovered correctly, in less than 2 minutes each, that the programs contained mapped functions that do not mutually terminate. An example is a function called INT_VALUE(), which receives a pointer to a node in a syntax tree. The old version compared the type of the node to several values, and if none of them matched it simply returned the input node.

In the new code, a 'default' branch was added, that called INT_VALUE() with the node's subtype. In an arbitrary context, it is possible that the syntax 'tree' is not actually a tree, rather a cyclic graph, e.g., owing to data aliasing. Hence, there is a context in which the old function terminates whereas the new one is trapped in infinite recursion. The full version of this article [1] includes the code of this function as well as an additional example in which mutual termination is not preserved.

In the remaining two comparisons RVT marked correctly, in less than a minute each, that all mapped functions are mutually terminating.

Conclusion and Future Research. Listing the functions that changed their termination behavior owing to code updates may be valuble to programers. In this article we made several steps towards achieving this goal. We showed a proof rule for mutual termination, and a bottom-up decomposition algorithm for handling whole programs. This algorithm calls a model-checker for discharging the premise of the rule. Our prototype implementation of this algorithm in RVT is the first to give an automated (inherently incomplete) solution to the mutual termination problem.

An urgent conclusion from our experiments is that checking mutual termination under free context is possibly insufficient, especially when it comes to programs that manipulate a global structure on the heap. Developers would also want to know whether their programs mutually terminate under the context of their specific program. Another direction is to interface RVT with an external tool that checks termination: in those cases that they can prove termination of one side but not of the other, we can use the results of Sec. 5 to prove termination in the other side. We can also benefit from knowing that a pair of functions terminate (not just mutually terminate) because in such a case they should be excluded from the call-equivalence check of their callers. Finally, it seems plausible to develop methods for proving termination by using the rule (M-TERM$^+$). One needs to find a variant of the input program that on the one hand is easier to prove terminating, and on the other hand is still call-equivalent to the original program.

References

1. Full version available from http://ie.technion.ac.il/~ofers/hvc-full.pdf
2. http://ie.technion.ac.il/~ofers/rvt.html
3. http://code.google.com/p/betik
4. Bradley, A.R., Manna, Z., Sipma, H.B.: Linear ranking with reachability. In: Etessami, K., Rajamani, S.K. (eds.) CAV 2005. LNCS, vol. 3576, pp. 491–504. Springer, Heidelberg (2005)
5. Clarke, E., Kroening, D.: Hardware verification using ANSI-C programs as a reference. In: Proceedings of ASP-DAC 2003, pp. 308–311. IEEE Computer Society Press (January 2003)
6. Cook, B., Podelski, A., Rybalchenko, A.: Abstraction refinement for termination. In: Hankin, C., Siveroni, I. (eds.) SAS 2005. LNCS, vol. 3672, pp. 87–101. Springer, Heidelberg (2005)

7. Cook, B., Podelski, A., Rybalchenko, A.: Proving program termination. Commun. ACM 54(5), 88–98 (2011)
8. Eén, N., Sörensson, N.: Translating pseudo-boolean constraints into sat. JSAT 2(1-4), 1–26 (2006)
9. Floyd, R.: Assigning meanings to programs. Proc. Symposia in Applied Mathematics 19, 19–32 (1967)
10. Garner, L.E.: On the Collatz 3n + 1 algorithm. Proceedings of the American Mathematical Society 82(1), 19–22 (1981)
11. Godlin, B., Strichman, O.: Inference rules for proving the equivalence of recursive procedures. Acta Informatica 45(6), 403–439 (2008)
12. Godlin, B., Strichman, O.: Regression verification. Technical Report IE/IS-2011-02, Technion (2011), http://ie.technion.ac.il/tech_reports/1306207119_j.pdf
13. Godlin, B., Strichman, O.: Regression verification. In: 46th Design Automation Conference, DAC (2009)
14. Kawaguchi, M., Lahiri, S.K., Rebelo, H.: Conditional equivalence. Technical Report MSR-TR-2010-119, Microsoft Research (2010)

Knowledge Based Transactional Behavior*

Saddek Bensalem[1], Marius Bozga[1], Doron Peled[2], and Jean Quilbeuf[1]

[1] UJF-Grenoble 1 / CNRS, VERIMAG UMR 5104, Grenoble, F-38041, France
[2] Department of Computer Science, Bar Ilan University, Ramat Gan 52900, Israel

Abstract. Component-based systems (including distributed programs and multiagent systems) involve a lot of coordination. This coordination is done in the background, and is transparent to the operation of the system. The reason for this overhead is the interplay between concurrency and non-deterministic choice: processes alternate between progressing independently and coordinating with other processes, where coordination can involve multiple choices of the participating components. This kind of interactions appeared as early as some of the main communication-based programming languages, where overhead effort often causes a restriction on the possible coordination. With the goal of enhancing the efficiency of coordination for component-based systems, we propose here a method for coordination-based on the precalculation of the knowledge of processes and coordination agents. This knowledge can be used to lift part of the communication or synchronization that appears in the background of the execution to support the interaction. Our knowledge-based method is orthogonal to the actual algorithms or primitives that are used to guarantee the synchronization: it only removes messages conveying information that knowledge can infer.

1 Introduction

Component-based systems are a generalization of distributed systems. In concurrent languages like CSP and ADA processes allow binary interactions between processes, often with the choice between outgoing communication restricted to be deterministic. Modern distributed systems may involve more general multi-party coordination, e.g., robots that need to coordinate temporarily on a certain task. While such a system may reveal a behavioral model that is based on interaction primitives, often in the back, there are algorithms that are based on more basic primitives such as asynchronous message passing or shared variables. Algorithms for obtaining synchronization primitives are complicated and require nontrivial overhead. Theoretical results also show some inherent restrictions: a well known result on the dinning philosophers [12] shows that a completely symmetric nonprobabilistic solution cannot exist.

We present here a method for improving the behavior of synchronous interactions by removing some of the overhead for guaranteeing the correct synchronization of components based on knowledge calculation. The main principle is based on the observation that such algorithms need to allow for a very general interaction, but can provide a much

---

* The research leading to these results has received funding from the European Community's Seventh Framework Programme [FP7] under grant agreements no 248776 (PRO3D) and no 257414 (ASCENS) and from ARTEMIS JU grant agreement 2009-1-100230 (SMECY).

A. Biere, A. Nahir, and T. Vos (Eds.): HVC 2012, LNCS 7857, pp. 40–55, 2013.

more efficient behavior for more limited cases. Analyzing the system before its execution based on model checking of knowledge properties allows us to utilize the particular behavior that is actually needed for the implementation of the synchronization. Knowledge, basically, refers to the facts that hold in all the global states that are consistent with the current local state of some process. A precalculated knowledge, embedded in the processes, allows exploiting the easier cases of behavior, when relevant.

Our method is general, independent of the actual synchronization algorithm or primitives used to obtain it. However, the actual implementation of the method depends on the specific details of the algorithm. We present its implementation on a well known generic synchronization algorithm called α-core [14].

The paper is organized as follows. Section 2 recalls cellular automata, as the underlying semantic model for synchronizing systems, and the α-core protocol, as one possible solution for distributed implementation of such systems. Section 3 presents the key results on exploiting knowledge to reduce the communication overhead for distributed implementation. We provide techniques for using knowledge independently for components and coordinators as well as for combining them. Section 4 reports experimental results obtained using a prototype implementation realized on top of the BIP framework [3]. Finally, Section 5 provides conclusions and future work directions.

2 Preliminaries

2.1 Cellular Automata

The model of execution that we want to obtain is that of synchronizing systems. To describe such systems we are using cellular automata. This model involves several processes, represented as automata with transitions labeled by action names, where the execution of all the actions that share the same name has to be synchronized by all processes. Formally, the cellular automata model is defined as follows:

Definition 1. *An automaton is a tuple $\langle S, A, \delta, s_0 \rangle$ where S is the set of states, A is the set of actions, $\delta : S \times A \to S$ is the transition relation, $s_0 \in S$ is the initial state. An execution of an automaton is a maximal sequence of states $s_0 s_1 s_2 \ldots$ such that for each $i \geq 0$, there exists $a \in A$ such that $\delta(s_i, a) = s_{i+1}$.*

Definition 2. *A cellular automaton is a set of n automata $\mathcal{A}^i = \langle S^i, A^i, \delta^i, s_0^i \rangle$, $i \in \{1, \ldots, n\}$, such that the sets of states are mutually disjoint, and the sets of actions may have common occurrences (corresponding to interactions).*

Example 1. Figure 1 shows a cellular automaton made of three automata. Each automaton $\mathcal{A}^i$ represents the ith bit of a binary counter (here modulo 8). The most significant bit is represented by the rightmost automaton. Interactions are named after the higher bit that changes during the interaction (e.g., s_1 corresponds to the setting of bit 1 and synchronizes $\mathcal{A}^1$ and $\mathcal{A}^0$, r_2 corresponds to the reset of bit 2 and synchronizes $\mathcal{A}^2$, $\mathcal{A}^1$ and $\mathcal{A}^0$). Each interaction involves either one (s_0), two (s_1) or three (s_2, r_2) automata.

We denote by $S = S^1 \times \ldots \times S^n$ the set of global states of a cellular automaton. A global state $g \in S$ is defined by the state of each automaton $\mathcal{A}^i$ from the cellular automaton. The state of the automaton $\mathcal{A}^i$ at global state g is denoted $g[i]$.

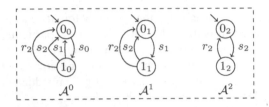

Fig. 1. Example of Cellular Automaton

Fig. 2. Global Behavior

Definition 3. *An execution of a cellular automaton is a maximal sequence of global states $g_0 g_1 \dots$ such that:*

- *g_0 is the tuple made of initial states: $\forall i \in \{1..n\}, g_0[i] = s_0^i$.*
- *For adjacent tuples g_j and g_{j+1} there is an action $a \in \cup_{i \in \{1..n\}} A^i$ such that for each $i \in \{1..n\}$, either $g_{j+1}[i] = \delta^i(g_j[i], a)$ or $a \notin A^i$ and $g_{j+1}[i] = g_j[i]$.*

It is easy to see that the projection of an execution into a single automaton is a prefix of an execution of that automaton.

We denote by $g \xrightarrow{a} g'$ if the action a can be executed from global state g and leads to global state g'. This notation is trivially extended to sequences of interactions, that is for $\sigma = a_1 a_2 \cdots a_k$ we denote by $g \xrightarrow{\sigma} g'$ if there exists global states $g_1, g_2, \cdots g_{k-1}$ such that $g \xrightarrow{a_1} g_1 \xrightarrow{a_2} g_2 \cdots g_{k-1} \xrightarrow{a_k} g'$. We denote by $\sigma|_{A^i}$, the sequence of interactions obtained by removing from σ all occurrences of interactions that are not in A^i.

The set of executions, i.e. global behavior, of the cellular automaton can be represented as a labeled transition system $\mathcal{A} = (S, A, T, g_0)$, where S is the set of global states, $A = \cup_{i \in \{1..n\}} A^i$ is the set of actions (or labels), $T \subseteq S \times A \times S$ is the set of valid transitions (as defined by Definition 3) and g_0 is the initial global state.

Example 2. The global behavior of the cellular automaton depicted in Figure 1 is shown in Figure 2. Any global state $g \in \{0, ..., 7\}$ denotes the tuple of local states $(g[2]g[1]g[0])$ obtained from the representation of g as a binary number.

Cellular automata are perhaps the simplest model to describe synchronizing systems. Nonetheless, this model is expressive enough to underlie higher-level frameworks with similar synchronization-based communication. In particular, we focus hereafter on the relation between cellular automata and the BIP framework [3], which will be used later in section 4 for concrete experiments. BIP (Behavior-Interaction-Priority) is a component-based framework which allows the construction of hierarchically structured component-based systems. In BIP, atomic components are characterized by their interface, that is, a set of ports (similar to action names) and their behavior, that is, an automaton with transitions labeled by ports. Components are composed by layered application of interactions and priorities. Interactions express synchronization constraints between ports of the composed components. An interaction is a set of ports, every one belonging to a different component, that has to be jointly executed. BIP provides (hierarchical) connectors as a mean to structure and express sets of interactions in a compact manner. Finally, priorities are used in BIP to filter amongst the set of enabled interactions. Priorities provide an additional coordination mechanism to control the system evolution. A significant part of BIP systems can be structurally represented as cellular automata. That is, any BIP system without priorities can be equally represented as a cellular automaton by mapping BIP interactions into cellular automata interactions. Since a port may be involved in several interactions, BIP atomic components can be transformed into automata by duplicating transitions labeled by a port into a set of transitions labeled by the corresponding interactions.

2.2 The α-Core Protocol

The α-core protocol [14] was developed to schedule multiprocess interaction. It generalizes protocols for handshake communication between pairs of processes. For each multiprocess interaction, there is a dedicated coordinator on a separate process. To appreciate the difficulty of designing such a protocol, recall for example the fact that the language CSP of Hoare [8] included initially an asymmetric construct for synchronous communication; a process could choose between various incoming messages, but had to commit on a particular send. This constraint was useful for achieving a simple implementation. Otherwise, one needs to consider the situation in which a communication is possible between processes, but one of them may have performed an alternative choice. Later Hoare removed this constraint from CSP. The same constraint appears in the asymmetric communication construct of the programming language ADA. The Buckley and Silberschatz protocol [5] solves this problem for the case of synchronous communication between pairs of processes, where both sends and receives may have choices. Their protocol uses asynchronous message passing between the processes to implement the synchronous message passing construct. The α-core protocol solves the more general problem of synchronizing any number of processes, using only asynchronous message passing. Alternative solutions for this problem have been proposed, using managers [6,1], a circulating token [11], or a randomized algorithm without managers [9]. Contrarily to other manager-based solutions, α-core does not need unbounded counters. The version presented below includes corrections from [10].

In α-core, the following messages are sent from a participant to a coordinator:

PARTICIPATE A participant is interested in a single particular interaction (hence it can commit on it), and notifies the related coordinator.

OFFER A participant is interested in one out of several potentially available interactions (a non-deterministic choice).

OK Sent as a response to a **LOCK** message from a coordinator (described below) to notify that the participant is willing to commit on the interaction.

REFUSE Notify the coordinator that the previous **OFFER** is not valid anymore. This message can respond to a **LOCK** message from the coordinator.

Messages from coordinators are as follows:

LOCK A message sent from a coordinator to a participant that has sent an **OFFER**, requesting the participant to commit on the interaction.

UNLOCK A message sent from a coordinator to a locked participant, indicating that the current interaction is canceled.

START Notifying a participant that it can start the interaction.

ACKREF Acknowledging a participant about the receipt of a **REFUSE** message.

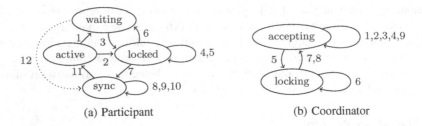

(a) Participant   (b) Coordinator

Fig. 3. State machines

Fig. 3(a) describes the extended state machine of a participant. Each participant process keeps some local variables and constants:

IS: a set of coordinators for the interactions the participant is interested in.
locks: a set of coordinators that have sent a pending **LOCK** message.
unlocks: a set of coordinators from which a pending **UNLOCK** message was received.
locker: the coordinator that is currently considered.
n: the number of **ACKREF** messages required to be received from coordinators until a
      new coordination can start.
α: the coordinators that asked for interactions and subsequently refused.

The actions according to the transitions are written as a pair *en* → *action*, where *en* is the condition to execute the transition, which may include a test of the local variables, a message that arrives, or both of them (then the test should hold *and* the message must arrive). We denote the reception of a message **MSG** from process *p* by *p*?**MSG**. The action is a sequence of statements, executed when the condition holds. The statement *p*!**MSG** means "send message **MSG** to process *p*". In addition, each transition is enabled from some state, and upon execution changes the state according to the related extended finite state machine. The participant's transitions, according to the numbering of Fig. 3(a) are:

1. $|IS > 1| \rightarrow \{$ foreach $p \in IS$ do $p!$**OFFER** $\}$
2. $|IS = 1| \rightarrow \{ locker:=p$, where $IS = \{p\}$; $locker!$**PARTICIPATE**; $locks, unlocks:=\emptyset \}$
3. $p?$**LOCK** $\rightarrow \{locker:=p$; $locks, unlocks:=\emptyset$; $p!$**OK** $\}$
4. $p?$**LOCK** $\rightarrow \{locks:=locks \cup \{p\}\}$
5. $locks \neq \emptyset \wedge p?$**UNLOCK** $\rightarrow \{locker:=q$ for some $q \in locks$; $q!$**OK**; $locks:=locks \setminus \{q\}$; $unlocks:=unlocks \cup \{p\}\}$
6. $locks = \emptyset \wedge p?$**UNLOCK** $\rightarrow \{$ foreach $q \in unlocks \cup \{p\}$ do $q!$**OFFER**$\}$
7. $p?$**START** $\rightarrow \{\alpha:=IS \setminus (unlocks \cup \{locker\})$; foreach $q \in \alpha$ do $q!$**REFUSE**; $n := |\alpha|$; start participating in the joint action managed by $locker\}$
8. $p?$**LOCK** $\rightarrow \{\}$ 9. $p?$**UNLOCK** $\rightarrow \{\}$ 10. $p?$**ACKREF** $\rightarrow \{n:=n-1\}$
11. $n = 0 \rightarrow \{$ Let IS be the new set of interactions required from the current state. $\}$

For a coordinator, whose extended finite state machine appears in Fig. 3(b), we have the variables *waiting*, *locked*, *shared* and α, holding each a set of processes, and *n* is a counter for the number of processes that indicated their wish to participate in the interaction. The constant *C* holds the number of processes that need to participate in the interaction (called, the *cardinality* of the interaction), and the variable *current* is the participant the coordinator is trying to lock. The transitions, according to their numbering from Fig. 3(b) are as follows:

1. $n < C \wedge p?$**OFFER** $\rightarrow$ $\{n:=n+1;\ shared:=\ shared \cup \{p\}\ \}$
2. $n < C \wedge p?$**PARTICIPATE** $\rightarrow$ $\{n:=n+1;\ locked:=\ locked \cup \{p\}\ \}$
3. $p?$**REFUSE** $\rightarrow$ $\{$ if $p \in shared$ then $n:=n-1;\ p!$**ACKREF**; $shared:=shared \setminus \{p\}\}$
4. $n = C \wedge shared = \emptyset \rightarrow \{$ foreach $q \in locked$ do $q!$**START**; $locked, shared:=\emptyset;\ n:=0\}$
5. $n = C \wedge shared \neq \emptyset \rightarrow \{current:=$ min$(shared);\ waiting:=shared \setminus \{current\};$ $current!$**LOCK**$\}$
6. $waiting \neq \emptyset \wedge p?$**OK** $\rightarrow$ $\{locked:=locked \cup \{current\};\ current:=min(waiting);$ $waiting:=waiting \setminus \{current\};\ current!$**LOCK**$\}$
7. $waiting = \emptyset \wedge p?$**OK** $\rightarrow \{locked:=locked \cup \{current\};$ foreach q in $locked$ do $q!$**START**; $locked, waiting, shared:=\emptyset;\ n:=0\}$
8. $p?$**REFUSE** $\rightarrow \{\alpha:=(locked \cap shared) \cup \{current, p\};$ foreach $q \in \alpha \setminus \{p\}$ do $q!$**UNLOCK**; $p!$**ACKREF**; $shared:=shared \setminus \alpha;\ locked:=locked \setminus \alpha;\ n:=n - |\alpha|\}$
9. $p?$**OK** $\rightarrow \{\}$

We propose to characterize the correctness of the implementation by using execution trace equivalence. We assume that the network is reliable and that there is no message loss. We say that the interaction a occurs in a distributed execution of α-core whenever the transition 7 in the coordinator for a is executed. The correctness of α-core guarantees that the executions of the original cellular automaton and the executions of its implementation are the same.

3   Knowledge-Based Optimization

Synchronization algorithms such as α-core impose a lot of overhead in order to guarantee correct interaction. We want to utilize knowledge in order to reduce the overhead in coordination messages. Knowledge appears naturally in distributed systems, as it represents what a process knows from its obseravtions. Halpern and Moses [7] defined a logic to reason about knowledge. Van der Meyden [13] introduced knowledge with perfect recall. Knowledge has been applied to control distributed discrete event systems [15] and to implement priorities between multiparty interactions [2,4]. However, the previous works assume a conflict resolution mechanism. We propose here a knowledge-based optimization of such a mechanism, which has not been done, at least to our knowledge. Based on [2], we construct a support automaton, which is a controller that either supports or blocks actions, based on precalculated knowledge. There are two kinds of controllers here. The first type is for each process of the system, and the second is per each α-core synchronizing process. The support automaton for a system automaton can reduce overhead by calculating when a component can actually commit to an interaction (offer a **PARTICIPATE** call to α-core), which requires less confirmation messages than simply declaring its participation (by the alternative **OFFER** call). In this case, the knowledge gathered in the precalculated stage can distinguish between the cases when one has an alternative possibility of coordination or does not. While we could benefit from syntactically distinguishing between these cases based on the code of the system, the use of knowledge, and in particular, knowledge of perfect recall [13], can distinguish the cases where syntactically there can be alternative collaborations, but at this stage of the executions, the alternatives are not available.

Let $\langle \mathcal{A}^1, \mathcal{A}^2, ..., \mathcal{A}^n \rangle$ be a cellular automaton and $\mathcal{A} = (S, A, T, g_0)$ its associated global behavior as defined in section 2.1.

3.1   Knowledge for Participants

Let $\mathcal{A}^i = \langle S^i, A^i, \delta^i, s_0^i \rangle$ be a participant. As in [13,2], we define the *knowledge with perfect recall* of this participant as the facts it can infer based on its local history. Recall that we denote by $\sigma|_{A^i}$ the sequence of interactions obtained by removing from the sequence σ all occurrences of interactions that are not in A^i.

Definition 4 (Indistinguishability of execution sequences for $\mathcal{A}^i$). *Two sequences of interactions σ and σ' are indistinguishable by $\mathcal{A}^i$, denoted $\sigma \equiv_i \sigma'$, iff $\sigma|_{A^i} = \sigma'|_{A^i}$.*

Definition 5 (Knowledge with perfect recall). *Let σ be a sequence of interactions , $\mathcal{A}^i$ be a participant and φ be a predicate. After executing σ, $\mathcal{A}^i$ knows φ if φ holds after any execution σ' that is indistinguishable by $\mathcal{A}^i$ from σ. Formally, $\mathcal{A}^i$ knows φ after executing σ if $\varphi(g)$ holds for every state g in $\{g \in S | \exists \sigma', \sigma' \equiv_i \sigma \wedge g_0 \xrightarrow{\sigma'} g\}$.*

In order to compute the knowledge with perfect recall of the participant $\mathcal{A}^i$, we build its support automaton $\mathcal{K}_i$ as in [2]. The support automaton $\mathcal{K}_i$ will follow the execution of observable interactions for $\mathcal{A}^i$, that is, all interactions in A^i. The remaining interactions in $U^i = A \setminus A^i$ are not observable by $\mathcal{K}_i$. Informally, the state reached in $\mathcal{K}_i$ after any sequence $\sigma \in A^*$ summarizes all the global states that can be reached in $\mathcal{A}$ after any sequence $\sigma' \in A^*$ such that σ and σ' are indistinguishable by $\mathcal{A}^i$. Formally, $\mathcal{K}_i$ is defined as the deterministic automaton $\langle S_i, A^i, \delta_i, s_{0i} \rangle$ where:

- The set of states $S_i = 2^S$ correspond to subsets of the global states S.
- The transition function δ_i is defined as $\delta_i(s, a) = \{g' \mid \exists g \in s, \exists \sigma \in A^*, g \xrightarrow{\sigma} g'$ and $\sigma|_{A^i} = a\}$. Informally, for any state s, its successor s' through interaction a contains the set of global states g' that are reached in $\mathcal{A}$ from global states g in s by executing any sequence of unobservable interactions and exactly one a.
- The initial state $s_{0i} = \{g \in S | \exists \tilde{\sigma} \in (U^i)^*, g_0 \xrightarrow{\sigma} g\}$. Informally, s_{0i} contains all global states reachable in $\mathcal{A}$ by executing any sequence of unobservable interactions starting from the initial global state g_0.

Example 3. We illustrate the construction above on each automaton of the binary counter example from Figure 1. For $\mathcal{A}^0$, we have $\mathcal{K}_0 = \mathcal{A}$, since $\mathcal{A}^0$ observes all interactions. The support automata obtained for $\mathcal{A}^1$ and $\mathcal{A}^2$ are depicted in Figure 4. Even if by construction, the state $\emptyset$ might be reachable, we do not consider it. Note that $\mathcal{K}_2$ is the same as $\mathcal{A}^2$ up to the name of the states.

The support automaton is used to reduce coordination overhead in α-core as follows. For every $\mathcal{A}^i$, the support automaton $\mathcal{K}_i = \langle S_i, A^i, \delta_i, s_{0i} \rangle$ is *embedded* in the corresponding participant behavior. For our application, there is no need to explicitly keep track of the set of global states corresponding to the states of $\mathcal{K}_i$. There-

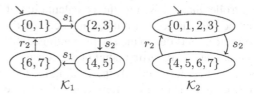

Fig. 4. Support automata for participants $\mathcal{A}^1$ and $\mathcal{A}^2$ of Figure 1

fore, once the automaton $\mathcal{K}_i$ is constructed, states in S_i can be replaced by elements of any arbitrary finite domain. The participant uses one extra local variable s to record the state of the support automaton. This variable is initialized as s_{0i}. Then, this variable is updated when the participant executes an interaction (transition 7) and is used to filter the set *IS* before entering the *active* state (transition 11). The original transitions 7 and 11 are therefore modified into transition $7'$ and $11'$ as follows:

$7'$. $p?\mathbf{START} \rightarrow \{\alpha := IS \setminus unlocks \setminus \{locker\}$; foreach $q \in \alpha$ do $q!\mathbf{REFUSE}$; $n := |\alpha|$; start participating in the joint action a managed by *locker*; $\boxed{s := \delta_i(s,a)}$ $\}$

$11'$. $n = 0 \rightarrow \{$ Let *IS* be the required interactions; $\boxed{IS := IS \cap \{a \in A | \delta_i(s,a) \neq \emptyset\}}$ $\}$

That is, the optimization restricts the sending of offer messages for interactions that are enabled according to the support automaton. Clearly, this restricts the number of exchanged messages. Moreover, in cases where no conflict exists in the filtered behavior (such as in the binary counter example, the size of the *IS* set is always reduced to 1), **OFFER** messages are replaced by **PARTICIPATE** messages, thus removing the need for further locking by coordinators.

Example 4. As an example, from the state 1 in $\mathcal{A}^1$, two interactions (s_2 and r_2) are possible. In $\mathcal{K}_1$ this state is split in two states that separate the case where s_2 is possible from the case where r_2 is possible.

Proposition 1. *The executions of the distributed implementation with knowledge-optimized participants are the same as the executions of the original automaton.*

3.2 Knowledge for Coordinators

Coordinators of the α-core can also gain information about the global context by recording the offers received from different components. That is, new offers are issued by participants only at the initial state and after every successful participation in an interaction. Therefore, offer reception provides to coordinators some (indirect and definitely incomplete) information about the evolution of the system. Nonetheless, this information can be exploited in order to avoid some useless coordination of the α-core protocol. For example, a coordinator may detect that some offers are obsolete (their locking will always be refused) or stable (on the contrary, their locking will always be accepted by the corresponding participant).

The construction of the support automata for coordinators is a bit more intricate than for participants. We want to benefit from the same approach by constructing a controller that is based on the precalculation of knowledge. However, such calculation can be quite intricate if it takes into account the structure of the α-core algorithm. The complication is due to the above mentioned difference in observation, that is, offers *vs.* interactions. The starting point of the construction is the global behavior $\mathcal{A}$. Clearly, $\mathcal{A}$ does not mention explicitly the sending/reception of offers by participants/coordinators. But, communication of offers can still be inferred from $\mathcal{A}$ knowing the behavior of the α-core protocol. We present hereafter a systematic construction that allows to progressively *refine* $\mathcal{A}$ such that to make visible (relevant) offers communication for any selected coordinator. The construction involves (1) offer generation, as response to execution of (conflicting) interaction, (2) asynchronous offer reception by the coordinator, (3) determinization into a support automaton to be used by the coordinator.

Let a be a fixed interaction. We construct the support automaton $\mathcal{K}_a$ by applying a sequence of transformations on the global behavior $\mathcal{A} = (S, A, T, g_0)$ as follows:

Offer generation: We construct the labelled transition system $\mathcal{A}' = (S, 2^{\{a, 1..n\}}, T', g_0)$ by replacing labels of each transition, so that they contain information about the offers concerning a. For an interaction a' and a global state g', we denote by $I(a', g') = \{i \mid a, a' \in A^i \wedge \exists s'' \in S^i, \ \delta^i(g'[i], a) = s''\}$ the set of indices of automata that can participate in a after executing a'. Intuitively, this corresponds to set of offers that the coordinator for a will receive after execution of a'. We relabel the transition $g \xrightarrow{a'} g'$ by $g \xrightarrow{\{a\} \cup I(a, g')} g'$ if $a' = a$ and by $g \xrightarrow{I(a', g')} g'$ otherwise. It might be the case that some transitions have $\emptyset$ as label after this step, which means that they have no observable effect on the a-coordinator and thus are unobservable.

Asynchronous offer reception: We construct the labelled transition system $\mathcal{A}'' = (S'', \{a, 0, 1, ..., n\}, T'', g_0'')$ obtained by breaking transitions in $\mathcal{A}'$ such that there is at most one action (either a or offer reception i) per transition. Formally, we take $S'' = S \times \{0, 1, 2\}^n$, that is, a state of $\mathcal{A}''$ is defined by a global state g of the cellular automaton and a vector v of n integers in $\{0, 1, 2\}$. For any participant i, the value v_i gives the number of *pending* offers, that is, potentially sent by i and not yet received by the coordinator. Given the specific behavior of the α-core, the number of pending offers is always between 0 and 2. For a given set of indices $I \subseteq \{1, ..., n\}$, we denote by $\mathbb{1}_I$ the characteristic vector of I that is 1 if $i \in I$ and 0 otherwise. We define the initial state $g_0'' = (g_0, \mathbb{1}_{I(a, g_0)})$. Transitions in T'' are constructed from the following rules, where I denotes an arbitrary index set:

$$\frac{g \xrightarrow{\{a\} \cup I} g' \in T'}{(g, 0) \xrightarrow{a} (g', \mathbb{1}_I)} \qquad \frac{g \xrightarrow{I} g' \in T' \quad \forall i \in I, \ v_i \leq 1}{(g, v) \xrightarrow{0} (g', v + \mathbb{1}_I)} \qquad \frac{v_i > 0}{(g, v) \xrightarrow{i} (g, v - \mathbb{1}_{\{i\}})}$$

Projection and determinization: Finally, we construct the support automaton $\mathcal{K}_a = (S_a, \{a, 1, ..., n\}, \delta_a, g_{a0})$ as the deterministic automaton constructed from $\mathcal{A}''$ by eliminating $\emptyset$ actions which are unobservable. The construction is essentially the same as the one introduced in section 3.1 for participants and is not repeated here.

The previous construction guarantees that whenever an offer from participant $\mathcal{A}^i$ is received by the coordinator, the action i is possible from the current state of the support automata. This is stated in Lemma 1.

Lemma 1. *For any distributed execution σ, its restriction $\sigma|_{\{a, 1, ..., n\}}$ to actions observable by $\mathcal{K}_a$ is the trace of an execution of $\mathcal{K}_a$.*

Example 5. In Figure 5, we present the different steps leading to the construction of $\mathcal{K}_{s_1}$. To obtain the automaton $\mathcal{A}'$, we relabel the transitions in $\mathcal{A}$. For instance, the transition $0 \xrightarrow{s_0} 1$ in $\mathcal{A}$ brings $\mathcal{A}^0$ in a state where it can take part in s_1. From the s_1-coordinator point of view, this corresponds to receiving an offer from $\mathcal{A}^0$. Thus, the transition is relabelled by $\{0\}$ in $\mathcal{A}'$. In the non-deterministic automaton $\mathcal{A}''$, each state is labelled by a couple (g, v), where g is a global state from $\mathcal{A}$, and $v = v_0 v_1$ is a vector where v_i is the number of offers to receive from $\mathcal{A}^i$. The dotted transitions correspond to unobservable actions. Note that we depicted only the half of $\mathcal{A}''$, the other half (corresponding to states 3,4,5,6) shows the same pattern between states $(3, 10)$ to $(6, 00)$ as between states $(7, 10)$ and $(2, 00)$. Finally, the determinized and minimized version of $\mathcal{A}''$ is the automaton $\mathcal{K}_{s_1}$. It states that between two executions of s_1, two offers from $\mathcal{A}^0$ and one offer from $\mathcal{A}^1$ are to be received, in any order.

The coordinator for interaction a observes the offers sent from all participants in a and computes the set of known stable and obsolete components (or offers). We say that a component (offer) $\mathcal{A}^i$ is *stable* at state s in $\mathcal{K}_a$ iff for all paths starting at s, a transition labelled by i cannot be reached without going through a transition labelled by a. Whenever an offer from $\mathcal{A}^i$ is stable, the coordinator *knows* that $\mathcal{A}^i$ can not send a new offer until the interaction a takes place. More precisely, $\mathcal{A}^i$ can only participate in a and the information received from $\mathcal{A}^i$ is up to date. If stable, $\mathcal{A}^i$ can be considered as if it were locked. In a dual manner, we say that a component (offer) $\mathcal{A}^i$ is *obsolete* at state s in $\mathcal{K}_a$ iff for all paths starting at s, a transition labelled by a cannot by reached without going through a transition labelled by i. In this case, the coordinator *knows* that it has to receive a new offer from $\mathcal{A}^i$ before starting the interaction. This information can be used to avoid tentative executions based on obsolete offers.

Example 6. Let us consider the support automaton for the coordinator of s_1 in the binary counter. At state C, the coordinator may have received two offers from $\mathcal{A}^0$ and $\mathcal{A}^1$ and the default behavior is to attempt execution for interaction s_1. However, the offer from $\mathcal{A}^0$ is obsolete. Using the support automaton, the coordinator can therefore detect this situation and silently remove that offer, which avoids the execution attempt. At state D, both $\mathcal{A}^0$ and $\mathcal{A}^1$ are stable and there is no need to lock them before executing s_1.

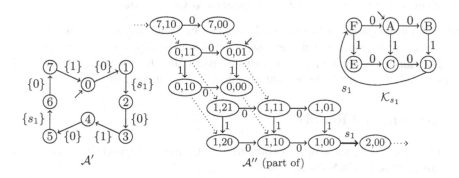

Fig. 5. Construction of the support automaton for the coordinator of s_1

The above optimizations are implemented as follows. The coordinator for a follows the automaton $\mathcal{K}_a$ when receiving offers[1] (transitions 1 and 2) and executing a (transitions 4 or 7, from Figure 3(b)). Formally, the coordinator uses an extra variable s tracking the state of the support automaton. The transitions 1,2,4 and 7 of the coordinator are modified into transitions 1',2',4' and 7' as follows:

1'. $n < C \wedge p?\mathbf{OFFER} \rightarrow \{n:=n+1;\ shared:= shared \cup \{p\};\ \boxed{s := \delta_a(s,p);\ update()}\ \}$

2'. $n < C \wedge p?\mathbf{PARTICIPATE} \rightarrow \{n:=n+1;\ locked:= locked \cup \{p\};\ \boxed{s := \delta_a(s,p);\ update()}\ \}$

4'. $n = C \wedge shared = \emptyset \rightarrow \{$ foreach $q \in locked$ do $q!\mathbf{START};\ locked, shared:=\emptyset;\ n:=0;$ $\boxed{s := \delta_a(s,a)}\ \}$

7'. $waiting = \emptyset \wedge p?\mathbf{OK} \rightarrow \{locked:=locked \cup \{current\};$ foreach q in $locked$ do $q!\mathbf{START};$ $locked, waiting, shared:=\emptyset;\ n:=0;\ \boxed{s := \delta_a(s,a);}\ \}$

The *update* function above is used to modify the *shared* and *locked* sets, given the current support automaton state s as follows:
foreach $p \in shared$

   if $p \in stable_a(s)$ { $shared := shared \setminus \{p\}$; $locked := locked \cup \{p\}$ }
   if $p \in obsolete_a(s)$ { $shared := shared \setminus \{p\}$; $n = n - 1$; $p!\mathbf{LOCK}$; $p!\mathbf{UNLOCK}$ }

Since a component can now be considered as locked even if it sent an **OFFER** message, it may receive a **START** message while waiting to be locked. Therefore, we add a transition 12 from the waiting to the sync state, as depicted in Figure 3(a). We also modify transition 7 into transition $7'$ as follows:

7'. $p?\mathbf{START} \rightarrow \{\alpha:=IS \setminus unlocks \setminus \{\boxed{p}\};$ foreach $q \in \alpha$ do $q!\mathbf{REFUSE};\ n := |\alpha|;$ start participating in the joint action managed by $\boxed{p}\}$

12. $p?\mathbf{START} \rightarrow \{\alpha:=IS \setminus unlocks \setminus \{p\};$ foreach $q \in \alpha$ do $q!\mathbf{REFUSE};\ n := |\alpha|;$ start participating in the joint action managed by $p\}$

Proposition 2. *The executions of the distributed implementation with knowledge-optimized coordinators are included in the executions of the original automaton.*

3.3   Combining Knowledge for Participants and Coordinators

Optimization for participants and coordinator can be combined. In this case, the construction of the support automata for coordinators has to be done on the system obtained using the support automata for participants. In particular, the relabelling step depends on the actual offers sent by participants and thus on their support automata.

4   Experimental Results

We present experimental results for computing and using the support automata for participants as presented in Section 3.1.

---

[1] Here we consider only *new* offers that we need to distinguish from offers sent when participant executes transition 6. This can be done by using a new message name for offers that are re-sent.

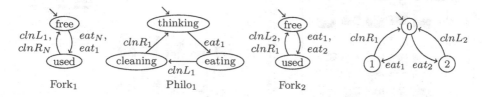

Fig. 6. A fragment of the dining philosophers example

Fig. 7. Support automaton for participant $Fork_2$

Examples. The first example presented in Figure 6 is a variation of the classical dining philosophers problem. Each philosopher $Philo_i$ may eat during the interaction eat_i involving its two neighbor forks. Then $Philo_i$ clean first its left fork, then its right fork through interactions $clnL_i$ and $clnR_i$ respectively. We denote philoN an instance with N philosophers.

The second example is called Master/Slave. We assume a set of N masters and M slaves. Each master wants to perform a task for which it needs two slaves that it can chose amongst a pool of size K. We denote msNMK such an instance. If the slave j is in the pool of the master i, then the interaction acq^i_j allows master i to acquire slave j, which brings the slave in state i so that it remembers that i acquired it. On completion on the task, the master i releases simultaneously the two acquired slaves j_1 and j_2 through the $rel^i_{j_1,j_2}$ interaction. Figure 8 shows respectively, the behavior of masters and slaves.

The third example models a transmission protocol that propagates values amongst a chain of memories. At every time, each memory node stores a single value. A fragment of this example is shown in Figure 9. The rule is to propagate (copy) the new value (from the left) only if the memory on the right has already copied the local value. Propagation steps are implemented as ternary interactions denoted by mv_{i,v_1,v_2}, which correspond to the case where memory i changes its value from v_1 to v_2. As an example, the interaction $mv_{i,1,0}$ in the Figure 9 changes the value in $Node_i$ from 1 to 0 if $Node_{i+1}$ already changed its value to 1 and the next value (in $Node_{i-1}$) is 0. For our experiment, the memories form a ring, thus the sequence of values seen by each memory depends only on the initial state of the system. Note that propagation is enabled at places where the ring contains two consecutive nodes holding the same value. We denote by tpN (resp. tpN′) an example with N nodes and one (resp. two) enabled propagations.

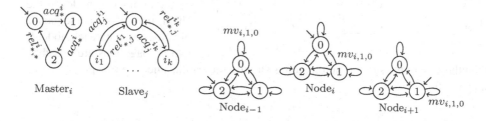

Fig. 8. Master Slave example   **Fig. 9.** Three consecutive nodes of the transmission protocol

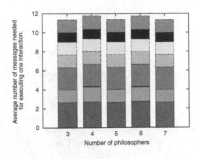

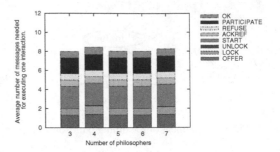

Fig. 10. Dining philosophers: messages per interaction, standard version

Fig. 11. Dining philosophers: messages per interaction, optimized version

Building support automata for participants. We implemented the support automaton computation for each participant by using analysis tools of the BIP framework. In Table 1, we present the results of this analysis by giving the average number of states in the original automata and in the support automata. This gives an indication on the size needed to store the knowledge, and the memory needed for execution of the support automata. For the philo$N$ instances, the support automaton of philosophers is the same as the original automaton. For the forks, there is only one additional state, as shown in Figure 7. The added state allows to distinguish who acquired the fork (left or right) and to send only one offer accordingly, thus avoiding unneeded conflict resolution.

In the Master/Slave example, the automaton describing a master is very generic. The corresponding support automaton contains all the possible sequences for acquiring two slaves and then releasing them. In particular, after having acquired two slaves, there is only one possible release interaction, thus only one offer is sent. Finally, in the transmission protocol example, the size of each support automaton is much larger since it depends on the number of nodes in the chain, that is on the sequence of values seen by each node. If two propagations are possible, then the size of the support automaton is slightly increased, since the two propagations may conflict.

Table 1. Results: average size of original and support automaton and performance of the obtained implementation, for each test instance

Name	Components	Average number of states in $\mathcal{A}^i$	in $\mathcal{K}_i$	Number of interactions during 60s Standard	Optimized
philo3	6	2.5	3	1129	2251
philo4	8	2.5	3	1811	2499
philo5	10	2.5	3	2261	4448
philo6	12	2.5	3	2624	4542
philo7	14	2.5	3	3093	4603
ms232	5	2.6	3	1491	1504
ms233	5	3	4.6	1128	1129
ms342	7	2.7	3.1	642	1885
ms343	7	3.1	4.9	1278	1265
ms344	7	3.6	7	1256	1251
tp3	3	3	6	750	1499
tp6	6	3	15	750	1500
tp6'	6	3	16	1498	1557
tp9	9	3	24	750	1509
tp9'	9	3	28	1497	3725
tp12	12	3	33	749	1513

Performance of distributed implementation. Using the BIP component framework, we built a transformation that replaces multiparty interactions by the α-core protocol. We obtain a distributed BIP model representing participants and coordinators communicating through asynchronous message passing. From this model, we generate a set of C++ programs communicating through Unix sockets. We ran the obtained code for both standard α-core and knowledge-optimized α-core on a UltraSparcT1 allowing parallel execution of 24 processes. In Table 1, we provide the number of interactions executed during 60 seconds of execution (not including initialization) for both standard and optimized version of each test instance. On the dining philosopher instances, the optimized version is up to twice faster than the standard version. On the Master/Slave instances, except for one, the performance is the same for both versions. On the transmission protocol instances, we have a speedup of at least two, except for the tp6′ example.

In order to evaluate the distributed execution of standard *vs.* optimized versions, we compare the average number of messages needed to perform an interaction for the three examples. For the dining philosophers, these average numbers are shown in Figures 10 and 11. We can observe a reduction of approximatively 25%, mainly because some **OFFER** messages from the fork participants are transformed in **PARTICIPATE** messages. In turn, this reduces the number of participants to lock, and thus the number of messages. For the Master/Slave, the average number of messages needed to complete one interaction for standard and optimized α-core are shown in Figures 12 and 13. Here the number of conflicts depends on the size of the pool of slaves assigned to each master. Since there are many conflicts, the number of offers sent to execute an interaction is quite big. Recall that on this example, performance of both versions is comparable. However, the number of exchanged message is smaller in the optimized version, because less offers are sent. For the transmission protocol, the average number of messages exchanged to execute one interaction for standard and optimized executions is shown in Figures 14 and 15. For the non-primed versions, since there is no dynamic conflict, each participant sends only **PARTICIPATE** messages and each coordinator can directly answer a **START** message. This reduces drastically the number of exchanged messages (6 per interaction, since they are ternary interactions). For the primed version, in some cases a node may participate in two interactions and thus send two **OFFER** messages, which is still much less than in the original version.

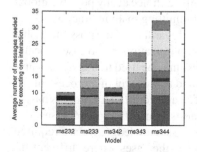

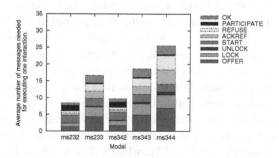

Fig. 12. Master/Slave: messages per interaction, standard version

Fig. 13. Master/Slave: messages per interaction, optimized version

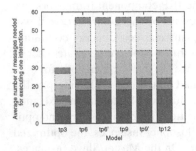 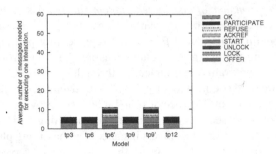

Fig. 14. Transmission protocol: messages per interaction, standard version

Fig. 15. Transmission protocol: messages per interaction, optimized version

5 Discussion

An architecture for component-based system can provide a very powerful tool for distributed software development. It assumes some underlying mechanism that provides support for the components to interact and to choose from several alternative actions. It is highly beneficial to develop code at this level, rather than to consider the lower level architecture that uses message passing, or shared variables. On the other hand, obtaining this level of abstraction is expensive: the overhead needed to allow both multiparty interaction and non-deterministic choice requires some nontrivial amount of lower level message exchange.

In this paper we looked at a technique to reduce the overhead needed for supporting high level architecture for component-based systems, such as the BIP systems. Observing a popular algorithm for interaction coordination, the α-core protocol, we remarked that additional information about the amount of overhead makes a lot of difference. The coordination protocol distinguishes the case where there is no non-deterministic choice; then, there are fewer messages sent, as an intent to participate in an interaction is a committed intention. It is often not known in advance how many conflicting choices there are: syntactically, there can be several, but at runtime, there are quite fewer cases available (enabled) at each particular instance. Our method is based on performing a preliminary model checking analysis of the system for detecting such situations. When we find that the local situation admits no non-deterministic choice at any possible global situation, we can employ the more efficient case of committing to an interaction.

This analysis is based on the knowledge of a process, regarding all the possible global states consistent with its local situation. We apply this optimization in two cases: locally at the process level, where the knowledge of the process may be used to transfer a seamingly non-deterministic case into a committing case, and at the level of a process of the coordination algorithm. The latter case is very powerful, as a coordinator process has, to some extent, a more global view, having received requests from different processes. Experiments show that rather than using simple memoryless knowledge, we are required to use history-based knowledge. The reason is that it is the cases where different instances of non-deterministic choice during runtime, rather than a history independent case, are the interesting ones. This can be explained intuitively by the fact that the history independent case actually hides a coding error, where not committing to an interaction although there are no alternatives should have been replaced by a commitment to the single possible interaction.

We performed experiments on three different examples. Our experiments show a considerable improvement in the number of messages needed to be exchanged. It is important to note that due to the use of history-based knowledge, additional memory is needed to encode the possible histories. In the worst case, the amount of added memory is quite nontrivial, exponential in the size of the system, for each process. However, our experiments show a much better and balanced memory consumption. We intend to conduct further experiments and to apply the knowledge-based technique for reducing message passing in a more aggressive way.

References

1. Bagrodia, R.: Process synchronization: Design and performance evaluation of distributed algorithms. IEEE Transactions on Software Engineering (TSE) 15(9), 1053–1065 (1989)
2. Basu, A., Bensalem, S., Peled, D., Sifakis, J.: Priority scheduling of distributed systems based on model checking. Formal Methods in System Design 39, 229–245 (2011)
3. Basu, A., Bozga, M., Sifakis, J.: Modeling heterogeneous real-time components in BIP. In: Software Engineering and Formal Methods (SEFM), pp. 3–12 (2006)
4. Bensalem, S., Bozga, M., Quilbeuf, J., Sifakis, J.: Knowledge-based distributed conflict resolution for multiparty interactions and priorities. In: Giese, H., Rosu, G. (eds.) FMOODS/FORTE 2012. LNCS, vol. 7273, pp. 118–134. Springer, Heidelberg (2012)
5. Buckley, G.N., Silberschatz, A.: An effective implementation for the generalized input-output construct of CSP. ACM Trans. Program. Lang. Syst. 5, 223–235 (1983)
6. Chandy, K.M., Misra, J.: Parallel program design: a foundation. Addison-Wesley Longman Publishing Co., Inc., Boston (1988)
7. Halpern, J.Y., Moses, Y.: Knowledge and common knowledge in a distributed environment. J. ACM 37, 549–587 (1990)
8. Hoare, C.A.R.: Communicating sequential processes. Commun. ACM 21, 666–677 (1978)
9. Joung, Y.-J., Smolka, S.A.: Strong interaction fairness via randomization. IEEE Trans. Parallel Distrib. Syst. 9(2), 137–149 (1998)
10. Katz, G., Peled, D.: Code mutation in verification and automatic code correction. In: Esparza, J., Majumdar, R. (eds.) TACAS 2010. LNCS, vol. 6015, pp. 435–450. Springer, Heidelberg (2010)
11. Kumar, D.: An implementation of n-party synchronization using tokens. In: International Conference on Distributed Computing Systems (ICDCS), pp. 320–327. IEEE (1990)
12. Lehmann, D., Rabin, M.O.: On the advantages of free choice: a symmetric and fully distributed solution to the dining philosophers problem. In: Principles of Programming Languages, POPL (1981)
13. Der Meyden, R.V.: Common knowledge and update in finite environments. Information and Computation 140, 115–157 (1997)
14. Pérez, J.A., Corchuelo, R., Toro, M.: An order-based algorithm for implementing multiparty synchronization. Concurrency and Computation: Practice and Experience 16(12), 1173–1206 (2004)
15. Ricker, S.L., Rudie, K.: Know means no: Incorporating knowledge into discrete-event control systems. IEEE Trans. on Automatic Control 45(9), 1656–1668 (2000)

Repair with On-The-Fly Program Analysis*

Robert Könighofer and Roderick Bloem

Institute for Applied Information Processing and Communications (IAIK),
Graz University of Technology, Austria

Abstract. This paper presents a novel automatic repair approach for incorrect programs. It applies formal methods and analyzes program behavior only on demand. We argue that this is beneficial, especially if exhaustive program analysis is infeasible. Our approach computes repair candidates and refines them based on counterexamples. It can be used with various verification techniques and specification formats to check a candidate's correctness. This includes test suites, model checkers verifying assertions, or even the user checking candidates manually, in which case no explicit specification is needed at all. We use concolic execution to analyze programs and SMT-solving to compute repair candidates. We implemented our approach in the open-source debugging environment FoREnSiC and present first experimental results.

Keywords: Program Repair, Formal Methods, Abstraction-Refinement, Concolic Execution, SMT-Solving.

1 Introduction

Debugging is a labor-intensive and costly activity in every software and hardware development process. Errors must be detected, located and fixed. Clearly, automation can reduce effort and costs dramatically. Automatic error detection is already widely used (e.g., model checking or test case generation). Also, automatic error localization is increasingly applied. The actual correction of the error, however, is usually done manually. Yet, fixing an error is often difficult, even if its location is known. This is especially true in other people's code, and if the error has not been tracked down manually. As an illustration, consider the algorithm to compute the greatest common divisor in Section 6.2. There is a bug in line 35, now try to think of a fix. Other difficulties in fixing bugs manually are the danger of eliminating only (some but not all) symptoms, or even introducing new errors. Automatic error correction methods aim to improve this situation.

Formal methods for automatic error correction typically suffer from limited scalability. They often model the correctness of the *entire* program with respect to a given specification in a logic formula [15,19] or game structure [12,13] to compute repairs. More scalable approaches are usually less systematic. They are

---

* This work was supported in part by the European Commission through project DIAMOND (FP7-2009-IST-4-248613), and by the Austrian Science Fund (FWF) through the national research network RiSE (S11406-N23).

A. Biere, A. Nahir, and T. Vos (Eds.): HVC 2012, LNCS 7857, pp. 56–71, 2013.

often based on brute-force search guided by genetic mechanisms [1,8] or other heuristics [7,16]. In this work, we attempt to close this gap a little further.

We present a new formal program repair method that addresses the scalability issue by not transforming the entire program into a formula at once. Instead, program analysis is done on-the-fly whenever information about program behavior is missing. We compute repairs by refining a candidate as long as it is still incorrect. If incorrect, we extract a counterexample, i.e., inputs for which the specification is violated, and analyze only program behavior that is possible under this counterexample. This information is then used to refine the repair candidate such that the counterexample is resolved. Our experience shows that, often, a few counterexamples (and corresponding refinements) suffice. This implies that the program needs to be analyzed for a few inputs only.

The main advantage of our new approach is that program analysis focuses on the information needed for repair. For complex programs, exhaustive analysis is usually infeasible or at least inefficient. When setting a bound on the analysis depth (e.g., by limiting the number of loop unrollings) one runs the risk of abstracting away the wrong information. In contrast, the on-the-fly approach is aware of which program behavior can safely be ignored until further notice. Another advantage is the flexibility regarding the verification technique used to check repair candidates and extract counterexamples. It can be a model checker, a test suite, or even a human checking candidates manually. Consequently, there is also flexibility in the specification format. Possibilities are assertions in the code or test vectors together with expected outputs. Assertions can also be used to check a program against a reference implementation. In case of the user checking candidates manually, no explicit specification is needed at all.

We do not expect a complete specification right from the beginning, nor do we suggest to replace humans in the debugging process. We rather strive to assist the user and keep her in the loop. If only incorrect repairs are found due to an incomplete specification, the user needs to refine the specification with additional properties or test cases. This has the nice side-effect that the quality of the specification is improved at the same time.

From a technical perspective, our new program repair method builds on the template-based method introduced in [15], from which we inherit many features. The input is an incorrect program, a specification, and a set of potentially faulty components. The output is a set of replacements of the components such that the specification is satisfied. We assume that the faulty components are identified in a preceding automatic error localization phase. In our implementation we use model-based diagnosis [15], but other diagnosis methods are also possible. Not only single-faults but also multiple faulty components can be handled. Replacements follow templates, which ensures the understandability and maintainability of the repaired program. This is important for keeping the user in the loop. Program analysis is done with concolic execution, repair candidates are computed using a Satisfiability Modulo Theories (SMT) solver. We see the main application of our method in debugging simple software programs, e.g., first software models of hardware designs. Our implementation works on C programs. It is integrated in the open-source debugging environment FoREnSiC [2] and can be downloaded[1]. We also present first experimental results.

This paper is structured as follows. Section 2 discusses related work, and Section 3 briefly explains existing techniques underlying our approach. Our new repair method is presented Section 4. The sections 5 and 6 describe our implementation and present first experimental results. Section 7 concludes the paper.

2   Related Work

The repair method presented in [15] uses templates to synthesize new expressions, symbolic or concolic execution for program analysis, and counterexample-guided refinements for repair. We adopt these strategies and their benefits. However, in [15], program analysis transforms the entire program (and specification) into one large correctness constraint before the repair starts. If complete analysis is infeasible, the number of examined program paths can be limited. Depending on what was omitted, the approach may then find incorrect repairs or no repair at all. Nothing ensures that only irrelevant program behavior is omitted. The novelty of our new approach is that program analysis is done on-the-fly during the repair process, focused towards the required information. Moreover, while [15] only allows `assert` statements in the code, our new approach is flexible regarding the specification and verification technique.

The repair method in [12,13] transforms a finite-state program into a finite-state game and computes repairs as strategies for this game. In [11], this idea is extended to programs with virtually infinite state space using predicate abstraction. To the best of our knowledge, this is the only existing formal error correction method which does not consider the entire program, but uses abstraction instead. Its main shortcoming is that it only considers the predicates found during the preceding verification phase; there is no mechanism to refine the abstraction if it is too coarse for finding a repair. Our method of performing program analysis on-the-fly for one counterexample after the other can also be seen as an abstraction mechanism. The abstraction captures the program behavior for certain inputs only. Our method can also refine an abstraction, simply by analyzing more inputs. Besides the different way of abstracting, we also use a different repair computation method (SMT-based instead of game-based).

Program repair is also related to program sketching [19,18], where a program with missing parts has to be completed in such a way that a given specification is satisfied. In [19], this problem is solved using counterexample-guided refinements, just like in our approach. But also here, program correctness is encoded into one large formula before synthesis starts. The counterexamples are applied to this formula and not to the program to refine candidates. The repair method of [4] also uses counterexample-guided refinements, but for combinational circuits. Less formal repair approaches include methods of repeatedly mutating the incorrect program and checking if it becomes correct [7,16]. Genetic programming methods typically combine mutation with crossing and selection according

---

[1] http://www.informatik.uni-bremen.de/agra/eng/forensic.php

to some notion of fitness [1,8,10]. The work in [6] infers preconditions of methods from passing test cases, and fixes errors by deleting or inserting method calls such that precondition violations are resolved. An extension [21] uses contracts, Boolean query abstraction, and various heuristics.

3 Preliminaries

3.1 Symbolic and Concolic Execution

Symbolic execution [5,14] is a program analysis technique which executes a program using symbols instead of concrete values as inputs. Symbols are placeholders for any concrete value from a given domain. Symbolic execution tracks the symbolic values of all program variables. If a branching point is encountered, a constraint solver is used to check if both branches are feasible. If so, the execution forks. For each execution path, a *path condition* is computed. It evaluates to true iff the respective path is activated. For a path that results in a specification violation, the corresponding path condition states when the problem occurs.

Concolic execution [9,17] is a variant of symbolic execution where the program is simultaneously executed on concrete and symbolic input values. The execution path is determined by the concrete values. In parallel, the symbolic values of all program variables are tracked and a symbolic path condition is computed. After one execution run, one conjunct of the path condition is negated and all succeeding conjuncts are discarded. Solving this constraint with a constraint solver gives inputs that trigger a different execution path. A systematic method to negate the different conjuncts of the path condition makes sure that all execution paths are analyzed, or at least a high coverage is obtained [3].

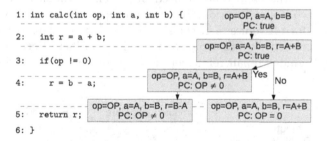

Fig. 1. Illustration of the concept of symbolic execution

Example 1. Fig. 1 illustrates symbolic execution on a simple program. This program will be used as a running example. It is a simple calculator which can only add and subtract. Boxes contain the state of the symbolic execution, upper-case letters are input symbols, and "PC" indicates the path condition. Concolic execution of this program could start with the concrete values op = 0, a = 0, and b = 0. It would execute the path that skips line 4 and compute the path condition OP = 0. Negating the only conjunct in this path condition and solving the constraints could give the next concrete input values op = 1, a = 0, and b = 0. This triggers the other path with the path condition OP $\neq$ 0.

3.2 Template-Based Repair

We briefly summarize the repair approach of [15], since our current work builds on it. The approach targets simple software, the implementation works on C[2]. assert-statements serve as specification. The error is assumed to be an incorrect expression. That is, bugs like missing code or incorrect control flow (like having an if instead of a while) cannot be handled. The main reason is efficiency.

In a first step, the program is executed symbolically. If an assertion violation is encountered, model-based diagnosis is used to compute sets of potentially faulty expressions. For every set of expressions, error correction then attempts to synthesize replacements. This is reduced to the search for integer constants using repair templates. A repair template is an expression involving program variables and template parameters, which are the unknown constants.

Example 2. Assume that the program in Fig. 1 is supposed to compute a+b if op=0, and a-b otherwise. This specification can be formalized with the assertion assert(op==0 ? r==a+b : r==a-b). Assume further that model-based diagnosis identifies the expression b-a in line 4 as potentially faulty. This expression is now replaced with a template like k0 + op*k1 + a*k2 + b*k3 + r*k4. Finally, the approach computes constant values for the template parameters k0 to k4 such that the program satisfies its specification.

Template parameter value computation works as follows. Let $\bar{i}$ be a vector of program inputs, and let $\bar{k}$ be the vector of template parameters. The program and its specification are first transformed into a formula $\mathsf{correct}(\bar{i}, \bar{k})$ which evaluates to true iff the program satisfies the specification when executed on input $\bar{i}$ and repaired with the expression induced by $\bar{k}$. The formula is computed using symbolic or concolic execution. To obtain a repair, one needs to find values for $\bar{k}$ such that for all values of $\bar{i}$, $\mathsf{correct}(\bar{i}, \bar{k})$ holds true. This corresponds to solving $\exists \bar{k} . \forall \bar{i} . \mathsf{correct}(\bar{i}, \bar{k})$. To avoid solving this quantifier alternation directly, counterexample-guided repair refinement is performed as illustrated in Fig.2.

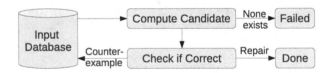

Fig. 2. Counterexample-guided repair refinement, as done in [15]

There is a database I of concrete input vectors $\overline{v_i}$, which is initially empty. In a loop, the following steps are performed. First, a repair candidate is computed as a satisfying assignment $\overline{v_k}$ for the variables $\bar{k}$ in $\bigwedge_{\overline{v_i} \in I} \mathsf{correct}(\overline{v_i}, \bar{k})$. This candidate is correct for the inputs $\overline{v_i} \in I$. Next, the method checks whether the

---

[2] The implementation handles certain features like pointer arithmetic only approximatively and does not guarantee the repair to be correct in this case.

candidate is correct for *all* inputs by computing a satisfying assignment $\overline{v_i}$ for $\overline{i}$ in $\neg\,\mathsf{correct}(\overline{i}, \overline{v_k})$. If no such $\overline{v_i}$ exists, a correct repair has been found. Otherwise, the vector $\overline{v_i}$ is a counterexample for the correctness of the repair candidate $\overline{v_k}$. It is added to I to render the next candidate correct also for this input.

Example 3. For the specification and template from Example 2 we have $\overline{i} = (\mathsf{OP}, A, B)$, $\overline{k} = (k_0, k_1, k_2, k_3, k_4)$, and $\mathsf{correct}(\overline{i}, \overline{k}) = (\mathsf{OP} = 0) \vee (k_0 + k_1 \cdot \mathsf{OP} + k_2 \cdot A + k_3 \cdot B + k_4 \cdot (A + B) = A - B)$. The first candidate is arbitrary and could be $\overline{v_k} = (0, 0, 0, 0, 0)$, which corresponds to replacing b-a in line 4 by 0. This is not correct and a counterexample is $\overline{v_i} = (1, 3, 2)$. The next candidate must satisfy $(k_0 + k_1 \cdot 1 + k_2 \cdot 3 + k_3 \cdot 2 + k_4 \cdot 5 = 1)$. A solution, and hence a refined repair candidate, is $\overline{v_k} = (0, 0, 0, -2, 1)$. Since $\neg(\mathsf{OP} = 0 \vee -2 \cdot B + A + B = A - B)$ is unsatisfiable, no counterexample exists for this candidate. Hence, the method would suggest to replace b-a in line 4 by r-2*b.

A limit to the number of iterations and a time-out for all constraint solving steps ensures termination within reasonable time. If no repair is found using a particular template, the approach switches to a more expressive one. The current implementation includes the linear template of Example 2 and also templates involving bitwise operations and bit shifts. Templates for conditions are currently of the form $t_e\,\mathsf{OP}\,0$ where t_e is a template for a non-Boolean expression and $\mathsf{OP} \in \{<, \leq, >, \geq, =, \neq\}$. The template-based approach ensures that the repairs are understandable, which is crucial for keeping the user in the loop and for the maintainability of the corrected program. Our new approach with on-the-fly program analysis inherits these advantages.

4   Repair with On-The-Fly Program Analysis

The repair method outlined in the previous section first analyzes the entire program and computes one large correctness condition covering the program behavior for all possible inputs and for all possible implementations of the expressions to be synthesized. However, for non-trivial programs, complete program analysis is typically not feasible. Even if feasible, it may take long and produce an unnecessarily large condition. When limiting the program analysis depth (e.g., the maximum number of loop unrollings or execution paths) information needed for finding a correct repair may be missing. Yet, for computing a repair candidate with iterative refinements, the correctness condition needs to be accurate for some inputs only. Only for candidate verification, all inputs need to be covered. However, candidate verification need not be performed on the same formula as candidate computation. A completely different method can be used instead.

We remedy these shortcomings by doing program analysis on-the-fly, analyzing the program only for the counterexamples that have been encountered. Furthermore, we decouple the repair candidate computation from the verification. This allows us to use various verification techniques and specification formats.

4.1 Overview

Fig. 3 outlines our approach. As input, it takes a specification and an incorrect program. The output are repairs in form of expression replacements such that the specification is satisfied. First, potentially faulty expressions are inferred using existing techniques like [15] or [16]. In this work, we focus on repair, i.e., computing replacements. This is sketched in the dashed box of Fig. 3.

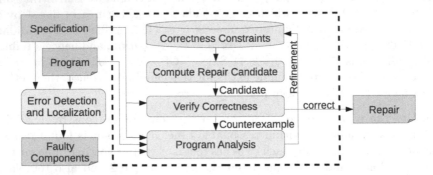

Fig. 3. Overview of our new error correction method

We maintain a database of correctness constraints that must be satisfied by any repair. This database is initially empty. In a loop, we first compute a repair candidate that satisfies these constraints using an SMT-solver. Next, we verify if this candidate satisfies the specification. If not, the verification step returns a counterexample. We analyze the program behavior on this counterexample using concolic execution and add constraints ensuring correctness for this input to the database. In this way, our method keeps analyzing the program for more and more inputs, and improving the repair candidates until a correct one is found. Our experience shows that often a few iterations are enough (see also Section 6).

The next subsections explain the different steps of our method in more detail. Then, we give an example and discuss benefits and limitations of our approach.

4.2 Repair Candidate Computation

Our database contains correctness constraints $\varphi(\overline{k})$ over the template parameter values $\overline{k}$ in some logic (our implementation supports linear integer arithmetic and bitvector arithmetic). We use an SMT-solver with appropriate theory to find a satisfying assignment for these constraints. The concrete values of the template parameters $\overline{k}$ can be mapped back to concrete expressions using the repair templates. This gives a candidate program that can be checked.

4.3 Repair Candidate Verification

The verification of repair candidates can be performed in many ways. The prerequisite is that the verification method is able to produce a counterexample in case of incorrectness. One possibility is to execute a test suite. In our setting, a test suite is a set of input vectors together with corresponding expected output vectors. In addition to the expected outputs, assertions in the code can be used. A counterexample is an input vector together with the corresponding expected output vector such that the actual output does not match the expected one, or an assertion is violated. In case of assertions in the code, the test suite can also consist of input vectors only. A counterexample is then an input vector (together with an empty vector of expected outputs) that triggers an assertion violation.

Another possibility is a model checker taking assertions in the code as specification. Model checkers typically prove incorrectness by giving a counterexample. In our case, this is an input vector for which an assertion is violated. The candidate verification can even be performed by a human. Here, a counterexample could be an input vector together with the expected output. In this case, no explicit specification is needed at all. The repair engine simply learns a fix using the input-output examples given by the user in response to the candidates.

The flexibility in the verification comes with flexibility in the specification. Test cases and assertions have already been mentioned. Assertions can also be used to compare a program with a reference implementation. One simply executes the program and the reference implementation on the same inputs and compares the outcome using suitable assertions. This allows the user to flexibly define what equivalence between the programs means.

4.4 Program Analysis

The crucial step of our approach is program analysis, which is incomplete in our case. We only look at behavior that is possible under one particular input assignment, namely the counterexample found in the preceding verification step.

We take the program where incorrect expressions have already been replaced by templates for new ones, and infer correctness constraints using concolic execution. The inputs are fixed to the concrete values given by the counterexample. Only the template parameters $\overline{k}$ are left open. Symbols represent their yet unknown values. The idea is to execute all feasible paths in this program, and to compute the respective path conditions, which are predicates over $\overline{k}$. Assertions in the code are handled just like other branching points: If an encountered assertion holds for the concrete values of the concolic execution run, the symbolic condition under which it holds is added to the path condition and concolic execution continues. If the assertion is violated, the condition under which this is the case is added and the execution run terminates. Program outputs are handled similarly. Whenever the program outputs a value (which can be modeled by a call to a special function output(x)), a conjunct is added to the path condition. If the concrete output matches the expected value, the conjunct states when this is the case. Otherwise, the conjunct expresses when the output does not match and the execution run terminates. If no expected output values are included in the counterexample (see Section 4.3), the output of the program is ignored.

The concolic execution runs are now divided into failing and passing runs. A *failing run* is one that either terminates in an assertion violation or with a mismatch between the actual and expected output. The corresponding path condition states when this happens. A *passing run* terminates without violating the specification. Let F be the set of failing runs and $PC^r(\overline{k})$ be the path condition of run r. We compute a necessary condition for program correctness as

$$\varphi(\overline{k}) = \neg \bigvee_{r \in F} PC^r(\overline{k}).$$

This condition is added to the database of correctness constraints. It will exclude candidates that fail on the input vector for which the program has been analyzed.

Since the inputs to the program are fixed, typically many execution paths become infeasible. Nevertheless, the set of execution paths may still be very large or even infinite. One reason for an infinite number of paths can be a loop where the termination condition depends on the implementation of the components to be synthesized, i.e., on the template parameter values. This problem arises also in [15], with the open inputs making the situation even worse. Just like [15], we address this problem by limiting the program analysis depth with a user-given bound on the number and length of execution paths to consider. A consequence of these limits can be that the repair refinement loop does not converge. However, since there is also a bound on the number of refinement iterations, the program will terminate and the user can try again with higher limits. In general, our approach is tailored towards finding repairs efficiently for many cases instead of having a sound and complete method that does not scale.

4.5   Example

Example 4. Assume that the program from Example 1 is specified with the test cases (op=0, a=3, b=5 → r=8), (1, 5, 3 → 2), and (1, 6, 1 → 5). We use the template from Example 2. Initially, the database of correctness constraints is empty, so the first repair candidate is arbitrary. It could be $\overline{v_k} = (0, 0, 0, 0, 0)$, which means that b-a in line 4 of the program is replaced by 0. Verifying this candidate with the test cases, we get (1, 5, 3 → 2) as counterexample. We now use concolic execution to analyze the program behavior for the input vector (1, 5, 3). Only the execution path including line 4 is feasible. After line 4, r has the symbolic value $k_0 + k_1 \cdot 1 + k_2 \cdot 5 + k_3 \cdot 3 + k_4 \cdot 8$, because b-a has been replaced by the template. Taking r as the output and 2 as expected value, concolic execution distinguishes two cases, which are activated with two concolic execution runs r_1 and r_2. The run r_1 is passing and has the path condition $PC^{r_1}(\overline{k}) = k_0 + k_1 \cdot 1 + k_2 \cdot 5 + k_3 \cdot 3 + k_4 \cdot 8 = 2$. The run r_2 is failing and has $PC^{r_2}(\overline{k}) = k_0 + k_1 \cdot 1 + k_2 \cdot 5 + k_3 \cdot 3 + k_4 \cdot 8 \neq 2$. Since $F = \{r_2\}$, we add $\varphi_1(\overline{k}) = k_0 + k_1 + k_2 \cdot 5 + k_3 \cdot 3 + k_4 \cdot 8 = 2$ to the database of correctness constraints. The next iteration starts. Now, the candidate has to satisfy $\varphi_1(\overline{k})$. A solution is $\overline{v_k} = (2, 0, 0, 0, 0)$, which corresponds to replacing b-a in line 4 by 2. This candidate fails on the test case (1, 6, 1 → 5). For this counterexample, concolic execution produces the correctness constraint $\varphi_2(\overline{k}) = k_0 + k_1 + k_2 \cdot 6 + k_3 \cdot 1 + k_4 \cdot 7 = 5$. It is added to the database and another iteration starts. The next repair candidate must fulfill $\varphi_1(\overline{k})$ and $\varphi_2(\overline{k})$.

A solution is $\overline{v_k} = (0, 0, 1, -1, 0)$, which means that b-a is replaced by a-b. This candidate passes all tests and is presented to the user.

4.6   Discussion

This section discusses the main benefits and limitations of our new repair method.

More Focused Program Analysis: The main advantage of our new repair method is that program analysis is very focused towards the information needed for computing repair candidates. Complete analysis is infeasible for complex programs. In [15], this issue is addresses by setting a limit on the number and length of the execution paths to consider. However, since there is no guidance on what to analyze, this limit can render the probability of obtaining the information relevant for finding a repair very low. In contrast, our new repair method analyzes the program only for the counterexamples that are relevant for the repair finding process. There is also a bound on the number and length of the execution paths. However, since these limits apply locally for each invocation, our new approach learns at least something about the behavior under each counterexample.

Simpler Program Analysis: Compared to [15], our new method renders program analysis with concolic execution simpler because the inputs are always fixed to one counterexample at a time. This does not only drastically reduce the number of feasible execution paths, it also simplifies the analysis per concolic execution run. We can start to track the symbolic values of the program variables only after a repair template with unknown parameters has been executed for the first time. In particular, if a reference implementation is used as a specification, our new approach needs to execute the entire reference code with concrete variable values only (see Section 6.2 for such a scenario). The approach without on-the-fly analysis needs to track the symbolic values right from the beginning because the inputs are not fixed but have a symbolic value.

Flexibility in the Specification: From the user's perspective, the most important benefit is probably the flexibility in the specification of the desired behavior. Existing formal correction approaches often support assertions only. However, writing assertions which accurately reflect the desired behavior and do not only check for basic properties is difficult. Test cases (possibly together with some assertions) are often more natural. This flexibility is also important for keeping the user in the loop. Writing additional test cases if only incorrect repairs are produced is often simpler than coming up with better assertions.

Better Scalability: Our method addresses the scalability issue, which is common for all formal error correction approaches, from several sides. Doing program analysis for typically only a few concrete counterexamples has already been mentioned. The flexibility in the technique for verifying repair candidates is another factor. Where formal approaches like model checking or symbolic execution fail, test case execution can still produce meaningful results.

Limitations: A drawback of the separation of concerns is that little information (only the counterexample) is passed from the verification phase to the program analysis phase. Furthermore, certain program paths may be feasible under several counterexamples, and may thus be analyzed multiple times using concolic execution. The limitation of the approach to incorrect expressions can be easily weakened in principle, but at the cost of efficiency. Whenever there are finitely many (and not too many) options to replace a certain construct in the program, we can analyze all of them. This way, we could handle bugs like having an if instead of a while, or bugs in the left-hand side of an assignment.

5   Implementation

We implemented our new repair method as a proof-of-concept in the open-source debugging environment FoREnSiC [2], re-using the provided infrastructure and parts of the implementation of [15]. Our new repair engine is integrated with the existing error localization engine. So far, we implemented two mechanisms to verify the correctness of repair candidates. The fist one is test case execution, operating on a given set of input vectors together with corresponding expected output values. Assertions in the code can be used in addition or as alternative to the expected outputs. The second verification mechanism uses concolic execution to compute one large correctness condition, just like [15], and uses this condition to verify correctness with an SMT-solver query. This second mechanism was implemented mainly to have a fair comparison with the existing technique. In the future, we also plan to implement verification engines using software model checkers such as CBMC or SATABS. We also want to implement an interface which asks the user to verify correctness. It would be interesting to see whether this way of doing semi-automatic program repair is useful and not too laborious.

Our implementation is able to use the SMT-solvers Yices and Z3, either via their C-API or via the SMT-LIBv2 format. We support linear integer arithmetic as well as bitvector arithmetic. The concolic execution engine we use for program analysis is an extension of CREST [3]. Our repair method also implements the heuristics of [15] for preferring simple repairs using Maximum Satisfiability (MAX-SAT) solving. Besides the source code, the FoREnSiC archive also contains the scripts to reproduce our experimental results.

6   Experimental Results

In this section, we experimentally compare our new repair method with the method of [15] to support the following informal claim.

Claim. *If program analysis is done before repair starts, the analysis needs to be fairly detailed to deliver the information required for finding a repair with counterexample-guided refinements. Repair with on-the-fly program analysis requires only a fractional amount of this information about the program behavior.*

This property is important because complex programs cannot be analyzed exhaustively. Section 6.2 shows an example were the method of [15] even fails because upfront program analysis does not produce the required information within reasonable time.

One could expect that our new repair method is also significantly faster because the constraints that are used for computing repair candidates are typically much smaller, and should hence be easier to solve. Unfortunately, if the constraints do not lack information that is needed for repair, this does not hold true. The reason is that modern constraint solvers, especially SMT-solvers, are good in ignoring information that is not needed. The additional time they require for parsing and simplifying the large formula is usually not so significant.

6.1 Performance Results

Table 1 summarizes performance results for repairing different faulty versions of the `tcas` program from the Siemens suite [20]. The `tcas` program implements a traffic collision avoidance system for aircrafts. It has about 180 lines of code, 12 integer inputs and one output. It comes in 41 faulty versions, together with a reference implementation and 1608 test cases. Table 1 only contains those faulty versions for which our fault model (incorrect expressions) applies. Versions with missing code or incorrect control flow are not considered. An exception are the versions `tcas21`, `tcas22`, and `tcas23`. They feature a missing function call, but this can be compensated by modifying an expression. Table 1 only compares the error correction step, assuming perfect information about the error location.

The columns 1 to 4 contain results for our on-the-fly repair method using test case execution to verify repair candidates. Column 1 indicates whether a repair could be found. Column 2 gives the number of execution paths that had to be analyzed using concolic execution to find a correct repair candidate. The number of iterations of the repair refinement loop is listed in Column 3. Column 4 shows the overall repair time (including program analysis and candidate verification). The columns 5 to 8 contain exactly the same information for the on-the-fly method that verifies candidates using a correctness formula expressing equivalence with the reference implementation (see Section 5). Finally, the columns 9 to 12 show results of the method without on-the-fly analysis. The specification is the same, namely an assertion requiring equivalence with the reference implementation. Column 10 gives the minimum number of execution paths that need to be analyzed for the method to find a repair. For this number of analyzed execution paths, the last two columns list the number of iterations of the repair refinement loop and the overall repair time, respectively.

All experiments were performed on an Intel P7350 processor with 2 × 2.0 GHz and 3 GB RAM, running 32-bit Linux. As SMT-solver we used Z3 version 3.1 with linear integer arithmetic, interfaced via its SMT-LIBv2 interface. A time-out of 60 seconds was set for all SMT-solver calls.

Discussion

What stands out in Table 1 is that repair with on-the-fly program analysis and test cases is able to fix all benchmarks, and is significantly faster than the

Table 1. Performance results

Col.	1	2	3	4	5	6	7	8	9	10	11	12
	On-the-fly with testing				On-the-fly with equivalence checking				Method of [15]			
	repair found	# paths analyzed	# iterations	repair time	repair found	# paths analyzed	# iterations	repair time	repair found	min. # paths	# iterations	repair time
	[-]	[-]	[-]	[sec]	[-]	[-]	[-]	[sec]	[-]	[-]	[-]	[sec]
tcas01	yes	16	9	23	no	-	-	-	yes	337	8	65
tcas02	yes	40	11	30	yes	8	3	12	yes	753	5	26
tcas06	yes	32	5	12	yes	60	8	79	yes	1393	7	55
tcas07	yes	4	3	10	yes	2	2	6	yes	305	3	11
tcas08	yes	12	7	18	yes	32	17	38	yes	305	5	17
tcas09	yes	6	4	13	yes	8	5	28	yes	593	6	41
tcas10	yes	104	10	32	no	-	-	-	no	-	-	-
tcas13	yes	14	8	33	no	-	-	-	no	-	-	-
tcas14	yes	24	13	71	no	-	-	-	no	-	-	-
tcas16	yes	2	2	9	yes	2	2	6	yes	305	2	9
tcas17	yes	4	3	10	yes	2	2	6	yes	305	3	12
tcas18	yes	2	2	8	yes	34	18	40	yes	305	4	14
tcas19	yes	12	7	18	yes	32	17	37	yes	305	5	18
tcas20	yes	10	6	15	yes	8	5	26	yes	593	9	85
tcas21	yes	32	17	206	no	-	-	-	no	-	-	-
tcas22	yes	32	17	206	no	-	-	-	no	-	-	-
tcas23	yes	22	12	113	no	-	-	-	no	-	-	-
tcas24	yes	22	12	112	no	-	-	-	no	-	-	-
tcas25	yes	10	6	17	yes	14	8	100	yes	337	7	82
tcas28	yes	8	3	10	yes	20	6	35	yes	1329	4	34
tcas35	yes	8	3	9	yes	20	6	46	yes	1329	5	41
tcas36	yes	2	2	7	yes	2	2	6	yes	305	2	8
tcas39	yes	10	6	17	yes	14	8	101	yes	337	7	82
avg.	100%	18.6	7.3	43	65%	17.2	4.7	38	70%	397	5.1	38

other methods. Of course, the 1608 test cases form a less restrictive specification than equivalence with the reference implementation. However, manual analysis of the computed repairs showed that they are reasonable – they do not just exhibit "holes" in the test suite. This illustrates that repair with test cases as specification can be useful and has the potential to scale better.

The columns 3, 7, and 11 show that a few iterations of the repair refinement loop are often enough to find a repair. Our new repair method with on-the-fly program analysis exploits this circumstance by doing program analysis only for the few counterexamples that show up. On average, it analyzes only 18 execution paths (see Column 2 and 6). Without on-the-fly analysis, at least 397 execution paths need to be analyzed on average (Column 10). These observations confirm the Claim about analysis depth postulated earlier. With the same mechanism to verify the correctness of repair candidates, the running times are almost the same (Column 8 vs. 12). The scalability benefits of our new method become more evident when exhaustive program analysis is not feasible anymore, as illustrated in the next section.

6.2 Greatest Common Divisor Example

The tcas example in the previous section fits the repair method with upfront program analysis well because it has only a finite (and small) number of execution paths. Let us now increase the level of difficulty. Consider the following C code implementing a sophisticated algorithm to compute the Greatest Common Divisor of two integers in the function gcd. The code also contains the Euclidean algorithm as reference implementation (gcdR), and an equivalence assertion in line 19. The gcd implementation contains a bug which is not easy to see and even more difficult to fix: line 35 should read u - v instead of u >> 1.

```
1   #include <assert.h>
2   #include <forensic.h>
3   #define UI unsigned int
4
5   //<ASSUME_CORRECT>
6   UI gcd(UI u, UI v);
7   UI gcdR(UI a, UI b) {
8     if(a == 0)      return b;
9     while(b != 0){
10      if(a > b)       a = a - b;
11      else            b = b - a;
12    }
13    return a;
14  }
15  void main() {
16    UI a, b;
17    FORENSIC_input_UI(a);
18    FORENSIC_input_UI(b);
19    assert(gcdR(a,b) ==
             gcd(a,b));
20  } //</ASSUME_CORRECT>
```

```
21  UI gcd(UI u, UI v) {
22    UI s = 0;
23    if(u == 0 || v == 0)
24      return u | v;
25    for(;((u|v)&1)==0;++s){
26      u >>= 1; v >>= 1;
27    }
28    while((u & 1) == 0)
29      u >>= 1;
30    do {
31      while((v & 1) == 0)
32        v >>= 1;
33      if(u <= v) { v -= u;
34      } else {
35        UI tmp = u >> 1;
36        u = v; v = tmp;
37      }
38      v >>= 1;
39    } while(v != 0);
40    return u << s;
41  }
```

We first apply our new repair method with on-the-fly program analysis and test-based repair candidate verification. As test inputs, we simply take all pairs a, b with $0 \leq a, b < 100$. The number 100 was chosen arbitrarily, the correct repair is also found with lower numbers like 15. For program analysis, we do not limit the number of execution paths to analyze, but rather their length. With two or three invocations of our method, we found out that a length of 55 is enough.[3] Using these parameters and Z3 with bitvector arithmetic, our new

---

[3] This number roughly corresponds to the number of executed statements.

method found the sequence of repair candidates "873", "85", "u - 2", and "u - v" in 101 seconds. The last one, "u - v", was found to be correct. Only 1570 program paths had to be analyzed. With a more careful choice of the parameters, a correct repair can also be found with less than 1000 paths analyzed.

We failed in applying the method with upfront program analysis to find a repair. Again, we experimented with an increasing maximum execution path length during program analysis. With a maximum length of 75, the faulty statement was not even executed in such a way that a wrong result was produced. With a maximum length of 80, we were already analyzing 10 402 execution paths, which took more than half an hour. Still, the program analysis was so inaccurate that only incorrect repairs (usually replacing the faulty expression with some constant) were found.[4]

Discussion

This example nicely demonstrates the scalability benefits of our new approach. Complete program analysis is simply infeasible for the gcd program. The many loops and branching points lead to huge numbers of possible execution paths, even if one considers only paths of relatively short length. Hence, one can only analyze small parts of the program behavior. When doing random program analysis before repair starts, it is very unlikely that the information needed for repair is obtained. With on-the-fly program analysis one cannot completely analyze the program either, not even for the counterexamples of interest. However, focusing on these counterexamples helps to extract enough information to find repairs.

7   Conclusion

In this work, we presented a novel method for automatic error correction in simple software programs using on-the-fly program analysis. In contrast to existing repair methods which perform program analysis before the repair process starts, our approach analyzes only those parts of the behavior of the program that are relevant for finding a repair. This is important if exhaustive program analysis is infeasible. Not looking at the entire program right from the beginning can be seen as an abstraction method. Unlike existing methods that use abstraction for repair [11], our method can also refine the abstraction. Compared to existing formal methods, our new approach is also more flexible regarding the form of specification and the correctness verification method. Assertions and test cases can be used as well as on-line feedback from the user. All this contributes towards making automatic error correction more practicable.

In the future, we plan to address limitations of the approach and its implementation by experimenting with fault models that go beyond incorrect expressions,

---

[4] The reader may wonder why no repair is found although the path length is already higher than with on-the-fly analysis. The reason is that we only consider symbolic operations for the path length, so the absolute values cannot be compared. In the on-the-fly approach, the symbolic computation begins only when the repair template (i.e., line 35) is executed for the first time. See also Section 4.6.

interfacing additional verification engines, and implementing memory models to accurately reason about array operations and pointer arithmetic.

References

1. Arcuri, A.: On the automation of fixing software bugs. In: ICSE, pp. 1003–1006. ACM (2008)
2. Bloem, R., Drechsler, R., Fey, G., Finder, A., Hofferek, G., Könighofer, R., Raik, J., Repinski, U., Sülflow, A.: FoREnSiC – An automatic debugging environment for C programs. In: Biere, A., Nahir, A., Vos, T. (eds.) HVC 2012. LNCS, vol. 7857, pp. 260–265. Springer, Heidelberg (2013)
3. Burnim, J., Sen, K.: Heuristics for scalable dynamic test generation. In: ASE, pp. 443–446. IEEE (2008)
4. Chang, K.-H., Markov, I.L., Bertacco, V.: Fixing design errors with counterexamples and resynthesis. In: ASP-DAC, pp. 944–949. IEEE (2007)
5. Clarke, L.A.: A system to generate test data and symbolically execute programs. IEEE Trans. Software Eng. 2(3), 215–222 (1976)
6. Dallmeier, V., Zeller, A., Meyer, B.: Generating fixes from object behavior anomalies. In: ASE, pp. 550–554. IEEE (2009)
7. Debroy, V., Wong, W.E.: Using mutation to automatically suggest fixes for faulty programs. In: ICST, pp. 65–74. IEEE (2010)
8. Forrest, S., Nguyen, T., Weimer, W., Le Goues, C.: A genetic programming approach to automated software repair. In: GECCO, pp. 947–954. ACM (2009)
9. Godefroid, P., Klarlund, N., Sen, K.: DART: Directed automated random testing. In: PLDI, pp. 213–223. ACM (2005)
10. Le Goues, C., Nguyen, T., Forrest, S., Weimer, W.: GenProg: A generic method for automatic software repair. IEEE Trans. Software Eng. 38(1), 54–72 (2012)
11. Griesmayer, A., Bloem, R., Cook, B.: Repair of Boolean programs with an application to C. In: Ball, T., Jones, R.B. (eds.) CAV 2006. LNCS, vol. 4144, pp. 358–371. Springer, Heidelberg (2006)
12. Jobstmann, B., Griesmayer, A., Bloem, R.: Program repair as a game. In: Etessami, K., Rajamani, S.K. (eds.) CAV 2005. LNCS, vol. 3576, pp. 226–238. Springer, Heidelberg (2005)
13. Jobstmann, B., Staber, S., Griesmayer, A., Bloem, R.: Finding and fixing faults. Journal of Computer and System Sciences 78(2), 441–460 (2012)
14. King, J.C.: Symbolic execution and program testing. Communications of the ACM 19(7), 385–394 (1976)
15. Koenighofer, R., Bloem, R.: Automated error localization and correction for imperative programs. In: FMCAD, pp. 91–100. IEEE (2011)
16. Raik, J., Repinski, U., Hantson, H., Jenihhin, M., Di Guglielmo, G., Pravadelli, G., Fummi, F.: Combining dynamic slicing and mutation operators for ESL correction. In: ETS, pp. 1–6. IEEE (2012)
17. Sen, K., Marinov, D., Agha, G.: CUTE: A concolic unit testing engine for C. In: ESEC/FSE, pp. 263–272. ACM (2005)
18. Solar-Lezama, A.: The sketching approach to program synthesis. In: Hu, Z. (ed.) APLAS 2009. LNCS, vol. 5904, pp. 4–13. Springer, Heidelberg (2009)
19. Solar-Lezama, A., Tancau, L., Bodik, R., Saraswat, V., Seshia, S.A.: Combinatorial sketching for finite programs. In: ASPLOS, pp. 404–415. ACM (2006)
20. Siemens suite, http://pleuma.cc.gatech.edu/aristotle/Tools/subjects
21. Wei, Y., Pei, Y., Furia, C.A., Silva, L.S., Buchholz, S., Meyer, B., Zeller, A.: Automated fixing of programs with contracts. In: ISSTA, pp. 61–72. ACM (2010)

Computing Interpolants without Proofs*

Hana Chockler, Alexander Ivrii, and Arie Matsliah

IBM Research – Haifa

Abstract. We describe an incremental algorithm for computing interpolants for a pair φ_A, φ_B of formulas in propositional logic. In contrast with the common approaches, our method does not require a proof of unsatisfiability of $\varphi_A \wedge \varphi_B$, and can be realized using any SAT solver as a black box. We achieve this by combining model enumeration with the ability to easily generate interpolants in the special case that one of the formulas is a cube.

1 Introduction

Craig's interpolation theorem [Cra57] states that for any pair of propositional formulas φ_A, φ_B, if φ_A implies $\neg\varphi_B$ ($\varphi_A \Rightarrow \neg\varphi_B$) then there exists a formula φ_I, so that $\varphi_A \Rightarrow \varphi_I \Rightarrow \neg\varphi_B$, and in addition $\mathrm{Vars}(\varphi_I) \subseteq \mathrm{Vars}(\varphi_A) \cap \mathrm{Vars}(\varphi_B)$. The formula φ_I is called a *Craig interpolant of φ_A and φ_B*.

Starting with the seminal work of McMillan [McM03], interpolants have a central role in formal verification (and beyond) – various application include hardware model checking [McM03, McM05], detection of functional dependency [LJHM07], Boolean function decomposition [LJH08], and model checking of sequential programs [McM10].

The most common technique for computing an interpolant for a pair of formulas φ_A, φ_B in propositional logic is based on a resolution refutation for $(\varphi_A \wedge \varphi_B)$ produced by a DPLL-like SAT solver [ZM03, ANORC10]. Once obtained, the proof can be transformed into an interpolant in the form of a Boolean circuit having the same structure as the proof itself [Kra97, Pud97, McM03, KW10].[1]

Even though this scheme is generally very successful in practice, its main limitation is the need for a refutation (proof of unsatisfiability) that is of manageable size. Since modern SAT solvers are not specifically aimed to produce short refutations, even for simple problems the interpolants produced are often too big to handle. In addition, the interpolants constructed in this way are usually highly redundant, and for practical applications it is often beneficial to minimize/simplify them. However, such minimization can be very costly – and thus in practice one might not succeed to construct a small interpolant even if

---

* This work is partially supported by the European Community under the call FP7-ICT-2009-5 – project PINCETTE 257647.

[1] There are efficient algorithms known to compute interpolants based on refutations in proof systems other than resolution (e.g., in Cutting Planes [Kra97]), but the one based on resolution is the canonical one from practical perspective.

A. Biere, A. Nahir, and T. Vos (Eds.): HVC 2012, LNCS 7857, pp. 72–85, 2013.
© Springer-Verlag Berlin Heidelberg 2013

one exists. In the worst case, the input formula $(\varphi_A \wedge \varphi_B)$ might not have a resolution refutation of polynomial (in the number of variables) size at all.

The problem boils down to the dependency of the method on a particular type of SAT solving algorithm. In other words, even if the ultimate SAT solver was given to us as an oracle that answers any satisfiability query instantly, we would not know how to use it to produce interpolants efficiently.

1.1   Our Contribution

In this paper we present a SAT-based incremental algorithm for computing interpolants. Our algorithm can be easily implemented on top of any complete SAT-solver with the minimal interface to return *SAT / UNSAT* and a satisfying assignment in case of *SAT*, and in particular the solver does not need to produce proofs or be DPLL-based. Even though this minimal interface in principle suffices, for practical reasons we will want from the solver a bit more: the (now standard) incremental interface that allows adding clauses between calls and solving under assumptions (see Section 3).

The core idea of our algorithm is to compute an interpolant φ_I incrementally by taking the disjunction of "point" interpolants φ_p for all $p \in A$ (where A denotes the set of models of φ_A). Each point interpolant φ_p contains p, is disjoint from B, and is defined in terms of common variables of φ_A and φ_B. It follows that the union of these interpolants for all $p \in A$ contains all of A and is still disjoint from B – thus constituting a valid interpolant for (φ_A, φ_B). An important observation here is that computing a point interpolant, or more generally an interpolant between a cube $c = \ell_1 \wedge \cdots \wedge \ell_k$ (containing up to 2^{-k} fraction of the points in A) and any propositional formula φ_B is trivial: one can simply remove from c the literals referring to variables local to A. From the practical viewpoint, it is crucial to further generalize these cubes to cover as many points of A as possible while still being disjoint from B. The difference between our approach and the traditional (monolithic) interpolation is depicted graphically in Figure 1.

A more general method of computing an interpolant for (φ_A, φ_B) is the following two-stage process. First, we show that $\varphi_A \wedge \varphi_B$ is unsatisfiable by means of a certain *partition-based* algorithm (by this we mean an algorithm in which one solver is run on φ_A, another solver is run on φ_B, and the two solvers are allowed to exchange constraints consisting only of common variables). Second, we show how to construct an interpolant based on these exchanged constraints (see Section 3.3 for details).

Our approach is somewhat similar in spirit to the classic algorithm that extracts a satisfying assignment from a SAT decision procedure, viewing the procedure as an oracle. In this algorithm, the variables are ordered, and then the first one is assigned at random. The algorithm then queries the SAT oracle for the existence of a satisfying assignment for the rest of the formula; it continues in this way until all variables are assigned.

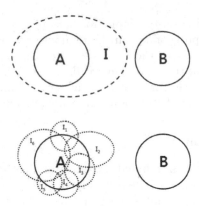

Fig. 1. Comparison between monolithic and incremental interpolants

1.2   Related Work

This work is tightly related to various methods for finding all models (satisfying assignments) of a given formula, or more specifically finding all assignments to the common variables of φ_A and φ_B possessing extensions satisfying φ_A. We refer to the papers [McM02, JS05, BKK11, GM12] containing efficient algorithms for this task and references to earlier work. In particular we also follow the widely used blocking clause approach to prevent the algorithm from discovering the same point again and again, and we try to generalize cubes as much as possible to get quick coverage of A (the set of models of φ_A). However, our setting allows an additional twist on the generalization process which makes convergence of interpolant computation quicker than that of computing all satisfying assignments: we can additionally generalize each cube as long as it remains disjoint from B, allowing wider coverage of points in A.

An alternative partition-based algorithm for detecting whether $\varphi_A \wedge \varphi_B$ is unsatisfiable appears in [PG00]. In the cited work, all the assignments to the common variables are checked, and $\varphi_A \wedge \varphi_B$ is unsatisfiable if and only if for every such assignment c either $c \wedge \varphi_A$ or $c \wedge \varphi_B$ is unsatisfiable. In contrast, our algorithm only considers those assignments to the common variables which admit a satisfiable extension for φ_A (and in practice this number is much smaller due to generalization).

Last but not least, an important source of inspiration for this work are the papers [BKK11, Bra11] which demonstrate the general power of an incremental approach for solving difficult problems. Note that in the context of model checking, IC3 (the recent breakthrough model-checking technique by Bradley [Bra11]) can be also viewed as a method which generates interpolants without proofs. However our setting is more general, allowing to compute an interpolant for any pair of propositional formulas.

2   Preliminaries

As usual, a *literal* is either a variable or its negation, a *clause* is a disjunction of literals, and a *cube* is a conjunction of literals. A *CNF* is a conjunction of clauses and a *DNF* is a disjunction of cubes.

Given a (propositional) formula φ_A, we denote by V_A the set of all variables that occur in φ_A. Given two formulas φ_A and φ_B, we denote by $V_{A\cap B} \triangleq V_A \cap V_B$ the set of *common* variables of φ_A and φ_B, and by $V_{A\setminus B} = V_A \setminus V_B$ the set of all variables *local* to φ_A.

With each formula φ_A we associate a subset of $\{0,1\}^{V_A}$ containing all assignments to V_A satisfying φ_A (models of φ_A). Slightly abusing notation, we sometimes refer to formulas as subsets and vice versa; in particular, $\varphi_A = \emptyset$ means that φ_A is unsatisfiable.

Definition 1 (Interpolant). [2] *Let φ_A, φ_B be a pair of formulas that cannot be simultaneously satisfied ($\varphi_A \wedge \varphi_B = \emptyset$). An* interpolant *$\varphi_I = Itp(\varphi_A, \varphi_B)$ of (φ_A, φ_B) is a formula satisfying: 1) $\varphi_A \Rightarrow \varphi_I$; 2) $\varphi_I \wedge \varphi_B = \emptyset$; and 3) $V_I \subseteq V_{A\cap B}$.*

Our algorithm makes use of a SAT solver to decide satisfiability of a propositional formula. For most of the paper this solver is viewed as a black box; the only requirements are that it should output *SAT* or *UNSAT* depending on the status of the formula, and in the case of *SAT* the solver should also return an assignment (model) satisfying the formula. Note that a model is a conjunction of unit clauses, or simply a cube.

We denote by $P^A_{A\cap B}$ the projection of the set (of all assignments satisfying) φ_A to $V_{A\cap B}$. $P^B_{A\cap B}$ is defined similarly. Clearly, $\varphi_A \wedge \varphi_B = \emptyset$ if and only if $P^A_{A\cap B} \cap P^B_{A\cap B} = \emptyset$.

3   Algorithm

In this section we present the main contribution of this paper – an incremental algorithm for computing an interpolant φ_I of (φ_A, φ_B). In the following subsections we describe a basic version of the algorithm, an efficient implementation of this algorithm on top of a modern CDCL solver (e.g. MiniSat), and various extensions and optimizations which seem crucial for real-life instances.

3.1   Basic Algorithm

The algorithm (described in Algorithm 1) accepts a pair (φ_A, φ_B) of propositional formulas, and, in the case under consideration that $\varphi_A \wedge \varphi_B$ is unsatisfiable, returns an interpolant φ_I (in DNF). The algorithm also detects the case that $\varphi_A \wedge \varphi_B$ is satisfiable, and can in principle return a satisfying assignment to $\varphi_A \wedge \varphi_B$.

---

[2] This definition slightly deviates from the original definition of Craig, but is now standard in the context of formal methods.

The interpolant φ_I is constructed incrementally; initially it is empty. Roughly speaking, the algorithm searches for points $p \in \varphi_A$ not yet covered by φ_I and then generalizes these points to cubes by omitting assignments to all variables local to φ_A and to as many common variables as possible, while still keeping these cubes disjoint from φ_B. Each such generalized cube represents a new incremental knowledge and is added to φ_I. For convenience we introduce the set $\varphi'_A = \varphi_A \wedge \neg \varphi_I$ corresponding to the set of assignments in φ_A not yet covered by φ_I; the algorithm terminates when φ'_A becomes empty.

Algorithm 1. Iterative computation of the interpolant

Input: A pair (φ_A, φ_B) of propositional formulas
Output: An interpolant φ_I for (φ_A, φ_B) (in DNF) if $\varphi_A \wedge \varphi_B = \emptyset$, or a satisfying assignment otherwise

1: $\varphi_I \leftarrow \emptyset$
2: $\varphi'_A \leftarrow \varphi_A$
3: **while** TRUE **do**
4:      **if** φ'_A is unsatisfiable **then**
5:         **return** φ_I
6:      **else**
7:         Let p be a model of φ'_A
8:         $p' \leftarrow$ projection of p to $V_{A \cap B}$
9:         $p'' \leftarrow$ generalization of p' w.r.t. φ_A
10:        **if** $(p'' \wedge \varphi_B)$ is satisfiable **then**
11:           **return** SAT + model
12:        **else**
13:           $p''' \leftarrow$ generalization of p'' w.r.t. φ_B
14:           $\varphi_I \leftarrow \varphi_I \vee p'''$
15:           $\varphi'_A \leftarrow \varphi'_A \wedge \neg p'''$
16:        **end if**
17:      **end if**
18: **end while**

We now describe a single iteration of the main loop (lines 4-17) in detail. On line 4 we call a SAT solver to check whether φ'_A is empty. If so, then $\varphi_A \subseteq \varphi_I$ and the algorithm terminates providing φ_I as the final interpolant. Otherwise (line 7), the SAT solver returns a model p for φ'_A, that is an assignment to variables in V_A. First we project this assignment to $V_{A \cap B}$ by omitting the variables local to φ_A (line 8); this projection corresponds to the cube p'.

We can (on line 9) further generalize the cube p' to p'' as long as it satisfies the following property: for any extension $\tilde{p}'$ of p'' to $V_{A \cap B}$ there is a further extension $\tilde{p}$ of $\tilde{p}'$ to V_A which satisfies φ_A. In other words, consider the projection $P_{A \cap B}^A$ of all assignments satisfying φ_A to $V_{A \cap B}$. By construction, $p' \in P_{A \cap B}^A$, and we seek to generalize it to p'' so that as sets of assignments $p' \in p'' \subseteq P_{A \cap B}^A$, thus enumerating more than one (projection of a) satisfying assignment to φ_A to $V_{A \cap B}$ at once. We describe the existing methods for such a generalization in

Section 3.3. Also note that this generalization is performed with respect to the original set φ_A.

Next (on line 10), we make another call to a SAT solver to check whether $\varphi_B \wedge p''$ is satisfiable (note that the cube p'' can be passed to the solver as a set of unit assumptions). If this is the case, then $\varphi_A \wedge \varphi_B$ is satisfiable, and in fact we can obtain an explicit satisfying assignment to $\varphi_A \wedge \varphi_B$ by extending the assignment satisfying $p'' \wedge \varphi_B$ to $V_{A \setminus B}$ which satisfies φ_A (which is possible by the property above). If the generalization step on line 9 is omitted, a satisfying assignment to $\varphi_A \wedge \varphi_B$ can be obtained immediately by unifying the assignment to $p'' \wedge \varphi_B$ and the assignment p (since the two assignments match on the common variables).

In the main case under consideration, $p'' \wedge \varphi_B$ is unsatisfiable, and we seek (on line 13) to generalize p'' even further to p''' by dropping the assignments to some of the variables in $V_{A \cap B}$ while keeping p''' disjoint from φ_B. The difference between this generalization and the one on line 9 is that now we can let p''' represent non-$P^A_{A \cap B}$ points provided that they are also non-$P^B_{A \cap B}$ points (see definitions above). In particular, p''' can also describe additional $P^A_{A \cap B}$-points, not previously described by p''. From the practical viewpoint, this is a very important optimization (details follow).

Note that we can view p''' as an interpolant of p and φ_B. We update $\varphi_I \leftarrow \varphi_I \vee p'''$ (thus keeping φ_I in DNF) and prevent the solver from rediscovering points in $p''' \wedge \varphi_A$ (and in particular p) by adding the blocking clause $\neg p'''$ to φ'_A.

Claim 1. *(1) Algorithm 1 always terminates. (2) If $\varphi_A \wedge \varphi_B = \emptyset$ it outputs a valid interpolant φ_I for (φ_A, φ_B).*

Proof. (1) Initially $\varphi'_A = \varphi_A$, and in each iteration its size (as set of assignments) shrinks by ≥ 1. (2) By construction, $V_I \subseteq V_{A \cap B}$. In addition, φ_I is a disjunction of cubes that are disjoint from φ_B, hence $\varphi_I \wedge B = \emptyset$. To see that $\varphi_A \Rightarrow \varphi_I$, observe that the algorithm terminates only when $\varphi'_A \triangleq \varphi_I \setminus \varphi_A$ becomes empty.

3.2   Implementation Details

Now we describe how the algorithm proposed in the last section can be efficiently implemented on top of MiniSat or any other SAT solver that provides an interface to incrementally add new clauses into the solver, and to solve under a set of additional unit assumptions [ES03]. In the case of a satisfiable result, such a solver should return a model satisfying all of the clauses in the solver as well as all of the unit assumption literals. In the case of an unsatisfiable result, the solver should return a subset of the assumptions used in the proof of unsatisfiability.

We keep two instances of the SAT solver: *A-solver* holding the CNF for φ'_A and *B-solver* holding the CNF for φ_B. Thus the SAT call on line 4 corresponds to $A.Solve()$ and the SAT call on line 10 corresponds to $B.Solve(p'')$ with the cube p'' passed as the set of unit assumptions. In the simplest version of the algorithm we can skip the generalization on line 9, and the generalization on line 13 of p'' to p''' is obtained for free by taking p''' to be the subset of the assumptions in p'' used for unsatisfiability. Finally, the strengthening of φ'_A on line 15 corresponds to $A.add(\neg p''')$.

We found that this (somewhat primitive) implementation already performs quite well on many instances.

3.3   Extensions

For some real-life instances originating from hardware model checking problems, the basic algorithm described above often takes too many iterations to converge in reasonable time. By experimentation, we found that the following heuristics/optimizations work well for those hard cases.

Exhaustive Generalization of p'' to p'''. Even though the MiniSat-like "solve under assumption" mechanism is highly successful at detecting which subset of the assumptions is important for unsatisfiability, this subset is very often far from minimal. Thus, after obtaining a reduced set from the solver's "final" conflict analysis, one can try to shrink this set further. It is natural to look for $minimal^3$ or even $minimum\text{-}sized$ subsets.

We implemented the following greedy approach for finding a minimal subset of the conflicting assumptions, similar to a basic destructive algorithm for MUS computations [DGHP09, Nad10, SL11]. Remove one of the assumptions – if the remaining formula is satisfiable then this assumption is deemed as $necessary$ and must be present in all minimal assumption subsets from this point on. If the remaining formula is unsatisfiable, then the assumption is $redundant$ and is deleted from the set of assumptions under consideration. Also note that in the case of an unsatisfiable answer, one can immediately trim the set of non-processed assumptions further (when this functionality is supported by the solver). After all of the assumptions are processed, we end up with a minimal subset as required. We refer to this approach as $exhaustive\ B\text{-}generalization$.

In general this optimization has a significant overhead on the running time of a single iteration of the loop since in the worst case it resorts to one additional SAT call for each of the assumptions in the initial set. However as we will see in the experimental section, the smaller clauses produced by this minimization are of better quality and the algorithm takes significantly fewer iterations to converge (in the same spirit as generalization of counterexamples and inductive clauses in IC3).

Forall-Exists Generalization of p' to p''. Turning to generalization of p' with respect to φ_A (on line 9), several methods have been proposed in earlier works in the context of finding all satisfying assignments to a formula (see for example [JS05]) or existential quantification (e.g. [BKK11] and [GM12]).

We implemented several variations, based on [BKK11]. We apply the following "dual-rail" construction. For each of the common variables $v \in V_{A \cap B}$, we introduce two additional fresh variables v^+ and v^-, and we replace each occurrence

---

[3] I.e. the formula would become satisfiable if any of the assumptions were dropped.

of v in φ_A by v^+, and each occurrence of $\neg v$ in φ_A by v^-. In addition, we add the binary clause $(\neg v^+, \neg v^-)$ to prevent the solver from assigning both v^+ and v^- to *true*. In the simpler variant to which we refer as *trivial A-generalization* we create the cube p'' from the model p of φ'_A by including the literals v for which v^+ is set to *true*, and the literals $\neg v$ for which v^- is set to *true*. In the more complicated variants, we seek the shortest possible cubes p''. To this end, we create additional variables $v^\pm = v^+ \wedge v^-$ for $v \in V_{A \cap B}$, and put a sequential counter construction [Sin05] on top of $v^\pm$. This allows (passing additional assumptions to the A-solver) to look for cubes in A which are of size at most k, for any given k, and one can find a shortest cube by setting increasing values to $k = 1, 2, \ldots$. By experimenting with various parameter settings, we limit the maximum value of the counter to $\min(15, |V_{A \cap B}|)$ and we do a binary search to find the minimal $k \in [1..15]$ if it exists. In other words we are guaranteed to end up with a shortest cube whenever it has length at most 15, and otherwise we resort to the trivial A-generalization from above. We refer to this version as *counter-based A-generalization*.

In general, the dual-rail construction has a negligible overhead, but searching for a shortest cube is expensive, both due to the extra logic pertaining to the sequential counter construction and the increased number of SAT-calls.

Exchanging Roles of the Two Solvers. In certain cases φ_B has fewer satisfying assignments than φ_A or it is easier to enumerate them. Then it might be easier to solve the "dual" problem first: compute φ_J – interpolant for (φ_B, φ_A), and then set $\varphi_I \leftarrow \neg \varphi_J$. This way the final interpolant is in CNF, but in most applications the precise form of the interpolant is not important (in case it is, see [BKK11] for an efficient method to convert between the two forms).

Exchanging Clauses of Common Variables. One can consider a general algorithm which uses the partitioning of $\varphi_A \wedge \varphi_B$ into (φ_A, φ_B) and allows to exchange learned clauses between the two solvers as long as they consist of common variables only. In particular, such an algorithm might use a scenario when the roles of the two solvers are switched periodically, or a scenario with the two solvers running in parallel, each producing satisfying assignments and/or blocking the satisfying assignments found by the other solver.

Of course, if the clauses are passed from φ_A to φ_B and back freely, more care should be taken when assembling the final interpolant. Luckily this is not too hard due to the following (here φ_G and φ_H correspond to (sets of) clauses learnt from φ_A and φ_B respectively).

Claim 2. *Suppose that $\varphi_A \Rightarrow \varphi_G$ and $\mathrm{Vars}(\varphi_G) \subseteq V_{A \cap B}$. Then an interpolant $\varphi_I = Itp(\varphi_A, \varphi_B)$ can be computed as $\varphi_I = Itp(\varphi_A, \varphi_B \wedge \varphi_G) \wedge \varphi_G$.*

Proof. Let $\varphi_J = Itp(\varphi_A, \varphi_B \wedge \varphi_G)$. By definition, $\varphi_A \Rightarrow \varphi_J$ and $\varphi_A \Rightarrow \varphi_G$, hence $\varphi_A \Rightarrow \varphi_I$. Also, φ_J is disjoint from $\varphi_B \wedge \varphi_G$, hence $\varphi_J \wedge \varphi_G$ is disjoint from φ_B.

Claim 3. *Suppose that $\varphi_B \Rightarrow \varphi_H$ and $\mathrm{Vars}(\varphi_H) \subseteq V_{A \cap B}$. Then an interpolant $\varphi_I = Itp(\varphi_A, \varphi_B)$ can be computed as $\varphi_I = Itp(\varphi_A \wedge \varphi_H, \varphi_B) \vee \neg \varphi_H$.*

Proof. Let $\varphi_J = Itp(\varphi_A \wedge \varphi_H, \varphi_B)$. $\varphi_A \wedge \varphi_H \Rightarrow \varphi_J$, hence $\varphi_A \Rightarrow \varphi_J \vee \neg \varphi_H = \varphi_I$. Also, since both φ_J and $\neg \varphi_H$ are disjoint from φ_B, so is φ_I.

We can keep track of the sets of clauses passed from φ_A to φ_B and vice versa and to reconstruct the interpolant by following the two rules above. This procedure leads to more general definitions of interpolants (not only CNF or DNF). However, if the only clauses passed from φ_A to φ_B are unit clauses, then the interpolant can be still computed in DNF as $(\vee C_i) \wedge (x) = \vee (C_i \wedge x)$ by distributivity.

Remark 1. Note that the blocking clauses $\neg p'''$ of Algorithm 1 are implied by φ_B, and thus can be viewed as clauses passed from φ_B to φ_A. In other words, Algorithm 1 can be seen as employing the incremental interpolant computation dictated by Claim 3 only.

We implemented a variant of this technique which periodically instructs the A-solver to look for unit clauses of common variables (by running the A-solver with a small time-limit and a small backtrack-limit) and passing these clauses to the B-solver. In many cases we saw a big reduction in the total number of iterations (in several cases passing unit clauses from φ_A to φ_B made φ_B directly unsatisfiable). The cons of this technique is that not all of the units passed from φ_A to φ_B are really required for unsatisfiability, while our construction adds all of these units into the interpolant. We refer to this optimization as *flp* (since it is reminiscent of failed literal probing in SAT-solving).

Interpolant Strength. We make a theoretical digression. In the discussion above we strove to generalize p' as much as possible, that is to describe the largest set in the projection. The motivation for this is clear – a smaller blocking clause can potentially block more points of φ'_A, thus allowing the algorithm to converge faster. However for various applications the loosest possible interpolant might not be good, and it could be helpful to compute the *largest* blocking clause which blocks the same points in φ'_A as $\neg p'''$. In other words, we can seek for a subcube q with $p' \subseteq q \subseteq p'''$ and $\varphi'_A \wedge \neg q = \varphi'_A \wedge \neg p'''$. After such subcube q is found, we can modify the line 14 of the algorithm to include q instead.

We illustrate this on an example. Suppose $\{x_1, x_2, x_3, x_4, x_5\} \subset V_{A \cap B}$ is a subset of common variables, $p'' = x_1 \wedge x_2 \wedge x_3 \wedge x_4 \wedge x_5$, and $p''' = x_1 \wedge x_2$. Suppose further that $p''' \wedge P_{A \cap B}^{A'}$ consists of the three points $(1, 1, 1, 1, 1, \cdot)$, $(1, 1, 1, 0, 1, \cdot)$, $(1, 1, 0, 1, 1, \cdot)$, where $\cdot$ represents the remaining variables in $V_{A \cap B}$. Note that the variable x_5 takes the same value on $P_{A \cap B}^{A'}$ and thus we can use $q = x_1 \wedge x_2 \wedge x_5$ instead of $x_1 \wedge x_2$ in the interpolant.

Finding the maximal set of variables which are constant on $p''' \wedge \varphi'_A$ can be done in at most $|p''| - |p'''|$ SAT calls. We illustrate this procedure on our example. We ask the SAT solver whether $\varphi'_A \wedge x_1 \wedge x_2 \wedge \neg(x_3 \wedge x_4 \wedge x_5)$ is satisfiable, that is we are looking for a point in $p''' \wedge P_{A \cap B}^{A'}$ with at least one different value out of

$\{x_3 = 1, x_4 = 1, x_5 = 1\}$. Let's say that the solver returns the point $(1,1,1,0,1,\cdot)$ which means that the variable x_4 is not constant on $p''' \wedge P_{A \cap B}^{A'}$. We refine the query asking whether $\varphi_A \wedge x_1 \wedge x_2 \wedge \neg(x_3 \wedge x_5)$ is satisfiable. Now the solver returns the point $(1,1,0,1,1,\cdot)$ which means that the variable x_3 is also not constant on $p''' \wedge P_{A \cap B}^{A'}$. Finally the query $\varphi_A \wedge x_1 \wedge x_2 \wedge \neg x_5$ is unsatisfiable, and the remaining set of variables are constant on $p''' \wedge P_{A \cap B}^{A'}$.

4   Experiments

Before discussing concrete experimental results, let us think when we expect the suggested approach to succeed. As mentioned before, Algorithm 1 and its variations might perform well if enumerating all satisfying assignments of φ_A (or φ_B) is not too hard, or whenever there exists a successful partition-based algorithm for solving $\varphi_A \wedge \varphi_B$. In particular we expect our algorithm to be successful for simple formulas with a small number $|V_{A \cap B}|$ of common variables[4].

We have evaluated our algorithm on the 465 single-property benchmarks used in the 2011 Hardware Model Checking Competition. For each of these benchmarks we unrolled the design for 11 cycles to represent the bounded model checking formula $J(x_0) \wedge T(x_0, x_1) \wedge \bigwedge_{i=1}^{10} T(x_i, x_{i+1}) \wedge \bigvee_{i=1}^{11} \neg P(x_i)$, where J, T, and P denote respectively the initial states of the design, the transition relation and the property being verified (see [McM03] for details). We define[5] $\varphi_A = \bigwedge_{i=1}^{10} T(x_i, x_{i+1}) \wedge \bigvee_{i=1}^{11} \neg P(x_i)$, $\varphi_B = J(x_0) \wedge T(x_0, x_1)$, and cnf-ize these propositional formulas using a variant of the approach described in [CMV09]. As the underlying SAT solver we use *Mage*, an IBM SAT solver which supports both the incremental interface of MiniSat and the ability to compute interpolants from proofs. In all of the experiments, the time-limit was set to 1800 seconds.

In the following tables we compare the performance of standard interpolation (building an interpolant from the proof of unsatisfiability of $\varphi_A \wedge \varphi_B$, in this and only in this case the proof generation capabilities of the solver are turned on) and various schemes based on Algorithm 1. We distinguish between three versions of generalization with respect to φ_A: no generalization at all (no A-gen), trivial A-generalization (triv A-gen) and counter-based A-generalization (cntr A-gen). The latter two versions are described in Section 3.3 and require dual-rail encoding. We also consider three versions of generalization with respect to φ_B: no generalization at all (no B-gen), the generalization based on the conflicting assumptions returned by the solver (std B-gen) and exhaustive B-generalization from Section 3.3 (exh B-gen). The results are summarized in Table 1. The second, third and fourth columns respectively denote the numbers of satisfied, unsatisfied and time-out instances, and the last column denotes the total time of the run. First of all, we see that generalizing with respect to B is crucial and that counter-based A-generalization is mostly unhelpful (in fact,

---

[4] In the worst case, all interpolants (expressed in terms of $V_{A \cap B}$) might be of size exponential in $|V_{A \cap B}|$: consider formulas φ_A, φ_B which enforce the parity of assignments to $V_{A \cap B}$ to be even and odd, respectively.

[5] The benefits of this "opposite" splitting are discussed later.

even the version of A-generalization with the unrestricted counter size on average only removes at most 5% - 10% of the literals of p', while the exhaustive B-generalization usually removes 90% of the literals and more). We also note that the standard interpolation performs best in terms of time (however, there was in fact one testcase where the version (no A-gen, std B-gen) finished in 1184 seconds, while the standard interpolation timed out). It should be noted that in this and subsequent experiments all the observed phenomena are consistent across individual instances (and not only in the bulk).

Table 1. Comparison of runtimes on 465 single property benchmarks from HWMCC11

Variant	SAT	UNSAT	TO	Total Running Time (s)
standard interpolation	14	429	22	49,153
no A-gen, no B-gen	1	22	442	767,678
no A-gen, std B-gen	14	420	31	79,686
no A-gen, exh B-gen	14	421	30	79,754
triv A-gen, no B-gen	1	25	439	762,135
triv A-gen, std B-gen	13	419	33	83,759
triv A-gen, exh B-gen	14	420	31	79,599
cntr A-gen, no B-gen	1	17	447	783,311
cntr A-gen, std B-gen	10	393	62	124,170
cntr A-gen, exh B-gen	10	399	56	115,312

We omit the inferior configurations and restrict to the test cases on which each configuration returned with a SAT or UNSAT answer - there are 430 such configurations. The comparison of the total number of iterations (column 2), the total interpolant size (column 3) and the total running time (column 4) are provided in Table 2. For the standard interpolation the number of iterations is meaningless and the size represents the number of gates in the *non-optimized* circuits (i.e. no structural hashing, etc. has been performed). For the remaining configurations the size represents the total number of literals in the computed interpolants (in CNF). Even though it is clear that the 4 schemes based on Algorithm 1 are on average 7 times slower than standard interpolation, it is interesting to note that they produce interpolants of much smaller size (up to 900 times). In particular, they require no need for further minimization. Next, it seems that on our test cases the extra time spent by a round of exhaustive generalization is compensated by fewer iterations required for the algorithm to converge. Finally, the dual-rail encoding and the trivial version A-generalizations seem to have a small positive impact on the size of the interpolant.

We have performed an additional experiment to see the value of periodically passing unit clauses from φ_A to φ_B (the flp technique described in Section 3.3). To this end we compare the (no A-gen, exh B-gen) configuration with a version of itself, where at the start and every 100 iterations the A-solver is instructed to look for unit clauses of common variables and to pass them to the B-solver. The results are summarized in Table 3. As usual, we restrict only to the benchmarks

Table 2. Comparison of numbers of iterations and interpolant sizes on 430 benchmarks

Variant	Total #iters	Total itp size	Total Running Time (s)
standard interpolation	0	90,922,242	3,842
no A-gen, std B-gen	129,506	837,273	19,138
no A-gen, exh B-gen	80,764	119,975	22,603
triv A-gen, std B-gen	133,903	857,081	22,286
triv A-gen, exh B-gen	77,752	117,105	22,637

where both versions complete – there are 407 such test cases. The interpolant size now measures the total number of literals in all the passed clauses (this corresponds to the previous definition when flp is disabled, and includes the number of unit clauses when flp is enabled). Activation of flp increases the running times (and the number of time-outs), but reduces the total number of iterations by about 4 times. On the other hand, most of the unit clauses detected during flp are irrelevant for the algorithm, and they increase the interpolant size.

Table 3. Measuring the effect of flp on 407 benchmarks

Variant	Total #iters	Total itp size	Total Running Time (s)
no A-gen, exh B-gen	73,071	147,358	15,532
no A-gen, exh B-gen, flp	18,685	184,619	43,374

A couple of additional remarks are in order. First, the size of the final interpolant can serve as a rough estimate for the total memory consumption of an algorithm. Second, in our experience enabling proof-logging techniques for the standard interpolation takes a very small overhead (around 5%), while the overhead of recording blocking (or more generally exchanged) clauses is absolutely negligible. Thus, the running times really represent a comparison between showing unsatisfiability of $\varphi_A \wedge \varphi_B$ using a single call to a SAT-solver and using various variants of a partition-based algorithm. Finally, these experiments should be taken only as a proof of concept of the methods presented. In fact, the current setup benefits our approach in two ways: 1) φ_B is a more restricted formula and so potentially has less satisfying assignments than φ_A, and 2) φ_A is a much simpler formula and so potentially allows for shorter explanation of the inconsistency between a satisfying assignment to φ_B and φ_A, that is for shorter cubes p'''. Indeed, the experiments with roles of φ_A and φ_B reversed resulted in inferior performance (nearly on all instances).

5   Conclusions and Future Work

We described an incremental algorithm for computing Craig interpolants for a pair of mutually unsatisfiable formulas. The most significant advantage of this algorithm is its simplicity – it does not depend on the underlying solver's ability to produce refutations and thus can be quickly implemented on top of any SAT-solver. In particular, it has the advantage of immediately benefiting from rapid improvements of modern SAT solvers which do not produce proofs.

At this stage, the main contribution of this work is theoretical, rather than practical. We have observed the need for better partition-based algorithms. We have suggested several heuristics towards this goal, but the experimental results show inferior performance (in terms of runtime) compared to a single monolithic call. If more efficient partition-based algorithms are discovered, this work shows how an interpolant may be easily and efficiently reconstructed afterwards. We have also described a technique to vary the strength of the computed interpolant.

On ther other hand, our algorithms are much lighter in terms of memory consumption (even though the size of a proof is linear in the running time of the solver, such proofs are usually huge), and as seen in experiments, the sizes of the interpolants produced are several orders of magnitude smaller than the sizes of the interpolants constructed from proofs. With this in mind (and in the spirit of [PG00]), we can view the algorithm as *the last resort* for computing interpolants, when all of the conventional techniques have failed.

One especially interesting direction for further study is to see how much the proposed technique for computing interpolants can be used inside the original interpolation algorithm for model checking [McM03]. The source of inspiration for this is the success of the IC3 technique [Bra11], which shows that it is often possible to efficiently characterize an over-approximation to states reachable within a certain number of cycles as a conjunction of clauses defined on state-variables only. Note that by splitting the bounded model checking formula as we described – with $\varphi_A = \bigwedge_{i=1}^{k} T(x_i, x_{i+1}) \wedge \bigvee_{i=1}^{k+1} \neg P(x_i)$, and $\varphi_B = J(x_0) \wedge T(x_0, x_1)$, the interpolant φ_I for (φ_A, φ_B) is computed as a DNF, and hence $\neg \varphi_A$ representing an over-approximation of states reachable in one step is precisely in CNF form.

References

[ANORC10] Achá, R.J.A., Nieuwenhuis, R., Oliveras, A., Rodríguez-Carbonell, E.: Practical algorithms for unsatisfiability proof and core generation in SAT solvers. AI Commun. 23(2-3), 145–157 (2010)

[BKK11] Brauer, J., King, A., Kriener, J.: Existential quantification as incremental SAT. In: Gopalakrishnan, G., Qadeer, S. (eds.) CAV 2011. LNCS, vol. 6806, pp. 191–207. Springer, Heidelberg (2011)

[Bra11] Bradley, A.R.: SAT-based model checking without unrolling. In: Jhala, R., Schmidt, D. (eds.) VMCAI 2011. LNCS, vol. 6538, pp. 70–87. Springer, Heidelberg (2011)

[CMV09] Chambers, B., Manolios, P., Vroon, D.: Faster SAT solving with better CNF generation. In: DATE, pp. 1590–1595 (2009)

[Cra57] Craig, W.: Linear reasoning. A new form of the Herbrand-Gentzen theorem. J. Symb. Log. 22(3), 250–268 (1957)

[DGHP09] Desrosiers, C., Galinier, P., Hertz, A., Paroz, S.: Using heuristics to find minimal unsatisfiable subformulas in satisfiability problems. J. Comb. Optim. 18(2), 124–150 (2009)

[ES03]   Eén, N., Sörensson, N.: An extensible SAT-solver. In: Giunchiglia, E.,
           Tacchella, A. (eds.) SAT 2003. LNCS, vol. 2919, pp. 502–518. Springer,
           Heidelberg (2004)
[GM12]   Goldberg, E., Manolios, P.: Quantifier elimination by dependency se-
           quents. CoRR, abs/1201.5653 (2012)
[JS05]   Jin, H., Somenzi, F.: Prime clauses for fast enumeration of satisfying
           assignments to Boolean circuits. In: DAC, pp. 750–753 (2005)
[Kra97]   Krajícek, J.: Interpolation theorems, lower bounds for proof systems, and
           independence results for bounded arithmetic. J. Symb. Log. 62(2), 457–
           486 (1997)
[KW10]   Kroening, D., Weissenbacher, G.: Verification and falsification of pro-
           grams with loops using predicate abstraction. Formal Asp. Com-
           put. 22(2), 105–128 (2010)
[LJH08]   Lee, R.-R., Jiang, J.-H.R., Hung, W.-L.: Bi-decomposing large Boolean
           functions via interpolation and satisfiability solving. In: DAC, pp. 636–
           641 (2008)
[LJHM07]   Lee, C.-C., Jiang, J.-H.R., Huang, C.-Y., Mishchenko, A.: Scalable explo-
           ration of functional dependency by interpolation and incremental SAT
           solving. In: ICCAD, pp. 227–233 (2007)
[McM02]   McMillan, K.L.: Applying SAT methods in unbounded symbolic model
           checking. In: Brinksma, E., Larsen, K.G. (eds.) CAV 2002. LNCS,
           vol. 2404, pp. 250–264. Springer, Heidelberg (2002)
[McM03]   McMillan, K.L.: Interpolation and SAT-based model checking. In: Hunt
           Jr., W.A., Somenzi, F. (eds.) CAV 2003. LNCS, vol. 2725, pp. 1–13.
           Springer, Heidelberg (2003)
[McM05]   McMillan, K.L.: Applications of Craig interpolants in model checking.
           In: Halbwachs, N., Zuck, L.D. (eds.) TACAS 2005. LNCS, vol. 3440, pp.
           1–12. Springer, Heidelberg (2005)
[McM10]   McMillan, K.L.: Lazy annotation for program testing and verification. In:
           Touili, T., Cook, B., Jackson, P. (eds.) CAV 2010. LNCS, vol. 6174, pp.
           104–118. Springer, Heidelberg (2010)
[Nad10]   Nadel, A.: Boosting minimal unsatisfiable core extraction. In: FMCAD,
           pp. 221–229 (2010)
[PG00]   Park, T.J., Van Gelder, A.: Partitioning methods for satisfiability testing
           on large formulas. Inf. Comput. 162(1-2), 179–184 (2000)
[Pud97]   Pudlák, P.: Lower bounds for resolution and cutting plane proofs and
           monotone computations. J. Symb. Log. 62(3), 981–998 (1997)
[Sin05]   Sinz, C.: Towards an optimal CNF encoding of Boolean cardinality con-
           straints. In: van Beek, P. (ed.) CP 2005. LNCS, vol. 3709, pp. 827–831.
           Springer, Heidelberg (2005)
[SL11]   Marques-Silva, J., Lynce, I.: On improving MUS extraction algorithms.
           In: Sakallah, K.A., Simon, L. (eds.) SAT 2011. LNCS, vol. 6695, pp. 159–
           173. Springer, Heidelberg (2011)
[ZM03]   Zhang, L., Malik, S.: Validating SAT solvers using an independent
           resolution-based checker: Practical implementations and other applica-
           tions. In: DATE, pp. 10880–10885 (2003)

MaxSAT-Based MCS Enumeration

Antonio Morgado[1], Mark Liffiton[2], and Joao Marques-Silva[1,3,⋆]

[1] CASL/CSI, University College Dublin, Dublin, Ireland
ajrm@ucd.ie
[2] Illinois Wesleyan University, Bloomington, IL, USA
mliffito@iwu.edu
[3] INESC-ID/IST, Lisbon, Portugal
jpms@ucd.ie

Abstract. Enumeration of *Minimal Correction Sets* (MCS) finds a wide range of practical applications, including the identification of Minimal Unsatisfiable Subsets (MUS) used in verifying the complex control logic of microprocessor designs (e.g. in the CEGAR loop of Reveal^{TM} [1,2]). Current state of the art MCS enumeration exploits core-guided MaxSAT algorithms, namely the so-called MSU3 [16] MaxSAT algorithm. Observe that a MaxSAT solution corresponds to a minimum sized MCS, but a formula may contain MCSes larger than those reported by a MaxSAT solution. These are obtained by enumerating all MaxSAT solutions. This paper proposes novel approaches for MCS enumeration, in the context of SMT, that exploit MaxSAT algorithms other than the MSU3 algorithm. Among other contributions, the paper proposes new blocking techniques that can be applied to different MCS enumeration algorithms. In addition, the paper conducts a comprehensive experimental evaluation of MCS enumeration algorithms, including both the existing and the novel algorithms. Problem instances from hardware verification, the SMT-LIB, and the MaxSAT Evaluation are considered in the experiments.

Keywords: AllMaxSAT, AllMaxSMT, MCS.

1 Introduction

A Minimal Correction Subset (MCS) of an unsatisfiable CNF formula is an irreducible set of clauses whose removal causes the formula to become satisfiable (thus "correcting" it). MCSes can be naturally extended for Satisfiability Modulo Theories (SMT) formulas expressed in clausal form.

The connection between all MCSes of a formula and its MUSes was first highlighted in the context of model-based diagnosis [10,23]. Namely, the enumeration of all MCSes of an unsatisfiable formula finds practical application in MUS enumeration [11]. One concrete example is the verification of hardware designs [2], for which enumeration of MCSes has been used in an industrial setting. Another

⋆ This work is partially supported by SFI grant BEACON (09/IN.1/I2618), and by FCT grants ATTEST (CMU-PT/ELE/0009/2009) and POLARIS (PTDC/EIA-CCO/123051/2010).

A. Biere, A. Nahir, and T. Vos (Eds.): HVC 2012, LNCS 7857, pp. 86–101, 2013.

example of application of MCS enumeration is in the context of design debugging [24]. A related problem is the enumeration of all *minimal* MCSes, those with the smallest cardinality. An example application is solving Boolean Multilevel Optimization by minimal MCS enumeration [3].

State of the art algorithms for MCS enumeration [12] are based on model enumeration of Maximum Satisfiability (MaxSAT) solvers, and the most effective approaches are based on core-guided algorithms, more concretely the so-called MSU3 algorithm [15,16]. Nevertheless, in practical MaxSAT solving, the MSU3 algorithm is not as effective as other core-guided MaxSAT algorithms. Therefore, it is natural to ask how MCS enumeration can be extended to other MaxSAT algorithms. This question further motivates the investigation of different approaches for implementing model enumeration in MaxSAT algorithms.

This paper proposes improvements to MSU3-like MCS enumeration algorithms, and it shows how to implement MCS enumeration with other well-known MaxSAT algorithms, namely (W)MSU1 [9,13]. Experimental results, obtained on a representative set of benchmarks, show that the proposed improvements are effective. The remainder of the paper is organized as follows. Section 2 introduces the definitions and notation used throughout the paper. Afterwards, section 3 summarizes the application of MCS enumeration in verification with counterexample-guided abstraction refinement (CEGAR). Section 4 investigates improvements to existing MCS enumeration algorithms, and shows how other core-guided MaxSAT algorithms can be used for MCS enumeration. Experimental results are presented in Section 5, and the paper concludes in Section 6.

2   Preliminaries

This section provides basic definitions on SMT and MCSes and surveys some of the existing work on MaxSMT.

The problem of determining the satisfiability of a formula with respect to a background theory $\mathcal{T}$ is called the *Satisfiability Modulo Theory* (SMT) problem. Current SMT solvers are able to handle a variety of different theories and even conjunctions of theories. One example SMT theory is the theory of *Equality with Uninterpreted Functions* ($\mathcal{T}_\varepsilon$), in which no restriction is imposed on the way the formulas or the predicates of a signature are interpreted.

Another example of a theory often seen in SMT instances is the theory of *Linear Integer Arithmetic* ($\mathcal{T}_\mathcal{Z}$), also know as the quantifier free *Presburger arithmetic*. Given the signature $(0, 1, +, -, \le)$, $\mathcal{T}_\mathcal{Z}$ is the theory of models that interprets these symbols in the usual way over the integers [5]. Further details on SMT, theories and SMT solving can be obtained in [20,25,5].

This paper addresses the problems of finding all *Minimal Correction Sets* (MCSes) in SMT. Despite focusing on SMT, all the algorithms and techniques described in the paper can be applied in the SAT domain. Before presenting the definition of the enumeration problems, some notation is introduced.

Given an unsatisfiable constraint system φ, a minimal correction set M of φ is a set of constraints whose removal yields a satisfiable formula $\varphi' = \varphi - M$

("correcting" the infeasibility) and that is minimal in the sense that adding any constraint from M back into φ' will make it unsatisfiable.

In the paper we refer to the MaxSMT problem [18]. The input of the MaxSMT problem is a CNF SMT formula φ, which is a conjunction of clauses. A clause is a disjunction of literals, where the literals are either atomic formulas or the negation of atomic formulas. The output of MaxSMT is an assignment $\mathcal{A}$ (consistent with $\mathcal{T}$) that minimize the number of falsified clauses of φ.

Generalizations of MaxSMT, include *Partial* MaxSMT, *Weighted* MaxSMT and *Weighted Partial* MaxSMT. In Partial MaxSMT the set of clauses in φ is divided in two separated sets: *hard* clauses and *soft* clauses. The goal is to minimize the number of soft clauses that are falsified while still satisfying all the hard clauses. Weighted MaxSMT allow weights on the clauses, with the objective of minimizing the sum of the weights of the falsified clauses, and Weighted Partial MaxSMT combines the previous two.

Two different enumeration problems are addressed in the paper and are defined as in Definition 1.

Definition 1. *Given a constraint system φ, the AllMinMCS problem consists of finding all the minimum size MCSes of φ. The AllMCS problem consists of finding all the MCSes of φ (independent of their size).*

Both AllMinMCS and AllMCS can be generalized to partial or/and weighted variants, analogous to MaxSMT. Observe that any MaxSMT solution indicates an MCS, in that the constraints not satisfied by that solution must be an MCS, and any such solution is a *smallest* MCS. The definition of an MCS requires minimality (not minimum cardinality), however, an instance can contain MCSes larger than those indicated by a MaxSMT solution, as well. Therefore, one can consider the problem of AllMinMCS to be similar to "AllMaxSMT", finding all MaxSMT solutions, and AllMCS is a somewhat broader problem.

The algorithms proposed in Section 4 are based on unsatisfiable cores. In SMT, as in the SAT domain, a *core* of an unsatisfiable CNF SMT formula φ is an unsatisfiable subset of clauses of φ. The SMT solver used in the experiments (Yices [8]) is capable of extracting cores from unsatisfiable instances.

2.1 MaxSMT

To the best of our knowledge, the first attempt to solve optimization problems using SMT (and in particular MaxSMT) was due to Nieuwenhuis & Oliveras [18]. This work extends the *Abstract DPLL Modulo Theories* [19] framework in order to be able to *strengthen* the theory. The strengthening of the theory allows the inclusion of new information (for example the improvement of a bound). Nieuwenhuis & Oliveras [18] applied their framework for the case of weighted MaxSMT. Initially, each clause C_i (with a weight w_i) receives a new Boolean variable p_i, and the constraints $(p_i \rightarrow (k_i = w_i))$, and $(\neg p_i \rightarrow (k_i = 0))$ are added to the theory. Also the constraint $(k_1 + \ldots + k_m \leq B)$ is added to the theory together with the relation $(B < B_0)$ (where B_0 is an estimation of the

---

Algorithm 1. The MSU3-SMT Algorithm (based on [16,15])

MSU3-SMT(φ)

```
1   φ_W ← φ                                        ▷ φ_W is the working formula
2   RV ← ∅                                          ▷ Set of relaxation variables
3   λ ← 0                                    ▷ Lower bound on true relaxation variables
4   while true
5       do (st, φ_C, A) ← SMT(φ_W ∪ Enc(∑_{r∈RV} r ≤ λ))
6           ▷ "φ_C" is an unsat core if st is false
7           ▷ "A" is satisfying assignment if st is true
8           ▷ "Enc" encodes cardinality constraint
9           if st = true then return A          ▷ Solution to MaxSMT problem
10          if |RV| < |soft(φ)|
11              then for each ω ∈ φ_C ∩ soft(φ)
12                  do RV ← RV ∪ {r}             ▷ r is new relax. var. created
13                      ω_R ← ω ∪ {r}
14                      φ_W ← φ_W \ {ω} ∪ {ω_R}
15              λ ← λ + 1
16          ▷ [[ Additional code for enumeration of MCS inserted here ]]
```

---

initial cost). Each time a new cost B_j is found, the theory is strengthened by adding the relation $(B < B_j)$ to the theory.

In 2010, Cimatti et al. [6] proposed a new theory called the theory of *Costs* $\mathcal{C}$ that allows modeling multiple cost functions, and they developed a decision procedure for $\mathcal{C}$. Using the theory $\mathcal{C}$, Cimatti et al. [6] showed how to address the problem of minimizing the value of one cost function subject to the satisfaction of a SMT($\mathcal{T}$) formula, which they called the *Boolean Optimization Modulo Theory* (BOMT) problem. The optimization itself is obtained by linear search or binary search, asserting atoms of $\mathcal{C}$ that bound the cost, and using an incremental SMT solver. Cimatti et al. [6] encoded the weighted partial MaxSMT into BOMT by adding a new Boolean variable A_j^i to each soft clause. Then, the cost function is the sum of the weights of the soft clauses, whose variable A_j^i is assigned true.

Other work on MaxSMT algorithms includes [17,26]. The work in [17] addresses the concrete problem of Maximum Quartet Consistency, where an SMT solver is used as a black box, and optimizes a cost function either using linear or binary search binary. The work in [26] addresses optimization in SMT formulas when the variables in the cost function are rational.

An early MCS enumeration algorithm by Liffiton & Sakallah [11] followed an iterative approach, checking for MCSes of size 1, 2, etc. and blocking solutions as they were found. This algorithm was later extended to exploit unsatisfiable cores [12], closely following the approach of the MSU3 MaxSAT algorithm of Marques-Silva & Planes [16,15] but extending it to enumerate MCSes. The core-guided enumeration algorithm, generalized to SMT, is reviewed in detail in Section 4, while the SMT version of the MSU3 MaxSAT algorithm on which it is based is presented briefly here.

Algorithm 2. The FM-SMT Algorithm [9]

FM-SMT(φ)

1   $\varphi_W \leftarrow \varphi$ ▷ φ_W is the working formula
2   $\lambda \leftarrow 0$ ▷ Bound on the number of iterations
3   **while true**
4   **do** (st, φ_C, $\mathcal{A}$) $\leftarrow$ SMT(φ_W)
5   ▷ "φ_C" is an unsat core if st is **false**
6   ▷ "$\mathcal{A}$" is a satisfying assignment if st is **true**
7   **if** st = **true then return** $\mathcal{A}$ ▷ Solution to MaxSMT problem
8   **if** $\lambda = |soft(\varphi)|$ **then return false**   ▷ No MaxSMT solution
9           $\lambda \leftarrow \lambda + 1$
10          $RV \leftarrow \emptyset$
11   **for each** $\omega \in \varphi_C$, ω tagged as *soft*
12   **do** $RV \leftarrow RV \cup \{r\}$ ▷ r is a new relax. var. created
13                  $\omega_R \leftarrow \omega \cup \{r\}$ ▷ ω_R is tagged *soft*
14                  $\varphi_W \leftarrow \varphi_W \setminus \{\omega\} \cup \{\omega_R\}$
15   **if** $RV = \emptyset$ **then false**   ▷ No MaxSMT solution
16          $\varphi_W \leftarrow \varphi_W \cup \text{Enc}(\sum_{r \in RV} r = 1)$ ▷ Encodes card. const. tagged *hard*

Algorithm 1 presents the pseudo-code of the MSU3-SMT algorithm for MaxSMT. MSU3-SMT iteratively expands the *set* of relaxable clauses to encompass each extracted core while constraining the *number* of clauses that are allowed to be relaxed. The advantage of MSU3-SMT over other core-guided approaches is that it only adds a maximum of one relaxation variable per clause and one additional constraint to restrict the number of clauses relaxed.

Other MaxSAT algorithms can be extended to compute MaxSMT solutions as well. In particular, this paper considers the FM-SMT algorithm, based on the MaxSAT algorithm of Fu&Malik [9]. The approach taken by FM-SMT is to iteratively neutralize cores as they are found by adding fresh relaxation variables to the soft clauses of each core. Because the objective is to minimize the number of falsified clauses, the algorithm adds a constraint to allow relaxing exactly one clause in each core per iteration, thus allowing one of the clauses in the core to be falsified. The pseudo-code of FM-SMT is depicted in Algorithm 2.

This paper also considers a variation of the FM-SMT algorithm that uses an atMost1 constraint instead of the exactly1 cardinality constraint on line 16 of Algorithm 2. This algorithm is referred to as MSU1-SMT (similarly to the MSU1 MaxSAT algorithm [15,14]).

3   AllMCS in CEGAR

One direct application of the AllMCS problem, and one for which Section 5 contains empirical results, is verification via counterexample-guided abstraction refinement (CEGAR). Reveal^{TM}[1] is one such formal verification system that

---

Algorithm 3. The ALLMCS-MSU3-SMT Algorithm

ALLMCS-MSU3-SMT(φ)

1   $\varphi_W \leftarrow \varphi$
2   $RV \leftarrow \emptyset$
3   $\lambda \leftarrow 0$
4   **while true**
5   **do** $(\text{st}, \mathcal{A}) \leftarrow$ MSU3-SMT $(\varphi, \varphi_W, RV, \lambda)$
6   **if** st = **true**
7   **then** ReportMCS($\varphi, \mathcal{A}$)
8   BlockMCSbyRV($\varphi_W, RV, \mathcal{A}$)
9   **else exit**

---

employs AllMCS in the process of verifying digital logic designs. Reveal performs datapath abstraction on a design and relies heavily on refinement, the dual of abstraction, to dynamically bridge between the abstract model and the original design throughout the verification process. Specifically, when a violation is found in the abstract model, the flow produces a conjunction of bit-vector constraints representing the violation that indicate either a potential bug in the design or a "false alarm" resulting from the abstraction. Each violation must be checked against the original design to determine whether it is spurious, and this is done by checking the satisfiability of the violation's constraints V conjoined with the constraints of the original design C. If $V \wedge C$ is satisfiable, then the violation indicates a potential bug, and the flow exits with that result, but if $V \wedge C$ is UNSAT, then the violation is spurious and the abstraction must be refined. Each minimal subset of the violation $V' \subseteq V$ such that $V' \wedge C$ is UNSAT provides a concise reason for the contradiction in the form of a refinement core or lemma that can be used to refine the abstract model (by blocking it).

It is here that AllMCS is applied. Every minimal unsatisfiable subset (MUS) of $V \wedge C$ indicates a minimal V' that can be used for refinement, and AllMCS is used in the first phase of the CAMUS algorithm for computing all MUSes of an unsatisfiable constraint system [11]. Extracting all MUSes is a core component of Reveal's algorithm during refinement, providing 1 to 4 orders of magnitude speedup in run-time compared with other refinement techniques as observed in academic benchmarks [2]. Efficient all-MUS extraction, and thus efficiently solving AllMCS is expected to be essential in practical abstraction/refinement-based implementations of formal verification on real-life designs. An open research topic corresponds to investigate the use of union of MUSes as in [21].

4   All(Min)MCS Algorithms

This section develops new algorithms for AllMinMCS/AllMCS. The MaxSAT-based approach proposed in [11,12] is briefly reviewed first. Then, the new algorithms are detailed.

Algorithm 4. Additional code to include in Algorithm 1 for AllMCS

---

1 $(st, \varphi_C) \leftarrow SMT(\varphi_W)$ $\triangleright \varphi_C$ is an unsat core if φ_W is unsat
2 **if** st = **UNSAT**
3   **then if** $|RV| = |soft(\varphi)|$
4          $\triangleright$ if all soft clauses are relaxed and φ_W is UNSAT,
5          $\triangleright$ then all MCSes have been found
6   **then return false**
7   **if** $\varphi_C \cap soft(\varphi) = \emptyset$
8   **then return false** $\triangleright$ nothing to relax; thus, no more solutions

---

The current state of the art approach for enumerating MCSes is due to Liffiton & Sakallah [12]. The algorithm enumerates MCSes in increasing order of size, essentially by solving MaxSAT iteratively, blocking each solution as it is found. The most recent, core-guided version is an extension of the MSU3 algorithm that follows this procedure. As with MaxSAT algorithms, this MCS enumeration algorithm is easily extended to SMT, and the pseudo-code for the ALLMCS-MSU3-SMT algorithm is presented in Algorithm 3. In the pseudo-code, the input of the algorithm has been extended with extra arguments to initialize the variables of the algorithm with the additional input arguments (between calls to the algorithm). The function *ReportMCS*() reports the MCS found, and the function *BlocksMCSbyRV*() blocks the current MCS from reappearing by adding a blocking constraint to the working formula:

$$\varphi_W \leftarrow \varphi_W \cup \bigvee_{\mathcal{A}(r)=1, \ r \in RV} \neg r \tag{1}$$

Blocking MCSes in this way, creating a clause with the negation of the satisfiable relaxation variables, is referred to in the paper as *blocking by using relaxation variables*. One requirement for the extension of MSU3-SMT to enumerating MCSes is a guarantee that the algorithm stops once it has found and blocked all the MCSes. This is done by adding the code shown in Algorithm 4 to line 16 in Algorithm 1, The motivation is that once all MCSes have been blocked, calling the SMT solver without cardinality constraints will return false. Observe that, the ALLMCS-MSU3-SMT algorithm always reports the MCSes in increasing size, because it iteratively asks for a MaxSMT solution on the current φ_W. As such, the same algorithm can be used to solve AllMinMCS by additionally stopping if the size of a newly found MCS is larger than the previous.

MSU3-SMT is based on the MSU3 MaxSAT algorithm of Marques-Silva & Planes [16,15]. MSU3 is a *core*-guided MaxSAT algorithm (once that it relies on unsatisfiable cores) that iteratively improves a lower bound. In the MaxSAT domain, another core-guided algorithm that also improve a lower bound is the FM MaxSAT algorithm of Fu & Malik [9]. For MaxSAT, and for some industrial applications, the FM algorithm performs better than MSU3. Indeed, in recent

MaxSAT Evaluations[1], the algorithms that follow the approach of Fu & Malik [9] abort on fewer instances than MSU3 in the MS-Industrial and in the WPMS-Industrial categories. Moreover, section 2 describes how to use the FM MaxSAT algorithm to create the FM-SMT algorithm.

Following the approach of Liffiton & Sakallah for MCS enumeration, enumerating MCSes using the FM-SMT algorithm corresponds to iteratively asking the FM-SMT solver for a MaxSMT solution and blocking each until no more solutions can be found. Since FM-SMT also uses relaxation variables, then the blocking of MCSes by using relaxation variables can be considered. The algorithm would be similar to ALLMCS-MSU3-SMT but using FM-SMT instead of MSU3-SMT. Nevertheless, using FM-SMT to enumerate MCSes presents some additional complications. One problem that arises with this approach is the termination of the algorithm. The original FM MaxSAT algorithm *does not include* the check done in line 8 of Algorithm 2. Suppose that FM-SMT does not make the check in line 8 and that the underlying SMT solver always returns as a core the full formula (that is $\varphi_C = \varphi_W$). Then after blocking all the MCSes, the FM-SMT algorithm should be able to report that the formula does not have any MaxSMT solution and exit on line 15 of the FM-SMT algorithm. Nevertheless, since the core obtained is the full formula, then the algorithm is always able to add new relaxation variables (line 12), and it enters a new loop where it continues with new relaxation variables.

Thus, in order to guarantee that enumerating MCSes with FM-SMT always terminates, the check done in line 8 of Algorithm 2 has to be performed. In the original FM MaxSAT algorithm (or also for solving MaxSMT with FM-SMT), this problem does not arise, since in MaxSAT (MaxSMT) the algorithm returns after finding the first solution (and not blocking it as in enumeration).

Another problem that arises with the FM-SMT algorithm for enumeration is the presence of duplicates and supersets of MCSes (which are not themselves MCSes) as shown in Example 1.

Example 1. Consider for example the CNF SMT formula with 5 soft clauses $\varphi = \{(x \geq 1), (x < 1), ((x < 1) \vee (y < 1)), (y < 1), (y \geq 1)\}$. On the first call to the FM-SMT algorithm, the solver finds two cores before returning a solution. Suppose the cores founds are $\varphi_C^1 = \{(x \geq 1), (x < 1)\}$ and $\varphi_C^2 = \{(y \geq 1), (y < 1)\}$. The algorithm updates λ twice (that is $\lambda = 2$) and the working formula to:

$$\varphi_W = \{((x \geq 1) \vee r_1), ((x < 1) \vee r_2), ((x < 1) \vee (y < 1)),$$
$$((y < 1) \vee r_3), ((y \geq 1) \vee r_4)\} \cup$$
$$\text{Enc}(r_1 + r_2 = 1) \cup$$
$$\text{Enc}(r_3 + r_4 = 1)$$

Suppose the solution reported is such that $\mathcal{A}(r_1) = \mathcal{A}(r_4) = 1$ and $\mathcal{A}(r_2) = \mathcal{A}(r_3) = 0$, then the enumerating algorithm will report the MCS $\{(x \geq 1), (y \geq 1)\}$ and add the blocking constraint $(\neg r_1 \vee \neg r_4)$ to the working formula.

---

[1] MaxSAT Evaluations, http://www.maxsat.udl.cat

Algorithm 5. The ALLMCS-FM-SMT Algorithm

ALLMCS-FM-SMT(φ)

1 $\varphi w \leftarrow \varphi$
2 $\lambda \leftarrow 0$
3 **while true**
4   **do** $(st, \mathcal{A}) \leftarrow$ FM-SMT $(\varphi, \varphi w, \lambda)$
5   **if** $st =$ **true**
6   **then if** ($!$isSuperSet$(\varphi, \mathcal{A})$)
7   **then** ReportMCS$(\varphi, \mathcal{A})$
8   BlockMCSbyRV$(\varphi w, \mathcal{A})$
9   **else exit**

In the next two iterations of the enumerating algorithm, the FM-SMT algorithm will always report a MaxSMT solution without adding any relaxation variable, and the enumerating algorithm will report the two MCSes $\{(x \geq 1), (y < 1)\}$ and $\{(x < 1), (y \geq 1)\}$, which after blocking the MCSes the working formula is as follows:

$$\varphi w = \{((x \geq 1) \vee r_1), ((x < 1) \vee r_2), ((x < 1) \vee (y < 1)),$$
$$((y < 1) \vee r_3), ((y \geq 1) \vee r_4)\} \cup$$
$$\text{Enc}(r_1 + r_2 = 1) \cup$$
$$\text{Enc}(r_3 + r_4 = 1) \cup$$
$$\{(\neg r_1 \vee \neg r_4)\} \cup \{(\neg r_1 \vee \neg r_3)\} \cup \{(\neg r_2 \vee \neg r_4)\}$$

Now φw is unsatisfiable and the core returned by the SMT solver contains all the clauses. The FM-SMT algorithm adds fresh relaxation variables to each of the soft clauses and a new constraint on the new relaxation variables. Also λ is updated to 3. The resulting working formula is as follows:

$$\varphi w = \{((x \geq 1) \vee r_1 \vee r_5), ((x < 1) \vee r_2 \vee r_6), ((x < 1) \vee (y < 1) \vee r_7),$$
$$((y < 1) \vee r_3 \vee r_8), ((y \geq 1) \vee r_4 \vee r_9)\} \cup$$
$$\text{Enc}(r_1 + r_2 = 1) \cup$$
$$\text{Enc}(r_3 + r_4 = 1) \cup$$
$$\text{Enc}(r_5 + r_6 + r_7 + r_8 + r_9 = 1) \cup$$
$$\{(\neg r_1 \vee \neg r_4)\} \cup \{(\neg r_1 \vee \neg r_3)\} \cup \{(\neg r_2 \vee \neg r_4)\}$$

The current working formula is satisfiable and one of the solutions of φw is such that $\mathcal{A}(r_2) = \mathcal{A}(r_3) = \mathcal{A}(r_9) = 1$ and all the other relaxation variables are assigned 0. This MaxSMT solution would make the enumeration algorithm to report $\{(x < 1), (y < 1), (y \geq 1)\}$ as an MCS, which is wrong, because this set corresponds to a superset of a previous MCS.

The previous example shows the necessity of removing supersets and duplicated MCSes that may arise when enumerating MCSes with the FM-SMT algorithm. The pseudo-code of ALLMCS-FM-SMT is shown in Algorithm 5. In the pseudo-code, the input of the algorithm has been extended with extra arguments to initialize the variables of the algorithm with the additional input arguments (between calls to the algorithm). The function *isSuperSet*() obtains the current MCS and checks if it corresponds to a superset of a previous MCS, in which case it returns true. As such, an MCS is only reported as an MCS if it is not a superset of a previous MCS.

The problem of enumerating MCSes with the FM-SMT algorithm is that it may add relaxation variables to the same clause more than once. When relaxing a clause that has participated in an MCS that has been blocked, then it allows for the clause to re-occur in a new MaxSMT solution using the new variable.

The next section presents two new blocking techniques that do not require the enumeration of MCSes with FM-SMT to check for supersets or duplicates.

4.1 New Techniques for Blocking MCSes

This section proposes two new techniques for blocking MCSes. The motivation is to eliminate the need to use relaxation variables for blocking MCSes, as is done with *Blocking by using Relaxation Variables*. With these new techniques, MCSes will remain "blocked" independently of the way the MaxSMT solver manipulates the relaxation variables.

The first technique is inspired by the relaxation variables and is called *Blocking by using Auxiliary Variables*. Blocking by using auxiliary variables consists of initially transforming each soft clause into a hard clause after adding a fresh Boolean variable called an *auxiliary variable*. Additionally, a set of unit soft clauses is added that corresponds to the negation of each auxiliary variable. Consider the previous formula of Example 1, and suppose that blocking by using auxiliary variables is to be used. Then the formula given to the MaxSMT solver is the formula containing the set of soft clauses:

$$\varphi^{soft} = \{(\neg a_1), \ (\neg a_2), \ (\neg a_3), \ (\neg a_4), \ (\neg a_5)\}$$

and the set of hard clauses:

$$\varphi^{hard} = \{((x \geq 1) \vee a_1), \ ((x < 1) \vee a_2), \ ((x < 1) \vee (y < 1) \vee a_3),$$
$$((y < 1) \vee a_4), \ ((y \geq 1) \vee a_5)\}$$

When the enumeration solver calls the function to block an MCS, then the blocking constraint to add to the working formula is as in the following Equation 2, where a_i are auxiliary variables.

$$\varphi_W \leftarrow \varphi_W \cup \{(\bigvee_{\mathcal{A}(a_i)=1} \neg a_i)\} \tag{2}$$

The second technique proposed does not require the addition of extra Boolean variables or the transformation of soft clauses into hard clauses. Instead, in *Blocking by using Original Literals*, the original literals in the clauses are used for blocking the MCSes. Consider once more the previous formula of Example 1 and suppose that blocking by using original literals is being used for blocking

MCSes. Suppose the algorithm has just found the MCS $\{(x < 1), ((x < 1) \lor (y < 1)), (y < 1)\}$, then the blocking clause added to the working formula is the clause $((x < 1) \lor (y < 1))$. In the general case, when the enumeration solver calls the function to block an MCS, then the blocking constraint to add to the working formula is as in the following Equation 3, where $(l_{i_1} \lor \ldots \lor l_{i_j})$ is the original literals in a clause that belongs to the current MCS found.

$$\varphi_W \leftarrow \varphi_W \cup \{(\bigvee_{\mathcal{A}(l_{i_1} \lor \ldots \lor l_{i_j})=0} l_{i_1} \lor \ldots \lor l_{i_j})\} \tag{3}$$

Note that since these two techniques deal directly with the MCSes, and not with the relaxation variables, then enumeration with the FM-SMT algorithm using these techniques will not report supersets of previous MCSes and as such does not require the check if the reported MCS is a superset of a previous MCS.

Observe that these two new blocking techniques can be applied not only in enumeration with the FM-SMT algorithm (and the MSU1-SMT algorithm) but also with the MSU3-SMT algorithm.

4.2   AllMCS with Costs

The AllMCS problem can be extended to weighted variants of MaxSAT/MaxSMT. Namely, each soft constraint can be associated with a weight. This weight represents the cost of adding the constraint to a MCS, i.e. of not satisfying the clause.

The goal is then to enumerate all of the MCSes taking into account the sums of the weights of their clauses. Two approaches can be considered. The first approach consists of extending the AllMCS algorithms to handle weights. For example, this can be done by using a weighted MaxSMT solver with an AllMCS algorithm. However, recent results from the MaxSAT Evaluations confirm that weighted MaxSAT is in practice harder to solve than non-weighted MaxSAT, and confirms the different complexity classes of these problems.

Nevertheless, a simpler solution exists. Observe that the MCSes of a CNF formula are *independent* of the weights associated with the clauses. That is, an MCS of a weighted CNF formula is also an MCS of the corresponding unweighted formula and vice-versa. Thus, for the case of weighted formulas, it suffices to use one of the unweighted AllMCS algorithms outlined in earlier sections. Afterwards, one just needs to sort the MCSes by increasing (or decreasing) weight.

5   Experimental Results

This section presents a complete experimental evaluation of the enumeration algorithms described in earlier sections. In what follows, the instances used in the experiments are described, along with the experimental setup.

Three classes of instances have been used in this work. The *Reveal* instances were generated in the Reveal digital logic verification flow as described in Section 3. These instances are characterized by having a single hard clause, with

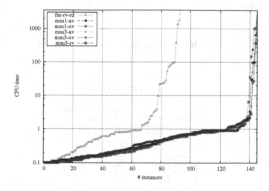

Fig. 1. Cactus plot for Reveal instances

Table 1. Statistics for Reveal instances

	#Sol.	Sum NA (91)	Sum NA (143)
fm-rv-rd	92	2823.02	–
msu1-av	144	**146.72**	**302.13**
msu1-ov	144	285.35	1575.03
msu3-av	**145**	352	554.67
msu3-ov	144	410.48	455.79
msu3-rv	144	430.38	550.65

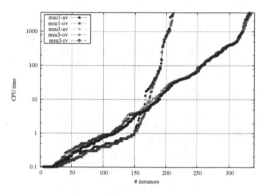

Fig. 2. Cactus plot for non-weighted MaxSAT instances

Table 2. Statistics for non-weighted MaxSAT industrial instances

	#Sol.	Sum NA (183)
msu1-av	210	7495.95
msu1-ov	211	**6981.32**
msu3-av	**335**	8457.76
msu3-ov	**335**	7276.02
msu3-rv	332	7467.42

all other clauses being soft. A total of 145 unsatisfiable instances were obtained from Reveal Design Automation, Inc. The second class of instances is referred to as MaxSAT, and it consists of all *industrial* instances from the MaxSAT Evaluations from 2009 to 2011. Both weighted and unweighted industrial instances are considered, making a total of 1323 instances, where 12 instances are satisfiable. The instances were considered in two sets, weighted and non-weighted, giving 233 weighted instances (6 satisfiable) and 1090 non-weighted instances (6 satisfiable). The last class of instances considered, referred to as *SMT-LIB*, was obtained from the SMT-LIB [4], a library of SMT benchmarks developed for testing and validating SMT algorithms. The instances selected are in the SMT-LIB 1.2 format and belong to one of the following logics: QF_IDL, QF_LIA, QF_LRA, QF_RDL, QF_UF, QF_UFIDL, QF_UFLIA, QF_UFLRA, QF_UF. All clauses in this class of instances are considered *soft*.

Each instance (obtained from SMTLIB) was given to the MSU1-SMT algorithm, and the instances for which MSU1-SMT reported a MaxSAT solution

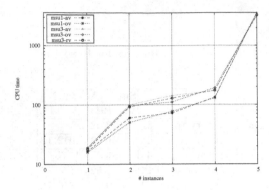

Fig. 3. Cactus plot for weighted MaxSAT instances

Table 3. Statistics for weighted MaxSAT industrial instances

	#Sol.	Sum NA (4)
msu1-av	4	281.52
msu1-ov	4	**272.5**
msu3-av	**5**	431.2
msu3-ov	**5**	415.84
msu3-rv	**5**	412.54

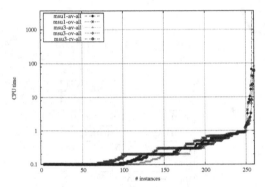

Fig. 4. Cactus plot of SMTLIB instances

Table 4. Statistics about the results with SMTLIB instances

	#Sol.	Sum NA (257)
msu1-av	257	184.29
msu1-ov	257	**171.2**
msu3-av	**260**	214.78
msu3-ov	**260**	219.4
msu3-rv	**260**	208.83

were then ordered by CPU time used. The first 808 instances in that order were selected for these experiments.

For the experimental results, both FM-SMT and MSU3-SMT have been implemented on top of yices [8]. We have also implemented the variant of FM-SMT that uses atMost1 constraints, referred to as MSU1-SMT.

In the experiments, all algorithms were configured to enumerate the complete set of MCSes. The algorithms make use of cardinality constraints, and in these experiments, the pairwise cardinality network encoding of Codish & Zazon-Ivry [7] was used for encoding each of the cardinality constraints into Boolean CNF. The only exception is for the FM-SMT algorithm, which uses the bitwise encoding [22], as it provided better results for this algorithm.

All the three techniques described in Section 4) for blocking one MCS (blocking by using *relaxation variables*, blocking by using *auxiliary variables* and blocking by using *original literals*), have been considered in the experiments, depending on the underlying MaxSMT algorithm used. For the ALLMCS-FM-SMT algorithm, only the blocking by using relaxation variables technique was used. Note that this is the only algorithm in the experiments which requires a verification of duplicated MCSes. The resulting algorithm is referred to as *fm-rv-rd*, and it was only tested with the Reveal instances. For the ALLMCS-MSU1-SMT algorithm, both blocking by using auxiliary variables and blocking by using original literals were considered for all instances. The resulting algorithms are referred to as *msu1-av* and *msu1-ov*, respectively. For the ALLMCS-MSU3-SMT algorithm, all the blocking techniques were tried, and the algorithms obtained are referred to as *msu3-av*, *msu3-ov* and *msu3-rv*. Observe that msu3-rv corresponds to the approach of Liffiton & Sakallah [12]. The algorithms were run on a cluster of Intel Xeon E5450 (3 GHz) nodes running RedHat Linux v.5 x86-64 with a timeout of 3600 seconds and a memory limit of 4GB.

Figure 1 shows a cactus plot obtained from the Reveal instances, while Table 1 shows a summary of the results for each of the algorithms. In the table, *#Sol.* represents the number of instances solved by each of the algorithms, *Sum NA (91)* represents the sum of cputimes taken by each algorithm on 91 instances for which all of the algorithms finished within the timeout. Finally, *Sum NA (143)* represents the sum of cputimes taken by each algorithm on 143 instances which were solved by all algorithms except for fm-rv-rd. As can be seen from the cactus plot and from the number of solved instances in Table 1, the fm-rv-rd is the worst performing algorithm, aborting in more instances and requiring more cputime to enumerate even on the 91 instances solved by all the algorithms. This is due to the need to remove duplicated MCSes and supersets of current MCSes. The algorithm that solves the largest number of the Reveal instances is msu3-av, able to solve one more instance than the other msu algorithms. Considering all the 143 instances where none of the msu algorithms aborts, msu1-av is the fastest enumerating algorithm.

For the non-weighted industrial MaxSAT instances, Figure 2 shows the cactus plot, while Table 2 summarizes the results for this class of instances. As before, column *#Sol.* shows the number of instances solved by each of the algorithms, and *Sum NA (183)* represents the sum of cputimes taken by each algorithm on 183 instances that were solved by all algorithms. From the cactus plot, it can be seen that overall, the msu3 algorithms perform better than the msu1 algorithms in this class of instances. Table 2 confirms that msu3 algorithms abort on fewer instances, and among the msu3 algorithms, msu3-av and msu3-ov are able to solve 3 more instances than msu3-rv. For the sum of cputimes on instances solved by all the algorithms, the fastest algorithm for these instances is msu1-ov, as the msu1 algorithms tend to be faster on the instances solved by all algorithms.

The results with weighted instances are presented in a the cactus plot of Figure 3 and summarized in Table 3. Despite these instances being weighted, the algorithms disregard the weights as suggested in Section 4.2. Column *#Sol* show the same type of result as the in previous tables. Column *Sum NA (4)* represents the sum of cputimes taken by each algorithm on 4 instances which were solved by all algorithms. From the figure and table, it can be seen that msu3 algorithms actually solve one more instance than msu1 algorithms but, for the 4 instances solved by all, msu1 algorithms are faster than msu3 algorithms, where msu1-ov is the fastest algorithm (over these 4 instances).

The last plot, Figure 4, shows the cactus plot with the results obtained from the SMTLIB instances, while Table 4 summarizes. For these instances, the msu3 algorithms are able to solve 3 more instances than the msu1 algorithms. Nevertheless, considering only the 257 instances solved by all the algorithms, the fastest algorithm is msu1-ov.

Overall, it can be seen from the results that the msu3 algorithms solve the greatest number of instances, and in particular, msu3-av is the only algorithm that solved all of the Reveal instances. On the other hand, when considering only instances that are solved by all algorithms, the results suggest that the fastest algorithms are the msu1 algorithms, indicating that the easier instances are solved more quickly by msu1 algorithms than msu3 variants. On these, msu1-av is the fastest for the reveal instances, while for the other three classes, the fastest algorithm is msu1-ov. There is no substantial difference between the different blocking techniques when applied to a given algorithm (msu1 or msu3).

6   Conclusions and Future Work

State of the art algorithms for MCS enumeration of SAT and SMT instances are based on one concrete instantiation of core-guided MaxSAT algorithms [12]. This paper proposes improvements to MCS enumeration algorithms, and shows how these algorithms can integrate other core-guided MaxSAT algorithms. Experimental results, obtained on a wide range of practical instances of SAT and SMT, show that the proposed improvements reduce overall running times and allow solving more problem instances.

The proposed algorithms have been implemented on top of SMT solvers, using available interfaces. Direct access to the internal state of the SMT solver is expected to allow further performance improvements.

References

1. Andraus, Z.S.: Automatic Formal Verification of Control Logic in Hardware Designs. PhD Dissertation, University of Michigan (2009)
2. Andraus, Z.S., Liffiton, M.H., Sakallah, K.A.: Reveal: A formal verification tool for verilog designs. In: Cervesato, I., Veith, H., Voronkov, A. (eds.) LPAR 2008. LNCS (LNAI), vol. 5330, pp. 343–352. Springer, Heidelberg (2008)
3. Argelich, J., Lynce, I., Marques-Silva, J.: On solving Boolean multilevel optimization problems. In: International Joint Conference on Artificial Intelligence, pp. 393–398 (2009)
4. Barrett, C., Stump, A., Tinelli, C.: The Satisfiability Modulo Theories Library (SMT-LIB) (2010), http://www.SMT-LIB.org
5. Barrett, C.W., Sebastiani, R., Seshia, S.A., Tinelli, C.: Satisfiability modulo theories. In: Biere, A., Heule, M., van Maaren, H., Walsh, T. (eds.) Handbook of Satisfiability, pp. 825–885. IOS Press (2009)
6. Cimatti, A., Franzén, A., Griggio, A., Sebastiani, R., Stenico, C.: Satisfiability modulo the theory of costs: Foundations and applications. In: Esparza, J., Majumdar, R. (eds.) TACAS 2010. LNCS, vol. 6015, pp. 99–113. Springer, Heidelberg (2010)

7. Codish, M., Zazon-Ivry, M.: Pairwise cardinality networks. In: Clarke, E.M., Voronkov, A. (eds.) LPAR-16. LNCS (LNAI), vol. 6355, pp. 154–172. Springer, Heidelberg (2010)
8. Dutertre, B., de Moura, L.: A fast linear-arithmetic solver for DPLL(T). In: Ball, T., Jones, R.B. (eds.) CAV 2006. LNCS, vol. 4144, pp. 81–94. Springer, Heidelberg (2006)
9. Fu, Z., Malik, S.: On solving the partial MAX-SAT problem. In: Biere, A., Gomes, C.P. (eds.) SAT 2006. LNCS, vol. 4121, pp. 252–265. Springer, Heidelberg (2006)
10. de Kleer, J., Williams, B.: Diagnosing multiple faults. Artificial Intelligence 32(1), 97–130 (1987)
11. Liffiton, M.H., Sakallah, K.A.: Algorithms for computing minimal unsatisfiable subsets of constraints. Journal of Automated Reasoning 40(1), 1–33 (2008)
12. Liffiton, M.H., Sakallah, K.A.: Generalizing core-guided Max-SAT. In: Kullmann, O. (ed.) SAT 2009. LNCS, vol. 5584, pp. 481–494. Springer, Heidelberg (2009)
13. Manquinho, V., Marques-Silva, J., Planes, J.: Algorithms for weighted Boolean optimization. In: Kullmann, O. (ed.) SAT 2009. LNCS, vol. 5584, pp. 495–508. Springer, Heidelberg (2009)
14. Marques-Silva, J., Manquinho, V.: Towards more effective unsatisfiability-based maximum satisfiability algorithms. In: Kleine Büning, H., Zhao, X. (eds.) SAT 2008. LNCS, vol. 4996, pp. 225–230. Springer, Heidelberg (2008)
15. Marques-Silva, J., Planes, J.: On using unsatisfiability for solving maximum satisfiability. Computing Research Repository abs/0712.0097 (2007)
16. Marques-Silva, J., Planes, J.: Algorithms for maximum satisfiability using unsatisfiable cores. In: Design, Automation and Test in Europe, pp. 408–413 (2008)
17. Morgado, A., Marques-Silva, J.: Combinatorial optimization solutions for the maximum quartet consistency problem. Fundam. Inform. 102(3-4), 363–389 (2010)
18. Nieuwenhuis, R., Oliveras, A.: On SAT modulo theories and optimization problems. In: Biere, A., Gomes, C.P. (eds.) SAT 2006. LNCS, vol. 4121, pp. 156–169. Springer, Heidelberg (2006)
19. Nieuwenhuis, R., Oliveras, A., Tinelli, C.: Abstract DPLL and abstract DPLL modulo theories. In: Baader, F., Voronkov, A. (eds.) LPAR 2004. LNCS (LNAI), vol. 3452, pp. 36–50. Springer, Heidelberg (2005)
20. Nieuwenhuis, R., Oliveras, A., Tinelli, C.: Solving SAT and SAT Modulo Theories: From an abstract Davis–Putnam–Logemann–Loveland procedure to DPLL(T). Journal of the ACM 53(6), 937–977 (2006)
21. Nöhrer, A., Biere, A., Egyed, A.: Managing SAT inconsistencies with HUMUS. In: Workshop on Variability Modelling of Software-Intensive Systems, pp. 83–91 (2012)
22. Prestwich, S.: Variable dependency in local search: Prevention is better than cure. In: Marques-Silva, J., Sakallah, K.A. (eds.) SAT 2007. LNCS, vol. 4501, pp. 107–120. Springer, Heidelberg (2007)
23. Reiter, R.: A theory of diagnosis from first principles. Artificial Intelligence 32(1), 57–95 (1987)
24. Safarpour, S., Mangassarian, H., Veneris, A., Liffiton, M.H., Sakallah, K.A.: Improved design debugging using maximum satisfiability. In: Formal Methods in Computer-Aided Design (November 2007)
25. Sebastiani, R.: Lazy satisfiability modulo theories. Journal on Satisfiability, Boolean Modeling and Computation 3(3), 141–224 (2007)
26. Sebastiani, R., Tomasi, S.: Optimization in SMT with $\mathcal{LA}(\mathbb{Q})$ cost functions. In: Gramlich, B., Miller, D., Sattler, U. (eds.) IJCAR 2012. LNCS, vol. 7364, pp. 484–498. Springer, Heidelberg (2012)

Automated Reencoding of Boolean Formulas*

Norbert Manthey[1], Marijn J.H. Heule[2,3], and Armin Biere[3]

[1] Institute of Artificial Intelligence, Technische Universität Dresden, Germany
[2] Department of Computer Science, The University of Texas at Austin, United States
[3] Institute for Formal Models and Verification, Johannes Kepler University, Austria

Abstract. We present a novel preprocessing technique to automatically reduce the size of Boolean formulas. This technique, called Bounded Variable Addition (BVA), exchanges clauses for variables. Similar to other preprocessing techniques, BVA greedily lowers the sum of variables and clauses, a rough measure for the hardness to solve a formula. We show that cardinality constraints (CCs) can efficiently be reencoded: from a naive CC encoding, BVA automatically generates a compact encoding, which is smaller than sophisticated encodings. Experimental results show that applying BVA can improve SAT solving performance.

1 Introduction

SAT solvers are used in many applications in electronic design automation (EDA), including combinational [1,2] and sequential equivalence checking [3,4], bounded [5] and unbounded model checking [6], and debugging [7]. State-of-the-art solvers commonly expect their input to be a Boolean formula in conjunctive normal form (CNF), which also serves as data structure for storing the formula internally and maintaining a cache of learned facts in form of clauses [8]. This restriction is on one hand a strength: it allows fast algorithms and compact data structures [9]. On the other hand being forced to use CNF instead of high-level constraints is also a weakness of current SAT solvers: it requires complex synthesis [10] and encoding algorithms [11,12] in order to take full advantage of the raw speed of CNF level solving. There have been several attempts to produce hybrid solvers [13,14], which combine CNF and circuit reasoning. These approaches typically involve a considerable overhead at least from the software engineering perspective. An alternative is to use CNF level preprocessing techniques [15,16,17] to efficiently and effectively simulate certain constraint encoding and reasoning techniques. As example, consider the combination of variable elimination [16] and blocked clause elimination [17], which is able to achieve the same effect as sophisticated encoding algorithms [12].

Starting from a problem to solve, the first step is to encode it into CNF. Next, *preprocessing* techniques are used to simplify the formula, before search is

---

* The second and the third author are supported by the Austrian Science Foundation (FWF) NFN Grant S11408-N23 (RiSE). The second author is supported by DARPA contract number N66001-10-2-4087.

A. Biere, A. Nahir, and T. Vos (Eds.): HVC 2012, LNCS 7857, pp. 102–117, 2013.

started. Recently, *inprocessing* was introduced [18,19] that applies preprocessing on a partially solved formula (i.e., during search), linking back in the tool chain. Here, we investigate another link back by *reencoding* clauses. This technique can be applied on the original set of clauses, but also on partially solved and inprocessed formulas. Thus, this paper adds to this discussion of which way to go another argument in favor of CNF level preprocessing. We show that it is possible to simulate sophisticated constraint *encoding* techniques with a rather simple CNF level technique, and thus create the missing link in the picture.

The basic idea is to reencode parts of the CNF by introducing new variables, if the size of the CNF *decreases*. The size of the CNF is measured by the sum of the number of variables and clauses. This is in essence a reverse application of variable elimination. Bounded variable elimination (BVE), as proposed in [16,20,21], essentially eliminates a variable in a CNF by clause distribution, if the size of the CNF *does not increase*. In many applications, BVE is currently one of the most effective CNF level preprocessing techniques.

We show improvements in SAT solving time after using our preprocessing on various application benchmarks and recent SAT competitions. We also show, that our technique theoretically and empirically simulates optimized encodings of cardinality constraints starting from a naive standard encoding. These constraints occur frequently in many applications [22,23,24] and have been studied by the CP and SAT communities [25,26,27,28,29,16,30,31]. Furthermore, our preprocessing technique is not restricted to cardinality constraints, but it is also able to factor out common logic in arbitrary formulas without cardinality constraints.

The closest related work is an attempt [32] to speed-up SAT solving by allowing extension steps of extended resolution. The idea is to factor out a common prefix of (learned) clauses by replacing it with a new variable. These extension steps never decrease the number of clauses. If applied to original clauses, BVE would eliminate the extensions again, which renders this technique [32] useless in combination with BVE. In contrast, BVE cannot undo our new method. Another rewriting technique [33] partitions the formula and removes gate definition clauses. The other clauses are clustered based on shared variables. Each cluster is then transformed into a Gröbner basis, reduced and finally transformed back into CNF. Combined with BVE, this transformation can lead to a faster solving process. However, the rewriting itself can be quite expensive [33].

We do not claim that high-level reasoning is useless in general. Clearly, there are situations where such reasoning should be combined with CNF level reasoning. This paper adds to the arsenal of preprocessing techniques a new algorithm, which allows to simulate additional sophisticated encoding and reasoning techniques on the CNF level. This is particularly useful for inprocessing, as used in PrecoSAT and Lingeling [18], so new learned facts can be taken into account. As future work, we want to extend these ideas to capture even more high-level techniques such as AIG rewriting [10], compact encoding techniques based on technology mapping [11], and Gaussian elimination of XOR constraints [34].

The remainder of this paper is structured as follows: the next section provides background information. In Section 3 we present our novel technique Bounded

Variable Addition (BVA). Automated reencoding of cardinality constraints is one of the possible applications of BVA, which is discussed in Section 4. Experimental results are described in Section 5. Finally, we draw conclusions in Section 6.

2   Preliminaries

In this section we review necessary background concepts: conjunctive normal form level Boolean satisfiability (SAT), resolution and variable elimination.

2.1   Conjunctive Normal Form

For a Boolean variable x, there are two *literals*, the positive literal, denoted by x, and the negative literal, denoted by $\bar{x}$. A *clause* is a disjunction of literals and a CNF formula a conjunction of clauses. A clause can be seen as a finite set of literals and a CNF formula as a finite set of clauses. A clause is a *tautology* if it contains both x and $\bar{x}$ for some x. The set of literals occurring in a CNF formula F is denoted by $\mathrm{LIT}(F)$. Formulas are *logically equivalent* if they have the same set of satisfying assignments over the common variables.

2.2   Resolution and Variable Elimination

The resolution rule states that, given two clauses $C_1 = \{x, a_1, \ldots, a_n\}$ and $C_2 = \{\bar{x}, b_1, \ldots, b_m\}$, the implied clause $C = \{a_1, \ldots, a_n, b_1, \ldots, b_m\}$, called the *resolvent* of C_1 and C_2, can be inferred by *resolving* on the variable x. We write $C = C_1 \otimes C_2$. This notion can be lifted to sets of clauses: for two sets S_x and $S_{\bar{x}}$ of clauses which all contain x and $\bar{x}$, respectively, we define

$$S_x \otimes S_{\bar{x}} = \{C_1 \otimes C_2 \mid C_1 \in S_x, C_2 \in S_{\bar{x}}, \text{ and } C_1 \otimes C_2 \text{ is not a tautology}\}.$$

The Davis-Putnam procedure [35] (DP) can be used as a basic simplification technique, referred to as *variable elimination by clause distribution* [20,21,36]. The elimination of a variable x in the whole CNF formula can be computed by pair-wise resolving each clause in S_x with every clause in $S_{\bar{x}}$. Replacing the original clauses in $S_x \cup S_{\bar{x}}$ with the set of *non-tautological* resolvents $S = S_x \otimes S_{\bar{x}}$ gives the formula $(F \setminus (S_x \cup S_{\bar{x}})) \cup S$ that is logically equivalent to F.

Notice that DP is a complete proof procedure for CNF formulas, with exponential space complexity. Hence for practical applications of variable elimination by clause distribution as a simplification technique for CNF formulas, variable elimination needs to be bounded [20,21,36].

3   Bounded Variable Addition

Closely following the heuristics applied in the SatElite preprocessor [36] for applying variable elimination, in this paper we study the bounded variant of variable elimination (VE) by clause distribution (BVE) as a simplification technique.

In BVE, a variable x can be eliminated only if $|S| \leq |S_x \cup S_{\bar{x}}|$, i.e., when the resulting CNF formula $(F \setminus (S_x \cup S_{\bar{x}})) \cup S$ will not contain more than $|F|$ clauses, where F is the formula before the elimination step.

Example 1. Consider a CNF formula F with

$$S_x = (x \vee c) \wedge (x \vee \bar{d}) \wedge (x \vee \bar{a} \vee \bar{b}) \quad \text{and} \quad S_{\bar{x}} = (\bar{x} \vee a) \wedge (\bar{x} \vee b) \wedge (\bar{x} \vee \bar{e} \vee f)$$

for the variable x. Applying VE to eliminate x, we have

$$\begin{aligned} S = S_x \otimes S_{\bar{x}} = &(a \vee c) \wedge (b \vee c) \wedge (a \vee \bar{d}) \wedge (b \vee \bar{d}) \wedge \\ &(\bar{a} \vee \bar{b} \vee \bar{e} \vee f) \wedge (c \vee \bar{e} \vee f) \wedge (\bar{d} \vee \bar{e} \vee f). \end{aligned}$$

Since $|S_x| + |S_{\bar{x}}| = 6$ and $|S| = 7$, BVE cannot eliminate the variable x. Notice that the clauses $(x \vee \bar{a} \vee \bar{b})$, $(\bar{x} \vee a)$, and $(\bar{x} \vee b)$ in F are equivalent to the Tseitin encoding of the gate $x = \text{AND}(a, b)$. This is why resolving $(x \vee \bar{a} \vee \bar{b})$ with $(\bar{x} \vee a)$ and $(\bar{x} \vee b)$ on x produces only tautological clauses that are not in S [36].

The global heuristic used for bounding VE –substitute only if the sum of variables and clauses decreases– appears to be a powerful metric to simplify a Boolean formula. This heuristic inspired us to develop the technique *Bounded Variable Addition* (BVA). As the name suggests, BVA is complementary to BVE: instead of exchanging variables for clauses BVA exchanges clauses for variables. Yet the same bounding heuristic is used: substitute to decrease the size of the CNF.

Example 2. The smallest formula for which adding a variable can decrease the size of the CNF consists of six clauses. Such a formula contains the pattern

$$E = (a \vee c) \wedge (a \vee d) \wedge (a \vee e) \wedge (b \vee c) \wedge (b \vee d) \wedge (b \vee e)$$

By adding a new variable x, E can be reencoded to the logically equivalent formula E' which has one clause less:

$$E' = (a \vee x) \wedge (b \vee x) \wedge (c \vee \bar{x}) \wedge (d \vee \bar{x}) \wedge (e \vee \bar{x})$$

However, it is not always easy to find patterns that reduce the number of clauses. Consider for instance the resulting S consisting of seven clauses in Example 1. Based on the global heuristic, one would like to replace S by $S_x \cup S_{\bar{x}}$ because the size of the latter is smaller. Given S, however, how can we compute that there exists a $S_x \cup S_{\bar{x}}$ such that $S = S_x \otimes S_{\bar{x}}$ and $|S_x| + |S_{\bar{x}}| < |S|$? Even for this small set of clauses, this question is far from trivial. Since practical SAT instances are huge, say $100{,}000$ clauses, the number of possibilities for S_x and $S_{\bar{x}}$ are enormous. Hence, general BVA until fixpoint will be very costly.

3.1   The *SimpleBoundedVariableAddition* Algorithm

The number of patterns to add a Boolean variable in order to decrease the size of the CNF is very large. To reduce the computational cost, we limited the search to detect only some specific patterns. We focus on those patterns for which the new variable x occurs positively in binary clauses only, while the occurrences of the complement are unrestricted.

Two sets will be used during the detection: a set of literals M_{lit} and a set of clauses M_{cls}. A pair $\langle M_{\text{lit}}, M_{\text{cls}} \rangle$ is called a *replaceable matching* w.r.t. F if for all $l \in M_{\text{lit}}$ and $C \in M_{\text{cls}}$ the clauses $(C \setminus \{M_{\text{lit}}\}) \cup \{l\}$ are either in F or tautological. Given a replaceable matching $\langle M_{\text{lit}}, M_{\text{cls}} \rangle$, we can apply the *matching-to-clauses* construction method which creates the sets S_x and $S_{\bar{x}}$ as follows: $S_x = \{(l \vee x) \mid l \in M_{\text{lit}}\}$ and $S_{\bar{x}} = \{(C \setminus M_{\text{lit}}) \cup \{\bar{x}\} \mid C \in M_{\text{cls}}\}$. The final step is to remove all clauses $(C \setminus \{M_{\text{lit}}\}) \cup \{l\}$ with $l \in M_{\text{lit}}$ and $C \in M_{\text{cls}}$ and replace them with $S_x \cup S_{\bar{x}}$.

Consider Example 2 again: For the formula E there exists a replaceable matching: $M_{\text{lit}} = \{a, b\}$ and $M_{\text{cls}} = \{(a \vee c), (a \vee d), (a \vee e)\}$. Applying the matching-to-clauses construction method of S_x and $S_{\bar{x}}$ gives $E' = S_x \cup S_{\bar{x}}$.

Theorem 1. *Given a replaceable matching $\langle M_{\text{lit}}, M_{\text{cls}} \rangle$ w.r.t. a CNF formula F, a formula F' can be constructed by adding a Boolean variable such that (1) F' is logically equivalent to F and (2) F' contains $|F| + |M_{\text{lit}}| + |M_{\text{cls}}| - |M_{\text{lit}}| \cdot |M_{\text{cls}}|$ clauses if none of the resolvents is a tautology.*

Proof. Given a replaceable matching $\langle M_{\text{lit}}, M_{\text{cls}} \rangle$, we can construct F' as follows: remove from F all clauses $(C \setminus \{M_{\text{lit}}\}) \cup \{l\}$ with $l \in M_{\text{lit}}$ and $C \in M_{\text{cls}}$ and replace them with $S_x \cup S_{\bar{x}}$ which are obtained using the matching-to-clauses construction method. The number of removed clauses is $|M_{\text{lit}}| \cdot |M_{\text{cls}}|$, while the number of added clauses is $|M_{\text{lit}}| + |M_{\text{cls}}|$ showing (2). Applying VE on x in F' produces F. (1) holds because VE preserves logical equivalence.

We refer to the *reduction* of a replaceable matching $\langle M_{\text{lit}}, M_{\text{cls}} \rangle$ with respect to the number of clauses as $|M_{\text{lit}}| \cdot |M_{\text{cls}}| - |M_{\text{lit}}| - |M_{\text{cls}}|$. Notice that for each $l \in \text{LIT}(F)$ holds that $M_{\text{lit}} := \{l\}$ and $M_{\text{cls}} := F_l$ is a replaceable matching. However, it is not useful because the reduction is -1. Heuristically the most interesting replaceable matching is the one with the largest reduction.

We developed the *SimpleBoundedVariableAddition* algorithm, see Fig. 1, to find and replace matchings with a positive reduction. In order to find matchings with large reductions first, a priority queue Q is used that sorts literals $l \in \text{LIT}(F)$ in descending order of the number of occurrences of l in F (line 1). While Q is not empty (line 2), the top element l is used to initialize $M_{\text{lit}} := \{l\}$ and $M_{\text{cls}} := F_l$ (line 3).

In the next seven lines a sequence P of literal-clause pairs $\langle l', C \rangle$ is created such that $C \in M_{\text{cls}}$ and $C \setminus \{l\} \cup \{l'\} \in F$. After initialization (line 4), we loop through the clauses $C \in M_{\text{cls}}$ and select in each of them the literal $l_{\min}$ that occurs least frequently in F to reduce the computational cost (line 5). Now we try to extend P by looping through the clauses $D \in F_{l_{\min}}$ (line 7) and check whether C and D differ in exactly one literal (line 8). Let the different literal be l' (line 9), so we extend P with $\langle l', C \rangle$ (line 10).

Now, we try to add a literal to the matching such that the reduction would increase. The best candidate for this addition is $l_{\max}$ the literal occurring most

SimpleBoundedVariableAddition (CNF formula F)

```
 1    let Q be a priority queue of l ∈ LIT(F) sorted by |F_l|
 2    while Q ≠ ∅ do
 3        l := Q.top(), Q.pop(), M_lit := {l}, M_cls := F_l
 4        P := ∅
 5        foreach C ∈ M_cls do
 6            let l_min ∈ C \ {l} be least occurring in F
 7            foreach D ∈ F_{l_min} do
 8                if |C| = |D| and C \ D = l then
 9                    l' := D \ C
10                    P := P ∪ ⟨l', C⟩
11        let l_max be occurring most frequently in P
12        if adding l_max to M_lit further reduces |F| then
13            M_lit := M_lit ∪ {l_max}, M_cls := ∅
14            foreach ⟨l_max, C⟩ ∈ P do
15                M_cls := M_cls ∪ {C}
16            goto 4
17        if |M_lit| = 1 then continue
18        let x be a new variable not occurring in F
19        foreach l' ∈ M_lit do
20            F := F ∪ {l', x}
21        foreach C ∈ M_cls do
22            F := F \ {(C \ {l}) ∪ {l'}}
23        foreach C ∈ M_cls do
24            F := F ∪ {(C \ {l}) ∪ {x̄}}
25        Q.push(l), Q.push(x), Q.push(x̄)
26    return F
```

Fig. 1. Pseudo code of the *SimpleBoundedVariableAddition* algorithm

frequently in P (line 11). If adding l_{max} increases the reduction (line 12), then l_{max} is added to M_{lit} (line 13) and M_{cls} is updated s.t. M_{lit} and M_{cls} is a replaceable matching (line 14–15). Afterwards, we try to further increase the matching by rebuilding P (line 16).

The last part of the algorithm implements the replacement, if M_{lit} contains multiple literals (line 17). Variable x is added (line 18) and all clauses $(C \setminus \{M_{lit}\}) \cup \{l\}$ with $l \in M_{lit}$ and $C \in M_{cls}$ are removed from F and replaced by $(l' \vee x)$ with $l' \in M_{lit}$ and $(C \setminus \{l\}) \cup \{x̄\}$ with $C \in M_{cls}$ (lines 19–24). Last, but not least, l, x and $x̄$ are inserted in Q for possible future replacements.

3.2 Extensions

Several extensions of the BVA algorithm as shown in Fig. 1 are possible. In this subsection we discuss four of them. First, we observed that for some problems it occurs that $l = \bar{l}_{max}$. In this special case, the resolvent between the clauses $C \in F_l$ and $D \in F_{l_{max}}$ such that $|C| = |D|$ and $C \setminus D = l$ subsume the antecedents. This is also known as self-subsumption [36]. We can simply remove l from the corresponding clause in $C \in F_l$, and remove the clause $D \in F_{l_{max}}$. So even if $\bar{l}$ occurs only once in P, it can be selected as l_{max} to reduce the number of clauses without adding a new variable. Since this check is straight forward, it has been added to the algorithm for the experimental evaluation.

The most natural extension is to search for more (less limited) patterns. For instance consider the following formula:

$$H = (a \vee d) \wedge (a \vee e) \wedge (a \vee f) \wedge (b \vee c \vee d) \wedge (b \vee c \vee e) \wedge (b \vee c \vee f)$$

The BVA algorithm as presented in Fig. 1 cannot reduce the number of clauses. However, if one would allow to have pairs of literals (or even more) in M_{lit}, then substitution is possible. Now consider $M_{lit} = \{\{a\}, \{b, c\}\}$ and $M_{cls} = \{(a \vee d), (a \vee e), (a \vee f)\}$, applying the replacement code (lines 19–24) results in the following formula:

$$H' = (a \vee x) \wedge (b \vee c \vee x) \wedge (\bar{x} \vee d) \wedge (\bar{x} \vee e) \wedge (\bar{x} \vee f)$$

Enhancing *SimpleBoundedVariableAddition* with these and other patterns will be part of future research.

The third extension is exploring how to reduce the cost to detect patterns. For instance, all literals $l \in Q$ which occur less than three times in F can be removed because the check on line 12 would fail for those literals. Also, all clauses in M_{cls} must have at least one literal occurring in Q. These observations can be used to speed-up detection which would be important for more complex patterns in particular. The first part of this extension is also used in the evaluated implementation, because of its simplicity. We simply do not add variables back into Q if they occur less than three times.

The fourth extension deals with taking into account tautological clauses.

Example 3. Consider the following CNF formula G

$$G = (a \vee \bar{b} \vee \bar{c}) \wedge (\bar{a} \vee b \vee \bar{c}) \wedge (\bar{a} \vee \bar{b} \vee c) \wedge (\bar{b} \vee \bar{c} \vee d) \wedge$$
$$(\bar{a} \vee \bar{c} \vee d) \wedge (\bar{a} \vee \bar{b} \vee d) \wedge (a \vee \bar{d}) \wedge (b \vee \bar{d}) \wedge (c \vee \bar{d})$$

The *SimpleBoundedVariableAddition* algorithm as described above cannot reduce the size of G. However, BVA can be applied using $M_{lit} = \{\{a\}, \{b\}, \{c\}, \{d\}\}$ and $M_{cls} = \{(\bar{b} \vee \bar{c} \vee d), (\bar{a} \vee \bar{c} \vee d), (\bar{a} \vee \bar{b} \vee d), (\bar{d} \vee d)\}$ resulting in G':

$$G' = (a \vee x) \wedge (b \vee x) \wedge (c \vee x) \wedge (d \vee x) \wedge$$
$$(\bar{b} \vee \bar{c} \vee \bar{x}) \wedge (\bar{a} \vee \bar{c} \vee \bar{x}) \wedge (\bar{a} \vee \bar{b} \vee \bar{x}) \wedge (\bar{d} \vee \bar{x})$$

Our current algorithm cannot reduce G because it cannot match tautological clauses such as $(\bar{d} \vee d)$. In order to find these more complex patterns, one should assume that all tautological clauses are implicitly in a formula. Patterns that include tautological clauses also require a different equation to count the reduction of the number of clauses. For instance, with $|M_{lit}| = 4$ and $M_{cls} = 4$, one would expect a reduction of 8, while the actual reduction is only 1.

4   Cardinality Constraints

For encoding applications, e.g. routing, scheduling, verification or code-generation [22,23], as well as for encoding instances from product configuration or radio frequency assignment or the domain of a CSP variable [37,38], it is necessary to encode numerical bounds. These numerical bounds can be notated as follows: $\leq k(x_1, \ldots, x_n)$ where n is the number of variables and k is the number of variables that are allowed to be assigned true. A naive encoding into propositional logic of this constraint is

$$\bigwedge_{\substack{M \subseteq \{1,\ldots,n\} \\ |M|=k+1}} (\bigvee_{i \in M} \bar{x}_i).$$

Many encodings for cardinality constraints have been proposed [29,31,16]. In the following two subsections we will show that BVA can be used to reencode cardinality constraints that are encoded naively efficiently. The comparison to sophisticated encodings is based on applying BVA to the naive encoding of cardinality constraints. To the best of our knowledge we name all proposed encodings for this constraint and then focus on the most promising encodings that maintain arc consistency, since reencoding with BVA also preserves arc consistency. Arc consistency means that if k variables are already assigned to true, than all the other variables will be mapped to false by Boolean constraint propagation.

There exist SAT solvers that handle cardinality constraints within the solver, for example Sat4J [39] or clasp [40]. This feature is used for solving MaxSAT and PB problems. However, these solvers do not extract cardinality constraints from the formula and exploit their special mechanisms. In general it is hard to judge whether handling cardinality constraints natively or encoding them to SAT results in the higher performance. Yet the strongest SAT solvers tend to not support native cardinality constraints. MiniSAT [41] for instance supported native cardinality constraints up to version 1.12, but dropped support in all later versions. Recent approaches to incorporate cardinality constraint reasoning into the solver again are in an early stage [42]. For example, this solver cannot compete with a SAT solver that performs preprocessing and inprocessing.

Encoding cardinality constraints into SAT and then using BVA has the advantage that any SAT solver can be applied. Due to recent portfolio systems [43] the most promising solver can be picked, whereas the set of candidate solvers is much smaller for solvers that handle these constraints natively.

4.1   The At-Most-1 Constraint

A special case of cardinality constraints is $k = 1$ that is applied whenever a finite domain is encoded, for example when CSP is translated into SAT. Several encodings have been proposed with lower number of clauses, for example the *log encoding* (LE) [44] or the *2-product encoding* (PE) [45]. Furthermore, for $k = 1$ the *sequential counter encoding* (SE) [29] can be adopted. The naive encoding for $k = 1$ is referred to as the direct encoding (DE). For each encoding the lower

Table 1. Encoding the *at-most-one* constraint

Encoding	Clauses	Variables
DE	$\frac{n \cdot (n-1)}{2}$	n
LE [44]	$n \cdot \lceil \log n \rceil$	$n + \log n$
PE [45]	$2n + 4 \cdot \sqrt{n} + O(\sqrt[4]{n})$	$n + \sqrt{n} + O(\sqrt[4]{n})$
SE [29]	$3n - 4$	$2n - 1$
DE + BVA	$3n - 6$	$\sim 2n$
LE + BVA	$\sim 3n$	$\sim 1.5n$

bound on the number of clauses and variables for a given value for n are given in Table 1. The values have been taken from the corresponding publications.

Neither of the encodings PE and SE can be processed by BVA. However, applying BVA to the naive encoding yields major benefit with respect to the number of clauses and variables. Although PE has the best asymptotic number of clauses, DE + BVA produce less clauses until the value for n reaches 47. The same effect can be seen for the number of variables as long as $n < 45$. Note, that for cardinality constraints in real instances the value of n usually is smaller than 45. Applying BVA to LE does not give better results than using PE. Table 1 also shows that using a naive encoding and applying BVA results in a very good encoding for the *at-most-1* constraint.

Example 4. Consider the DE of $\leq 1(a, b, c, d, e, f)$:

$$D = (\bar{a} \vee \bar{b}) \wedge (\bar{a} \vee \bar{c}) \wedge (\bar{a} \vee \bar{d}) \wedge (\bar{a} \vee \bar{e}) \wedge (\bar{a} \vee \bar{f}) \wedge (\bar{b} \vee \bar{c}) \wedge (\bar{b} \vee \bar{d}) \wedge$$
$$(\bar{b} \vee \bar{e}) \wedge (\bar{b} \vee \bar{f}) \wedge (\bar{c} \vee \bar{d}) \wedge (\bar{c} \vee \bar{e}) \wedge (\bar{c} \vee \bar{f}) \wedge (\bar{d} \vee \bar{e}) \wedge (\bar{d} \vee \bar{f}) \wedge (\bar{e} \vee \bar{f})$$

Applying BVA on D replaces nine clauses by six using $M_{\text{lit}} = \{\bar{a}, \bar{b}, \bar{c}\}$ and $M_{\text{cls}} = \{(\bar{a} \vee \bar{d}), (\bar{a} \vee \bar{e}), (\bar{a} \vee \bar{f})\}$:

$$(\bar{a} \vee \bar{b}) \wedge (\bar{a} \vee \bar{c}) \wedge (\bar{b} \vee \bar{c}) \wedge (\bar{d} \vee \bar{e}) \wedge (\bar{d} \vee \bar{f}) \wedge (\bar{e} \vee \bar{f}) \wedge$$
$$(\bar{a} \vee x) \wedge (\bar{b} \vee x) \wedge (\bar{c} \vee x) \wedge (\bar{d} \vee \bar{x}) \wedge (\bar{e} \vee \bar{x}) \wedge (\bar{f} \vee \bar{x})$$

Fig. 2 shows the number of clauses that are needed to encode the at-most-1 constraint with the mentioned encodings. The value on the x-axis gives the number of Boolean variables where a single one has to be set to true. It can be seen clearly that both DE and LE use more clauses than any of the special encodings. Applying BVA to the naive encoding results in almost the same number of clauses as if a special encoding is used. Until the number of elements reaches 47, using DE + BVA results in the smallest number of clauses for the at-most-1 constraint.

4.2   The At-Most-K Constraint

The more generic case of the cardinality constraint does not bind k to a specific value. Thus, it is not possible to easily adopt a special encoding as for the

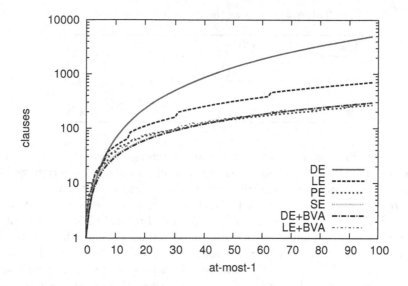

Fig. 2. Clauses needed to encode the *at-most-1* constraint

case $k = 1$. In general, for the mentioned applications a value of k that is larger than 1 is required. Still, special encodings have been proposed to encode general cardinality constraints efficiently. Again, we consider only encodings that preserve arc consistency.

Encoding cardinality constraints based on a unary number representation and a binary tree with comparators has been proposed [30] which we refer to as TREE. Sinz introduced a sequential counter encoding and a parallel counter encoding, where the latter one does not preserve arc consistency. Eén and Sörrensen [16] introduced three possibilities to encode a cardinality constraint, namely by using (i) binary decision diagrams, (ii) networks of sorters or (iii) networks of adders [16], where only the first two encoding preserve arc consistency. Encoding the BDD into CNF has been done by the Tseitin transformation. There are two small sized encodings for cardinality constraints that do not provide arc consistency: the *parallel counter* [29] and the *hybrid perfect hashing function* based encoding [46]. Although the properties of the latter are very nice, it cannot guarantee arc consistency for all possible cardinality constraints. The arc consistent variant of *perfect hashing function* based encoding [46] uses slightly more clauses than the sequential counter, but needs less auxiliary variables. Since we focus on the number of clauses, we do not consider this encoding. Table 2 shows the asymptotic number of clauses and variables that are needed by using the different encodings. Notice that the number of clauses that are required by the naive encoding is significantly higher than for the other encodings.

Discussing the effect of BVA on the naive encoding of *at-most-k* constraints is not as simple as for the special case $k = 1$, because non-binary clauses are involved in these encodings.

Table 2. Encoding the *at-most-k* constraint

Encoding	Clauses	Variables
naive	$\binom{n}{k+1}$	n
TREE [30]	$O(n^2)$	$\Theta(n \log n + 1)$
SE [29]	$2nk + n - 3k - 1$	$(n-1) \cdot k$
BDD [16]	$2nk + n - k^2$	$(n-k+1) \cdot k + n$

Due to the limit of BVA to detect only matchings where M_{lit} is restricted to a set of single literals, many potential matchings cannot be recognized and replaced. The following example illustrates this statement. Although matchings with a reduction of 3 are part of formula K, only reductions of size 2 can be recognized. By increasing the number of matching literals in BVA, this limit can be overcome. Still, applying BVA to the naive at-most-k encoding reduces the number of clauses significantly. The smaller the value k, the closer the number of clauses after BVA gets to the number of clauses of the special encodings. We present some exemplary values for the number of clauses and variables after applying BVA to the naive encoding in Table 3 to support this statement. The formulas for SE and BDD have been generated by using the tools that have been provided with the corresponding publications. For $n = 10$ using BVA results in the smallest formula. For $n = 20$ the special encodings are almost always more effective than BVA.

Example 5. Consider the encoding of $\leq 3(a, b, c, d, e, f)$:

$$K = (\bar{a} \vee \bar{b} \vee \bar{c} \vee \bar{d}) \wedge (\bar{a} \vee \bar{b} \vee \bar{c} \vee \bar{e}) \wedge (\bar{a} \vee \bar{b} \vee \bar{c} \vee \bar{f}) \wedge (\bar{a} \vee \bar{b} \vee \bar{d} \vee \bar{e}) \wedge$$
$$(\bar{a} \vee \bar{b} \vee \bar{d} \vee \bar{f}) \wedge (\bar{a} \vee \bar{b} \vee \bar{e} \vee \bar{f}) \wedge (\bar{a} \vee \bar{c} \vee \bar{d} \vee \bar{e}) \wedge (\bar{a} \vee \bar{c} \vee \bar{d} \vee \bar{f}) \wedge$$
$$(\bar{a} \vee \bar{c} \vee \bar{e} \vee \bar{f}) \wedge (\bar{a} \vee \bar{d} \vee \bar{e} \vee \bar{f}) \wedge (\bar{b} \vee \bar{c} \vee \bar{d} \vee \bar{e}) \wedge (\bar{b} \vee \bar{c} \vee \bar{d} \vee \bar{f}) \wedge$$
$$(\bar{b} \vee \bar{c} \vee \bar{e} \vee \bar{f}) \wedge (\bar{b} \vee \bar{d} \vee \bar{e} \vee \bar{f}) \wedge (\bar{c} \vee \bar{d} \vee \bar{e} \vee \bar{f})$$

Applying BVA on the formula K will find the matching $M_{\mathrm{lit}} = \{\bar{a}, \bar{b}\}$ and $M_{\mathrm{cls}} = \{(\bar{a} \vee \bar{d} \vee \bar{e} \vee \bar{f}), (\bar{a} \vee \bar{c} \vee \bar{d} \vee \bar{e}), (\bar{a} \vee \bar{c} \vee \bar{e} \vee \bar{f}), (\bar{a} \vee \bar{c} \vee \bar{d} \vee \bar{f})\}$ with a reduction of 2 clauses. Yet the more interesting case is to use $M_{\mathrm{lit}} = \{\{\bar{a}, \bar{b}\}, \{\bar{a}, \bar{c}\}, \{\bar{b}, \bar{c}\}\}$ and $M_{\mathrm{cls}} = \{(\bar{a} \vee \bar{b} \vee \bar{d} \vee \bar{e}), (\bar{a} \vee \bar{b} \vee \bar{d} \vee \bar{f}), (\bar{a} \vee \bar{b} \vee \bar{e} \vee \bar{f})\}$ which has reduction 3.

5   Experiments

We implemented the algorithm of Fig. 1 in a new tool[1]. Although applying *SimpleBoundedVariableAddition* until fixpoint requires less than a second on most benchmarks, we observed that BVA was sometimes very expensive – even in case no replaceable matching can be found. Therefore, we limited the execution of BVA as follows: when the check on line 8 of Fig. 1 is executed 10,000,000 times,

---

[1] The sources of the tool are available at http://fmv.jku.at/bva

Table 3. Encoding the *at-most-k* constraint

k	n	naive		naive + BVA		SE [29]		BDD [16]	
		#var	#cls	#var	#cls	#var	#cls	#var	#cls
2	10	10	120	18	32	28	43	33	59
3	10	10	210	18	47	37	60	37	70
4	10	10	252	19	51	46	77	39	75
5	10	10	210	17	53	55	94	39	74
2	20	20	1140	40	80	58	93	73	139
3	20	20	4845	44	209	77	130	87	180
4	20	20	15504	66	326	96	167	99	215
5	20	20	38760	60	768	115	204	109	244
6	20	20	77520	130	1104	134	241	117	267
7	20	20	125970	113	2051	153	278	123	284
8	20	20	167960	227	2247	172	315	127	295
9	20	20	184756	104	3175	191	352	129	300
10	20	20	167960	191	2892	210	389	129	299

the algorithm is aborted. Then, the formula is returned with all substitutions
until that point. This limit ensures that the preprocessing runtime is only a few
seconds for the more costly formulas. Note, that all the experiments use the first
and third extension that have been mentioned in Section 3.2. For the experiments
we selected the SAT solver Lingeling (version SAT11 Competition[2]) because of
its strong performance during SAT10 Race and SAT11 Competition.

5.1 Bio-informatics

One family of benchmarks for which we observed that BVA could significantly
decrease the size of the instances originates from bio-informatics. These formulas
encode computing evolutionary tree measures into SAT [47]. The results of these
instances are shown in Table 4. The selected benchmarks are very hard and no
solver was able to tackle any of the _09 or _10 instances (within the CPU timeout
of 40,000 seconds). After applying our BVA tool –which on average reduces the
size of a factor ten– Lingeling could solve all instances. Of the original instances
only rpoc_08 could be solved, yet 36 times slower.

5.2 FPGA Routing

As discussed in prior sections, several benchmarks arising from EDA consist of
cardinality constraints. A family of this type used in recent SAT competitions
encodes FPGA routing problems [22]. This family consists of six routing configurations (chnlXX_YY) in which one tries to route (a) 11, 12 or 13 connections
through 10 tracks, and (b) 12, 13 or 20 connections through 11 track. Table 5

---

[2] http://www.satcompetition.org

Table 4. Results on bio-informatics benchmarks. TO is 20,000 seconds

instance	original			BVA preprocessed			
	#var	#cls	solve	#var	#cls	pre	solve
ndhf_09	1910	167476	TO	3098	14588	1.47	**187**
ndhf_10	2112	191333	TO	3418	16756	1.70	**1272**
rbcl_08	1278	67720	TO	1981	8669	0.29	**16**
rbcl_09	1430	79118	TO	2192	10157	0.39	**101**
rbcl_10	1584	91311	TO	2443	11811	0.43	**604**
rpoc_08	1278	74454	8628	2011	8494	0.39	**237**
rpoc_09	1430	86709	TO	2252	10063	0.47	**3590**
rpoc_10	1584	99781	TO	2474	11667	0.66	**11945**

shows the results. BVA decreases the size of the CNF by more than a factor two. The preprocessed formulas are easier to solve. FPGA routing can also be solved with special purpose solvers that perform well on these instances. Techniques that are used in these solvers are for example symmetry breaking [22]. Since symmetry breaking and BVA are orthogonal, it is a reasonable choice to measure the effect of BVA also on this instance family. Furthermore, it would be possible to combine symmetry breaking and BVA.

Table 5. Results on FPGA routing problems. TO is 20,000 seconds

instance	original			BVA preprocessed			
	#var	#cls	solve	#var	#cls	pre	solve
chnl10_11	220	1122	9372	302	562	0.00	**69.3**
chnl10_12	240	1344	7279	340	624	0.00	**15.0**
chnl10_13	260	1586	2682	380	686	0.00	**26.0**
chnl11_12	264	1476	TO	374	684	0.00	**41.6**
chnl11_13	286	1742	TO	418	752	0.00	**17.1**
chnl11_20	440	4220	TO	667	1228	0.00	**12.1**

5.3   Recent SAT Competitions

We observed that applying variable elimination (BVE) creates many patterns for variable addition (BVA). Therefore we preprocessed, using SatElite of MiniSAT 2.2 [36], the formulas of recent SAT competitions with BVE –which is default in the strongest SAT solvers– and applied our *SimpleBoundedVariableAddition* algorithm afterwards.

On the application benchmarks of SAT09, Lingeling solved 196 instances (75 SAT and 121 UNSAT) within 900 seconds (including all preprocessing time), while without BVA 190 instances (74 SAT, 116 UNSAT) were solved. The same experiment on the application benchmarks of SAT11 resulted in a similar picture:

with BVA 169 (79 SAT, 90 UNSAT) were solved, while without BVA, Lingeling solves 162 instances (80 SAT, 82 UNSAT).

On the crafted instances we noticed that BVA works particularly well on benchmarks from the Satisfiable Random High Degree Subgraph Isomorphism (SRHD) family [48]. Using BVA, Lingeling is able to solve several more instances of this family. However, even with the improved performance Lingeling requires minutes to solve these benchmarks, while local search SAT algorithms can find a solution in seconds.

6   Conclusions

We presented the preprocessing technique BVA that automatically reduces the size of CNF formulas by introducing new variables. BVA can shrink formulas containing for instance cardinality constraints. Experiments show that the smaller CNFs are generally solved faster, making BVA a useful technique. Also interestingly, the presented algorithm is orthogonal to BVE, which is one of the most powerful preprocessing techniques.

Future work in this direction will focus on enhancing BVA with more replacement patterns. Additionally, BVA will be studied in the context of inprocessing to observe the interaction with other techniques such as BVE and BCE.

We finally would like to thank the anonymous reviewers for detailed suggestions on how to improve the paper.

References

1. Goldberg, E.I., Prasad, M.R., Brayton, R.K.: Using SAT for combinational equivalence checking. In: DATE, pp. 114–121 (2001)
2. Mishchenko, A., Chatterjee, S., Brayton, R.K., Eén, N.: Improvements to combinational equivalence checking. In: Hassoun, S. (ed.) ICCAD, pp. 836–843. ACM (2006)
3. Baumgartner, J., Mony, H., Paruthi, V., Kanzelman, R., Janssen, G.: Scalable sequential equivalence checking across arbitrary design transformations. In: ICCD. IEEE (2006)
4. Kaiss, D., Skaba, M., Hanna, Z., Khasidashvili, Z.: Industrial strength SAT-based alignability algorithm for hardware equivalence verification. In: FMCAD, pp. 20–26. IEEE Computer Society (2007)
5. Biere, A., Cimatti, A., Clarke, E.M., Fujita, M., Zhu, Y.: Symbolic model checking using SAT procedures instead of bdds. In: DAC, pp. 317–320 (1999)
6. Sheeran, M., Singh, S., Stålmarck, G.: Checking safety properties using induction and a SAT-solver. In: Hunt Jr., W.A., Johnson, S.D. (eds.) FMCAD 2000. LNCS, vol. 1954, pp. 108–125. Springer, Heidelberg (2000)
7. Chen, Y., Safarpour, S., Marques-Silva, J.P., Veneris, A.G.: Automated design debugging with maximum satisfiability. IEEE Trans. on CAD of Integrated Circuits and Systems 29(11), 1804–1817 (2010)
8. Marques Silva, J.P., Sakallah, K.A.: Grasp: A search algorithm for propositional satisfiability. IEEE Trans. Computers 48(5), 506–521 (1999)
9. Moskewicz, M.W., Madigan, C.F., Zhao, Y., Zhang, L., Malik, S.: Chaff: Engineering an efficient SAT solver. In: DAC, pp. 530–535. ACM (2001)

10. Mishchenko, A., Chatterjee, S., Brayton, R.K.: Dag-aware aig rewriting a fresh look at combinational logic synthesis. In: DAC, pp. 532–535 (2006)
11. Eén, N., Mishchenko, A., Sörensson, N.: Applying logic synthesis for speeding up SAT. In: Marques-Silva, J., Sakallah, K.A. (eds.) SAT 2007. LNCS, vol. 4501, pp. 272–286. Springer, Heidelberg (2007)
12. Chambers, B., Manolios, P., Vroon, D.: Faster SAT solving with better CNF generation. In: DATE, pp. 1590–1595. IEEE (2009)
13. Guerra e Silva, L., Miguel Silveira, L., Marques Silva, J.P.: Algorithms for solving boolean satisfiability in combinational circuits. In: DATE, pp. 526–530. IEEE Computer Society (1999)
14. Ganai, M.K., Ashar, P., Gupta, A., Zhang, L., Malik, S.: Combining strengths of circuit-based and CNF-based algorithms for a high-performance SAT solver. In: DAC, pp. 747–750. ACM (2002)
15. Bacchus, F., Winter, J.: Effective preprocessing with hyper-resolution and equality reduction. In: Giunchiglia, E., Tacchella, A. (eds.) SAT 2003. LNCS, vol. 2919, pp. 341–355. Springer, Heidelberg (2004)
16. Eén, N., Sörensson, N.: Translating pseudo-boolean constraints into SAT. JSAT 2(1-4), 1–26 (2006)
17. Järvisalo, M., Biere, A., Heule, M.: Blocked clause elimination. In: Esparza, J., Majumdar, R. (eds.) TACAS 2010. LNCS, vol. 6015, pp. 129–144. Springer, Heidelberg (2010)
18. Biere, A.: Lingeling, Plingeling, PicoSAT and PrecoSAT at SAT Race 2010. FMV Report Series Technical Report 10/1, Johannes Kepler University, Linz, Austria (2010)
19. Järvisalo, M., Heule, M.J.H., Biere, A.: Inprocessing rules. In: Gramlich, B., Miller, D., Sattler, U. (eds.) IJCAR 2012. LNCS, vol. 7364, pp. 355–370. Springer, Heidelberg (2012)
20. Biere, A.: Resolve and expand. In: Hoos, H.H., Mitchell, D.G. (eds.) SAT 2004. LNCS, vol. 3542, pp. 59–70. Springer, Heidelberg (2005)
21. Subbarayan, S., Pradhan, D.K.: NiVER: Non-increasing variable elimination resolution for preprocessing SAT instances. In: Hoos, H.H., Mitchell, D.G. (eds.) SAT 2004. LNCS, vol. 3542, pp. 276–291. Springer, Heidelberg (2005)
22. Aloul, F.A., Ramani, A., Markov, I.L., Sakallah, K.A.: Solving difficult SAT instances in the presence of symmetry. In: DAC 2002, pp. 731–736. ACM, New York (2002)
23. Chai, D., Kuehlmann, A.: A fast pseudo-boolean constraint solver. IEEE Trans. on CAD of Integrated Circuits and Systems 24(3), 305–317 (2005)
24. Marques-Silva, J.P., Planes, J.: Algorithms for maximum satisfiability using unsatisfiable cores. In: DATE, pp. 408–413. IEEE (2008)
25. Quimper, C.-G., López-Ortiz, A., van Beek, P., Golynski, A.: Improved algorithms for the global cardinality constraint. In: Wallace, M. (ed.) CP 2004. LNCS, vol. 3258, pp. 542–556. Springer, Heidelberg (2004)
26. Quimper, C.-G., Walsh, T.: Beyond finite domains: The all different and global cardinality constraints. In: van Beek, P. (ed.) CP 2005. LNCS, vol. 3709, pp. 812–816. Springer, Heidelberg (2005)
27. Zanarini, A., Pesant, G.: Generalizations of the global cardinality constraint for hierarchical resources. In: Van Hentenryck, P., Wolsey, L.A. (eds.) CPAIOR 2007. LNCS, vol. 4510, pp. 361–375. Springer, Heidelberg (2007)
28. Régin, J.-C.: Combination of among and cardinality constraints. In: Barták, R., Milano, M. (eds.) CPAIOR 2005. LNCS, vol. 3524, pp. 288–303. Springer, Heidelberg (2005)

29. Sinz, C.: Towards an optimal CNF encoding of boolean cardinality constraints. In: van Beek, P. (ed.) CP 2005. LNCS, vol. 3709, pp. 827–831. Springer, Heidelberg (2005)
30. Bailleux, O., Boufkhad, Y.: Efficient CNF encoding of boolean cardinality constraints. In: Rossi, F. (ed.) CP 2003. LNCS, vol. 2833, pp. 108–122. Springer, Heidelberg (2003)
31. Asín, R., Nieuwenhuis, R., Oliveras, A., Rodríguez-Carbonell, E.: Cardinality networks and their applications. In: Kullmann, O. (ed.) SAT 2009. LNCS, vol. 5584, pp. 167–180. Springer, Heidelberg (2009)
32. Audemard, G., Katsirelos, G., Simon, L.: A restriction of extended resolution for clause learning SAT solvers. In: Fox, M., Poole, D. (eds.) AAAI. AAAI Press (2010)
33. Condrat, C., Kalla, P.: A gröbner basis approach to CNF-formulae preprocessing. In: Grumberg, O., Huth, M. (eds.) TACAS 2007. LNCS, vol. 4424, pp. 618–631. Springer, Heidelberg (2007)
34. Warners, J.P., van Maaren, H.: A two-phase algorithm for solving a class of hard satisfiability problems. Operations Research Letters 23(3-5), 81–88 (1998)
35. Davis, M., Putnam, H.: A computing procedure for quantification theory. Journal of the ACM 7(3), 201–215 (1960)
36. Eén, N., Biere, A.: Effective preprocessing in SAT through variable and clause elimination. In: Bacchus, F., Walsh, T. (eds.) SAT 2005. LNCS, vol. 3569, pp. 61–75. Springer, Heidelberg (2005)
37. Küchlin, W., Sinz, C.: Proving consistency assertions for automotive product data management. J. Autom. Reasoning 24(1/2), 145–163 (2000)
38. Cabon, B., de Givry, S., Lobjois, L., Schiex, T., Warners, J.P.: Radio link frequency assignment. Constraints 4(1), 79–89 (1999)
39. Le Berre, D., Parrain, A.: The sat4j library, release 2.2, system description. Journal on Satisfiability, Boolean Modeling and Computation (JSAT) 7, 59–64 (2010)
40. Gebser, M., Kaufmann, B., Schaub, T.: The conflict-driven answer set solver *clasp*: Progress report. In: Erdem, E., Lin, F., Schaub, T. (eds.) LPNMR 2009. LNCS, vol. 5753, pp. 509–514. Springer, Heidelberg (2009)
41. Eén, N., Sörensson, N.: An extensible SAT-solver. In: Giunchiglia, E., Tacchella, A. (eds.) SAT 2003. LNCS, vol. 2919, pp. 502–518. Springer, Heidelberg (2004)
42. Liffiton, M.H., Maglalang, J.C.: A cardinality solver: More expressive constraints for free - (poster presentation). In: Cimatti, A., Sebastiani, R. (eds.) SAT 2012. LNCS, vol. 7317, pp. 485–486. Springer, Heidelberg (2012)
43. Xu, L., Hutter, F., Hoos, H.H., Leyton-Brown, K.: Satzilla: portfolio-based algorithm selection for sat. J. Artif. Int. Res. 32(1), 565–606 (2008)
44. Prestwich, S.D.: Variable Dependency in Local Search: Prevention Is Better Than Cure. In: Marques-Silva, J., Sakallah, K.A. (eds.) SAT 2007. LNCS, vol. 4501, pp. 107–120. Springer, Heidelberg (2007)
45. Chen, J.: A New SAT Encoding of the At-Most-One Constraint. In: Proceedings of ModRef 2011 (2011)
46. Ben-Haim, Y., Ivrii, A., Margalit, O., Matsliah, A.: Perfect hashing and CNF encodings of cardinality constraints. In: Cimatti, A., Sebastiani, R. (eds.) SAT 2012. LNCS, vol. 7317, pp. 397–409. Springer, Heidelberg (2012)
47. Bonet, M.L., John, K.S.: Efficiently calculating evolutionary tree measures using SAT. In: Kullmann, O. (ed.) SAT 2009. LNCS, vol. 5584, pp. 4–17. Springer, Heidelberg (2009)
48. Anton, C.: An improved satisfiable SAT generator based on random subgraph isomorphism. In: Butz, C., Lingras, P. (eds.) Canadian AI 2011. LNCS (LNAI), vol. 6657, pp. 44–49. Springer, Heidelberg (2011)

Leveraging Accelerated Simulation
for Floating-Point Regression

John Paul[1], Elena Guralnik[2], Anatoly Koyfman[2], Amir Nahir[2], and Subrat K. Panda[1]

[1] IBM Systems & Technology Group in Bangalore, India
{john.paul,subratpanda}@in.ibm.com
[2] IBM Research in Haifa, Israel
{elenag,anatoly,nahir}@il.ibm.com

Abstract. Accelerated simulation (acceleration) platforms play a pivotal role in the verification of today's complex designs. Currently, acceleration is used with either adapted pre-silicon tools or post-silicon tools. We present a novel acceleration-only tool, which enables a fast and efficient methodology for floating-point regression. We overcome the lack of test-bench in this environment through self-checking.

1 Introduction

Functional verification is widely acknowledged as one of the main challenges of the hardware design cycle [12]. The growing size and complexity of modern hardware systems have turned the functional verification of these systems into a mammoth task [20]. Verifying such systems involves tens or hundreds of person years and requires the compute power of thousands of workstations. But even with all this effort, it is virtually impossible to eliminate all bugs in the design before it tapes-out. Despite advances in formal verification technologies [7], dynamic verification (a.k.a. simulation-based verification) remains the primary vehicle for the functional verification of hardware systems [20]. Today's state of the art verification methodologies include a highly automated process that incorporates stimuli generation, checking, and coverage collection—combined with islands of manual labor [20].

In the past, software simulation was (almost) the exclusive vehicle for executing the verified designs. But, the increasing complexity of designs, combined with shorter time-to-market requirements, raised the need for performing parts of the verification tasks on other platforms. Today, functional verification is performed on a variety of platforms, ranging from transaction-level modeling, via software simulation, acceleration, and emulation, to the silicon itself [18,4]. In some cases, verification is done in a heterogeneous environment involving a variety of platforms, as in the case of Hardware-Software Co-Simulation [6].

Acceleration and emulation platforms are somewhere in between software simulation and silicon. They are much faster than software simulation, but not as fast as silicon. Similarly, they provide better observability than silicon, but not the free and total observability provided by software simulators. Therefore, verification solutions, and specifically stimuli generators, for such platforms should combine requirements from both worlds.

A. Biere, A. Nahir, and T. Vos (Eds.): HVC 2012, LNCS 7857, pp. 118–131, 2013.

The acceleration platform is especially attractive because it can be leveraged very early in the process. It can serve to strengthen the pre-silicon verification effort and enable the early detection of bugs. In addition, acceleration products offer a simulation-like interface and are thus relatively easy to use. Some products go as far as offering live, seamless, migration between acceleration and simulation [1].

The high cost of developing unique verification solutions for acceleration platforms causes most of these solutions to be adaptations of existing solutions for software simulation or post-silicon tools. In this paper, we demonstrate how the acceleration platform can be utilized to address one of the more common use-cases in the development life cycle: regressing a change in the design logic.

As part of the logic development process, designers make frequent changes to the logic. These changes may originate from the need to fix a bug, improve timing, or simply implement a change in the specifications. One common concern is that making a change to the logic, as small as it may be, can introduce new bugs. It would greatly improve productivity if such bugs were detected shortly after their introduction. To validate that no new bugs were introduced in the process, the verification engineer, or the logic designer, runs a *regression suite* [8]. The regression suite is a large set of test-cases that provide high confidence regarding the functional correctness of the design. For complex units, running regression in software simulation can take days.[1]

Using our solution, the verification engineer can choose a large set of ready-made test-cases, such as the regression suite mentioned above, and convert them into a single, fully-contained, self-checking, program. Using an accelerator can speed up the execution time for the test case by several orders of magnitude. This not only leads to finding bugs faster but also has a significant effect on the time required to reach coverage closure.

We demonstrate the proposed solution on floating point (FP) data verification. Verifying the hardware implementation of the floating point unit (FPU) is known as an intricate problem. The numerous corner cases of the vast test space, coupled with the complexity of the implementation of floating point operations, turn the FPU verification effort into a unique challenge in the field of processor verification. It is not surprising that the most well known hardware bug is Intel's FDIV bug [2].

We present a tool that takes a large set of FP test-cases (pre-generated by FPgen [5,11]) and converts them into a single program that is then simulated at the core-level environment. This program is a concatenation of the original test-cases, where each test-case is preceded by a prolog and followed by an epilogue. The prolog mimics the required initializations specified in the original test-case. These initialization are typically handled in software simulation by the environment, which forces the initial values into the specified resources. We convert these initializations into a set of reloading instructions, which bring the required resources to the desired state. The epilog runs in two different modes: *simulator mode* and *hardware mode*. When running in simulator mode, we run the program to collect the expected results. Following that, we run the test-case on the accelerator in hardware mode. In this mode, the epilog is in charge of

---

[1] While an industrial simulation farm holds thousands of servers, the regression task is so common that it is impractical to expect to be assigned with sufficient machines to complete the regression task quickly

comparing the actual state of the design with the expected values obtained from the reference model, and flagging any discrepancies that may indicate a bug.

We show that using this tool, thousands of test-cases can be compressed into a single test-case and executed on an accelerator in a short amount of time, and report results of a field trial.

The rest of this paper is organized as follows. In Section 2 we provide background about floating point verification and test-generation, as well as on the accelerated simulation platform. Section 3 provides an in-depth review of our solution for floating point regression on the acceleration platform. Our results are described in Section 4. Section 5 concludes this paper.

2 Background

2.1 Acceleration

Accelerated simulation platforms (more commonly known as accelerators) are an important component in today's simulation-based verification [9]. Accelerators are special purpose massively-parallel machines, developed for the sole purpose of accelerating the simulation of hardware models. The accelerator is constructed of a large number of tightly synchronized parallel logic processors. To simulate a hardware model on an accelerator, the model must first be compiled in a process that converts the hardware model to a set of instructions for each of the accelerator's processors, schedules the instructions for the processors, and determines the synchronization points between them [16]. State of the art accelerators run over three orders of magnitude faster than software simulation (i.e., over 1000 times faster).

While accelerators offer much faster simulation, there are several challenges related to their use. First, any interaction between the accelerator and an external computer (termed host) requires stopping the acceleration engine. This means that using a traditional environment in which the test-bench runs on the host and the accelerator runs the hardware model severely under utilizes the accelerator due to the frequent communication. The transaction-based acceleration (TBA) [14] methodology overcomes this problem by having part of the test-bench compiled into the hardware model and reducing the interaction between the host and the accelerator.

However, the TBA approach encounters the second challenge in using accelerators. The speed of the accelerator, as well as the duration of the compilation process, heavily depend on the size of the hardware model. That is, the more logic is added to the hardware model, the slower the accelerator runs. This limits the ability to use techniques such as TBA or checker synthesis [10].

We note that for the case of floating point data path verification presented in this paper, neither TBA nor checker synthesis is applicable. Moving input data operands from the host to the accelerator and output values in the other direction is unreasonable due to the extensive amount of data. The complexity of the floating point algorithms and the required accuracy needed to verify the results prohibit the creation of hardware realizable checkers.

2.2   Floating Point Test Generation

The complexity of the floating point data path implementation and the numerous corner cases that should be addressed not only call for a dedicated test generator, but also demand a comprehensive test plan. The FPgen [5] verification solution provides these two components.

FPgen generation capabilities are primarily based on constraint satisfaction technology [17]. As part of the verification process, FPgen produces a large set of test-cases in the form of input data operands for floating point instructions, targeting the areas outlined by the test plan.

The primary focus of the FPgen generator is to solve data constraints on operands of individual floating point instructions. A data constraint on an operand is defined as the set of values that can be selected for this operand. An individual instruction may have independent data constraints for each one of its operands. Solving all the instruction constraints is equivalent to selecting a value from each given set, such that the instruction semantics are satisfied. FPgen provides engines that solve these constraints within a reasonable amount of time. Moreover, when multiple solutions exist for a constraint, one should be selected at random, with uniform probability where possible. This randomness is important because the constraints only reflect a suspected area. One instance in this area might reveal a problem, while another might not.

Constructing an appropriate set of such constraints is of utmost importance to ensure successful verification. Exhaustive checking implies testing an enormous, practically unbounded, number of different calculation cases; practical computational resources suffice only to simulate a meager fraction of these. We need to choose these cases very carefully in order to obtain a representative sample of the state space. In particular, a proper focus on the corner cases is a crucial factor in providing a sufficiently comprehensive set of test-cases. Continued analysis of the instructions themselves, and of the various bugs appearing in their implementations, has provided us with valuable knowledge, reflected as an integral part of FPgen's test plan template.

3   FP Regression Tool

We apply the concept of converting a set of pre-generated test-cases into a self-executing self-checking program for the floating-point data path regression problem. In this section we describe the tool's execution flow, the structure of the generated program, and the accompanying debug aids.

3.1   Execution Flow

The high level execution flow of the tool is described in Figure 1.

We start with a set of test-cases pre-generated by FPgen[5], as depicted in the leftmost section of the Figure 1. FPgen is a test-generation framework that provides a convenient platform for biasing and generating operand data for floating-point instructions. The verification engineer can choose the set of test-cases so they focus on a specific instruction or event (for example, *sqrt*) or opt for a set that provides broad coverage of

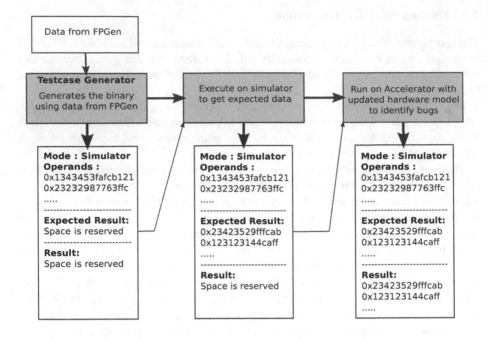

Fig. 1. Execution Flow

the entire floating point spectrum. Our tool outputs a single program that includes all the desired test-cases.

Next, our tool generates the initial program and then executes it on a software reference model that is instruction accurate[2], as depicted in the middle section of the Figure 1.

The purpose of this stage is to collect and store the expected results from the execution of the different test-cases. We assume the software reference model correctly implements the specification and provides accurate results[3]. After every test-case, epilog instructions are executed to store the results into empty arrays. This is done using instructions that are part of the generated program and does not require any involvement of the environment.

Once the program completes execution on the software reference model, our tool dumps the data from the arrays and modifies the program image. The program is modified in two ways: the expected results of the test-case execution are now stored in an array designated for storing expected results. In addition, we modify the execution mode to *hardware* mode so the subsequent execution of the program can also check the results.

---

[2] An instruction accurate reference model calculates the values that will appear in the registers and memory after each executed instruction, as specified in the architecture book.

[3] In reality, this may not be the case, and errors in the software reference model are often found. This makes the debugging of the failure a little more challenging, but does not significantly change anything that interferes with our solution.

Table 1. Program usage of registers

Register	Usage
GPR1, GPR2	base and offset pointers to input data table
GPR3, GPR4	base and offset pointers to input state table
GPR5, GPR6	base and offset pointers to actual/expected results data table
GPR7, GPR8	base and offset pointers to actual/expected state table
GPR9, GPR10	base and offset pointers to expected results data table
GPR11, GPR12	base and offset pointers to expected state table
GPR13	mode of operation (simulation/hardware)
GPR14, GPR15, GPR16	used for comparisons
GPR17, GPR18	base and offset pointers to comparison results table

Finally, we take the modified program and run it on an accelerator with an updated (potentially buggy) design model, as depicted in the rightmost section of the Figure 1. During this run, the program executes the test-cases and compares their results to the expected values. Any data related to results that are incorrect is saved to a debug report at the end of the run.

3.2 Program Structure

The generated program is constructed of three major parts: kernel, data tables, and the test program itself. Figure 2 depicts this structure.

Kernel. The program is designed to run on *bare-metal* [19], that is, we do not rely on an operating system (OS). This is important for two reasons. First, it significantly reduces all OS-related overheads and thus enables us to maximize the utilization of the accelerator (i.e., we spend minimum cycles executing "irrelevant" instructions). In addition, it enables us to have complete control of the system and switch freely between running modes (e.g., from hypervisor to user mode).

The kernel is in charge of initializing the relevant resources once the execution of the program begins. We demonstrate the concept on a real Power[TM] design, and thus, we make extensive use of General Purpose Registers (GPRs). We assign most of the processor's general purpose registers with fixed roles for managing the test program. Table 1 lists these roles. For example, we use GPR9 and GPR10 as base pointer and offset register, respectively, to the expected results table. After values are saved to the expected results table, GPR10 is incremented to point to the next available entry in the table. Note that GPR5, GPR6, GPR7 and GPR8 point to different tables in the two

```
Kernel:                                  Test Case:
0x100: # Initialize registers            # load FPSCR settings for each group
0x200:                                   lfdx FPR31, GPR3, GPR4
..........
0x3000: Mode of Operation                #clear Exception status bits
                                         mtmsf 0xFF,FPR31
Compare: #Routine to match expected
data with actual result.                 lfdx FPR1, GPR1, GPR2
                                         addi GPR2, GRP2, 8
Operands:                                lfdx FPR2, GPR1, GPR2
0xf1da9cd6d6421ff1                       addi GPR2, GRP2, 8
0xe3d69cd6d6421fe9
0xff7fffff                               fadd FPR8, FPR1, FPR2
0xf7ffdff3fcffffe597e5250f91925a64
..........................               #Save expected result
                                         stfdpx FPR8, GPR3, GPR4
Expected Result:                         addi GPR4, GPR4, 16
0x736aabbc04722342000000000000000000
0xf3adbc14722342abef18ff834311ff         #save FPSCR
..........................               mffs FPR30
Result:                                  stfdx FPR30, GPR7, GPR8
0x736aabbc04722342000000000000000000
0xf3adbc14722342abef18ff834311ff         #if mode == Hardware call Compare
..........................               cmpdi GPR13,0.
ComparissonResult:                       beq L3
0x0000000000000000                       mtlr GPR23
0x0000000000000000                       blrl
```

Fig. 2. Program structure

different modes of operation. When the tool runs in simulation mode, these registers point to the *expected* values tables and when it runs in hardware mode, they point to the *actual* values.

We chose to use load/store instructions that rely on two registers, as opposed to a single register and a value-base offset. This guarantees that the program can cope with very large tables. Because our program focuses on floating point verification, there's no harm in assigning program management roles to the GPRs, which are not needed for the test program itself. Furthermore, assigning fixed roles prevents us from having to re-initialize the registers as part of the programs' execution. We only need to increment the offset registers. This further increases the accelerator's utilization.

In addition to register initializations, the kernel also includes interrupt handlers for cases in which we expect the instructions to take exception.

A symbol in the kernel is allocated to hold the value of the mode of operation (simulation or hardware). We place this symbol in a pre-determined place ($0x3000$ in Figure 2) so we can modify its value in the program image without re-compiling.

Data Tables. The program includes four types of tables: input data and state tables, expected results data and state tables, actual results data and state tables, and a comparison results table. For simplicity, we chose to place data and state values in different tables.

When the program is first created, we populate its input data and state tables with the data collected from the FPgen pre-generated test-cases. The other tables are empty at this stage. Since we know the number of test-cases included in the program, we can determine the required size for each table.

When the program executes on the software reference model (in simulation mode), the kernel initializes the required registers to point to the expected results tables; the epilog instructions save the values into those tables. Once the program completes execution, we dump these values from the memory of the software reference model into the program image, populating the expected results tables there. At this stage, we also change the value of the mode of operation symbol.

When the program runs on the acceleration platform, the epilog instructions save the actual values into the actual results tables and the compare routine checks whether these values match the expected results. We do not really need to store these values, as we can do the comparison based on the test instruction's target register. However, we chose to store them into a table for later use in building a debug report.

Test Program. The test-program is in fact a concatenation of the FPgen pre-generated test-cases. Each FPgen test-case, typically consisting of one or two floating point instructions, is preceded by instructions that load the data inputs into the instruction source registers and set the required state. In addition, the pointer-offset registers are incremented to point to the entries of the next test-case.

Every test-case is followed by a set of instructions that save the target register and the new state to the relevant tables. In simulation mode these are the expected results tables, while in hardware mode these are the actual results tables. In hardware mode, we also branch from this part of the test-program to the compare routine in order to validate the accuracy of the results and mark any discrepancies in the comparison table.

At first glance, it may seem like our program has a significant overhead. For every test-case we have about 20 instructions required to set the input, save the output, and compare the results. However, this is not the case. First, not all instructions "are born equal." Although the *addi* (add immediate) instruction used to increment the offset pointer requires one cycle for execution, the actual floating point instruction requires a much longer execution time.

Furthermore, the placement of the input tables in memory, along with the test program's deterministic access pattern to these tables, enables the processor to activate its prefetching mechanisms, reducing the time required to reload the source registers.

Finally, we order the test-cases within the test program according to their required input state. This reduces the rate of state changes within the test program, increasing the test program's effectiveness.

3.3   Debugging

As stated above, when running in hardware mode on the accelerator, we compare the actual results with the expected ones. When the results of the test-case do not match the expected values, we store an error code into the comparison table. We use different error codes to designate different types of mismatches. Following that, the execution of the test program continues, allowing the detection of multiple errors in a single run.

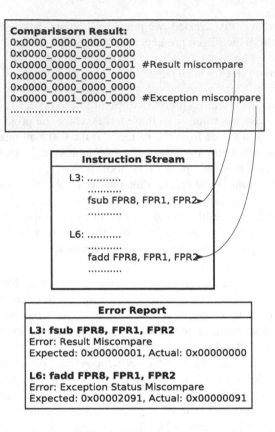

Fig. 3. Debug report

After the program completes execution, we analyze the comparison table. By providing the location of the error code in the table, we are able to cross-reference it with the expected and actual results tables, in order to provide a detailed report pinpointing the failure. This process is depicted in Figure 3. The bottom of the figure displays a snippet of the report. As can be seen, the report holds the ID of the failed instruction within the test program, the type of error, as well as the expected result and actual result.

In some cases, where debugging the failure with the accelerator proves difficult, the generated report is sufficient to find the original FPgen test-case and run it in simulation, where the environment eases the debugging work (either due to the better observability, or because of the presence of better checkers).

4   Results

The Power^{TM} architecture [15] supports various types of floating point data and instructions – binary floating point, decimal floating point and vector computation. In addition, the architecture also supports single/double precision values, normalized/denormalized

Table 2. Experimental setups

Experiment			Content			Program Size (KB)	
Config-uration	Instr-uction	Instr. per-model	Models	Total instr.	Binary Size	Operand Array
FADD50	fadd	50	56	2085	312	25
FADD100	fadd	100	56	3921	572	47
FADD500	fadd	500	56	16893	2400	210
FADD1000	fadd	1000	56	27663	3916	340
FADD2000	fadd	2000	56	47035	6648	581
FADD3000	fadd	3000	56	65889	9328	834
MIX10	All	10	134	1080	184	21
MIX50	All	50	134	5330	824	108
MIX100	All	100	134	10364	1520	209
MIX200	All	200	134	20648	3128	418

values and various kinds of rounding modes, all making the input space huge. Further-more, a wide variety of exceptions such as overflow, underflow, and zero-divide are supported. In the Power7 Processor core [13] the decimal floating-point (DFP) facility shares the 32 floating-point registers (FPRs) and status registers with the floating point units; the vector unit supports data with 128 bits. FPgen can generate input operand values for all instructions that execute on these units given any constraints on the input, output, and intermediate values, as explained in Section 2.2.

To validate the value of our tool, we've conducted a wide set of experimental results. In this section we report these results, as well as results of a field trial of this tool.

4.1 Experimental Results

For the purpose of experimentation and verifying the capability and usability of the tool, we performed experiments on a variety of cases. We divide our experiments into two extreme types: *single instruction* and *instruction mix*, where the former adheres to a case where a designer makes a localized change (relevant to a single instruction – *fadd* in our case, both in single-precision and double-precision forms), and is seeking to validate this fix. The latter type is of relevance when the designer makes a broader change, and thus must validate a large set of instructions. In reality, there is a wide range of cases in between these two extremes. We further refine our experiments to consider different numbers of instructions required to validate the change.

Table 2 and Table 3 describe the results of our experiments. Each row in these tables describes one setup.

Table 2 has two sections of columns. The leftmost part, titled **Content**, describes the contents put into the program as part of the experiments. It is combined of three values: the number of desired generation solutions requested of FPgen for each model, the number of models, and the total number of the generated floating point instructions. FPgen sometimes fails to find a solution, and so the total number of instructions is always less than the product of the former two fields. A model is a set of constraints used for FPgen's activation. For example, one model may call for generating *fadd* such

Table 3. Experimental results

Experiment		Run Time			
Config-uration	Instr-uction	FPGen Run (min)	Binary Gen (sec)	Ref Gen (sec)	Accel Run (sec)
FADD50	fadd	12	0.4	0.35	1150
FADD100	fadd	18	0.7	0.4	1122
FADD500	fadd	50	2.8	0.8	1233
FADD1000	fadd	93	4.4	1.2	1211
FADD2000	fadd	93	7.4	1.8	1284
FADD3000	fadd	248	10.2	2.4	1352
MIX10	All	29	0.4	0.5	1112
MIX50	All	122	1.8	0.5	1115
MIX100	All	258	3.5	0.6	1176
MIX200	All	493	6.8	1	1206

that the output triggers an *overflow*, while a different model may constrain both of *fadd*'s operands to be denormalized numbers.

The second column section, titled **Program Size**, provides details about the size of the generated program. We distinguish between the size of the generated program (Binary Size in the table) and the size of the input operands table. The total size of the program (the sum of these two values) is important because it impacts the time required to load the program into the memory of the accelerator. Note that we have a very efficient loader that is capable of loading data into the memory of the accelerator at a rate of over $100MB$ per minute.

Table 3 holds the data regarding the time required to run each of the phases of the tool's execution. Note that we provide the time required to run FPgen to generate the test-cases, while in reality it is very common to store these test-cases, so that in future executions, this phase is redundant. The columns show, from left to right, the time required by FPgen to generate the test-cases, the time required to parse the resulting test-cases and covert them to the initial program, the time required to executed the program on the software reference model to gather expected results, and the time required to run the program on the accelerator.

Our results indicate that, as expected, the program size grows linearly with the number of floating point instructions put into the program.

Interestingly, the accelerator run time is barely affected by the number of floating point instructions in the program. This is because this time is governed by overheads - the time required to reset the accelerator, upload the hardware model, and write the program to memory. This indicates that in order to properly utilize the accelerator, the verification engineer should strive to run as big a regression as possible.

Overall, our tool enables the verification engineer to run over $65,000$ test-cases, in under half an hour.

Fault Injection and Debugging. In order to demonstrate the tool's ability to discover bugs, we introduced random faults to different places in the program and observed whether they were detected by the tool and, if detected, whether the final report generated by our tool pointed to the source of the fault/error. We introduced the faults into the program after its execution on the software reference model (i.e., just before we ran it on the accelerator). We distinguish between three types of faults: input, output, and exception.

We introduced input faults by modifying the value of one of the input operands. This may represent a bug in one of the reloading instructions. In some rare cases, our tool fails to detects such faults. One example of this is the case of *division by zero*. In this case, a faulty value in the numerator may go undetected, since the data of the target FP register is not affected. We still consider this to be a problem, as this may cause intermediate events in the computation of the result to remain out of reach. Fortunately, our accelerators supported the collection of coverage data [4] and we were able to validate that the required events were indeed hit.

Output faults represent problems in computing the output values. We injected these by modifying the value of the expected results. Exception faults represent wrongful behavior, such as taking an exception when it should not have been taken or vice versa. For both of these types, our tool invariably detected all faults and was able to pin-point the problematic instruction.

Software bugs are an important issue that is a major concern in validation. Software bugs may trigger false positives and false negatives, resulting in a lot of menace in comparison to the real bugs. Our tool's framework has a certain degree of robustness against software bugs because of two important reasons: *(i)* We are able to run the program, when in hardware mode, on a software reference model to verify it and *(ii)* The program is rather generic, and the main changes between different runs are the data tables. In other words, once we verify that the reloading sequence is fully functional, it works regardless of the subsequent floating point instruction; same goes for the compare routine.

4.2 Field Trial

As part of the signoff process for one of the next IBM Power designs the need arised to run roughly 85 million test-cases in simulation. The verification team decided to, in order to meet the deadline, make use of our tool to run roughly 35 million of these test-cases on a single accelerator that was allocated to them (the same type of accelerator we used to gather the experimental results).

The test-cases were divided to 700 sets of 50,000 test-cases. Each set was converted to a single program using our tool, and then simulated using the acceleraor. The simulation time of each set was roughly 20 minutes. Overall, three weeks work were required to simulated all 35 million test-cases (we note that the net time required for this is 10 days, but the floating-point verification team shared the accelerator with other teams as well).

The verification team estimates that running the same set of test-cases in simulation would have required two and a half months[4]. Thus we clearly see the benefits of the suggested approach in the field.

---

[4] Since all design units have to go through the signoff process, allocating more simulation resources to this team was not an option.

5   Conclusions and Future Work

We introduced a method that enables the verification engineer to convert a large set of pre-generated test-cases into a self-contained self-checking program. Running this program on an accelerator provides the ability to quickly verify that modifications made to the hardware logic did not introduce new bugs. We demonstrated this technique on floating point data path verification.

Our solution focuses on the data path. We intend to augment it with irritator threads [3] to increase the quality of the test-cases.

References

1. Incisive simulation acceleration deployment,
   http://www.cadence.com/rl/Resources/application_notes/
   CDN_Incisive_Simulation_Acceleration_Deployment.pdf
2. FDIV replacement program (statistical analysis of floating point flaw). Technical report (1994), http://www.intel.com/support/processors/pentium/sb/
   CS-013007.htm
3. Ludden, J.M., Rimon, M., Hickerson, B.G., Adir, A.: Advances in simultaneous multithreading testcase generation methods. In: Barner, S., Kroening, D., Raz, O. (eds.) HVC 2010. LNCS, vol. 6504, pp. 146–160. Springer, Heidelberg (2011)
4. Adir, A., Nahir, A., Ziv, A., Meissner, C., Schumann, J.: Reaching coverage closure in post-silicon validation. In: Barner, S., Kroening, D., Raz, O. (eds.) HVC 2010. LNCS, vol. 6504, pp. 60–75. Springer, Heidelberg (2011)
5. Aharoni, M., Asaf, S., Fournier, L., Koyfman, A., Nagel, R.: FPgen - a deep-knowledge test generator for floating point verification. In: Proceedings of the 8th High-Level Design Validation and Test Workshop, pp. 17–22 (2003)
6. Chen, S.-H., et al.: Hardware/software co-designed accelerator for vector graphics applications. In: 2011 IEEE 9th Symposium on Application Specific Processors (SASP), pp. 108–114 (June 2011)
7. Clarke, E.M., Grumberg, O., Peled, D.A.: Model Checking. MIT-Press (1999)
8. Copty, S., Fine, S., Ur, S., Yom-Tov, E., Ziv, A.: A probabilistic alternative to regression suites. Theor. Comput. Sci. 404(3), 219–234 (2008)
9. Darringer, J., Davidson, E., Hathaway, D., Koenemann, B., Lavin, M., Morrell, J., Rahmat, K., Roesner, W., Schanzenbach, E., Tellez, G., Trevillyan, L.: EDA in IBM: past, present, and future. IEEE Transactions on Computer-Aided Design of Integrated Circuits and Systems 19(12), 1476–1497 (2000)
10. Das, S., Mohanty, R., Dasgupta, P., Chakrabarti, P.P.: Synthesis of system verilog assertions. In: Proceedings of the Conference on Design, Automation and Test in Europe: Designers' Forum, DATE 2006, Leuven, Belgium, pp. 70–75. European Design and Automation Association (2006)
11. Guralnik, E., Aharoni, M., Birnbaum, A.J., Koyfman, A.: Simulation-based verification of floating-point division. IEEE Trans. Computers 60(2), 176–188 (2011)
12. International technology roadmap for semiconductors 2009 edition - design. Website,
    http://www.itrs.net/Links/2009ITRS/2009Chapters_2009Tables/
    2009_Design.pdf
13. Kalla, R., Sinharoy, B.: POWER7: IBM's next generation balanced POWER server chip. In: Hot Chips 21 (2009)

14. Matalon, S., et al.: Building transaction-based acceleration regression environment using plan-driven verification approach,
    http://www.cdnusers.org/community/incisive/Vtp_dvcon2007
    _tbaregression.pdf
15. May, C., Silha, E., Simpson, R., Warren, H. (eds.): The PowerPC Architecture. Morgan Kaufmann (1994)
16. Moffitt, M.D., Günther, G.E.: Scalable scheduling for hardware-accelerated functional verification. In: ICAPS (2011)
17. Naveh, Y., et al.: Constraint-based random stimuli generation for hardware verification. In: AAAI (2006)
18. Singerman, E., et al.: Transaction based pre-to-post silicon validation. In: DAC, pp. 564–568 (2011)
19. Storm, J.: Random test generators for microprocessor design validation (2006),
    http://www.inf.ufrgs.br/emicro
20. Wile, B., Goss, J.C., Roesner, W.: Comprehensive Functional Verification - The Complete Industry Cycle. Elsevier (2005)

Coverage-Based Trace Signal Selection
for Fault Localisation in Post-silicon Validation

Charlie Shucheng Zhu[1,*], Georg Weissenbacher[2,**], and Sharad Malik[1]

[1] Princeton University
[2] Vienna University of Technology, Austria

Abstract. Post-silicon validation is the time-consuming process of detecting and diagnosing defects in prototype silicon. It targets electrical
and functional defects that escaped detection during pre-silicon verification. While the at-speed execution of test scenarios facilitates a higher
test coverage than pre-silicon simulation, this comes at the cost of limited
observability of signals in the integrated circuit. This limitation compli-
cates the localisation of the cause underlying a defect. Trace buffers,
designed to store a limited execution history, partially alleviate but do
not entirely remedy the problem. Since trace buffers typically record only
a small fraction of the system state over at most a few thousand cycles,
their utility is contingent on the cautious selection of traced signals.

This paper presents a technique for the automated selection of trace
signals. While the aim of existing selection strategies is typically to enable the (early) detection of defects or to maximise the recoverable state
information, our objective is to facilitate the subsequent automated localisation of faults using consistency-based diagnosis. To this end, we
use integer linear programming and automated test pattern generation
to identify a subset of state signals through which potential failures are
likely to propagate. We demonstrate that our technique complements our
previous work on SAT-based fault localisation using backbones. In that
context, we evaluate the utility of our results on two OpenCores designs.
We show that for this purpose, our technique generates a better selection
of trace signals than a related approach recently presented by Yang and
Touba.

1 Introduction

Post-Silicon validation deals with debugging early silicon prototypes with the
goal of detecting and diagnosing design faults. These faults may be functional,
i.e. logical bugs, or electrical, i.e. faults in the circuit design. Electrical faults tend
to be trickier to detect since these may be triggered only under very specific conditions and thus this behaviour may not be easily repeatable. In comparison to

* The author acknowledge the support of the Gigascale Systems Research Center, one
of six research centers funded under the Focus Center Research Program (FCRP),
a Semiconductor Research Corporation entity.
** Funded by the Vienna Science and Technology Fund (WWTF) through project
VRG11-005.

A. Biere, A. Nahir, and T. Vos (Eds.): HVC 2012, LNCS 7857, pp. 132–147, 2013.

pre-silicon validation using simulation and formal verification, post-silicon validation is no longer limited by slow software models, but rather can run substantially large traces at speed. However, unlike these software models, there is very limited signal observability. The observability at the chip outputs is typically enhanced by adding additional state to the chip, referred to as trace buffers, which buffer the values of a small set of carefully selected signals, referred to as trace signals, typically for a few thousand cycles. These buffered values are then used to both detect and diagnose/localise faults. Since the number of trace signals needs to be small to keep the trace buffer overhead low, these need to be carefully selected. This is generally done manually using key designer insight. While this may be justified for high volume parts such as processors, automation of this step is highly desirable for application to a broad range of designs. This paper addresses the problem of automatically selecting the set of trace signals for their application in aiding fault diagnosis in post-silicon validation. We present a coverage-based algorithm for this. The algorithm takes as input the design, the set of possible faults, the set of candidate trace signals and a set of test vectors. In this paper we limit the candidate set of trace signals to be the existing state bits in the design, though that is not a requirement of our approach. The algorithm first determines, for each fault and the set of test vectors, the set of candidate signals that the fault-effect, i.e., error, propagates to. It then selects a subset of candidates that maximally covers, i.e., detects, the fault set. This coverage problem is naturally framed as an integer linear programming (ILP) problem. This formulation is related to recent work done in trace signal selection by Yang and Touba [19]. However, the formulation in that paper is geared towards error detection and not fault diagnosis. For a given erroneous trace, the problem of fault diagnosis or localisation deals with identifying which gate had the fault and which cycle the fault was activated. In our recent work [21] we presented an algorithm for fault diagnosis that uses trace buffers. However, the focus of that paper was not on the trace signals, and thus these were arbitrarily selected in that work. The work in this paper is complementary in that it provides a systematic way to select trace signals. In our experimental evaluation in this paper we show that this coverage based trace selection compares favorably with the arbitrary selection in fault diagnosis. We also show that it compares favourably with the error detection based selection [19] by Yang and Touba applied to fault diagnosis. This evaluation is done using two microcontroller designs from OpenCores.

This paper is organized as follows. § 2 covers the background and related work. The technical contributions are presented in § 3 and the experimental evaluation in § 4. Finally § 5 provides some concluding remarks.

2   Background and Related Work

2.1   Automatic Test Pattern Generation

Automatic test pattern generation (ATPG) is concerned with the construction of test scenarios that make manufacturing faults surface if present (for a tutorial,

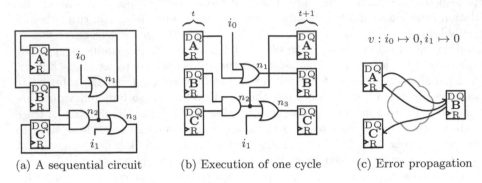

(a) A sequential circuit   (b) Execution of one cycle   (c) Error propagation

Fig. 1. Error propagation in a simple sequential circuit

see [5]). The approach is typically based on simple gate-level fault models, the most popular of which is the *single stuck-at fault* model, in which the output of a single gate is permanently stuck at a fixed logic value (0 or 1). For such a fault to become *observable*, its effect (i.e., the incorrect output signal of the gate) has to *propagate* through the circuit (along a *sensitised* path) to one of the primary outputs or to an observable latch. This may not happen with each trace, since the erroneous signal might be masked by other signals.

Example 1. Consider the propagation of errors in the sequential circuit in Figure 1a. The simple circuit comprises three latches (labelled **A**, **B**, and **C**) and a combinational part with two input signals i_0 and i_1. For the sake of simplicity, we omit the primary output signals and assume that latch **C** is observable. Assume that the output of the AND gate in Figure 1a is permanently stuck-at 1, leading to an erroneous result in case the values stored in the latches **B** and **C** are 0 and 1, respectively. For this error to propagate to the latch **C** in the current execution cycle, the input signal i_1 needs to be 0.

The aim of ATPG is to automatically generate input patterns that result in the activation and propagation of faults. In order to trigger the stuck-at 1 fault in Example 1, one of the latches **B** or **C** must hold the value 0. For the fault to propagate to latch **C** through the subsequent OR gate, it is necessary that i_1 is 0. Accordingly, we require input signals that result in different logic values for at least one of the observable signals of the original and the faulty circuit.

Test pattern generation for digital circuits can be formulated as a Boolean satisfiability problem (c.f. [5, §22.2.3]), which can be solved using efficient satisfiability checkers (e.g., [14,9]). For combinational circuits, this approach is illustrated in Figure 2. By using an XOR gate (or *miter*) to combine the outputs of the original circuit and a duplicate circuit into which a stuck-at fault has been injected, we obtain a new circuit whose output is one if and only if the values of the latches and input signals are chosen such that the fault is activated and propagates to an observable output. Using a satisfiability checker and a propositional encoding of the resulting circuit, we can derive appropriate logic values.

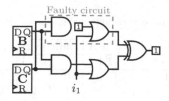

Fig. 2. ATPG as Boolean satisfiability problem

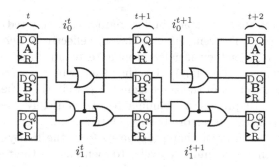

Fig. 3. Execution of two cycles

A similar technique can be applied for sequential circuits. In this setting, it is sufficient if the error propagates to an observable output or latch after several execution cycles. While the error in Example 1 may not propagate to latch **C** immediately, it does propagate to latch **A**, from where (in a favourable test scenario) it may propagate to latch **B** and eventually latch **C** in subsequent execution cycles. In Boolean satisfiability-based ATPG, this is taken into account by *unwinding* the circuit into an *iterative logic array* (ILA) [1], as shown in Figure 3 for two execution cycles. By encoding a sequence of execution cycles into a propositional formula, it is possible to obtain a multi-cycle test scenario in which the fault is activated and propagates. We refer to this approach as *sequential* ATPG.

Related Work. Mutation testing is a technique related to ATPG that is applied in software testing. The test-case generation technique for Simulink programs presented in [2], for instance, resembles the ATPG approach described above in that it uses fault models (such as stuck-at faults). The aim of mutation testing, however, is typically to evaluate or increase the coverage of a test suite. Moreover, unlike ATPG, mutation testing for software programs is typically based on syntactic modifications (*mutations*, respectively) of the source code rather than on fault models.

2.2   Trace Signal Selection Using Integer Linear Programming

In an integrated circuit of realistic dimensions only a fraction the system state (stored the in latches) can be recorded in a trace buffer. In Example 1, for

Table 1. Fault-free and erroneous executions of the circuit in Figure 1

	Fault-free		Fault in **A**		Fault in **B**		Fault in **C**	
	t	$t+1$	t	$t+1$	t	$t+1$	t	$t+1$
A	0	0	**1**	0	0	**1**	0	0
B	0	0	0	**1**	**1**	0	0	0
C	1	0	1	0	1	**1**	0	0
Functional vector $v : i_0 \mapsto 0, i_1 \mapsto 0$								

instance, we assume that the trace buffer maintains a (limited) history of the logic values of latch **C**. The remaining latches are effectively *unobservable*. Consequently, only errors that eventually propagate to an observable output (or latch) can be detected. Accordingly, whether (and when) an error is caught is contingent on the selection of the trace signals (as well as on the test scenario).

Yang and Touba [19] propose a technique to automatically select trace signals based on the propagation of errors between latches. The approach is based on the following insight: an error that propagates from the faulty gate to a latch may keep propagating over multiple cycles (depending on the test pattern that is applied) until it eventually corrupts an observable signal.

The authors of [19] construct an *error transmission matrix* which holds, for a fixed set of single-cycle test patterns, the information between which latches errors may propagate. The matrix is then transformed into an *integer linear programming* (ILP) problem whose optimal solution identifies a set of latches which capture as many errors propagated from latches in as many test scenarios as possible.

Example 2. We continue working in the setting of Example 1. Figure 1b illustrates one execution cycle in form of an ILA. The latches on the left side represent the state of the circuit in time-frame t, the latches to the right represent the subsequent time-frame $t+1$.

Table 1 shows four single-cycle executions of the circuit in Figure 1a, starting from a state in which the latches **A** and **B** hold the value 0, and latch **C** holds the value 1. The input test vector is the same in all executions ($i_0 \mapsto 0, i_1 \mapsto 0$). The first execution is fault-free, whereas we introduced transient errors by flipping the values of the latches **A**, **B**, and **C**, respectively, in the remaining three executions. Each of these errors represents a gate-level fault that propagated to the respective latch, whose bits are highlighted in bold in the table. Table 1 illustrates that in the given scenario, an error in **A** propagates to **B**, and an error in **B** propagates to **A** as well as to **C**. The error introduced in **C** does not propagate, since it is masked by the value of **B**. The error propagation between the three latches in this situation is indicated in Figure 1c.

Following the methodology presented by Yang and Touba [19], we obtain the error transmission matrix in Figure 4a. Additional test patterns can be encoded in the transmission matrix by adding more rows. For clarity, we omit the optimisation step described in [19] which reduces the size of the matrix by grouping together *independent* latches whose information can be compressed.

$$\text{max: } \sum_{i=0}^{2} R_i$$

$$
\begin{array}{ll}
\text{$\mathbf{A}$ $\mathbf{B}$ $\mathbf{C}$} & \\
\end{array}
$$

$$
\begin{array}{c}
\mathbf{A}\,\mathbf{B}\,\mathbf{C} \\
\begin{array}{c}
(\mathbf{A}, v) \\
(\mathbf{B}, v) \\
(\mathbf{C}, v)
\end{array}
\begin{bmatrix}
0 & 1 & 0 \\
1 & 0 & 1 \\
0 & 0 & 0
\end{bmatrix}
\end{array}
$$

$$
\begin{aligned}
S_{\mathbf{B}} &\geq & R_0 \\
S_{\mathbf{A}} + S_{\mathbf{C}} &\geq & R_1 \\
0 &\geq & R_2 \\
R_0, R_1, R_2 &\in & \{0, 1\} \\
S_{\mathbf{A}}, S_{\mathbf{B}}, S_{\mathbf{C}} &\in & \{0, 1\} \\
S_{\mathbf{A}} + S_{\mathbf{B}} + S_{\mathbf{C}} &= & 1
\end{aligned}
$$

(a) Transmission matrix   (b) ILP problem

Fig. 4. Selecting trace signals using integer linear programming

The ILP problem obtained from the transmission matrix in Figure 4a in order to select *one* signal to trace is shown in Figure 4b. Each R_i ($i \in \{0, 1, 2\}$) represents a row, and a value of 1 indicates that the corresponding error propagates to a selected latch in the respective test scenario. Consequently, the objective is to maximise the sum $R_0 + R_1 + R_2$. Whether an error is captured in a latch depends on the latches that are traced. In our example, we restrict the trace buffer to only one latch; accordingly, $S_{\mathbf{A}} + S_{\mathbf{B}} + S_{\mathbf{C}} = 1$. Finally, each row in the transmission matrix determines which errors can be captured. The line $S_{\mathbf{A}} + S_{\mathbf{C}} \geq R_1$, for instance, encodes that an error in latch **B** can be captured by either latch **A** or latch **C** in the test scenario v.

Note that this ILP problem does not have a unique optimal solution: assigning 1 to either $S_{\mathbf{A}}$, $S_{\mathbf{B}}$, or $S_{\mathbf{C}}$ maximises the objective. A solution $S_{\mathbf{A}} = 1$, $S_{\mathbf{B}} = 0$, and $S_{\mathbf{C}} = 0$ returned by the ILP solver indicates that we should trace the value in latch **A**. No matter which latch we choose, according to Table 1 we will only be able to track either the error in **A**, or the error in **B** (since faults of **C** do not propagate in this setting).

Related Work. Hung and Wilton [11] base their signal selection algorithm on the expected number of reachable system states that can be "ruled out" by observing these signals. This approach relies on a computationally expensive approximation of the reachable state space.

Yang et al. [20] propose to use unsatisfiable cores obtained from a test scenario that results in a failure and a propositional encoding of the circuit to identify signals that are relevant to the analysis of the failure. Moreover, they propose a SAT-based technique to select trace signals from which relevant signals that cannot be observed can be reconstructed.

Prabhakar and Hsiao [15] use a multiplexed trace signal scheme which enables them to effectively double the number of signals that can be traced. Moreover, the paper proposes a technique to identify signals that can be inferred from traced signals using logical implication and therefore need not be recorded.

Paula et al. [7] proposes to compute *signatures* of states to narrow down the set of predecessor states of the crash state, effectively enabling backwards state stepping. This allows them to identify the error in an earlier cycle in a subsequent test run. A follow-up paper [8] describes how repeated test runs can be used to arbitrarily increase the number of execution cycles which can be recorded by a trace buffer. Both techniques require that the erroneous behaviour can be reproduced repeatedly.

A detailed discussion of techniques that use compression techniques to increase observability is provided by [19].

2.3   SAT-Based Fault Localisation

The objective of the trace signal selection algorithm in [19] is to detect as many errors as early as possible. Detecting an error, however, is often the easy part of the post-silicon validation phase. Due to the observability limitations in integrated circuits, *locating* the cause of the error can be a formidable challenge.

Consistency-based diagnosis [16] is a technique that aims at locating the cause of an observed error by identifying fault candidates based on the *golden model* of a system and observations of its actual implementation. It relies on automated reasoning to identify the smallest set of components that explains the inconsistency between the hardware design and the behaviour of the manufactured prototype. The technique has seen a recent spike in popularity (e.g., [17,18,4,3,21]) due to the improved scalability of satisfiability solvers. The following example illustrates the idea underlying consistency-based diagnosis.

Example 3. Recall the setting from Example 1, in which we postulated a stuck-at 1 fault for the AND-gate in the circuit in Figure 1a. The ILA in Figure 1b which represents one execution cycle of this circuit can be encoded as a propositional formula in which $\mathbf{A}^t$, $\mathbf{B}^t$, $\mathbf{C}^t$ and $\mathbf{A}^{t+1}$, $\mathbf{B}^{t+1}$, $\mathbf{C}^{t+1}$ refer to the values held by the latches in time-frames t and $t+1$, respectively:

$$(\mathbf{A}^{t+1} = \mathbf{B}^t \cdot \mathbf{C}^t) \quad \cdot \quad (\mathbf{B}^{t+1} = \mathbf{A}^t + i_0) \quad \cdot \quad (\mathbf{C}^{t+1} = \mathbf{A}^{t+1} + i_1) \qquad (1)$$

As a result of the faulty AND gate, the logic values in $\mathbf{A}^{t+1}$ and $\mathbf{C}^{t+1}$ are corrupted during the execution of the manufactured chip. This fact as well as the initial state and the input values are encoded in the following propositional formula:

$$\left(\begin{array}{l} (\mathbf{A}^t = 0) \ \cdot \ (\mathbf{B}^t = 0) \ \cdot \ (\mathbf{C}^t = 1) \cdot \\ (\mathbf{A}^{t+1} = 1) \cdot (\mathbf{B}^{t+1} = 0) \cdot (\mathbf{C}^{t+1} = 1) \end{array} \right) \cdot (i_0 = 0) \cdot (i_1 = 0) \qquad (2)$$

Due to the discrepancy between the *golden model* in Figure 1a and the behaviour of the manufactured prototype the conjunction of the formulae 1 and 2 is unsatisfiable. In order to determine the cause of the discrepancy, we can use a *partial maximum-satisfiability* (MAX-SAT) solver (see [10], for instance) to identify a minimal set of conjuncts of Formula 1 that are responsible for the inconsistency of Formula 1 and Formula 2. In our example, dropping the constraint $(\mathbf{A}^{t+1} = \mathbf{B}^t \cdot \mathbf{C}^t)$ makes the formula satisfiable, which indicates that a faulty AND gate in Figure 1b is a possible explanation for the inconsistency.

In Example 3 we assume that all latches are observable. While this is a valid assumption in the context of *pre-silicon* debugging, where all signal values can be determined by means of simulation, this information is typically not available in the post-silicon setting. In this setting, the approach described in Example 3 may fail: eliminating the information about $\mathbf{B}^t$, $\mathbf{C}^t$, $\mathbf{B}^{t+1}$, and $\mathbf{C}^{t+1}$ from Formula 2 makes the conjunction of the formulae 1 and 2 satisfiable.

This problem can be addressed by means of unwinding the sequential circuit sufficiently often and constraining the resulting ILA with the information collected in the trace buffer.

Example 4. The two-cycle ILA in Figure 3 can be translated into the following propositional formula:

$$
\begin{aligned}
(\mathbf{A}^{t+1} = \mathbf{B}^t \cdot \mathbf{C}^t) \quad \cdot \quad (\mathbf{B}^{t+1} = \mathbf{A}^t + i_0^t) \;\cdot\; (\mathbf{C}^{t+1} = \mathbf{A}^{t+1} + i_1^t). \\
(\mathbf{A}^{t+2} = \mathbf{B}^{t+1} \cdot \mathbf{C}^{t+1}) \cdot (\mathbf{B}^{t+2} = \mathbf{A}^{t+1} + i_0^{t+1}) \cdot (\mathbf{C}^{t+2} = \mathbf{A}^{t+2} + i_1^{t+1})
\end{aligned}
\tag{3}
$$

Assume that the trace buffer recorded the information $(\mathbf{A}^t = 0)$, $(\mathbf{A}^{t+1} = 1)$, and $(\mathbf{A}^{t+2} = 1)$. Constraining Formula 3 with the information obtained from the trace buffer and the test pattern $i_0^t = 0$, $i_1^t = 0$, $i_0^{t+1} = 0$, and $i_1^{t+1} = 0$ results in an unsatisfiable SAT instance. A subsequent analysis yields that dropping either $(\mathbf{B}^{t+1} = \mathbf{A}^t + i_0^t)$ or $(\mathbf{A}^{t+2} = \mathbf{B}^{t+1} \cdot \mathbf{C}^{t+1})$ makes the instance satisfiable and identifies either the OR gate in time-frame t or the AND gate in time-frame $t+1$ as potential culprits.

Example 4 shows that a consistency-based diagnosis may report more than one fault candidate. In general, this problem cannot be avoided (even if all latches are observable), since both gates are valid fault candidates. Note, however, that the approach identified an exact time-frame in which the respective components may have failed, making it suitable for the analysis of intermittent or transient faults.

For large circuits, the number of execution cycles that can be analysed is limited by the scalability of the underlying logic solver. While in theory it is always sufficient to analyse the *entire* execution, in practice the size of the resulting propositional formula would likely be prohibitive. This problem is addressed in [12] and [21] by *sliding* a *window* of fixed size (backwards) along the execution trace, thus partitioning the execution trace into ILAs of fixed size. The technique presented in [12] targets design debugging and requires full observability to compute Craig interpolants [6], which are used to propagate information across windows. Zhu et al. [21] is aimed at post-silicon validation and relies on *backbones* (see, e.g., [13]) to propagate state information across windows. The backbone of a satisfiable propositional formula comprises all literals which take the *same* value in *all* satisfying assignments of the formula.

Example 5. We continue working in the setting of Example 4. Assume that the scalability of the solver limits the consistency-based analysis technique to windows of size one. As previously established, the information $(\mathbf{A}^{t+1} = 1)$, $(\mathbf{A}^{t+2} = 1)$ and $i_0^{t+1} = 0$, $i_1^{t+1} = 0$ is insufficient to yield an inconsistency in

Table 2. Fault-free and erroneous 2-cycle executions of the circuit in Figure 1

	Fault-free			Fault in $\mathbf{A}$		
	t	$t+1$	$t+2$	t	$t+1$	$t+2$
$\mathbf{A}$	0	0	0	1	0	1
$\mathbf{B}$	0	0	0	0	1	0
$\mathbf{C}$	1	1	0	1	1	1
	$i_0^t = 0,\ i_1^t = 1,\ i_0^{t+1} = 0,\ i_1^{t+1} = 0$					

time-frame $t+1$ of Figure 3. However, from $(\mathbf{A}^{t+2} = 1)$ and $(\mathbf{A}^{t+2} = \mathbf{B}^{t+1} \cdot \mathbf{C}^{t+1})$ (c.f. Formula 3) we can derive the *backbone* $\mathbf{B}^{t+1} = 1$ and $\mathbf{C}^{t+1} = 1$, which is inconsistent with $(\mathbf{A}^t = 0)$, $i_0^t = 0$, and time-frame t in Figure 3, resulting in the fault candidate $(\mathbf{B}^{t+1} = \mathbf{A}^t + i_0^t)$.

Similarly, from $(\mathbf{A}^t = 0)$, $i_0^t = 0$, and time-frame t in Figure 3 we can derive the backbone $\mathbf{B}^{t+1} = 0$, which is inconsistent with $\mathbf{A}^{t+2} = 1$ and time-frame $t + 1$. Accordingly, the analysis yields the AND gate corresponding to $\mathbf{A}^{t+2} = \mathbf{B}^{t+1} \cdot \mathbf{C}^{t+1}$ as a fault candidate.

Related Work. As previously mentioned, there are a number of papers that apply consistency-based diagnosis to address *pre-silicon* debugging (with full observability) by constraining a *faulty* RTL model with *correct* input/output pairs (given as a specification) [17,18,4,3].

3   Improving Coverage-Based Trace Signal Selection

In this section, we propose two improvements over the ILP-based signal selection approach of Yang and Touba [19]. Our modifications to the algorithm address the following limitations:

- The approach outlined in §2.2 does not directly take advantage of the *transitivity* of error propagation. As pointed out at the end of §2.1, an error may propagate through non-observable latches for several execution cycles until it corrupts a latch monitored by the trace buffer.
- The fault model of [19] is applied exclusively to latches. Depending on the structure of the circuit, however, some latches may have a higher probability of being corrupted/propagated by gate-level faults than others and thus also may be more useful for fault localisation.

3.1   Multi-cycle Coverage

The following example illustrates the limitation of a trace signal selection algorithm that is based on a propagation depth of one.

Example 6. Table 2 shows a correct and an erroneous execution of the sequential circuit in Figure 1a. As in Example 2, we introduce a transient error by flipping the value of one latch in the execution. Unlike in Example 2, however, the executions in Table 2 have two cycles. As mentioned previously, an error in latch **A** propagates to latch **B** within one cycle. After an additional execution cycle, however, the error corrupts both latch **A** and latch **C**. If we add this information to the error transmission matrix and the ILP encoding in Figure 4, we are able to derive that observing latch **A** or latch **C**, but not latch **B**, is the optimal solution.

3.2   Injecting Faults in Combinational Logic

The starting point of the analysis in [19] is that a gate-level fault has already propagated to a latch. Depending on the structure of the circuit, however, certain latches might be more susceptible to capturing an erroneous signal originating in the combinational logic and thus also have greater value in fault localisation.

Example 7. In the sequential circuit in Figure 1a, a fault in the AND gate may propagate to latches **A** and **C**. A fault in the OR gates may propagate to latch **B** and latch **C**, respectively. Accordingly, if all gates are equally likely to fail, then latch **C** has a higher probability of being corrupted.

Motivated by the concerns discussed in § 3.1 and § 3.2, the following section describes our modifications to the approach of [19].

3.3   Integer Linear Programming Encoding

To take the structure of the circuit into account (see §3.2), we inject faults in the gates of the combinational part of the circuit *as well as* in the latches. A set of fault simulations are applied on each injected fault repeatedly. Unlike the method proposed in [19], the test patterns used for fault simulation are multi-cycle and generated by sequential ATPG (as described in §2.1). ATPG helps to provide tests which result in the activation and the propagation of the fault to a latch (or primary output). From the fault simulations, we determine the set of latches to which the fault can propagate and add a row to the error transmission matrix accordingly. The corresponding ILP problem can then be built as described in §2.2.

Example 8. We continue working on the setting from Example 7. Suppose we have obtained a 2-cycle test pattern from ATPG. The same test pattern as in Example 6 are adopted. Transient faults are injected in both latches and gates. Table 3 shows the correct and erroneous execution of all injected faults. With the same approach as §2.2, we can obtain the equivalent ILP problem in Figure 5. For simplicity, we assume that trace signals can be observed with equal costs on all latches in this paper. In general, the cost for tracing certain signals depends on the structure of circuit. To favor certain latches, we can intentionally duplicate their corresponding rows in the transmission matrix. Duplicating rows in a transmission matrix is acceptable, because the ILP is not the bottleneck of scalability in our work. Additional details are provided at the end of §4.2.

Table 3. 2-cycle execution of faults in both latches and internal gates

	Fault-free			Fault in **A**			Fault in **B**			Fault in **C**		
	t	$t+1$	$t+2$	t	$t+1$	$t+2$	t	$t+1$	$t+2$	t	$t+1$	$t+2$
A	0	0	0	1	0	1	0	1	0	0	0	0
B	0	0	0	0	1	0	1	0	1	0	0	0
C	1	1	0	1	1	1	1	1	0	0	1	0
$i_0^t = 0,\ i_1^t = 1,\ i_0^{t+1} = 0,\ i_1^{t+1} = 0$												

	Fault-free			Fault in n_1			Fault in n_2			Fault in n_3		
	t	$t+1$	$t+2$	t	$t+1$	$t+2$	t	$t+1$	$t+2$	t	$t+1$	$t+2$
A	0	0	0	0	0	1	0	1	0	0	0	0
B	0	0	0	0	1	0	0	0	1	0	0	0
C	1	1	0	1	1	1	1	1	0	1	0	0
$i_0^t = 0,\ i_1^t = 1,\ i_0^{t+1} = 0,\ i_1^{t+1} = 0$												

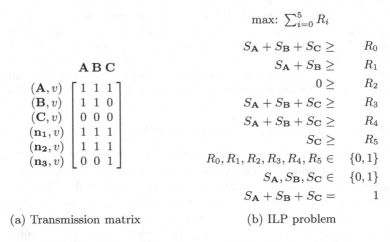

$$\max: \sum_{i=0}^{5} R_i$$

$$
\begin{array}{ABC}
 & \mathbf{A}\ \mathbf{B}\ \mathbf{C} \\
(\mathbf{A},v) & 1\ 1\ 1 \\
(\mathbf{B},v) & 1\ 1\ 0 \\
(\mathbf{C},v) & 0\ 0\ 0 \\
(\mathbf{n_1},v) & 1\ 1\ 1 \\
(\mathbf{n_2},v) & 1\ 1\ 1 \\
(\mathbf{n_3},v) & 0\ 0\ 1
\end{array}
$$

$$S_\mathbf{A} + S_\mathbf{B} + S_\mathbf{C} \geq R_0$$
$$S_\mathbf{A} + S_\mathbf{B} \geq R_1$$
$$0 \geq R_2$$
$$S_\mathbf{A} + S_\mathbf{B} + S_\mathbf{C} \geq R_3$$
$$S_\mathbf{A} + S_\mathbf{B} + S_\mathbf{C} \geq R_4$$
$$S_\mathbf{C} \geq R_5$$
$$R_0, R_1, R_2, R_3, R_4, R_5 \in \{0,1\}$$
$$S_\mathbf{A}, S_\mathbf{B}, S_\mathbf{C} \in \{0,1\}$$
$$S_\mathbf{A} + S_\mathbf{B} + S_\mathbf{C} = 1$$

(a) Transmission matrix   (b) ILP problem

Fig. 5. ILP problem with coverage on faults of internal gates

The fact that we use *sequential* ATPG to determine a set of latches to which a fault may propagate addresses the concerns described in §3.1. By injecting faults not only in latches but also in internal gates, we effectively obtain a larger set of latches that are potentially corrupted, which increases the intersection of latches that capture several faults. We use a fixed number of cycles for the generation of the test scenarios; details are provided in § 4.

4   Experimental Evaluation

4.1   Trace Signal Selection

In our experiments, we evaluated our methodology using the single stuck-at-fault model on two benchmarks from Opencores.org: the 68HC05 (127 latches)

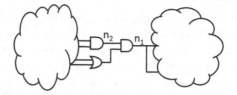

Fig. 6. Nodes with different fanout degrees

and 8051 (2794 latches) microcontrollers[1]. This fault model is chosen for its convenience as it is well understood. This is not a limitation of our approach. Faults are injected in both latches and internal gates and fault simulation is used to build an error transmission matrix. Two issues need careful consideration in constructing the error transmission matrix.

First, each row in the error transmission matrix represents the detection of a fault in the circuit. Including all possible faults, whose number is proportional to the size of the circuit, can result in very large matrices. To reduce the number of faults that need to be considered, we limit the fault sites to the outputs of fanout-free regions and take advantage of well-known results on fault equivalence. As shown in Figure 6, node n_1 has a fanout-degree of two, while the fanout-degrees for node n_2 is one. A stuck-at-1 fault occurs at node n_2. If this fault is activated by a vector and propagates to node n_1, it is equivalent to a stuck-at-1 fault at n_1. If the fault on node n_2 is not propagated to node n_1 for a vector, it is masked. Thus, the two rows corresponding to these two stuck-at-1 faults at n_1 and n_2 in the error transmission matrix are exactly the same. We refer to those nodes with fanout-degree larger than 1 as fanout-points. As a result, it is sufficient to consider faults on fanout-points without losing any error transmission information.

Second, to build the error transmission matrix, we need to know where each fault can propagate to. This is achieved by using fault simulation. Unlike the proposed method from [19], we use multi-cycle test patterns obtained from sequential ATPG for fault simulation. The test patterns were limited to 6-cycle tests to manage test generation time. A test generated for a fault is used in fault simulation for all the faults.

In our experiments, we limited the number of trace signals to be 5% of the total number of latches which is the candidate set of trace signals. We used the CPLEX ILP solver and AMPL modeling language[2]. For the 68HC05 benchmark, the ILP solver returns 6 optimized trace signals which can capture 63.75% of stuck-at faults. For the 8051 benchmark, 140 trace signals are identified that capture 31.70% of stuck-at faults. This coverage is strongly related to the length of the test vectors since some of the faults may not be covered at all using the 6-cycle tests.

---

[1] OpenCores projects available online at http://opencores.org/project

[2] CPLEX for AMPL available online at http://www.ampl.com/CPLEX

4.2   Evaluation Method

To evaluate the trace signals selected by our methodology, 30 single stuck-at faults are injected to both the 68HC05 and 8051 benchmarks to generate 60 faulty circuits. To mimic the post-silicon debug process, instead of running a real chip prototype, each faulty circuit is simulated by a tailored test vector. The aim of this tailored test vector is to cause the specific fault to be activated and observed at some latch or circuit output, just as an erroneous trace would. The rationale for this is as follows. As our experimentation is based on simulation rather than at-speed post-silicon validation, it is much slower and thus is limited to a length of a few thousand cycles. The likelihood of a bug being detected by a random trace of this length is quite low. As a result, we tailored one test vector for each faulty circuit. Each of these vectors are 3000 cycles long and the bug in the circuit is guaranteed to be activated roughly every 100 cycles. However, there is no guarantee the error will be observed at the outputs or in the trace buffers, and it is exactly this aspect of the fault propagation that we wish to observe. For this purpose, during simulation, the execution trace is recorded on the selected trace buffers and output pins. This is then used as constraints for the offline SAT-based analysis described in §2.3. By using the sliding window analysis along this execution trace, we can determine whether the bug can be localised. Our metric for the quality of the trace signals is the size of the window required to localise the fault. A smaller window indicates a higher quality of selection as it results in a more scalable localisation algorithm. This is because a smaller window means that a smaller number of circuit unfoldings need to be considered in the analysis. Thus with limited capacity of analysis engines such as SAT solvers, the size of the circuit that can be accommodated is much larger.

Compared to trace signal selection, the evaluation phase is more time-consuming. Selecting trace signals only involves one call to the ILP solver, which can easily handle our test cases. However, in the evaluation phase, the SAT solver is called repeatedly for each window and each call is potentially expensive.

4.3   Experimental Results

Three different sets of trace signals are compared in this evaluation process. The first set of trace signals are derived using random selection. The second set of trace signals are selected using the approach of Yang and Touba [19] (latch-fault propagation), i.e., the error transmission matrix is built based on bugs injected only on latches and single-cycle fault propagation. The last set of trace signals are selected based on our approach (all-fault propagation) described above. Further, as described in § 2.3, each set of trace signals is evaluated by sliding windows with backbones.

In Figure 7 and Figure 8, each graph represents one of the two sliding window analyses on different benchmarks. On the x axis, there are 30 randomly injected single faults for both benchmarks. The y axis represents the minimum window size required to detect the corresponding fault by the SAT-based fault localisation approach described in §2.3. We used a limit of 15 time-frames for the size of the sliding window to manage experimental run times.

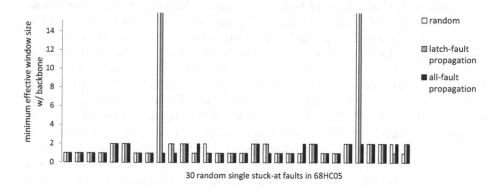

Fig. 7. Minimum window sizes to detect bugs randomly injected in 68HC05 with three different sets of selected trace signals

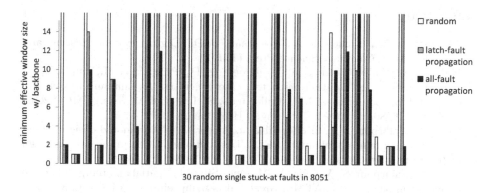

Fig. 8. Minimum window sizes to detect bugs randomly injected in 8051 with three different sets of selected trace signals

The 69hc05 benchmark was the easier case. 28 of the 30 faults could be localised with either random or latch-fault propagation based selection. Only the all-fault propagation method could localise all 30 of them. The 8051 benchmark was the harder case. Random selection allowed localisation for only 8 faults. Latch-fault propagation performed better, succeeding for 16 faults. All-fault propagation did much better by succeeding for 23 faults. Further, for most cases, all-fault propagation was able to localise a fault with a smaller window size compared to the other methods.

5 Conclusions

This paper considers the problem of selecting trace signals in post-silicon validation for use in fault-localisation. It uses a coverage based problem formulation that maximizes the number of faults that can be detected at the trace signals using a limited number of trace signals. In contrast to a the coverage based formulation of Yang and Touba, our formulation considers faults at all circuit sites, and not just latches. This increases the likelihood of fault localisation being able to isolate faults to these sites. Further, in our formulation we consider multi-cycle fault propagation, which more accurately captures real fault propagation compared to the single cycle propagation of Yang and Touba's method. The value of these differences is reflected in the experimental results where we compare various trace signal selection algorithms in terms of their ability to reduce the window size needed in sliding window consistency based fault-localisation. This metric is a proxy for scalability, as a smaller window size indicates that fewer time frames are needed and thus a larger circuit can be accommodated in each time frame. Our method performs much better than both random selection, as well as the Yang and Touba method. Specifically it can detect and localize 14 more faults of a total of 60 faults than the Yang and Touba method.

References

1. Abramovici, M., Breuer, M.A., Friedman, A.D.: Digital systems testing and testable design. Computer Science Press (1990)
2. Brillout, A., He, N., Mazzucchi, M., Kroening, D., Purandare, M., Rümmer, P., Weissenbacher, G.: Mutation-based test case generation for simulink models. In: de Boer, F.S., Bonsangue, M.M., Hallerstede, S., Leuschel, M. (eds.) FMCO 2009. LNCS, vol. 6286, pp. 208–227. Springer, Heidelberg (2010)
3. Chen, Y., Safarpour, S., Marques-Silva, J., Veneris, A.: Automated design debugging with maximum satisfiability. IEEE Transactions on Computer-Aided Design of Integrated Circuits and Systems (TCAD) 29, 1804–1817 (2010)
4. Chen, Y., Safarpour, S., Veneris, A., Marques-Silva, J.: Spatial and temporal design debug using partial MaxSAT. In: Great Lakes Symposium on VLSI, pp. 345–350. ACM (2009)
5. Cheng, K.-T., Wang, L.-C.: Automatic test pattern generation. In: EDA for IC System Design, Verification, and Testing. CRC Press (2006)
6. Craig, W.: Linear reasoning. A new form of the Herbrand-Gentzen theorem 22(3), 250–268 (1957)
7. De Paula, F.M., Gort, M., Hu, A.J., Wilton, S.J.E., Yang, J.: Backspace: formal analysis for post-silicon debug. In: Formal Methods in Computer-Aided Design (FMCAD), pp. 5:1–5:10. IEEE (2008)
8. de Paula, F.M., Nahir, A., Nevo, Z., Orni, A., Hu, A.J.: TAB-Backspace: unlimited-length trace buffers with zero additional on-chip overhead. In: Proceedings of the 48th Design Automation Conference (DAC), pp. 411–416. ACM (2011)
9. Eén, N., Sörensson, N.: An extensible SAT-solver. In: Giunchiglia, E., Tacchella, A. (eds.) SAT 2003. LNCS, vol. 2919, pp. 502–518. Springer, Heidelberg (2004)
10. Fu, Z., Malik, S.: On solving the partial MAX-SAT problem. In: Biere, A., Gomes, C.P. (eds.) SAT 2006. LNCS, vol. 4121, pp. 252–265. Springer, Heidelberg (2006)
11. Hung, E., Wilton, S.: On evaluating signal selection algorithms for post-silicon debug. In: Quality Electronic Design, ISQED (March 2011)
12. Keng, B., Safarpour, S., Veneris, A.G.: Bounded model debugging. IEEE Transactions on Computer-Aided Design of Integrated Circuits and Systems (TCAD) 29(11), 1790–1803 (2010)

13. Marques-Silva, J., Janota, M., Lynce, I.: On computing backbones of propositional theories. In: European Conference on Artificial Intelligence (ECAI), pp. 15–20. IOS Press (2010)
14. Moskewicz, M.W., Madigan, C.F., Zhao, Y., Zhang, L., Malik, S.: Chaff: engineering an efficient SAT solver. In: Design Automation Conference (DAC), pp. 530–535. ACM (2001)
15. Prabhakar, S., Hsiao, M.: Multiplexed trace signal selection using non-trivial implication-based correlation. In: Quality Electronic Design (ISQED), pp. 697–704 (2010)
16. Reiter, R.: A theory of diagnosis from first principles. Artificial Intelligence 32(1), 57–95 (1987)
17. Safarpour, S., Mangassarian, H., Veneris, A.G., Liffiton, M.H., Sakallah, K.A.: Improved design debugging using maximum satisfiability. In: Formal Methods in Computer-Aided Design (FMCAD), pp. 13–19. IEEE (2007)
18. Sülflow, A., Fey, G., Bloem, R., Drechsler, R.: Using unsatisfiable cores to debug multiple design errors. In: Great Lakes Symposium on VLSI, pp. 77–82. ACM (2008)
19. Yang, J.-S., Touba, N.A.: Efficient trace signal selection for silicon debug by error transmission analysis. IEEE Transactions on CAD of Integrated Circuits and Systems 31(3), 442–446 (2012)
20. Yang, Y.-S., Keng, B., Nicolici, N., Veneris, A.G., Safarpour, S.: Automated silicon debug data analysis techniques for a hardware data acquisition environment. In: International Symposium on Quality of Electronic Design. IEEE (2010)
21. Zhu, C.S., Weissenbacher, G., Malik, S.: Post-silicon fault localisation using maximum satisfiability and backbones. In: Formal Methods in Computer-Aided Design (FMCAD). IEEE (2011)

A Novel Approach for Implementing Microarchitectural Verification Plans in Processor Designs

Yoav Katz[1], Michal Rimon[2], and Avi Ziv[1]

[1] IBM Research - Haifa, Israel
{katz,aziv}@il.ibm.com
[2] IBM Server and Technology Group, Haifa, Israel
michalr@il.ibm.com

Abstract. The ever-growing microarchitecture complexity of processors creates a widening gap between the verification plan and the test generation technologies used in its implementation. This gap impacts the cost and quality of the verification process. To overcome this, we introduce a novel test generation platform for processor verification. This approach is based on a scenario description language that is close to the microarchitecture verification plan, and uses new test generation algorithms and a microarchitectural model to support this higher level of abstraction. Initial results on a high end industrial design show our approach reduces the effort of implementing a microarchitectural verification plan and improves the quality of verification.

1 Introduction

The goal of functional verification of processors is to establish the conformance of a processor design to its specification. Today's state of the art verification methodologies is based on a highly automated process that includes stimuli generation, checking, and coverage collection—combined with islands of manual labor [1]. Verification begins with the creation of a verification plan. The plan defines the aspects of the architecture and microarchitecture to be verified and the methods that will perform the verification. Test-case generators play a central role in such automated verification environments. The stimuli generated by these tools need to trigger architecture and microarchitecture events defined by the verification plan and ensure that all the dark corners of the verified design are exercised and the bugs hidden in them are exposed.

The input to a test-case generator is a test-template, which describes at a high level the desired characteristics of the generated test-cases. Given a test-template as input, the test-case generator generates a large set of architecturally valid test-cases that satisfy the template request and fill in the remaining details in a pseudo-random way.

Existing processor-level test-case generators (such as [2,3]) provide a rich language for specifying requests at the instruction-level and a powerful instruction-based solving scheme for generating test-cases that satisfy the instruction level

A. Biere, A. Nahir, and T. Vos (Eds.): HVC 2012, LNCS 7857, pp. 148–161, 2013.

requests. This generation scheme calls for generation of instructions in execution order, one instruction at a time. The generation is interleaved with execution on a software reference model (ISS). This generation scheme has many advantages. First, it breaks the generation problem into a set of smaller, manageable sub-problems. In addition, it allows the generation engine to use the current processor state when generating the next instruction. Many tools formulate the generation of each instruction as a Constraint Satisfaction Problem (CSP) and thus achieve a high level of randomness and user controllability [4].

Advanced microarchitecture techniques such as out-of-order execution, on-chip caching and multi-threading, exploit the growth of available transistor count to deliver improved performance. As processor microarchitecture complexity increases, there is a growing need to thoroughly exercise the microarchitecture and reach all its corner cases. Advances in the verification methodologies and test-generation tools led to new features that target the microarchitecture. For example, tools embed testing knowledge [2] to increase the probability of generating interesting microarchitectural events (e.g., creating register dependency between instructions to trigger pipeline forwarding). The tools also include elaborate user control in the test-template to help the test-case reach specific microarchitectural events, and address the challenges of multithreaded and multiprocessing designs [5, 6].

Nevertheless, we observe a growing gap between the goals of the verification plan, which now targets events deep inside the processor, and the available test generation tools. This impacts both the resulting verification quality and the effort required to complete the verification process. One cause of this gap is the limited support for specifying and generating interactions between instructions. Specifically, users have to invest significant effort in creating the test-templates to generate the required intra-instruction dependencies and adapt them to the specific microarchitecture.

Another outcome of this methodology is that verification know-how as to the best ways to address microarchitecture verification is embedded in the test-templates, but not in the tools. Therefore, applying this knowledge in new test-templates requires significant effort. Moreover, less experienced verification engineers may be unaware of this knowledge and will not apply it in subsequent verification efforts.

There are other approaches for addressing the complexity of modern microarchitectures. One approach calls for a test generator that is fully aware of all the microarchitectural implementation details. Armed with this knowledge and a strong solution engine, the test generator can generate test-cases that reach complex microarchitectural events [7,8]. The main problem with this approach is that creating and maintaining an accurate description of the microarchitecture can be impractical.

Coverage Driven Generation (CDG) is another way to addressing the difficulty of generating stimuli that targets complex microarchitectural events [9]. In this paradigm, machine learning techniques, such as Genetic Algorithms [10], Bayesian networks [9], Markov models [11] and inductive logic programming

(ILP) [12], are used to learn the relation between test-templates and coverage points and modify the test-templates to improve coverage. While there is much research in this area [13], there are few successful applications of CDG in real industrial designs.

Automatic ways to embed microarchitectural testing knowledge into existing test generators were explored by Katz et al. [14]. In this approach, information is collected from simulation traces and automatically converted into instruction-level testing knowledge using machine learning classification algorithms.

In this paper we introduce Test Plan Automation (TPA), a novel test generation approach for processor verification. The approach is based on formulating a scenario description language that is close to the microarchitecture verification plan and using new test generation algorithms and a microarchitectural model to support this higher level of abstraction. Initial results show our approach reduces the effort of implementing a microarchitectural verification plan and improves the quality of verification.

The rest of this paper is organized as follows: In Section 2 , we present the concept and main components of our proposed method. We then describe each of these components in-depth in Sections 3-6. Section 7 describes the experimental results and we conclude in Section 8.

2   Solution Concept

The main goal of TPA is to improve the stimuli generation aspects of the implementation of the microarchitectural verification plan. This goal is achieved in two ways. First, TPA raises the level of abstraction of the test-template language and brings it closer to the verification plan while relying on a microarchitectural model to provide specific details on microarchitecture behavior. In addition, TPA closes the gap between the test-template and the generated test-cases using new stream solving generation algorithms and scenario-level testing knowledge. These are depicted in Figure 1.

The test-template language used in TPA is designed to support the main ingredient of the verification plan, namely scenarios. The basic building blocks of the language are basic scenarios that target simple events that involve a single microarchitectural mechanism. A basic scenario is expressed as a set of instructions and the required constraints between them. An example of such scenario is two instructions that access the same cache line to create a cache hit. The language provides means, such as scenario combinations, to create more complex scenarios from the basic scenarios. For example, a cache hit and a cache miss scenarios can be combined to create a scenario that that hits on the L1 cache and misses on the L2 cache.

Many of the parameters in the scenarios TPA needs to generate come from the microarchitectural mechanisms they operate on and many of the events TPA targets are relevant to several mechanisms. For example, cache hit events are relevant to all the caches in the system. To allow reuse of the scenarios between mechanisms, TPA uses a microarchitectural model that contains the important

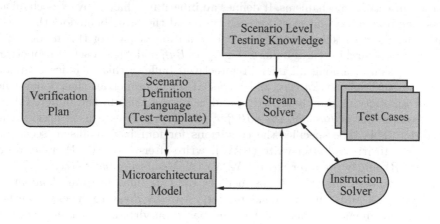

Fig. 1. TPA main components

parameters of these mechanisms. When a scenario is generated, this information is used for filling in scenario details to create a specific scenario that targets the requested event in a specific mechanism.

TPA includes a new test-case generation scheme that is able to effectively satisfy constraints between instructions [15]. It formulates an abstract constraint satisfaction problem (CSP) that captures the essence of the requested scenario. This abstract CSP is solved incrementally and the abstract CSP solution is interleaved with single instruction generation.

To improve the quality of the test-cases it generates, TPA extends the notion of testing knowledge from the instruction-level to the scenario-level. Testing knowledge is the embodiment of expert verification knowledge in the tool such that the tool biases the stimuli toward interesting verification events without the need for explicit direction by the verification engineer. Scenario level testing knowledge automatically elaborates and modifies the original scenario to reach variants of the targeted event or other related events.

3   Microarchitectural Model

TPA is a tool for generating microarchitectural scenarios and thus, information about the microarchitecture is required to reach the needed events. To facilitate maximal reuse of scenarios, we separate the scenario description from the microarchitectural information and use a microarchitectural model that contains all the needed microarchitectural information. TPA does not attempt to provide a fully accurate model that guarantees that microarchitectural events are reached by the scenarios. Instead, TPA aims to significantly increase the probability of reaching these events while minimizing the cost of model development and maintenance.

TPA captures the commonalities between microarchitecture mechanisms both within the design and among different designs by forming an ontology of microarchitectural mechanisms. It defines an inheritance hierarchy of mechanism types, the properties that exist for each type and the basic behaviors that pertain to it. Figure 2 shows a graphic representation of part of this model that describes microarchitectural buffers. The type *Buffer* defines a set of properties which are shared among all microarchitectural buffers, this includes common properties such as *numEntries*, and a special set of properties that denote the type of instructions that read, write, and remove entries in the buffer. Inheriting from Buffer is *RandomAccessBuffer*, in which entries can be accessed in any order. This type specifies the conditions for four basic collision scenarios that apply to it: read-after-write (RAW), write-after-read (WAR), read-after-read (RAR) and write-after-write (WAW). A *MemoryRandomAccessBuffer* is a random access buffer that keeps memory data. It inherits from *RandomAccessBuffer* and adds an additional property *inputAddress* to specify whether access to this memory buffer is calculated based on virtual or real address values. Cache mechanisms are special cases of *MemoryRandomAccessBuffer*, and therefore they are defined as a subtype of it. The figure uses a lighter color for the actual design mechanisms that are defined as instances in the model. For example, the L1DataCache, L2Cache are defined as instances of *CacheMechanism* whereas the Load-Miss-Queue and *StoreReorderQueue* are defined as instances of *MemoryRandomAccessBuffer*.

The ontology helps maximize the reuse of scenarios. For example, scenarios that target a 'buffer full' event can be applied to any mechanism derived from

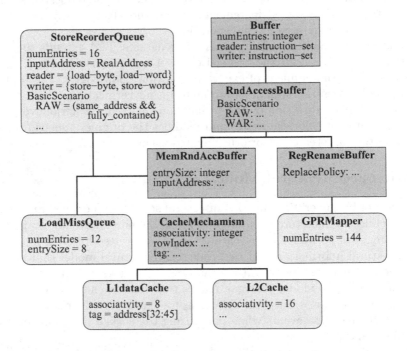

Fig. 2. Microarchitectural model ontology

Buffer, ranging from the store reorder queue (SRQ) to caches to register rename buffers. Localizing all the mechanism properties in a single location simplifies the overall maintenance effort of the verification process and encourages structure and rigor.

4   Scenario Input Language

TPA provides a high-level scenario description language. It has constructs for defining scenarios as a set of instructions and the constraints between them. In addition, given a collection of predefined scenarios the language has constructs for defining new scenarios that instantiate them in several combination options.

4.1   Scenario Definition

A scenario definition starts with a declaration of the instructions that participate in the scenario and the mechanisms to which the scenario applies. Each instruction declaration statement may specify a single instruction or a set of instructions. In the latter case, the user needs to specify lower and upper bounds on the number of instructions in the set. In addition, the declaration can restrict the instructions to a specified type. A mechanism declaration statement specifies a mechanism type or a specific mechanism instance. If the declaration specifies a mechanism type, each scenario instantiation can be restricted to a derived type or a particular instance of the specified mechanism type.

Consider a cache-replace event; caches are arranged into rows, where each row can contain multiple cache lines, depending on the cache associativity. Each memory address is mapped to a specific row which is calculated based on some bits in the address. Within the row, cache lines are identified by tags, which are formed by other bits in the address. A cache-replace event occurs when all the entries in the row are used, and a new address with a new tag is mapped to the same row. In this case, one of the existing cache lines needs to be evicted. The following is a high level description of a scenario that targets a cache-replace event:

1. Generate at least $n+1$ instructions that access memory, where n is the cache associativity
2. All instructions should access the same row in the cache
3. At least $n+1$ instructions should have a different tag

Figure 3 shows the TPA definition of the cache-replace scenario. The scenario can be applied to any mechanism M1 of type *CacheMechanism*. The instruction declaration of the scenario states that the scenario requires a set of instructions, with a size larger than the *associativity* of the cache. The scenario puts an upper limit on the number of instructions. Each instantiation of the scenario will generate a random number of instructions within the specified limits. All the instructions are of type *M1.Writer*. This type is defined in the mechanism, and includes all the instructions that can write to the cache (e,g., loads and stores).

```
ScenarioDefinition Cache-Replace
Mechanisms:
      M1            type=CacheMechanism;
Instructions:
      accessors  type=M1.Writer
                 size=[M1.associativity+1,2*M1.associativity]
Constraints:
      SomeDiff
                 mechanism=M1
                 instructions=accessors
                 lowerLimit=M1.associativity+1
                 property=tag
      AllSame
                 mechanism=M1
                 instructions=accessors
                 property=row
```

Fig. 3. Cache-replace scenario description

In addition, each scenario definition has to include a declarative description of the constraints between its instructions. We distinguish between two types of constraints: constraints that control the interactions between instructions and constraints that control the placement of instructions in the test.

Constraints that control the interaction between instructions are divided into two groups: *Property constraints* request that a property value be the same/different for all the instructions in the specified set and *Mechanism behavior constraints* target a basic mechanism behavior and are parameterized according to properties of the mechanism.

Constraints that control the placement of instructions in the test are divided into three groups. *Order constraints* specify a required partial order between two specific instructions in the generated test-case. Unlike traditional test generators, TPA does not assume that the order of appearance in the scenario implies any order in the resulting test. *Distance constraints* specify how many instructions are allowed between any two specified instructions. TPA fills the space between two instructions with "non-scenario" instructions. These instructions may belong to a different scenario or may be selected by testing knowledge. *Thread constraints* specify for any set of instructions whether they should be generated on the same or on different threads.

In the cache-replace example, two property constraints enforce the scenario restrictions on the instructions' cache row and tag properties. When the scenario is instantiated on a specific cache mechanism, the mechanism is accessed to obtain the row and tag calculation methods that apply to it.

Figure 4 shows a scenario for targeting a read-after-write collision event in a buffer using the *MemoryCollision* constraint. The constraint operates on pairs of instructions and a mechanism of type *MemoryRandomAccessBuffer*. It enforces collision conditions on the memory accesses of the instructions according to a set of parameters provided by the mechanism. For example, when this scenario is applied to the *StoreReorderQueue* shown at the bottom left of Figure 2, the mechanism parameters specify that instr1 that writes to the buffer is a store instruction and instr2 that reads from the buffer is a load instruction. In addition, the mechanism provides the *MemoryCollison* constraints the exact nature of the collision: same address and fully contained, meaning that the load and store instructions access the same memory location and the data of the load is contained in the data of the store.

```
ScenarioDefinition Read-After-Write
Mechanisms:
        M1              type=MemoryRandomAccessBuffer;
Instructions:
        instr1          type=M1.writer
        instr2          type=M1.reader
Constraints:
        Order(instr1, instr2)
        SameThread(instr1, instr2)
        MemoryCollision
                mechanism=M1
                instructions=(instr1 instr2)
                collisionType=RAW
```

Fig. 4. Read-After-Write scenario description

Note that the scenario can be applied as is to any other instance of *MemoryRandomAccessBuffer* such as the *LoadMissQueue*, resulting in a totally different sequence of instructions.

4.2   Scenario Instantiation

Given a scenario definition, each instantiation of the scenario can request that the scenario be applied to a desired subtype of the declared mechanism type or to a specific instance. Figure 5 shows several possible invocations of the Read-After-Write scenario. In the first invocation the user requests an instantiation of the Read-After-Write scenario to any arbitrary design mechanism. In this case, the user request is combined with the restrictions specified in the scenario definition and the generated test-cases will target any mechanism that is defined in the microarchitectural model as an instance of *MemoryRandomAccessBuffer*. In the subsequent invocations, the user requests that the Read-After-Write collision occur on one of the cache mechanisms, or specifically on the store reorder queue.

4.3   Scenario Combinations

Scenario combinations are important because they can cause several events to occur in a small time window by having the same instructions take part in multiple

Read-After-Write ()
Read-After-Write (CacheMechansim)
Read-After-Write (StoreReorderQueue)

Fig. 5. Possible Read-After-Write scenario instantiations

scenarios, or stress a specific mechanism by instantiating multiple scenarios for
that mechanism. TPA supports the definition of scenarios that instantiate previously defined scenarios. When a scenario is instantiated by another scenario,
the selection of instructions and mechanisms to use has to satisfy restrictions
expressed by both scenarios.

Consider the combined scenario depicted in Figure 6, which creates two different types of events on two mechanisms in a small time window: a cache replace
on some cache and a read-after-write collision on some internal buffer. Here, the
cache-replace scenario determines the set of instructions for the scenario and the
read-after-write scenario operates on two random instructions that participate
in the cache scenario.

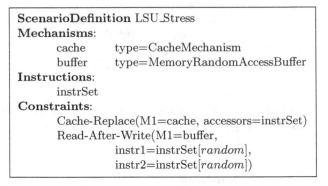

Fig. 6. Combining scenarios

5   Generation Scheme

TPA generates a scenario in two main steps. First, the scenario definitions are
parsed and several high level decisions are made. These decisions include the
selection of mechanism instances that were not completely specified and the
selection of instruction set sizes. Once these decisions are made, the number
of the instructions and the relevant constraints are known and TPA creates
a constraint graph that represents this particular scenario instantiation. The
nodes in the graph are instructions and the arcs represent scenario constraints
between sets of instructions. In the second part of the generation process, the
constraint graph is passed to a scenario solver for generating instruction streams
that satisfy the user request. The challenge lies in having the test generator

effectively generate test-cases that consist of sequences of instructions satisfying these constraints.

A test generation approach that generates instruction by instruction is not suitable for this problem because of its inability to consider constraints emanating from instructions later in the sequence when the current instruction is solved. This would cause the generator to make early decisions that may lead to generation failure of dependent instructions later in the stream. Trying to formulate and solve the entire scenario as a single CSP is not a feasible approach as the size of the resulting CSP would make this problem intractable.

To address this, TPA implements an abstraction-refinement approach to scenario generation [15]. It formulates an abstract constraint satisfaction problem that captures the essence of the requested scenario and interacts with an instruction-based test generator for single instruction generation.

The abstract CSP contains CSP variables that determine for each instruction its identity (mnemonic), identity of the thread for which it will be generated, and the location in the program order of that thread (timestamp). In addition the stream constraints add the relevant CSP variables to all the participating instructions. For example, in the CSP that is generated by the combined scenario in Figure 6, the *MemoryCollision* constraint which implements the read-after-write scenario adds variables to represent the real address and length of the memory access of each instruction, while the property constraints that implement the cache replace scenario add variables that represent the cache tag and row of the address.

The abstract CSP propagates constraints between all instructions, including constraints that influence earlier instructions based on restrictions from later instructions. When constraint propagation subsides, the instruction with lowest timestamp value is selected as the next instruction to be generated. The restrictions imposed by the stream constraints on the instruction are provided as input to a single instruction generator. This generator generates the specific instruction, taking into account all the instruction-level constraints necessary for generating an architecturally valid instruction. Once the first instruction is generated, all decisions that were made and are relevant to the rest of the scenario are propagated back to the abstract problem and the process continues.

Since the thread and location of the each instruction in program order are CSP variables they can be randomly selected. Hence instructions can be generated in many orders and interleavings in the final test-case. These instructions could have originated from the same scenario or from different scenarios that were combined.

6   Scenario Testing Knowledge

Testing knowledge is a way of embedding the knowledge and expertise of the verification engineer in a random stimuli generator that utilizes it to bias the generator towards interesting events. The raised level of abstraction in TPA opens the door for new, scenario-level, testing knowledge that can be used to improve the quality of the generated test-cases.

One area in which testing knowledge plays a major role is creating an interesting microarchitectural state for the requested scenario to operate in. This is done in TPA in two main ways: selecting an interesting order and placement for the instructions in the scenario and adding background instructions to vary the microarchitectural state. For example, TPA may choose to place two instructions involved in a collision close to each other to increase the probability of them fetching together. In addition, it may insert a background instruction that causes the first instruction in the collision to stall, so that the instructions are executed out-of-order.

Another important type of scenario level testing knowledge used in TPA is scenario mutations. The goal of mutations is to reach simulation events that are not the original intent of the scenario but are related to it. The tool supports several types of mutations such as microarchitectural model mutations that change the behavior of the mechanisms that the scenario applies to and mutations that execute parts of the scenario in a speculative path.

In addition to the scenario-level testing knowledge, TPA also takes advantage of instruction level testing knowledge provided to it by the single instruction generator. Users can control the application of both instruction-level and scenario-level testing knowledge as part of the scenario description and thus convey their own judgment as to what testing knowledge is more relevant to a given scenario at a given stage of the verification process.

7   Experimental Results

TPA implements the scenario-based generation approach described in the previous sections. TPA utilizes the instruction solving capabilities of Genesys-Pro, a leading commercial instruction-based test generator. We demonstrate the advantages of scenario-based generations of TPA over the instruction-based Genesys-Pro by comparing the two tools in their ability to cover the Store Reorder Queue (SRQ) microarchitectural feature of a high-end Power processor. The SRQ is a buffer found in the Load Store Unit (LSU) of processors. It keeps the data of each store instruction internally in the processor until the store instruction completes. This prevents wrong updates to the caches (and the rest of the system) when the store instruction does not complete for any reason and helps maintain the ordering rules between stores. One of the roles of the SRQ is to provide data to newer load instructions, thus avoiding stalling the processor until the store instruction completes. Therefore, read-after-write (RAW) collisions in the SRQ (also called load-hits-store and abbreviated to LHS in the rest of the section) are an important item in the verification plan of the processor.

The verification plan for LHS calls for test-cases that create all interesting read-after-write collisions in the SRQ, such as out-of-order collisions, simultaneous accesses to the buffer, and more. The implementation of the verification plan is monitored using a coverage model defined by the design team, whose goal is to ensure that all interesting events in the SRQ occur.

We compare the ease of creating test-templates for TPA and Genesys-Pro that implement the LHS item in the verification plan and the quality of the

Table 1. Comparison of ease in creating test-templates

	Genesys-Pro	TPA
Number of test-template	13	3
Encoding SRQ behavior	Test-templates	Model
Reusability across designs	Needs effort	Easy
Reusability across architectures	Impossible	Easy
Combinations with other scenarios	Hard	Easy

test-cases generated from these test-templates by both tools. Table 1 summarizes the first part of the comparison. In Genesys-Pro, each requested type of collision needs to be encoded specifically in the test-template. This encoding includes properties of the collision that originate from the SRQ mechanism. As a result, 13 test-templates, each handling a different type of collision or near collision of interest, are needed to cover this single item in the verification plan. While these test-templates are carried over between generations of the same architecture, adapting them to each generation takes effort because the test-templates need to be adapted to the microarchitecture in many places. The reliance on architectural and microarchitectural features of the design makes it virtually impossible to reuse these test-templates in different architectures.

In TPA, on the other hand, it is easy to stipulate specific collisions in a test-template and fit it to a specific mechanism in the microarchitectural model. As a result, only a small number of test-templates are needed to implement the LHS item in the verification plan. In this comparison, we used three test-templates: 1) a simple test-template, shown in Figure 4, that creates many instances of basic RAW collisions in the SRQ; 2) a test-template that combines these collisions with other scenarios, such as group formation and cache scenarios (similar to the test-template in Figure 6); and 3) a test-templates that includes mutations of the basic scenario and the mechanism to create interesting near-collisions. It is important to note that the three test-templates are needed only to illustrate the benefits of various features of TPA. For actual verification purposes, the last template suffices.

The simplicity of the TPA test-templates and the fact that most of the relevant information for the collisions comes from the architectural and microarchitectural models, makes reuse of this test-templates across design and architectures easy. In fact, we used the same test-templates to generate test-cases for several Power and zArchitecture designs.

The second part of the comparison evaluates the quality of the tests generated by both tools. Here we compared the ability of the tools to hit the LHS coverage events defined by the design team. A summary of the results is shown in Table 2.

The first two lines in the table provide information on the number of test-cases and simulation cycles used. We believe that the simulation cycles count, and not the number of test-cases, is a fairer base for comparison, so our goal was to have twice as many cycles for all the Genesys-Pro test-cases combined than cycles for test-cases from each of TPA test-templates.

Table 2. Comparison of the quality of generated tests

	Genesys-Pro	TPA			
		Simple	Comb	Mutation	Total
Test-cases	769	295	475	511	1281
Cycles	20M	11M	10M	10M	31M
LHS events covered	46	41	49	50	51
Other LSU events covered	1519	1063	1587	1523	1715
Generation time per instruction	1.50	1.28	1.45	1.52	1.43

Comparison of the LHS coverage results shows that the simple TPA test-template reaches lower coverage than Genesys-Pro. This can be explained by the fact that the simple test-template does not try to create near-collisions. Each of the two other TPA test-templates, which combine the basic LHS scenario with other scenarios and use mutations to create near-collisions, achieve better coverage than the 13 Genesys-Pro templates. This indicates better test-case quality. Another evidence for the superior quality of TPA test-cases is the coverage of other LSU events (that are not targeted by any of the templates) by the TPA test-cases. To show that the higher quality of the generated test-cases is not caused by increased generation time, the last row in Table 2 compares the average generation time per instruction for the compared test-templates. This time is calculated by dividing the total generation time of a test-case by the number of scenario instructions it contains. Therefore, for the TPA test-templates, this time includes the time needed to construct and solve the stream CSP as well as the time needed to generate each of the instructions. The row shows that despite using a more sophisticated generation scheme, the generation time per instruction in TPA is similar or lower. This can be explained by the planning done in the TPA generation scheme, which reduces the number of instruction generation failures.

8   Conclusions

The growing complexity of microarchitectures creates a widening gap between the verification plan and test generator input languages used to implement it. This impacts the cost and quality of the verification process. In this paper, we proposed a novel method of test generation. Our method is based on a high-level scenario description language that is close to the microarchitecture verification plan, and a new test generation algorithm and microarchitectural model to support this higher level of abstraction. Experimental results show that the proposed method is indeed capable of achieving test-cases with higher coverage, lower test-template development costs, and comparable generation time, when evaluated against the existing state-of-the-art test generation solution.

Future development directions of the technology include extension of the scenario-based testing knowledge to other areas such as multithreading, integration of automatic methods for populating the microarchitecture model, and full scale deployment in the verification of current high-end processor designs.

References

1. Wile, B., Goss, J.C., Roesner, W.: Comprehensive Functional Verification - The Complete Industry Cycle. Elsevier (2005)
2. Adir, A., Almog, E., Fournier, L., Marcus, E., Rimon, M., Vinov, M., Ziv, A.: Genesys-Pro: Innovations in test program generation for functional processor verification. IEEE Design and Test of Computers 21(2), 84–93 (2004)
3. Hennenhoefer, E., Typaldos, M.: The evolution of processor test generation technology, http://www.obsidiansoft.com/pdf/evolution.pdf
4. Naveh, Y., Rimon, M., Jaeger, I., Katz, Y., Vinov, M., Marcus, E., Shurek, G.: Constraint-based random stimuli generation for hardware verification. AI Magazine 28(3), 13–30 (2007)
5. Ludden, J.M., Rimon, M., Hickerson, B.G., Adir, A.: Advances in simultaneous multithreading testcase generation methods. In: Barner, S., Kroening, D., Raz, O. (eds.) HVC 2010. LNCS, vol. 6504, pp. 146–160. Springer, Heidelberg (2011)
6. Burns, D.: Pre-silicon validation of hyper-threading technology. Intel Technology Journal 6(1) (2002)
7. Adir, A., Bin, E., Ziv, A.: Piparazzi: A test generator for micro-architecture flow verification. In: Proceedings of the High-Level Design Validation and Test Workshop, pp. 23–28 (2003)
8. Mishra, P., Dutt, N.: Specification-driven directed test generation for validation of pipelined processors. ACM Trans. Design Autom. Electr. Syst. 13(3) (2008)
9. Fine, S., Ziv, A.: Coverage directed test generation for functional verification using Bayesian networks. In: Proceedings of the 40th Design Automation Conference, pp. 286–291 (2003)
10. Squillero, G.: MicroGP—an evolutionary assembly program generator. Genetic Programming and Evolvable Machines 6(3), 247–263 (2005)
11. Wagner, I., Bertacco, V., Austin, T.: Microprocessor verification via feedback-adjusted Markov models. IEEE Transactions on Computer-Aided Design of Integrated Circuits and Systems 26(6), 1126–1138 (2007)
12. Eder, K., Flach, P., Hsueh, H.-W.: Towards automating simulation-based design verification using ILP. In: Muggleton, S., Otero, R., Tamaddoni-Nezhad, A. (eds.) ILP 2006. LNCS (LNAI), vol. 4455, pp. 154–168. Springer, Heidelberg (2007)
13. Ioannides, C., Barrett, G., Eder, K.: Feedback-based coverage directed test generation: An industrial evaluation. In: Barner, S., Kroening, D., Raz, O. (eds.) HVC 2010. LNCS, vol. 6504, pp. 112–128. Springer, Heidelberg (2011)
14. Katz, Y., Rimon, M., Ziv, A., Shaked, G.: Learning microarchitectural behaviors to improve stimuli generation quality. In: Proceedings of the 48th Design Automation Conference, pp. 848–853 (2011)
15. Katz, Y., Rimon, M., Ziv, A.: Generating instruction streams using abstract CSP. In: Proceedings of the 2012 Design, Automation and Test in Europe Conference, pp. 15–20 (2012)

Statistical Model Checking for Safety Critical Hybrid Systems: An Empirical Evaluation

Youngjoo Kim[1], Moonzoo Kim[1], and Tai-Hyo Kim[2]

[1] CS Dept. KAIST
Daejeon, South Korea
{jerry88,moonzoo}@cs.kaist.ac.kr
[2] Formal Works Inc.
Seoul, South Korea
taihyo.kim@formalworks.com
http://www.formalworks.co.kr

Abstract. As more computing systems are utilized in various areas of our society, the reliability of computing systems becomes a significant issue. However, as the complexity of computing systems increases, conventional verification and validation techniques such as testing and model checking have limitations to assess reliability of complex safety critical systems. Such systems often control highly complex continuous dynamics to interact with physical environments. To assure the reliability of safety critical hybrid systems, *statistical model checking* (SMC) techniques have been proposed. SMC techniques approximately compute probabilities for a target system to satisfy given requirements based on randomly sampled execution traces. In this paper, we empirically evaluated four state-of-the-art SMC techniques on a fault-tolerant fuel control system in the automobile domain. Through the experiments, we could demonstrate that SMC is practically useful to assure the reliability of a safety critical hybrid system and we compared pros and cons of the four different SMC techniques.

1 Introduction

With the rapid advance of computing hardware, more computing systems are utilized in various areas of our society including avionics and automobiles. Consequently, the reliability of computing systems becomes a significant issue to our society. However, as computing power increases, the complexity of computing systems increases rapidly, which causes many challenges to assure reliability of computing systems. Conventional verification and validation (V&V) techniques such as testing and model checking have limitations to assess the reliability of complex safety critical computing systems, since such systems often control highly complex continuous dynamics to interact with physical environments.

To assure the reliability of safety critical hybrid systems, *statistical model checking (SMC)* techniques have been proposed [19,17,18,8,4,21,20,2]. SMC techniques *approximately* compute probabilities for a target system to satisfy given requirements based on randomly sampled execution traces. Thus, SMC techniques can check the reliability of a safety critical hybrid system without analyzing the complex internal logic of the target system.

A. Biere, A. Nahir, and T. Vos (Eds.): HVC 2012, LNCS 7857, pp. 162–177, 2013.

However, most literature on the SMC techniques focuses on theoretical aspects of suggested techniques, not their practical applicability to real-world safety critical systems.

In this paper, we empirically evaluated the *effectiveness* (in terms of the precision of the verification result) and *efficiency* (in terms of the verification time) of the following four representative state-of-the-art SMC techniques: *single sampling plan (SSP)*, *statistical probability ratio test (SPRT)*, *Bayesian hypothesis testing (BHT)*, and *Bayesian interval estimation testing (BIET)*.[1] We applied these four SMC techniques to a fault-tolerant fuel control system (FFCS), which is a safety critical system for automobiles.

Contributions of this paper are as follows:

- We demonstrated that SMC techniques can assess the reliability of a complex safety critical system.
- We made empirical evaluation of the four state-of-the-art SMC techniques systematically with carefully controlled experiment environments.
- We identified and compared characteristics of the four SMC techniques, based on which precise results can be obtained faster by applying multiple SMC techniques together.

The organization of the paper is as follows. Section 2 overviews the four SMC techniques. Section 3 explains the target FFCS system. Section 4 describes the verification results by using the four SMC techniques on a Matlab/Simulink model of FFCS. Section 5 discusses issues from the empirical study. Section 6 concludes this paper with future work.

2 Background

In general, a model checking technique [1] checks whether a given model $\mathcal{M}$ satisfies a given requirement property ϕ ($\mathcal{M} \models \phi$) or not. A statistical model checking (SMC) technique checks whether a probability for $\mathcal{M}$ to satisfy ϕ is greater than or equal to a given threshold parameter θ ($\mathcal{M} \models P_{\geq\theta}(\phi)$) or not. We specify ϕ in bounded linear temporal logic (BLTL) [20] and that a probability for $\mathcal{M}$ to satisfy ϕ is greater than or equal to a given threshold θ in probabilistic bounded linear temporal logic (PBLTL) [21] (see Section 2.1). To compute the probability, SMC techniques utilize random sampling of execution traces/paths of $\mathcal{M}$ based on statistical techniques.

Figure 1 illustrates the overview of SMC. SMC receives a target model $\mathcal{M}$ which is an executable simulation model and PBLTL formula ϕ with θ. In addition, SMC receives *precision parameters* based on which the accuracy of the calculated probability is decided. SMC consists of three components: *simulator*, *BLTL model checker*, and *statistical analyzer*. Simulator executes $\mathcal{M}$ and generates a sample execution trace σ_i. BLTL model checker determines if σ_i satisfies ϕ and passes the result (i.e., success if σ_i satisfies ϕ; failure, otherwise) to statistical analyzer. Statistical analyzer calculates a probability p that $\mathcal{M}$ satisfies ϕ by collecting the result regarding if σ_i satisfies ϕ.

---

[1] In this study, we did not evaluate Chernoff-Hoeffding bound SMC technique [4] due to excessive time cost.

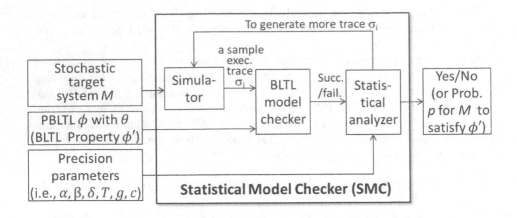

Fig. 1. SMC overview

Statistical analyzer requests simulator to generate σ_{i+1} repeatedly until the number of successful results of σs over the total number of σs is distributed within given precision boundary. Note that SMC does not analyze an internal logic of a target system, and thus SMC can validate complex safety critical systems without the state explosion problem.

More specifically, suppose that $X_1, ..., X_n$ are Bernoulli random variables (i.e., X_i can be either 0 or 1) of the model checking result of ϕ over an execution path σ of $\mathcal{M}$ and p indicates a probability of X_i to become 1 (i.e., $P(X_i = 1) = p$). Since we do not know p exactly, we should estimate p using random sampling techniques with user-given precision parameters. We pick a sample path σ_i from $\mathcal{M}$ by executing $\mathcal{M}$ and test whether σ_i satisfies ϕ or not. If σ_i satisfies ϕ, $x_i = 1$; $x_i = 0$ otherwise. Note that, for estimating p, we should determine a number of sample paths n to check ϕ using statistical techniques. We may obtain n statically by using heuristics or dynamically through iterative sampling.

There are two classes of statistical techniques: *hypothesis testing* (Section 2.2) and *estimation testing* (Section 2.3).

2.1 Probabilistic Bounded Linear Temporal Logic (PBLTL)

To define PBLTL, we first define a syntax and semantics of bounded linear temporal logic(BLTL) [20], and then extend BLTL to PBLTL [21].

For a target model $\mathcal{M}$, SV is a finite set of real-valued state variables. A Boolean predicate over SV is a constraint of the form $y \sim v$, where $y \in SV$, $\sim \in \{\geq, \leq, =\}$, and $v \in \mathbb{R}$. The syntax of the BLTL logic formula ϕ is given by the following grammar:

$$\phi ::= y \sim v \mid (\phi_1 \vee \phi_2) \mid (\phi_1 \wedge \phi_2) \mid \neg\phi_1 \mid (\phi_1 \mathbf{U}^t \phi_2),$$

where $y \in SV$, $\sim \in \{\geq, \leq, =\}$, $v \in \mathbb{R}$, and $t \in \mathbb{R}_{\geq 0}$.

For other temporal operators, we can define $\mathbf{F}^t\phi$ as $True\ \mathbf{U}^t\phi$ and $\mathbf{G}^t\phi$ as $\neg\mathbf{F}^t\neg\phi$. We denote a fact that an execution σ satisfies a property ϕ as $\sigma \models \phi$. We use σ^k to denote a suffix trace of σ starting at step k (σ^0 denotes the original execution σ). We denote the value of a state variable y in σ at step k by $V(\sigma, k, y)$. We define t_k as a time at step k and t as a time bound. The semantics of BLTL on a trace σ^k is defined as follows:

- $\sigma^k \models y \sim v$ iff $V(\sigma, k, y) \sim v$
- $\sigma^k \models \phi_1 \vee \phi_2$ iff $\sigma^k \models \phi_1$ or $\sigma^k \models \phi_2$
- $\sigma^k \models \phi_1 \wedge \phi_2$ iff $\sigma^k \models \phi_1$ and $\sigma^k \models \phi_2$
- $\sigma^k \models \neg\phi_1$ iff $\sigma^k \nvDash \phi_1$
- $\sigma^k \models \phi_1 \mathbf{U}^t \phi_2$ iff there exists $i \in \mathbb{N}$ such that
  1. $\sum_{0 \leq l < i} t_{k+l} \leq t$,
  2. $\sigma^{k+i} \models \phi_2$, and
  3. for each $0 \leq j < i, \sigma^{k+j} \models \phi_1$

A probabilistic bounded linear temporal logic (PBLTL) formula is a formula of the form $P_{\geq \theta}(\phi)$, where ϕ is a BLTL formula and $\theta \in (0, 1)$ is a probability threshold. We denote that a model $\mathcal{M}$ satisfies PBLTL property $P_{\geq \theta}(\phi)$ as $\mathcal{M} \models P_{\geq \theta}(\phi)$, which means that a probability for $\mathcal{M}$ to satisfy ϕ is greater than equal to θ (see [21] for detailed description).

2.2 Hypothesis Testing

For hypothesis testing, we build a hypothesis $H : p \geq \theta$ against an alternative hypothesis $K : p < \theta$ where θ is a threshold over (0,1) and p is a *true probability* that $\mathcal{M}$ satisfies ϕ. Hypothesis testing checks whether H is accepted or not based on the randomly sampled paths. In this paper, we utilize the following three hypothesis testing techniques - *single sampling plan (SSP)*, *sequential probability ratio test (SPRT)*, and *Baysian hypothesis testing (BHT)*.

Single Sampling Plan (SSP). SMC techniques cannot compute a true probability p exactly, but can estimate p within given error bounds. Precision parameters for SSP [17] are *error bounds* α and β, and a half size of *indifference region* δ. For testing a hypothesis H, there are two types of errors such as false negative (also known as a type I error) which rejects a true hypothesis H and false positive (also known as a type II error) which accepts a false hypothesis H. We can bound an error probability of a false negative error within α. Similarly, we can bound an error probability of a false positive error within β. The left side of Figure 2 presents the function of probability L_p of accepting the hypothesis H as a function of p with the probability of a type I error and type II error as exactly α and β. However, we want to give similar probability L_p with $p = \theta$ to $p = \theta - \epsilon$ for arbitrarily small $\epsilon > 0$ for reality. To solve this problem, we introduce *indifference region* (p_1, p_0) around θ where $p_0 = \theta + \delta$, $p_1 = \theta - \delta$, and δ is a half size of indifference region (see right side function in Figure 2). Therefore, instead of testing H against K, we use the modified hypothesis $H_0 : p \geq p_0$ against the alternative hypothesis $H_1 : p < p_1$. If the probability p is in (p_1, p_0), then since we cannot guarantee the error bounds α and β in (p_1, p_0), we do not care which hypothesis is accepted.

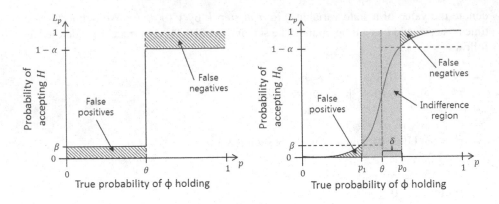

Fig. 2. Function of probability L_p of accepting the hypothesis $H : p \geq \theta$ (left side) and function of probability L_p of accepting the hypothesis $H_0 : p \geq p_0$ with indifference region (right side)

For SSP, a user can determine a maximum number of sample paths n and a threshold number of success sample paths c statically. After determining n and c, SSP executes a target program multiple times. If the number of success sample paths that satisfy ϕ are greater than c, then H is accepted; K is accepted otherwise. Then, we can express the probability that the number of success sample paths among n samples are less than c with the cumulative distribution function for binomial distribution $B(n, p)$:

$$F(c; n, p) = \sum_{i=0}^{c} \binom{n}{i} p^i (1 - p)^{n-i}.$$

Therefore, we accept H with $1 - F(c; n, p)$ using n and c, and accept K with $F(c; n, p)$ using n and c. We can obtain minimal value for n and c using binary search based algorithm with given p_0, p_1, α, and β. Note that SSP is the only SMC technique that computes the number of required sample paths statically among the SMC techniques utilized in this study.

Sequential Probability Ratio Test (SPRT). SPRT [19,17,18,15] determines a number of required sample paths dynamically at runtime. If another sample path is needed, SPRT generates one more sample path by executing a target system. If the information from generated sample paths are enough to determine hypothesis H_0, SPRT stops executing a target program and outputs the result that H_0 is accepted or not. SPRT uses precision parameter inputs α, β, and δ which are same in SSP.

SPRT operates as follows. After generating mth sample paths of the test, we calculate the quantity

$$\frac{p_{1m}}{p_{0m}} = \prod_{i=1}^{m} \frac{Pr[X_i = x_i | p = p_1]}{Pr[X_i = x_i | p = p_0]} = \frac{p_1^{d_m}(1 - p_1)^{m-d_m}}{p_0^{d_m}(1 - p_0)^{m-d_m}}$$

where $d_m = \sum_{i=1}^{m} x_i$ and x_i is ith observation of $\sigma_i \models \phi$. p_{jm} is the probability of the sequence $x_1, ..., x_m$ with $Pr[X_i = 1] = p_j$ for $j=0,1$. Therefore, the above quantity makes the ratio of two probabilities, the *probability ratio*. The hypothesis H_0 is accepted if

$$\frac{p_{1m}}{p_{0m}} \leq B,$$

and the hypothesis H_1 is accepted if

$$\frac{p_{1m}}{p_{0m}} \geq A.$$

Otherwise, we should generate $m + 1$th sample path of the test. A and B are selected to bound error probability α and β, with $A > B$. In practice, we choose $A = \frac{1-\beta}{\alpha}$ and $B = \frac{\beta}{1-\alpha}$(detailed description is found in [15,17]).

Bayesian Hypothesis Testing (BHT). BHT [8] dynamically determines the number of sample paths during simulation as same in SPRT. BHT uses two precision parameter inputs such as threshold T of determining H_0 and prior density g for p, the actual probability of satisfying ϕ. In Bayes' theorem, we get prior probability using current information first. After obtaining new information, we can obtain posterior probability refining prior probability. BHT uses Bayes' theorem to determine the number of sample paths of the test.

Let $P(H_0)$ and $P(H_1)$ be the strictly positive *prior probabilities* of accepting H_0 and H_1 and satisfying $P(H_0) + P(H_1) = 1$. Let $d = (x_1, ..., x_n)$ be a sequence of n sample paths of the test. Bayes' theorem states that the *posterior probabilities* of accepting H_0 and H_1 based on observations of d are

$$P(H_0|d) = \frac{P(d|H_0)P(H_0)}{P(d)} \quad P(H_1|d) = \frac{P(d|H_1)P(H_1)}{P(d)}$$

for every d with $P(d) = P(d|H_0)P(H_0) + P(d|H_1)P(H_1) > 0$.

BHT operates as follows. After generating mth sample paths of the test, we can calculate the quantity

$$\frac{P(H_0|d)}{P(H_1|d)} = \frac{P(d|H_0)}{P(d|H_1)} \cdot \frac{P(H_0)}{P(H_1)}$$

where $d = (x_1, ..., x_m)$. We call the above quantity as the ratio of the posterior probabilities. Here, we define the *Bayes factor* $\mathcal{B}$ of d and hypotheses H_0 and H_1 as follows:

$$\mathcal{B} = \frac{P(d|H_0)}{P(d|H_1)}$$

The *Bayes factor* $\mathcal{B}$ can be interpreted as a measure of the evidence in favor of H_0 and also $\frac{1}{\mathcal{B}}$ can be the evidence in favor of H_1. We introduce a Bayes factor threshold T to test H_0 against H_1 such that $T \geq 1$. The hypothesis H_0 is accepted if $\mathcal{B} > T$, and the hypothesis H_1 is accepted if $\mathcal{B} < \frac{1}{T}$. Otherwise, BHT generates $m + 1$th sample path using simulation [2] (detailed description is found in [8]).

---

[2] T corresponds to the inverse number of error bounds α and β for SSP and SPRT [21].

2.3 Estimation Testing

Estimation testing can approximately compute p, the probability that the model $\mathcal{M}$ satisfies the given property ϕ expressed by bounded linear temporal logic (BLTL). With p, we can determine whether the probabilistic bounded linear temporal logic (PBLTL) is satisfied or not. For that purpose, we use a following statistical estimation testing technique.

Bayesian Interval Estimation Testing (BIET). BIET [21] dynamically determines the number of sample paths for checking the satisfiability of the model $\mathcal{M}$ with the property ϕ during simulation as SPRT and BHT do. BIET also uses the Bayes' theorem. BIET uses four precision parameter inputs such as a half-size δ' of an estimation interval which will contain p with high probability, the coverage goal c of the estimation interval, and the parameters α', β' of the Beta prior. In fact, BIET estimates interval around the probability p instead of estimating p, but we regard the mean of the estimated interval as $\hat{p}$, the estimated value of *true probability* p, i.e., the estimated interval is $(\hat{p} - \delta', \hat{p} + \delta')$. We call the estimated interval as (t_0, t_1). We have a *coverage goal* such that the probability that the probability satisfying $\mathcal{M} \models \phi$ is in (t_0, t_1) should be over the coverage $c \in (\frac{1}{2}, 1)$. The exact description of the coverage goal is as follows:

$$\int_{t_0}^{t_1} f(u|x_1, ..., x_n)du = c$$

where x_i is ith observation of $\sigma_i \models \phi$ for $i = 1, ..., n$ and n is the number of sample paths. We call the coverage goal as a $100c$ percent *Bayesian interval estimate* of p. Since BIET uses the Bayes' theorem, we need prior information, i.e., prior density of p to obtain prior probability. For simplicity, we focus on the Beta prior with parameters α', β'(See [21] for details).

At mth stage of the test, by Beta prior with α', β', we can calculate the quantity

$$\hat{p} = \frac{x + \alpha'}{m + \alpha' + \beta'}$$

where $x = \sum_{i=1}^{m} x_i$ is the number of success sample paths during m number of sample paths. Next, using $t_0 = \hat{p} - \delta', t_1 = \hat{p} + \delta'$, we can calculate the quantity

$$\gamma = \int_{t_0}^{t_1} f(u|x_1, ..., x_m)du$$

where γ is the coverage of m number of sample paths for checking $\mathcal{M} \models \phi$. If $\gamma \geq c$, then BIET stops the simulation and outputs t_0, t_1, and $\hat{p}$. Otherwise, BIET generates $m + 1$th sample path and repeats.

3   Fault-Tolerant Fuel Control System

This section overviews a fault-tolerant fuel control system (FFCS) [12] in an automobile domain. We selected FFCS as a target system to apply the SMC techniques for the following reasons:

Table 1. Size and complexity of the FFCS Simulink/stateflow model in Halstead metrics

N_1: # of operators	N_2:# of operands	n_1:# of distinct operators	n_2:# of distinct operands	N:program length ($= N_1 + N_2$)	n: program vocabulary ($=n_1 + n_2$)	V: program volume ($N \times logn$)	D: program difficulty ($=n_1/2 \times N_2/n_2$)	E: program effort ($= D \times V$)
65	111	35	94	176	129	1234.0	20.7	25500.0

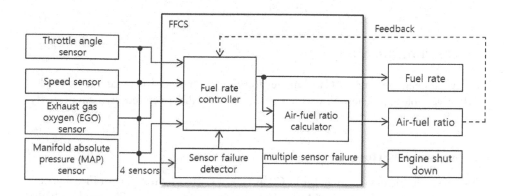

Fig. 3. Block diagram of FFCS

- FFCS is a safety critical system whose reliability is very important.
- FFCS is a complex real-world application, not a toy example such as ones in probabilistic symbolic model checker (PRISM) [11] benchmarks. Most SMC papers use PRISM benchmarks as their target examples.
- A Simulink/stateflow model of FFCS is publicly available. Thus, it is convenient to build prototypes of the SMC techniques for FFCS based on a Simulink/stateflow simulator.

Figure 3 is an overall diagram of FFCS. FFCS [12] controls a fuel rate to inject fuel based on sensor data for best performance, detects a sensor fault, and shuts down an engine for safety in the presence of multiple sensor failures. FFCS has the following four sensors: throttle angle sensor, speed sensor, exhaust gas oxygen (EGO) sensor, and manifold absolute pressure (MAP) sensor. FFCS receives these four sensor inputs and generates a proper fuel rate and an air-fuel ratio. FFCS consists of the following three components: fuel rate controller, air-fuel ratio calculator, and sensor failure detector. Fuel rate controller receives the four sensor data and calculates a proper fuel rate to make an air-fuel ratio optimal (i.e., 14.6). Air-fuel ratio calculator receives EGO sensor data and a fuel rate and calculates the air-fuel ratio. Sensor failure detector receives all four sensor data and controls the fuel rate controller to increase/decrease the fuel rate in the presence of a single sensor fault or shuts down the engine if multiple sensors fail, since the air-fuel ratio cannot be controlled with failures of multiple sensors.

The size and complexity of the Simulink/stateflow FFCS model in terms of Halstead [3] metrics are described in Table 1. We counted each atomic block (i.e., a module of a mathematical function or control logic) as an operator and each input of an atomic block as an operand of the Simulink/stateflow FFCS model. The automatically generated C code from the model has 8266 LOC in 222 functions.

A requirement property for FFCS is that a probability that the fuel rate does not become zero for one second in 100 seconds should be greater than equal to threshold θ. The property is crucial in a real world, because if the fuel rate is zero for one second, then the engine stops and can cause a serious accident. This property can be expressed by PBLTL as follows [21]:

$$P_{\geq\theta}(\neg(F^{100}G^1(fuelrate = 0)))$$

4 Experimental Study

We have applied the four SMC techniques to FFCS with precision parameters as independent variables and checked whether FFCS satisfies the given requirement property in PBLTL or not.

4.1 Experiment Setup

We set a stochastic environment for FFCS as follows. The environment of FFCS generates random faults at the EGO, MAP, and speed sensors as [21] does. The random faults are modeled by three independent Poisson processes with different arrival rates [16]. We assume one fault event remains for one second. When a fault event occurs in a sensor, FFCS remains in a failure mode for one second and returns to a normal mode. We utilize the following four inter-arrival fault rates (i.e., mean inter-arrival times of sensor fault) to the three sensors: (3,7,8), (10,8,9), (20,10,20) and (30,30,30).

For the SMC techniques, we use the following precision parameters:

- Hypothesis testing techniques
  - SSP:
    * threshold $\theta \in \{0.5, 0.7, 0.9, 0.99\}$
    * a half-size of indifference region $\delta \in \{0.01, 0.03, 0.05\}$
    * error bounds $\alpha, \beta \in \{0.1, 0.01, 0.001\}$
  - SPRT:
    * threshold $\theta \in \{0.5, 0.7, 0.9, 0.99\}$
    * a half-size of indifference region $\delta \in \{0.01, 0.03, 0.05\}$
    * error bounds $\alpha, \beta \in \{0.1, 0.01, 0.001\}$
  - BHT:
    * threshold $\theta \in \{0.5, 0.7, 0.9, 0.99\}$
    * Bayes factor threshold $T \in \{10, 100, 1000\}$
    * prior density g = uniform density over (0,1)
- Estimation testing technique
  - BIET:
    * interval coverage $c = \{0.9, 0.99, 0.999\}$
    * a half-size of estimation interval $\delta' = \{0.01, 0.03, 0.05\}$
    * parameters of Beta prior $\alpha' = \beta' = 1$ [3]

---

[3] $\alpha' = \beta' = 1$, since we assume the prior density to be a uniform density over $(0, 1)$.

Table 2. Experiment result of SSP with fault rate $(3, 7, 8)$ and $\delta = 0.03$

α, β	threshold θ															
	0.5				0.7				0.9				0.99			
	n	m	$acpt$	$time$	n	m	$acpt$	$time$	n	m	$acpt$	$time$	n	m	$acpt$	$time$
0.1	455	255.3	1.0	688.3	386	307.0	1.0	821.5	161	141.5	0.0	381.3	57	5.8	0.0	17.1
0.01	1501	857.8	1.0	2308.1	1261	1001.5	1.0	2686.7	531	468.8	0.0	1256.4	113	5.0	0.0	14.8
0.001	2649	1487.8	1.0	4013.2	2226	1764.3	1.0	4760.8	932	806.8	0.0	2172.5	170	6.0	0.0	20.3

We performed each experiment five times to obtain average verification result over $[0, 1]$ regarding whether the hypothesis H is accepted or not where H: a probability to satisfy $\phi (= \neg(F^{100}G^1(fuelrate = 0)))$ is greater than or equal to θ. In addition, we measured the average verification time for each experiment.

We built a statistical model checker as a Matlab module which runs together with a FFCS model. We use a Matlab simulator as a simulator component to generate an execution trace σ of a Matlab/Simulink FFCS model. Then, the BLTL model checker analyzes if σ satisfies the requirement property ϕ. After the BLTL model checker evaluates σ, the statistical analyzer calculates a required number of sample traces dynamically based on the precision parameters and the number of success/fail sample traces generated so far. If a number of the generated samples reaches the required number, the statistical model checker generates a verification result and terminates the SMC process. Note that all sub-components of SMC are independent from each other and can be re-used for other target systems without modification. Thus, it will not be difficult for practitioners to apply SMC techniques to their safety critical systems.[4]

We used Matlab R2010a for the experiments. All experiments were performed on 64 bit Windows 7 Professional K equipped with a 3 GHz Intel processor and 16 gigabytes of memory.

4.2 Experimental Results

Tables 2-4 describe the experiment results of applying the hypothesis testing techniques to FFCS with fault inter-arrival rate (3,7,8) and $\delta = 0.03$.[5] In these three tables,

- θ is a threshold of the hypothesis H for SSP, SPRT, and BHT
- n is a maximum number of required sample paths and m means an average number of sample paths generated for SSP. For SPRT and BHT, n is an average number of sample paths generated for SPRT and BHT.
- $acpt$ is an average result over $[0, 1]$ regarding the hypothesis H where 0 is 'reject' and 1 is 'accept'
- $time$ is an average verification time for each experiment in seconds

---

[4] We have released the statistical analyzers using SSP, SPRT, BHT, and BIET techniques publicly at http://pswlab.kaist.ac.kr/tools/SMC/

[5] Full experiment data with the other three fault inter-arrival rates and $\delta \in \{0.01, 0.05\}$ is available at http://pswlab.kaist.ac.kr/data/hvc2012-expr-results.zip

Table 3. Experiment result of SPRT with fault rate $(3, 7, 8)$ and $\delta = 0.03$

α, β	threshold θ											
	0.5			0.7			0.9			0.99		
	n	$acpt$	$time$	n	$acpt$	$time$	n	$acpt$	$time$	n	$acpt$	$time$
0.1	26.6	1.0	17.6	34.0	1.0	22.4	108.4	0.0	71.5	5.6	1.0	3.7
0.01	49.0	1.0	32.3	93.4	1.0	61.6	484.0	0.0	319.4	5.6	1.0	3.7
0.001	72.8	1.0	48.0	127.6	1.0	84.2	786.6	0.0	519.2	11.6	1.0	7.7

Table 4. Experiment result of BHT with fault rate $(3, 7, 8)$

T	threshold θ											
	0.5			0.7			0.9			0.99		
	n	$acpt$	$time$	n	$acpt$	$time$	n	$acpt$	$time$	n	$acpt$	$time$
10	3.6	1.0	2.4	5.0	1.0	3.3	42.2	0.8	27.9	21.0	0.2	13.9
100	7.6	1.0	5.0	26.0	1.0	17.2	3917.2	0.2	2585.4	27.0	0.0	17.8
1000	13.6	1.0	9.0	48.4	1.0	31.9	4013.2	0.2	2648.7	35.2	0.0	23.2

Table 5. Experiment result of BIET with fault rate $(3, 7, 8)$

δ'	interval coverage c								
	0.9			0.99			0.999		
	n	$\hat{p}$	$time$	n	$\hat{p}$	$time$	n	$\hat{p}$	$time$
0.05	104.8	0.8835	69.2	273.0	0.8849	180.2	475.5	0.8830	313.8
0.03	276.6	0.8944	182.6	729.4	0.8889	481.4	1191.5	0.8924	786.4
0.01	2733.8	0.8856	1804.3	6696.5	0.8861	4419.7	10924.2	0.8865	7210.0

Table 5 describes the experiment result of applying the estimation technique BIET to FFCS with fault inter-arrival rate $(3,7,8)$, where n is an average number of sample paths, $\hat{p}$ is an estimated probability to satisfy ϕ, and $time$ indicates an average verification time in seconds. Tables 2-5 show that n (m for SSP) increases as the precision parameters becomes smaller. For example, for SSP, when α and β decrease from 0.1 to 0.001 with threshold $\theta = 0.5$, m increases from 255.3 to 1487.8 (Table 2). Similar tendencies are observed for SPRT, BHT, and BIET.

Regarding Effectiveness (Precision of the Verification Results). All four techniques produce similar results. For hypothesis testing techniques SPRT, SSP, and BHT, the probability for FFCS with the fault inter-arrival rate of sensors $(3,7,8)$ and $\delta = 0.03$

to satisfy the requirement property ϕ is between 0.7 and 0.9. This is because $acpts$ are 1.0 when $\theta \leq 0.7$ while $acpts$ are close to 0 when $\theta \geq 0.9$ in Tables 2-4.[6] Also, note that n of SPRT and BHT increases exponentially as θ increases from 0.5 to 0.9, and decreases sharply from 0.9 to 0.99. For example, for SPRT with $\alpha=\beta=0.1$ (Table 3), n becomes 26.6, 34.0, 108.4 and 5.6 as θ becomes 0.5, 0.7, 0.9 and 0.99, respectively. In general, for the hypothesis testing techniques that generates sample paths dynamically (i.e., SPRT and BHT), if a true probability is close to the threshold θ, a large number of sample paths is required to determine whether a given hypothesis H is accepted or not. By the above results, we can conclude that a true probability that FFCS with the fault rate (3,7,8) satisfies the requirement property is close to 0.9. Furthermore, BIET computes the probability between 0.8830 (with $c = 0.999$ and $\delta' = 0.05$) and 0.8944 (with $c = 0.9$ and $\delta' = 0.03$) (Table 5), which is included in the estimated probability interval (0.7,0.9) of the hypothesis testing techniques. Therefore, based on the above analysis of the results, we can conclude that the verification results of the SMC techniques are precise.

Regarding Efficiency (Verification Time). The time taken for each experiment was moderate. The longest experiment took 7210.0 seconds (i.e., around 2 hours) to generate 10924.2 sample paths on average for BIET with $c = 0.999$ and $\delta' = 0.01$ (Table 5). Note that most other experiments took much less time. For example, the longest experiments in SSP, SPRT, and BHT took 4760.8 ($\alpha=\beta=0.001$ and $\theta=0.7$) (Table 2), 519.2 ($\alpha=\beta=0.001$ and $\theta=0.9$) (Table 3), and 2648.7 ($T=1000$ and $\theta=0.9$) (Table 4) seconds, respectively. Therefore, we can conclude that statistical model checking can assure reliability of a complex target system at modest cost.[7]

5   Discussion

5.1   Practicality of Statistical Model Checking

Through the empirical evaluation of the SMC techniques on FFCS, we believe that statistical model checking is practically useful for the following reasons:

- SMC can check a probability for a complex hybrid system to satisfy a given requirement property ϕ. In this project, we could statistically check the probability for FFCS to satisfy ϕ, since we just generated random sample execution paths without analyzing the internal structure of FFCS, which is a great advantage of SMC.
- SMC allows a user to select proper trade-off between verification precision and time cost by selecting appropriate precision parameter values (Section 4.2). In some cases, due to limited project time, it may be more valuable to obtain less precise verification in short time than more precise verification result in much longer time.

---

[6] The result of SPRT with $\theta = 0.99$ is not reliable, since the precision of SPRT is low when θ is close to 1. Also, note that n becomes very small (i.e., less than 12) with $\theta=0.99$ in Table 3.

[7] SSP takes much more time to generate one sample than the other techniques, since the heuristics of SSP to determine a maximum number of sample paths is very complex.

Table 6. Comparison of the four statistical model checking techniques

	Technique	Precision	Speed	# of sample decision	Applicability
Hypothesis testing	SSP	Low when θ is close to 1	Slow except when θ is close to 1	Static	Low
	SPRT	Low when θ is close to 1	Fast	Dynamic	Middle
	BHT	Middle	Slow when θ is close to *true probability*	Dynamic	High
Estimation testing	BIET	High	Slow	Dynamic	High

– The SMC techniques can obtain precise verification results in a moderate amount of verification time (i.e., less than two hours for the most experiments in Section 4.2).[8]

5.2 Necessity of Proper Precision Parameter Values

We found that, for SSP and SPRT to produce precise verification results, δ should be very small when θ is close to 1. For example, the verification result of SPRT was 'accept' for $\theta = 0.99$ with $\delta=0.03$ (see Table 3), which is considered as an incorrect result, since the other SMC techniques conclude that the estimated probability is between 0.7 and 0.9 (Section 4.2). The reason for these imprecise results of SSP and SPRT is due to the limited size of indifference region. For example, if the threshold θ is 0.99 and $\delta \geq 0.01$, then p_0 becomes 1, which causes the denominator of the probability ratio $\frac{p_{1m}}{p_{0m}}$ to be 0 when one false sample occurs for SPRT, which can cause imprecise result. For SSP, when $n=170$ with $\alpha = \beta = 0.001$ and $\delta= 0.03$, a number of success samples should be larger than 169 to accept H. In other words, if one sample path violates ϕ, then the verification finishes immediately with 'reject' result. Therefore, SSP and SPRT should be applied with very small δ when θ is close to 1.

In addition, BHT with threshold $\theta = 0.9$ produced different verification results with different T. With $T=10$, the verification result was 0.8 (i.e., almost 'accept') on average. However, with $T=100$ or 1000, the verification results were 0.2 (i.e., almost 'reject') on average. From the results of the other techniques which indicate the true probability $p \in (0.7, 0.9)$ (Section 4.2), we can conclude that the verification result with $T=10$ was imprecise. This is because T was not sufficiently small enough to obtain a precise verification result. Therefore, proper precision parameter values are important to obtain precise verification results.

5.3 Comparison of the SMC techniques

Table 6 summarizes characteristics of the four SMC techniques. The precision of SSP and SPRT is lower than the other techniques when θ is close to 1 because of the size

---

[8] If the required reliability goal is very high (i.e., from $1 - 10^{-4}$ to $1 - 10^{-5}$ for SIL 4 level [6]), SMC may take multiple weeks.

restriction of the indifference region (Section 5.2). The precision of BIET is higher than the other techniques by the *law of large numbers* [14], because BIET utilizes more samples than the other techniques. BHT achieves a middle level of precision compared to SSP/SPRT and BIET. Regarding verification speed, SSP is slow except when θ is close to 1; when θ is close to 1, SSP is fast (but imprecise) since a number of samples is small. BHT is slow by generating a large number of samples when θ is close to a true probability. BIET is relatively slow due to a large number of samples utilized. SPRT is relatively fast, since it does not have weaknesses of the other techniques in terms of the verification speed. By considering these aspects, the applicability of BHT and BIET is relatively higher than that of SPRT and SSP.

As shown in Table 6, there is no single best SMC technique for all aspects. Thus, a combination of different SMC techniques can achieve precise result faster. For example, many safety critical systems should satisfy requirement property ϕ with very high probability for reliable operations (i.e., θ should be larger than 0.9999). We know that SPRT is faster than BIET, but its precision is low when θ is close to 1. In such cases, we can first apply SPRT to a target system with low θ for fast verification speed. If the verification results for low θ values (i.e., $\theta \in [0.5, 0.7]$) are 'reject', then we do not need to verify a target system further. Otherwise, we use BIET for higher θ (i.e., $\theta \in [0.9, 0.99]$), which is more precise but slower than SPRT, since SPRT is imprecise for θ close to 1. Consequently, this combined method can achieve precise result faster than BIET only.[9]

6   Conclusion and Future Work

From our empirical study, we demonstrated that SMC techniques can assess the reliability of a complex safety critical system such as FFCS. Based on the statistical techniques, SMC techniques can estimate the reliability of a complex safety critical hybrid system, to which conventional V&V techniques often fail to apply due to high complexity of a target system.

Therefore, we believe that industries on safety critical system domain can benefit from the SMC techniques much. As market competition becomes severe, many companies try hard to improve the quality of their products and to obtain safety certificate such as ISO 26262 [7] for automobiles and DO178B/C [13] for avionics by validating the reliability of the products. However, it has been very difficult to validate the reliability of complex hybrid systems due to aforementioned reasons. SMC can be used to validate the reliability goal assigned to a target system/component effectively and efficiently. In [9], we have demonstrated that SMC can be a solution for validating software reliability at an early development stage to reduce the defect correction cost of conventional software reliability assessment procedures such as IEEE Std.1633 [5].

As future work, to improve the practicality of the SMC techniques further, we plan to collaborate with automobile companies like Hyundai or Kia on the application of

---

[9] From this observation, we have developed a hybrid SMC technique which combines SPRT, the fastest SMC technique and BIET, the most accurate SMC technique. We have showed that this hybrid SMC technique improves effectiveness and efficiency compared to a single SMC technique [10].

the SMC techniques on automobile controllers. In addition, we will develop a safety engineering process to validate software reliability based on the SMC techniques, which is essential to obtain safety certificate.

Acknowledgment. This work was supported by the Excellent Research Center (ERC) of Excellence Program of Korea MEST/NRF of Korea (Grant 2012-0000473), the IT R&D program of MKE/KEIT [10041752, Research and Development of Dual Operating System Architecture with High-Reliable RTOS and High-Performance OS], and Dual Use Technology Program in Korea.

References

1. Clarke, E., Biere, A., Raimi, R., Zhu, Y.: Bounded model checking using satisfiability solving. Formal Methods System Design (FMSD) 19(1), 7–34 (2001)
2. Clarke, E., Donzé, A., Legay, A.: Statistical model checking of mixed-analog circuits with an application to a third order $\Delta - \Sigma$ modulator. In: Chockler, H., Hu, A.J. (eds.) HVC 2008. LNCS, vol. 5394, pp. 149–163. Springer, Heidelberg (2009)
3. Halstead, M.H.: Elements of Software Science. Elsevier Science Ltd. (1977)
4. Hérault, T., Lassaigne, R., Magniette, F., Peyronnet, S.: Approximate probabilistic model checking. In: Steffen, B., Levi, G. (eds.) VMCAI 2004. LNCS, vol. 2937, pp. 73–84. Springer, Heidelberg (2004)
5. IEEE Computer Society. IEEE Std 1633: IEEE Recommend Practice on Software Reliability (2008)
6. International Electrotechnical Commission (IEC). IEC 61508: Functional safety of electrical/electronic/programmable electronic (E/E/PE) safety related systems (2005)
7. International Organization for Standardization (ISO). ISO 26262: Road vehicles – functional safety (2011),
   http://www.iso.org/iso/catalogue_detail?csnumber=43464
8. Jha, S.K., Clarke, E.M., Langmead, C.J., Legay, A., Platzer, A., Zuliani, P.: A bayesian approach to model checking biological systems. In: Degano, P., Gorrieri, R. (eds.) CMSB 2009. LNCS, vol. 5688, pp. 218–234. Springer, Heidelberg (2009)
9. Kim, Y., Choi, O., Kim, M., Baik, J., Kim, T.: Validating software reliability through statistical model checking: Safer, cheaper, and faster. IEEE Software (under review)
10. Kim, Y., Kim, M., Kim, T.: Hybrid statistical model checking technique for reliable safety critical systems. In: IEEE International Symposium on Software Reliability Engineering, ISSRE (2012)
11. Kwiatkowska, M., Norman, G., Parker, D.: PRISM 4.0: Verification of probabilistic real-time systems. In: Gopalakrishnan, G., Qadeer, S. (eds.) CAV 2011. LNCS, vol. 6806, pp. 585–591. Springer, Heidelberg (2011)
12. Lauber, J., Guerra, T.M., Dambrine, M.: Air-fuel ratio control in a gasoline engine. International Journal of Systems Science (IJSySc) 42(2), 277–286 (2011)
13. Radio Technical Commission for Aeronautics (RTCA). Do-178c: Software considerations in airborne systems and equipment certification (2012)
14. Sen, P.K., Singer, J.M.: Large sample methods in statistics: An Introduction with Applications. Chapman & Hall, New York (1993)
15. Wald, A.: Sequential tests of statistical hypotheses. Annals of Mathematical Statistics 16(2), 117–186 (1945)

16. Yi, S., Heo, J., Cho, Y., Hong, J.: Adaptive mobile checkpointing facility for wireless sensor networks. In: Gavrilova, M.L., Gervasi, O., Kumar, V., Tan, C.J.K., Taniar, D., Laganá, A., Mun, Y., Choo, H. (eds.) ICCSA 2006. LNCS, vol. 3981, pp. 701–709. Springer, Heidelberg (2006)
17. Younes, H.L.S.: Verification and Planning for Stochastic Processes with Asynchronous Events. PhD thesis, CMU (January 2005)
18. Younes, H.L.S., Kwiatkowska, M., Norman, G., Parker, D.: Numerical vs. statistical probabilistic model checking. Software Tools for Technology Transfer (STTT) 8(3), 216–228 (2006)
19. Younes, H.L.S., Musliner, D.J.: Probabilistic plan verification through acceptance sampling. In: AIPS Workshop on Planning via Model Checking (2002)
20. Younes, H.L.S., Simmons, R.G.: Statistical probabilistic model checking with a focus on time-bounded properties. Journal Information and Computation (JIC) 204(9), 1368–1409 (2006)
21. Zuliani, P., Platzer, A., Clarke, E.M.: Bayesian statistical model checking with application to stateflow/simulink verification. In: Hybrid Systems: Computation and Control, HSCC (2010)

A New Test-Generation Methodology for System-Level Verification of Production Processes*

Allon Adir, Alex Goryachev, Lev Greenberg, Tamer Salman, and Gil Shurek

IBM Research - Haifa, Haifa, Israel
{adir,gory,levg,tamers,shurek}@il.ibm.com

Abstract. The continuing growth in the complexity of production processes is driven mainly by the integration of smart and cheap devices, such as sensors and custom hardware or software components. This naturally leads to higher complexity in fault detection and management, and, therefore to a higher demand for sophisticated quality control tools. A production process is commonly modeled prior to its physical construction to enable early testing. Many simulation platforms were developed to assess the widely varying aspects of the production process, including physical behavior, hardware-software functionality, and performance. However, the efficacy of simulation for the verification of modeled processes is still largely limited by manual operation and observation. We propose a massive random-biased, ontology-based, test-generation methodology for system-level verification of production processes. The methodology has been successfully applied for simulation-based processor hardware verification and proved to be a cost-effective solution. We show that it can be similarly beneficial in the verification of production processes and control.

Keywords: Production processes / Manufacturing processes, Test generation, Transaction-based modeling, UML/SysML.

1 Introduction

Modern production processes are becoming smarter and more complex. Cheaper, smarter sensors allow for more informative control of production systems [1]. The traditional end-of-line quality control can filter out defective products for recycling. On the other hand, in-process quality control provides the ability to take action on defective workpieces within the production process [2]. In-process control is largely based on the incorporation of various sensors in the various stages of the manufacturing chain. This leads to more complex possible production "paths" that include the possibility of fixing or adjusting a defective workpiece, repeated application of one or more stages, possible in-process product sorting based on observed features, and more.

---

* The research leading to these results has received funding from the European Union Seventh Framework Programme (FP7/2007-2013) under grant agreement n° 285075.

A. Biere, A. Nahir, and T. Vos (Eds.): HVC 2012, LNCS 7857, pp. 178–192, 2013.

The growth in complexity poses a challenge to the design and construction of robust and error-free production processes. Smart and automated verification activities are required to ensure the correctness of process designs. In general, behavioral models are useful for pre-construction simulation and testing as well as for post-construction adaptation. Finding design errors in simulation environments before creating the actual system is easier and cheaper than looking for them in the system itself, due to better observability and controllability of the system. In addition, the actual construction of a production system can be very costly, making it highly desirable to correct as many faults as possible in a design before it is implemented. Some existing modeling environments of production processes [3–11] were devised to enable visualization [4, 7], while others produce executable behavioral models for simulation purposes [3, 6, 8, 10, 11]. However, testing in these environments focuses on structural coverage and time-related verification.

Nevertheless, such simulation platforms can help assess the system behavior and performance in different "situations" for functional verification purposes. These situations (i.e., tests) are the key to effective deployment of the simulator. The common approach of manually operating the simulator suffers both from the relatively small number of tests that are eventually used and from the difficulty of directing the system to situations that may be worthy of testing. For example, creation of scenarios that involve events occurring far from the system inputs may require complex analysis of the system operation. Automatic test generators exist for simulation, but these focus mainly on simulating the expected typical behavior of the system and lack controls to direct the testing toward the rare functional corner cases that may be required in the test plan.

In this paper, we focus on automatic and directed massive test generation for simulation environments that allow for functional and performance testing. A good test generator produces tests that exercise the possible paths of the system under various performance- and stress-related conditions. In addition, using verification testing-knowledge can enhance the coverage achieved by the generated tests and bring the simulated system to corner cases or stress scenarios according to a given test plan.

Our approach uses two separate models of the system. The first model is an executable behavioral model that is used for simulation. The second model, on which our test-generation expert system is based, serves as a repository for accumulating knowledge on how to generate tests. This knowledge includes information about the system structure and properties, which is required for generating valid tests and also knowledge as to how to best test the production system. This is typically a derivation and extension of the knowledge accumulated for past verification efforts [12].

Our proposed methodology of test generation for simulation environments of production processes is drawn from the field of processor hardware verification. The great advancements in processor hardware verification technologies were made possible due to the high cost of bugs in hardware, which brought large investments to the field. It is also due to the increasing use of formal languages in the hardware design process, which enabled increased automation in verification. Specifically, our test generation expert system uses the X-Gen test generator [13], originally developed and successfully used for testing IBM's processor hardware systems.

Our work is being conducted as part of the MuProD project [2] funded by the European Commission within the Seventh Framework Programme. MuProD is advancing solutions that avoid end-of-line (EOL) failures in production processes via intelligent and integrated in-process measurement techniques. These measurement techniques are immediately followed by reactions to generated defects, as they are detected. This novel type of production system can benefit much from our proposed test-generation methodology because of the large number of possible different paths and behaviors induced by the multiplicity of sensors, reworking stages, and in-process fault types.

Our proposed verification methodology also uses simulation monitors to track test coverage and identify possible problematic system behavior during the simulation of a test. The experiment reported in Sec. 6 used simulation-monitoring techniques to monitor the coverage of system simulations. These monitoring techniques were developed for the DANSE project [14], also funded by the European Commission within the Seventh Framework Programme. DANSE deals with the development of new methodology to support the evolving, adaptive, and iterative system-of-systems (SoS) life cycle models, including analysis and simulation support.

Our approach offers the following contributions to the verification methodologies of production processes: 1) Defining a testing ontology for production processes using (UML) [15] or (SysML) [16], following the concept described in [17]; 2) Performing functional and performance verification by massive random-biased testing; 3) Demonstrating how transaction-based testing can be applied to production processes; and 4) Enabling capture and accumulation of testing knowledge for functional and performance verification of production processes.

2   Methodology of Simulation-Based System-Level Verification of Production Processes

This section begins with a description of a working example of a production process design. We then describe our proposed methodology for system-level verification and show how it can be applied to the working example.

2.1   Working Example

The working example that accompanies this paper is a production process composed of 35 components. Most of these are generic components, including operators, buffers, sensors, tracks and track junctions (track joiners and splitters), a scrap heap, and product stocks. Some components are processing stages specific to our example production process (e.g., one shifter and one injector). The objects passing through the production process are packets. A packet contains three attributes: an ID for unique identification purposes of the packet and two attributes with integer values named X and Y (which may represent some dynamic physical attributes of the manipulated packet). The topology of the production process is depicted in Fig. 1, where the solid lines portray possible paths for the flow of packets and the dashed lines portray the flow of sensory information.

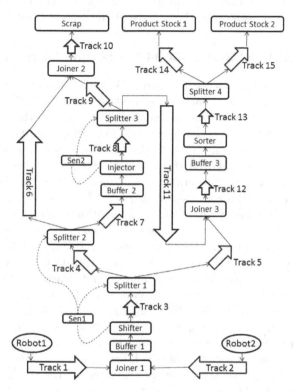

Fig. 1. A working example of a production process topology

In this working example, two operators, called Robot 1 and Robot 2, put packets on tracks toward processing by a shifter stage, which shifts some constant amount from the Y attribute of a packet to the X attribute. However, during shifting some amount could be lost (i.e., leakage). A sensor identifies the leakage during shifting and sends the information to corresponding splitters designed so that three different continuations are possible for the packet. A path (through Track 5) for successfully shifted packets for which the leakage is tolerated (according to some tolerance threshold parameter), a second path (through Tracks 4 then 6) for packets that are ruined by excessive leakage, and a third path (through Tracks 4 then 7) for packets for which the leakage is not tolerated, but may be corrected by a re-work. The re-work for the latter path is performed by another processing stage called the injector. The injector adds some constant amount to the X attribute of the packet. However, the injected amount might also suffer from leakage. Another sensor computes whether the leakage is small enough and whether or not it was able to bring the total leakage to a tolerated amount or not. If the re-work was successful, the packet is joined to the path leading to the product stocks (through Track 11). Otherwise, the packet is joined to the path leading to the scrap heap (through Track 9). Packets designated for the product stocks are sorted by another splitter according to the relation between their X and Y attributes. If X is larger than Y they arrive at the first product stock, otherwise they arrive at the second product stock.

2.2 Simulation-Based System-Level Verification Platform

The methodology under which our test generation solution operates is borrowed from the field of processor hardware verification (specifically verification of computer systems and SoCs) [13] and is described in Fig. 2. In this methodology, the verification engineer writes test templates according to a test plan. These test templates serve as the main input to the test generator. The test templates aim to generate tests that will drive the simulation towards desired states or scenarios in the design. The test generator is an expert system that includes both system-oblivious parts and system-specific parts. The test generator is based on a domain-specific ontology, in which an application engineer defines the terminology for specifying production systems and testing knowledge. Using this terminology, the application engineer then models a specific production process and its testing knowledge. The result of the test generation is a set of random-biased tests. These tests are fed into a simulator that simulates the design. The design's behavior while the test is running can be verified by various means. For example, verification could be done by using a reference model, or alternatively, by embedding simulation *checking monitors* to detect the occurrence of violations of system requirements. Such checking monitors give appropriate failure and pass reports. Another set of monitors, known as *coverage monitors*, can be used to detect the occurrence of the events targeted by the test plan. The coverage monitors produce coverage reports that are analyzed by the verification engineer. The verification engineer can be either satisfied with the testing results according to the test plan or can update the test templates to produce additional tests.

3 Modeling for Simulation and the Simulation Platform

Three types of components can be distinguished in the simulation platform that executes the tests (Fig. 3): designed components, behavioral components, and physical components.

The designed components are executable models that are direct representations of a designed element of the production system. These designs will later serve as the basis for implementation and, hence, finding problems in them is one of the main goals of the simulation-based testing.

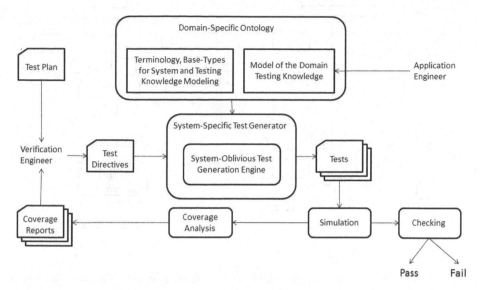

Fig. 2. High level description of the testing methodology for simulation based design verification

The behavioral components are behavioral representations of some element of the production system. These components behave like the real system element, but are designed differently. Typically, they involve a much simpler software implementation that has the same behavior as the real element. These behavioral models are needed for full-system simulation but are not the object of the testing procedure. A bug found in a behavioral model merely reflects a problem in the simulation and not in the system to be implemented. The behavioral models can represent components that have not yet been designed; components that cannot be designed, such as users or human operators; or alternatively, components that have already been thoroughly tested. A simulation environment can start with a few designed components and many behavioral components (Fig. 3(a)) that get replaced with their respective designed substitutes as the system design matures (Fig. 3(b)).

The physical components can be integrated in the simulation using classic system-integration-lab [18], or hardware-in-the-loop (HIL) platforms. Some of the designed components can be progressively replaced by the corresponding implemented physical components (Fig. 3(c)).

A production process can be modeled using any existing modeling platform that supports model simulation [3, 6, 8, 10]. For this work we chose SysML for modeling production processes. SysML is a general-purpose modeling language for systems engineering applications. It is an extension of a subset of UML, which originally targeted software or software-intensive systems. These modeling languages are object-oriented in nature and can be translated into executable languages using code generators. The executable models can then be run for simulation purposes.

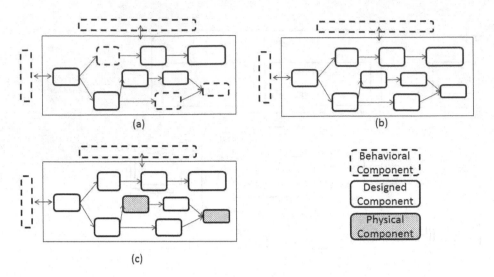

Fig. 3. High level description of the evolution of a simulation environment, where behavioral components are replaced with corresponding designed components and then by physical components as the production process model matures. (a) A production process model described using designed and behavioral components. (b) A production process described using designed components. (c) A production process described using designed components and integrating physical components. The remaining behavioral components after the model matures are input/output components and human operators.

We model components in a production process using SysML blocks. We model the behavior of components using statecharts and the interaction among component types using flowports and events. The topology of the production process is modeled in a SysML internal block diagram.

In addition to being able to transform the model into an executable program, the model should also be able to consume our generated tests. This means the behavioral components should be able to read the instructions given in a test and operate accordingly.

The software components of the simulated system are instantiated from a production-process ontology, which is basically an extendable and reusable library of component types. The component types are chosen either from an existing set of component types—such as tracks, track-junctions (splitters and joiners), buffers—or especially modeled for the specific production system such as models of in-line machining and sensors. The configuration of the model consists of configured instances of the component types and the topology of their connections. For example, a track can be configured to have a certain length and speed. In our working example, all tracks are configured to have a length with room for ten slots of packets, and they advance one slot every half a second.

4 Test Generation

We used X-Gen [13] to generate tests for production processes, such as the working example process shown in Fig. 1. X-Gen is a test-case generator originally developed and applied to computer systems and system on chip (SoCs). X-Gen adheres to the ontology-based paradigm [12]. The generator is partitioned into two separate layers. At the core of X-Gen is a system-oblivious test generation engine, which is capable of generating tests for a variety of systems. This generic engine, with the addition of the domain-specific ontology, is a system-specific test generator as shown in Fig. 2.

The abstract system model, which is a part of the domain-specific ontology, describes the system's components and its *interactions* (i.e., system scenarios that involve multiple components that collaborate to achieve some target). Testing knowledge is the verification expertise that biases the random test generation toward interesting areas for verification. Incorporating testing knowledge does not require explicit input from the user. An example of the testing-knowledge building blocks provided by X-Gen is its collision mechanism that biases tests toward the (possibly concurrent) reuse of certain system resources.

The topology of the system under test is described in a configuration file, while the verification scenario is defined in a test template file. The scenario definition is done using a proprietary special-purpose programming language developed for this task. The language allows verification engineers to define scenarios ranging from fully deterministic to totally random.

Once the test template is consumed by the test generator, a set of tests is created. These tests can be fed into the simulation to practice the different scenarios they represent in the model of the production process.

4.1 Test Template Definition Language

A test template describes the test characteristics required for specific verification goals. Through test templates, verification engineers can provide a full or partial specification of a required scenario and leave unspecified all the aspects that are not crucial to the scenario. This enables X-Gen to hit a targeted event in a large number of different ways. Thus, when a targeted scenario is defined by the verification engineer in loose terms, X-Gen, through its randomness and testing knowledge, can generate an interesting test around the loosely-defined scenario.

System interactions are the basic building blocks of the test template language. Verification engineers can constrain different interaction attributes, including the identity of the initiator and target(s) that participate in the interaction and their properties.

An interesting interaction in the context of production processes is one concerning a packet released by an operator and ending up in a sink, where a sink is either a scrap heap or a product stock. We call this interaction a *FullPath* interaction. When the operator or the sink are not specified as part of the interaction in the test template, then the decision is left for the random-biased generation engine to determine appropriate specific components.

The test template language contains several high-level statements used to group interactions or other high-level statements: AllOf statement generating all of its sub-statements; OneOf statement providing a weighted choice between its sub-statements; and Repeat statement generating multiple instances of its sub-statements. These high-level statements can be used to group single interactions or to group other high-level statements. Hence, a test template can be viewed as a tree with interactions as its leaves and high-level statements as its intermediate nodes.

In addition to the concepts described above, X-Gen's test-template language provides programming-language-like constructs that enables verification engineers to depict specific scenarios. These constructs include a rich expression language and support for variables with typed declarations, assignments, and constraining the selection of values for actors and properties. This enables the verification engineer to form practically any type of complex relationship among a set of interactions.

Consider the topology design of the working example shown in Fig. 1. Among the interesting behaviors to be tested in the production process are synchronized packets, i.e., packets that are released by the two different operators at the same time or a workload of packets arriving at the two different product stocks with some given ratio. A test template requesting tests that include both of the above-mentioned behaviors is shown in Fig. 4.

```
Integer: T
ComponentId: targetSink
AllOf
  Repeat(400)
    AllOf
      FullPath: {Robot1}; (T <- time); (targetSink <- target)
      FullPath: {Robot2}; (time <- T); (target <- targetSink)
  Repeat(200)
    OneOf
      FullPath: (target <- ProductStock1) weight=10
      FullPath: {target <- ProductStock2} weight=90
```

Fig. 4. Example test template

The test template in Fig. 4, when consumed by a test generator, should be able to yield many random tests. In each such test, 800 packets will be released by the 2 operators, Robot 1 and Robot 2. Each operator will release 400 packets synchronized with the packets of the other operator and reaching the same destination sink. Note that X-Gen generates the interactions in the same order they appear in the test template. The resolution of variables follows the order of the interactions' generation.

Following that, the test will include the release of 200 packets from random operators, such that 10% of the packets will end up in Product Stock 1 and the remaining 90% in Product Stock 2.

4.2   X-Gen Generation Scheme for Production Processes

For a given test template, X-Gen's generation process can be divided into two layers: traversing the high-level statement tree and generating the interactions at its leaves. Statement tree traversal is done in a hierarchical manner, in which each statement is responsible for the generation of all of its sub-statements. An AllOf statement, for example, would generate all its sub-statements, while a OneOf statement would randomly pick one of its sub-statements and then generate it.

X-Gen generates an interaction by constructing and solving a constraint network, also known as a *constraint satisfaction problem* (CSP). Testing knowledge is incorporated into the CSP as soft constraints that are activated with some preset probability. The network is solved using a variant of the well-known *maintaining arc consistency* (MAC) algorithm [19, 20].

An interaction is generated in two stages. In the first stage called *path selection*, X-Gen randomly chooses an interaction initiator and target(s). This is done by forming a CSP to choose the path used by the interaction. We create a CSP variable representing the path. The domain of the CSP variable is the set of all paths that initiate from one of the allowed initiators and terminate at one of the allowed targets. Additional constraints may be used to enforce path restrictions; soft constraints may be added to bias toward interesting paths (e.g., always going "left" from a certain Splitter).

Once the path is chosen, a second stage, referred to as *property selection*, constructs a second CSP network. The variables in the CSP are the properties of the interaction, including the properties of a packet. Some components along the chosen path impose restrictions on the properties of the packet and some modify them. The restrictions and modifications are naturally modeled through constraints on respective components. Soft constraints are added to bias random choices to interesting corner cases.

4.3   Tests

A test for the design of a production process is a collection of interactions between component types. The generated test is refined by creating a text file containing specific configurations and instructions to the simulator.

When refined into a text file, a test includes a configuration of the system, its initial state, and sets of instructions for the behavioral components in the system. The configuration of the system is the assignment of values to the various parameters of the different components. The initial state describes the state of the system when the test starts running, e.g., the packets that already exist in-flight in the different stages in the system. The sets of instructions for the initiating and behavioral components are directions for how these components should generate activity in the production process. Each instruction includes a time stamp in which it is to be performed, a command specifying what activity is to be generated, and a set of arguments for that activity.

Consider the topology design in Fig. 1 of the working example and the test template in Fig. 4. A partial snapshot of a possible test that could be produced from the given test template is shown in Fig. 5. The configuration of the shifter is given in the parameter defining the shifted amount, which is set to 10, while the configuration of the first sensor is given in the parameter defining the tolerance threshold, which is set to 3. The synchronized interactions are specified in the template to cause the two operators to put two different packets in the production line at the same time and so that they end up in the same sink. This may yield the first instructions in Robot 1 and Robot 2 in the test. Both packets are released to their corresponding tracks 20 seconds (TS = 20) into the test, and both will arrive at the scrap heap due to untolerated and unfixable leakage.

```
INITIALIZATIONS: Operator:Robot1
-------------------------------
B Put Packet=<ID=3,X=48,Y=67> TS=20
:

INITIALIZATIONS: Operator:Robot2
-------------------------------
B Put Packet=<ID=5,X=77,Y=11> TS=20
:

INITIALIZATIONS: Stage:Shifter
-------------------------------
C ShiftAmount 10
B Leak Leakage=<ID=3,amount=6>
B Leak Leakage=<ID=5,amount=7>
:

INITIALIZATIONS: Stage:Sensor1
-------------------------------
C Tolerance 3
:
```

Fig. 5. An example test

5   Checking and Coverage Analysis

In simulation-based verification, the simulation of the generated tests aims to reveal errors in the design under test. The occurrence of an error during a test simulation can be detected in various ways. One method is to generate tests that include their corresponding expected results (intermediate and final). This method requires some reference model that is able to "run" the test and predict the expected results. When the test is simulated on the design simulator, the actual results are compared with the expected results from the reference model.

Another approach is to use simulation monitors. A simulation monitor is a software module that observes the progress of simulation and can detect and report specified behaviors of the simulated model. Simulation monitors have diverse uses such as:

- *Checking monitors*: These monitors check for violations of system requirements as exhibited during simulation. These can originate from the system stakeholder requirements, from the designer, or from the verification engineer. They can include monitors to check for requirements relating to speed, power, heat, and more. They can also check for requirements relating to the functionality of the production system (e.g., that a production stage is performing its designated task correctly).
- *Coverage monitors*: These monitors check for the occurrence of scenarios targeted by the test plan. Coverage monitors are the main vehicle for assessing the progress or completeness of the testing phase. The coverage reports can help the verification engineer focus on uncovered areas or can lead to a managerial decision that enough testing has been done.
- Monitors that gather statistics for post-simulation analysis, such as an analysis of system performance, power consumption, scrap rates, and more.

In the following section, we compare the performance of different test generation approaches using simulation coverage monitors.

We show that our test generation method is able to reach significantly higher functional coverage than a random test generator with a smaller number of tests.

6   Experiments

A SysML model of a production process, as described in Section 2.1 and Fig. 1, was constructed to demonstrate the application of the proposed test-generation technology. The modeled production process topology includes 12 different end-to-end production paths. In addition, for demonstration purposes, we defined the following set of verification events for the production process as testing knowledge in the ontology:

A. **name:** *Almost total shift*
   definition: $Y \in \{0, 1\}$ after the shifter stage.
B. **name:** *Near-equilibrium at start*
   definition: $|X - Y| \leq 2$ when released by a robot.
C. **name:** *Near-equilibrium at end*
   definition: $|X - Y| \leq 2$ when entering a scrap or a product stock.
D. **name:** *Shifter tolerance leakage*
   definition: Leakage of the shifter is exactly the tolerance threshold.
E. **name:** *Injector tolerance leakage*
   definition: Leakage of the injector is exactly the tolerance threshold.

We set the verification goal to cover all the above five verification events for each of the 12 end-to-end production paths. This defines a coverage model with $12 \times 5 = 60$ coverage objectives. However, only 36 of the 60 coverage objectives are in fact possible in the defined production process. For example, event E can occur only for paths that go through the injector, and only 6 such paths exist. Next, given this coverage model, the following test templates were created. Each template was set to generate a test with 3000 packets. The total number of covered objectives as a function of the simulated packets is shown in Fig. 6 for the 4 test templates. The templates are ordered from the most constrained to the least constrained. As expected, the less constrained test templates, though easier to specify, resulted in a slower coverage rate.

1. The first test template explicitly specifies a test for each of the 60 coverage objectives. The 12 paths were precisely specified and the 5 verification events were requested by invoking the corresponding controls from the testing knowledge database. The activation of the testing knowledge was a nonmandatory specification, which means that the event will occur in the test only if it is possible when considering the mandatory constraints, such as the test validity and the path specifications.
2. The second template specifies only the five verification events from the testing knowledge, while the end-to-end production paths were left to be selected randomly by the test generator.
3. The third template merely directs the generator to generate tests with random packets, while activating the default settings of the testing knowledge.
4. The fourth template is purely random, i.e., un-biased tests will be generated, constrained only to be valid production paths with no application of any testing knowledge.

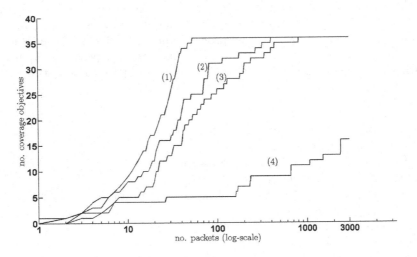

Fig. 6. Coverage progress for the four different test-generation approaches. (1) Directed towards all coverage goals. (2) Directed towards the verification events with random paths. (3) Random tests with default testing knowledge. (4) Random tests with no testing knowledge.

As shown in Fig. 6, the tests generated for the first template were the quickest to reach full coverage of the 36 coverage objectives. The second and third test templates took much longer to reach full coverage than the first. However, these less specific test templates have the advantage of giving more "room" for the test generator to apply its random testing knowledge and thus generate a greater variety of tests. X-Gen's test template specification language allows verification engineers to define templates ranging from fully deterministic to completely random. Yet even the completely random templates will be generated with the default random application of testing knowledge, which biases the random generation toward areas worthy of testing. In addition, Fig. 6 shows that the fourth template, which did not use any testing knowledge, made the slowest progress in coverage, as expected. In fact, some of the events were never covered, even after 3000 packets. These events have a naturally low probability of occurring but may still be important to test. An alternative to our approach would be to fill in these coverage holes by manually writing the missing test cases. However, this is obviously time-consuming and sometimes difficult to achieve. The events may refer to behaviors of the packet flow somewhere in mid-production, and therefore the test creation would require a detailed analysis of the manipulations carried out at the relevant processing stages.

7 Conclusions and Future Work

We presented a new test-generation methodology for system-level verification of production processes. Our methodology offers an alternative to manual and random test generation for functional and performance verification, by producing massive random-biased tests. The tests are generated from test templates stated in a rich high-level template language. The test generator uses a generic system-oblivious engine in addition to a domain-specific ontology and testing knowledge. We described an ontology of a production system using SysML, an industrial-standard modeling language. We built a simulator for this ontology, also using SysML, to run the generated tests. We presented an example of how to model a production process for the purpose of functional and performance testing. We demonstrated our methodology for generating tests that achieve coverage of a set of verification objectives and compared it to the coverage of a random test generator. We showed that our approach can achieve better coverage with a smaller number of tests than random test generation.

In the future, we plan to apply our methodology for test generation on a variety of types of production processes used by the industrial partners of the MuProd project. We expect that this methodology will prove beneficial to the field of production processes' design and verification.

References

1. Teti, R., Jemielniak, K., O'Donnell, G., Dornfeld, D.: Advanced monitoring of machining operations. CIRP Annals - Manufacturing Technology 59, 717–739 (2010)
2. MuProD, http://www.muprod.eu/

3. Köhler, H., Nickel, U., Niere, J., Zündorf, A.: Integrating UML Diagrams in Production Control Systems. In: International Conference on Software Engineering, pp. 241–251 (2000)
4. Rother, M., Shook, J.: Learning to See: Value-Stream Mapping to Create Value and Eliminate MUDA, Lean Enterprise Inst., Version 1.3, Cambridge, Mass. (2003)
5. Nickel, U., Niere, J., Zündorf, A.: The FUJABA Environment. In: International Conference on Software Engineering, pp. 742–745 (2000)
6. Specht, T., Drawehn, J., Thränert, M., Kühne, S.: Modeling Cooperative Business Processes and Transformation to a Service Oriented Architecture. In: 7th IEEE International Conference on ECommerce Technology, pp. 249–256 (2005)
7. Wen-xian, T., Yuan-yuan, X.: A Production Process Mixed Modeling for Marine Diesel Engine Based on IDEF0 and Petri Net. In: International Symposium on Information Science and Engineering, ISISE 2008, vol. 2, pp. 773–777 (2008)
8. Zor, S., Görlach, K., Leymann, F.: Using Modeling Manufacturing Processes. In: Sihn, W., Kuhlang, P. (eds.) Sustainable Production and Logistics in Global Networks - Proceedings of 43rd CIRP International Conference on Manufacturing Systems, pp. 515–522 (2010)
9. Campagna, D., Formisano, A.: ProdProc - Product and Production Process Modeling and Configuration. In: 26th Italian Conference on Computational Logic, pp. 261–279 (2011)
10. Organization for the Advancement of Structured Information Standards (OASIS), Web Services Business Process Execution Language Version 2.0 - OASIS Standard (2007)
11. Colledani, M., Terkaj, W., Tolio, T.: Product-Process-System Information Formalization. In: Tolio, T. (ed.) Design of Flexible Production Systems: Methodologies and Tools. Springer (2009)
12. Aharon, A., Lichtenstein, Y., Malka, Y.: Model-Based Test Generator for Processor Design Verification. In: Innovative Applications of Artificial Intelligence (IAAI) (1994)
13. Emek, R., Jaeger, I., Naveh, Y., Bergman, G., Aloni, G., Katz, Y., Farkash, M., Dozoretz, I., Goldin, A.: X-Gen: A Random Test-Case Generator for Systems and SoCs. In: 7th IEEE International High-Level Design Validation and Test Workshop (HLDVT), pp. 145–150 (2002)
14. DANSE, http://danse-ip.eu/home
15. http://www.omg.org/spec/UML/2.4.1/
16. http://www.omg.org/spec/SysML/1.3/
17. Bin, E., Ghanayim, A., Holtz, K., Marcus, E., Morad, R., Peled, O., Rimon, M., Shurek, G., Tsanko, E.: Ontology-Based Tools in the Service of Hardware Verification. In: 22nd International Conference on Software Engineering & Knowledge Engineering, pp. 303–308. Knowledge Systems Institute Graduate School (2010)
18. Brahme, D.S., Cox, S., Gallo, J., Glasser, M., Grundmann, W., Norris Ip, C., Paulsen, W., Pierce, J.L., Rose, J., Shea, D., Whiting, K.: The Transaction-Based Verification Methodology. Cadence Berkeley Labs (2000)
19. Bin, E., Emek, R., Shurek, G., Ziv, A.: Using constraint satisfaction formulations and solution techniques for random test program generation. IBM Systems Journal 41(3), 386–402 (2002)
20. Mackworth, A.: Consistency in Networks of Relations. Artificial Intelligence 8(1), 99–118 (1977)

Defining and Model Checking Abstractions of Complex Railway Models Using CSP||B

Faron Moller[1], Hoang Nga Nguyen[1], Markus Roggenbach[1],
Steve Schneider[2], and Helen Treharne[2]

[1] Swansea University, Wales, UK
[2] University of Surrey, England, UK

Abstract. The safety analysis of interlocking railway systems involves verifying collision and derailment freedom. In this paper we propose a structured way of refining track plans, in order to expand track segments so that they form collections of track segments. We show how the abstract model can be model checked to ensure the safety properties, which must also hold in the corresponding concrete track plan, so that we will never need to model check the concrete track plan directly. We also identify the minimal number of trains that needs to be considered as part of the model checking, and we demonstrate the practicality of the approach on various scenarios.

1 Introduction

Formal verification of railway control software has been identified as one of the "Grand Challenges" of Computer Science [11]. As is typical with Formal Methods, this challenge comes in two parts: the first addresses the question of whether the mathematical models considered are legitimate representations of the physical systems of concern. The modelling of the systems, as well as of proof obligations, needs to be *faithful*. The second part is the question of how to utilize available technologies, for example model checking or theorem proving. Whichever verification process is adopted, it needs to be both *effective* and *efficient*.

In [13,12] we proposed a new modelling approach for railway interlockings. We use CSP||B [15], which combines event-based with state-based modelling. This reflects the double nature of railway systems, which involves events such as train movements and, in the interlocking, state based reasoning. In this sense, CSP||B offers the means for the natural modelling approach we strive for: the formal models are close to the domain models. To the domain expert, this provides traceability and ease of understanding. This addresses the first of the above stated challenges: *faithful* modelling.

In this paper, we address the question of how to *effectively* and *efficiently* verify various safety properties within our CSP||B models. To this end we develop a set of abstraction techniques for railway verification that allow the transformation of complex CSP||B models into less involved ones, prove that they are

A. Biere, A. Nahir, and T. Vos (Eds.): HVC 2012, LNCS 7857, pp. 193–208, 2013.

correct, and demonstrate that they allow one to verify a variety of railway systems via model checking. The first set of abstractions reduces the number of trains that need to be considered in order to prove safety for an unbounded number of trains. Their correctness proof involves slicing of event traces. Essentially, these abstractions provide us with finite state models. The second set of abstractions simplifies the underlying track topology. Here, the correctness proof utilizes event abstraction specific to our application domain similar to the ones suggested by Winter in [17]. These abstractions make model checking faster.

Outline. We first introduce our modelling language CSP||B. In Section 3 we summarise our generic railway modelling approach using CSP||B, as described in [13,12]. In Section 4, we present our first set of abstraction techniques based on event traces. Then in Section 5 we present our data abstraction techniques. The application of the abstraction results is presented via a set of example scenarios in Section 6. In Section 7 we put our work in the context of related approaches.

2   Background to CSP||B

The CSP||B approach allows us to specify communicating systems using a combination of the B-Method [4] and the process algebra CSP (Communicating Sequential Processes) [9]. The overall specification of a combined communicating system comprises two separate specifications: one given by a number of CSP process descriptions and the other by a collection of B machines. Our aim when using B and CSP is to factor out as much of the "data-rich" aspects of a system as possible into B machines. The B machines in our CSP||B approach are classical B machines, which are components containing state and operations on that state. The CSP||B theory [15] allows us to combine a number of CSP processes Ps in parallel with machines Ms to produce $Ps \parallel Ms$ which is the parallel combination of all the controllers and all the underlying machines. Such a parallel composition is meaningful because a B machine is itself interpretable as a CSP process whose event-traces are the possible execution sequences of its operations. The invoking of an operation of a B machine outside its precondition within such a trace is defined as divergence [14]. Therefore, our notion of consistency is that a combined communicating system $Ps \parallel Ms$ is *divergence-free* and also *deadlock-free*.

A B MACHINE clause declares a machine and gives it a name. The VARIABLES of a B machine define its state. The INVARIANT of a B machine gives the type of the variables, and more generally it also contains any other constraints on the allowable machine states. There is an INITIALISATION which determines the initial state of the machine. The machine consists of a collection of OPERATIONS that query and modify the state. Besides this kind of machine we also define static B machines that provide only sets, constants and properties that do not change during the execution of the system.

The language we use to describe the CSP processes for B machines is as follows:

$$P ::= e?x!y \rightarrow P(x) \mid P_1 \;\Box\; P_2 \mid P_1 \;\sqcap\; P_2 \mid \text{if } b \text{ then } P_1 \text{ else } P_2 \text{ end} \mid$$
$$N(exp) \mid P_1 \parallel P_2 \mid P_1 \;_A\|_B\; P_2 \mid P_1 \;\|\|\; P_2$$

The process $e?x!y \rightarrow P(x)$ defines a channel communication where x represents all data variables on a channel, and y represents values being passed along a channel. Channel e is referred to as a *machine channel* as there is a corresponding operation in the controlled B machine with the signature $x \longleftarrow e(y)$. Therefore the input of the B operation y corresponds to the output from the CSP, and the output x of the B operation to the CSP input. Here we have simplified the communication to have one output and one input but in general there can be any number of inputs and outputs. The other CSP operators have the usual CSP semantics.

For reasoning of CSP∥B models we require the following notation.

- Since a B machine is interpretable as a CSP process, the various CSP refinements also apply to CSP∥B. In this paper we focus on trace refinement where $P \sqsubseteq_T Q$ if $traces(Q) \subseteq traces(P)$. This refinement preserves safety properties, such as collision freedom or derailment freedom as we shall discuss in Section 3.
- Furthermore, we apply CSP renaming $f(P)$ and CSP hiding $P \setminus A$ to CSP processes, B machines and to CSP∥B models, which all semantically represent sets of traces. Given a set of traces T, $f(T)$ represents the set of all traces $tr \in T$ where the events are replaced point-wise by the function f; $T \setminus A$ to represent the set of all traces $tr \in T$ where the events from the set A are removed from tr.
- A system run σ (of a CSP∥B model) of length $n \geq 0$ is a finite sequence

$$\sigma = \langle s_0, e_0, s_1, e_1, \ldots, e_{n-1}, s_n \rangle$$

where the s_i, $i = 0 \ldots n$, are states of the B machine, and the e_i, $1 \leq i \leq n - 1$, are events – either controlled by CSP and enabled in B when called, or B events. Here we assume that s_0 is a state after initialisation. Given a system run σ, we can extract its trace of events:

$$events(\sigma) = \langle e_0, \ldots, e_{n-1} \rangle.$$

3 Modelling and Safety Verification of Railway Systems Using CSP∥B

Together with railway engineers we developed a common view on the information flow in railways. In physical terms a railway consists of, at least, four different components. These components are shown in Figure 1. The *Controller* selects and releases routes for trains. The *Interlocking* serves as a safety mechanism with regards to the Controller and, in addition, controls and monitors the Track equipment. The *Track equipment* consists of elements such as signals, points, and track circuits (logical names for tracks and points from the track plan as discussed above; in the railway domain, tracks and track circuits are often confused): signals can show the aspects green or red; points can be in normal position (leading trains straight ahead) or in reverse position (leading trains to a different line) and track circuits detect if there is a train on a track. Finally, *Trains* have a driver who determines their behaviour. For the purposes of modelling, we make the assumption that track equipment reacts instantly and is free of defects. The information flow shown in Figure 1 is as follows: the controller sends a request message to the interlocking to which the interlocking responds; the interlocking sends signalling information to the trains; and the trains inform the interlocking about their movements. The interlocking serves as the system's clock: messages can be exchanged once per cycle.

In this paper, we study various track plans, one of which is a station illustrated in Figure 2(b). It depicts the *scheme plan* for the station, which comprises a track plan, a control table, and release tables. (We will discuss Figure 2(a) in Section 6).

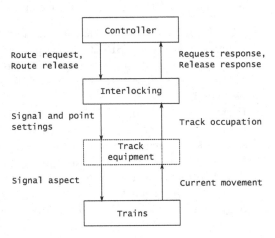

Fig. 1. Information flow

The *track plan* provides the topological information of the station which consists of 16 tracks (e.g., the track c_TAA), three signals (e.g., $S1$), and two points (e.g., P1). Note that the tracks include entry and exit tracks on which trains can "appear" and "disappear". These two kinds of tracks are specially treated during verification.

An interlocking system gathers train locations, and sends out commands to control signal aspects and point positions. The *control table* determines how the station interlocking system sets signals and points. For each signal, there is one row describing the condition under which the signal can show proceed. There are two rows for signal $S1$: one for the main line (Route A1) and one for the side line (Route B1). A route comprises tracks and points between two signals. For example, signal S1 for the main line can only show proceed when point P1 is in normal (straight) position and tracks $c\_TAA, c\_TAB, c\_TAC, c\_TAD, c\_TAE,$ c_TAF, c_TAG are all clear. Here we assume that trains are equipped with an Automatic Train Protection system which prevents trains from moving over a red light and therefore, overlaps are not needed, e.g., the overlap for Route A1 would be c_TAH. For further discussion on this see [10].

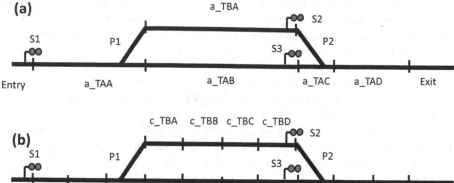

Control table				Release tables	

Control table

Route	Normal	Reverse	Clear
A1	P1		c_TAA, c_TAB, c_TAC, c_TAD, c_TAE, c_TAF, c_TAG
B1		P1	c_TAA, c_TAB, c_TAC, c_TBA, c_TBB, c_TBC, c_TBD
A2	P2		c_TAH, c_TAI, c_TAJ
B2		P2	c_TAH, c_TAI, c_TAJ

Release tables

P1	Occupied
A1	c_TAD
B1	c_TBA

P2	Occupied
A2	c_TAI
B2	c_TAI

Fig. 2. One Station - Abstract (a) and Concrete (b) Track Plan (Scenario 3 from Fig. 4)

The interlocking also allocates *locks* on points to particular route requests to keep them locked in position, and releases such locks when trains have passed. For example, the setting of Route A1 obtains a lock on point P1, and sets it to normal. The lock is released after the train has passed the point. *Release tables* store the relevant track.

In this setting, we consider two safety properties: *collision-freedom* excludes two trains occupying the same track; and *no-derailment* says that whenever a train enters a point, the point is set to cater for this; e.g., when a train travels from track c_TAG to track c_TAH, point P2 is set so that it connects c_TAG and c_TAH (and not c_TBD and c_TAH). The correct design for the control table and release tables is safety-critical: mistakes can lead to collision or derailment.

3.1 CSP||B Modelling of Railways

In previous work [12,13] we have demonstrated that CSP||B caters for railways. It is possible to read the actual models together with railway engineers in order to validate them. This review demonstrates that the models can be clearly understood by railway engineers. Here, we refrain from elaborating on the modelling approach and refer the interested reader to [13] for the details. However, the concepts from the models central for verification (in Section 4 and Section 5), namely static and dynamic state representation and also train movements, are discussed below.

The static state information of a CSP||B model is defined in context machines, i.e., machines that contain set and function definitions. For example, the names of all the track circuits is defined in a set called *ALLTRACKS*. The topology of the track plan is captured using a collection of relations that capture how the elements of the track plan are related. For example, $next : TRACK \leftrightarrow TRACK$ is a relation between tracks and possible successor tracks. Therefore, (c_TAC, a_TAD) and (c_TAC, c_TBA) are elements of the *next* relation within the one-station example in Figure 2.

The *Interlocking* machine models the dynamics of the system. Its state evolves over time. It consists of the following variables: *pos* representing the position of all trains, *nextd* representing the current position of all points (and thus the dynamic relation between tracks and their successors), *signalStatus* representing the aspect of each signal, *normalPoints* representing the points which are in normal position, *reversePoints* representing the points which are in reverse position, and *currentLocks* representing the current semaphores on points.

In the CSP||B models, a train a can perform one of the following events: *move.a.currp.newp* represents a moving from track *currp* to track *newp*, *nextSignal.a.aspect* represents a seeing the particular *aspect* (red or green) at the next signal, *enter.a.p* represents placing a on an entry track p, and *exit.a.p* represents a leaving the system. Trains that have left the system can be placed again on an entry track; we call this behaviour recurring trains. Note that in the situation where *currp* and *newp* are separated by a signal the event *move.a.currp.newp* is possible only if this signal shows green.

4   Providing Finite State Models

Our railway models are infinite state in nature. The reason for this is that we consider train identifiers explicitly. Therefore, it is essential to find bounds for the number of trains that we need to consider when analysing our models for safety. In this section we provide two methods: one tailored towards collision freedom, one designed for derailment freedom.

4.1   Minimum Number of Trains for Verifying Collision

The following theorem turns the question of whether a railway scheme plan is collision free into a finite state problem by reducing the – in principle – unbounded number of trains to be considered into a finite number:

Theorem 1. *Let S be a railway scheme plan with r routes. S is collision free iff all systems runs with $r + 1$ recurring trains are collision free.*

Proof. We prove the "if" direction only, as the other direction trivially holds.

We first note that if there are two trains on a route then a collision can occur (as these two trains are not separated by a signal). Therefore, as long as there is no collision there will be at most r trains on S. Assuming we have $r + 1$ trains there will always be one train available to move onto an entry track. Thus, $r + 1$ recurring trains are sufficient.   □

4.2   Minimum Number of Trains for Verifying Derailment

Regarding derailment, we obtain an even stronger result. The reduction argument, however, holds only for "reasonable" scheme-plans where the various tables are free of trivial mistakes with respect to the railway topology. Concretely, we say that a scheme plan is well-formed if the following conditions hold:

1. **Release-Table condition.** Locks of a route can only be released by a train movement on this route (e.g., in Figure 2, there is the lock c_TAD on P1 for route A1; c_TAD appears in the clear column of the control table for the route A1).
2. **Clear-Table condition.** The clear table of a route contains at least the tracks of this route (e.g., in Figure 2 route A1 topologically goes from signal S1 to signal S3 and all tracks from c_TAA to c_TAG are in the clear column of the control table for the route A1).
3. **Normal/Reverse-Table condition.** The normal table or the reverse table of a route contain at least the points on this route (e.g., in Figure 2 route A1 topologically goes from signal S1 to signal S3, it includes the only point P1, and P1 is in the normal column of the control table for the route A1).
4. **Route condition.** Topologically different routes are distinguishable by point positions in the control table (e.g., in Figure 2 route A1 and route B1 are topologically different, point P1 is in the normal column of the control table for route A1, point P1 is in the reverse column of the control table for route B1).
5. **Lock-Table condition.** Routes with different lock tables are distinguishable by point positions in the control table (e.g., in Figure 2 route A1 and route B1 have different lock table entries, namely, c_TAD and c_TBA respectively, in the control table the position of P1 distinguishes them as seen above).

The scheme plan of Figure 2 is well-formed.

Note that there is exactly one condition per table (release table, clear table, normal/reverse table, lock table) plus one condition which links routes as defined topologically with the route definition in the tables. All five conditions are static and can easily be decided for a given scheme-plan. It is worthwhile to point out that well-formedness does not imply the property "no-derailment":

Observation 1. *There exist well-formed scheme-plans with derailment.*

For example, altering the scheme plan of Figure 2 by exchanging the position of point P2 for route A2 and route B2 leads to derailment as explained in Section 3. This exchange, however, preserves well-formedness.

Our modelling characterizes only implicitly, which routes which are set. Therefore, we the following theorem is helpful:

Theorem 2. *For all system runs of a well-formed scheme-plans it holds: If a signal s shows green, then there exists a route r with signal(r) = s which is set.*

Then, we establish the following theorem which allows the reduction of the number of trains for proving derailment freedom:

Theorem 3. *For any collision free system run on a well-formed scheme plan involving $k \geq 1$ trains $Trains = \{a_1, \ldots, a_k\}$ and a train b which does not derail in this run, there exists a system run involving only the trains $\{a_1, \ldots, a_k\}$ with identical movements.*

Proof. (Sketch) Let σ be the system with trains in $\{a_1, \ldots, a_k, b\}$ where b does not derail. We shall construct another run σ' which

– does not speak about b, which,
– however, preserves the movement of all trains $a_i \in Trains$.

First, we define the set of all events $E(b)$ that are related with the train b:

$$E(b) := \{e \in \sigma \mid e = move.b.currp.newp$$
$$e = nextSignal.b.aspect$$
$$e = enter.b.p$$
$$e = exit.b.p\}$$

Intuitively, σ' is obtained from σ by either discarding or replacing events in $E(b)$. In order to determine how to treat these events, it is necessary to understand how the train b can influence the trains $a_i \in Trains$: (i) b might prevent a train $a \in Trains$ from moving (because a signal in front of a shows red because b uses a resource); (ii) b might allow a train in $Trains$ to move (a move from b releases a lock, so that the signal in front of a can change to green). When "taking away" b from σ our only concern is (ii): we wish to preserve moves. This insight leads to the definition of the following replacement function $replace_b$ concerning events (where ϵ stands for the empty word, i.e., for deletion of the event):

1. $replace_b(e) = e$ if $e \notin E(b)$
2. $replace_b(move.b.currp.newp) = release.r.bb$ if there exists a signal s with $currp = homeSignal(s)$. As **move** is only enabled if signal s shows green, Theorem 2 guarantees that there exists a route r which is set. Well-formedness of the scheme-plan guarantees uniqueness.
3. $replace_b(e) = \epsilon$ if e is any of $move.b.currp.newp$, where $currp \neq homeSignal(s)$ for any signal s, or $nextSignal.b.aspect$, or $enter.b.p$, or $exit.b.p$.

$replace_b$ keeps all events not related to b (1.), releases all locks related to b at the earliest possible opportunity (2.), and deletes all other events related to b.

In order to show that the constructed σ' is a system run, we relate states in σ with those in σ'. Informally, a state S in σ is related to a state T in σ', written as $S \geq_b T$, if (1) for all trains a_i it holds that in S and in T (i) their positions are the same and (ii) they are offerred the same possibilities to move; and (2) T does not speak about the train b. To capture these ideas formally, we define that $S \geq_b T$ if

1. Compared to S, T just deletes the information regarding b.
   $T(pos) = S(pos) \setminus \{b \mapsto track \mid track \in TRACK\}$
2. Track equipment is in the same state.

$$S(nextd) = T(nextd) \qquad\qquad S(signalStatus) = T(signalStatus)$$
$$S(normalPoints) = T(normalPoints) \quad S(reversePoints) = T(reversePoints)$$

3. A route r causes locks in T only if it does so in S:
   $S(currentLocks[\{r\}]) = \emptyset \Rightarrow T(currentLocks[\{r\}]) = \emptyset$ and
   $T(currentLocks[\{r\}]) \neq \emptyset \Rightarrow S(currentLocks[\{r\}]) = T(currentLocks[\{r\}])$

Let $\sigma = \langle S_0, e_0, S_1, e_1, \ldots, e_{n-1}, S_n \rangle$, we obtain σ' in two steps. First, we define the sequence of events:

$$events(\sigma') = \langle replace_b(e_0), \ldots, replace_b(e_{n-1}) \rangle$$

Then, we replace in each step $\langle S_i, e_i, S_{i+1} \rangle$ of σ the result state:

In case of "deletion", there is no state change in σ', e.g.,:			In case of "replacement", states can change in σ and σ', e.g.,		
T	ϵ	T	T	$release.R.bb$	T'
$\overset{b}{\wedge\!\shortmid}$		$\overset{b}{\wedge\!\shortmid}$	$\overset{b}{\wedge\!\shortmid}$		$\overset{b}{\wedge\!\shortmid}$
S	$move.b.currp.newp$	S'	S	$move.b.currp.newp$	S'

Finally, we prove that the so constructed σ' is indeed a system run by induction on the length of the system run σ. The base case is given by $S_0 \geq_b S_0$ where S_0 is the initial state which has no trains in and there are no locks for points. In the induction step we show: (i) if an event e is enabled in S then $replace_b(e)$ is enabled in the corresponding state; (ii) $\geq_b$ is preserved under the execution under an event e and its corresponding event $replace_b(e)$. Both arguments rely on the fact that σ is a system run, i.e., is a control flow allowed by the CSP processes. □

The condition "collision free" on the system run σ is required, as we "simulate" the movement of the train b by a route release request. Routes can only be released if there is no train on the track t directly in front of the corresponding signal. In the corresponding run σ', b will not be on track t, as b has been removed. There might, however, be another train a. We exclude this by the condition "collision freedom": if there was a train a on the same track t as train b, there would be a collision in σ.

Corollary 1. *For collision free and well-formed scheme plans holds: if they are derailment free for one train, then they are derailment free for any number of trains.*

5   Simplifying Scheme Plans

In this section we prove, by topological argument, that it is sufficient to check a simple scheme plan for safety in order to establish safety for a complex scheme plan. The technical means for this is to establish a B refinement.

Let us consider an example in order to demonstrate the effect that the number of tracks per route has on model checking. Figure 3 shows three track plans. Track plan (a) has one track per route, track plan (b) has two tracks per route, and track plan (c) has four tracks per route. Below, we show how the state space grows in the number of tracks per route (illustrated using 3 trains):

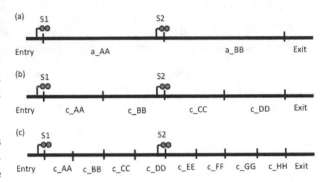

Fig. 3. Linear Scenario

number of tracks per abstract track	1	2	4	8	16
number of states	596	806	1472	3483	9615

In the following, we develop and formalise an abstraction mechanism which reduces the number of tracks per route and thus gives an advantage in model checking. Figure 2 illustrates our abstraction: part (b) shows a concrete track plan to which part (a) is the abstract counterpart.

As discussed in Section 3.1, a track plan is essentially given by the set *ALLTRACK* of its track circuits and a relation *next* between them. We use the prefix a_ for abstract, and c_ for concrete when considering two track plans and the relationship between them. Thus, *a_ALLTRACK* is the abstract set of track circuits (of tracks and points). Similarly, *c_ALLTRACK* is the concrete set of track circuits. We assume that these are disjoint, apart from the special element *nullTrack*. The relations *a_next* and *c_next* define how track circuits are connected. Each concrete track circuit is associated with one abstract track circuit, defined by the following total surjective function:

$$abs : c\_ALLTRACK \twoheadrightarrow a\_ALLTRACK$$

such that $abs(nullTrack) = nullTrack$.

The definition of *abs* for the one-station example is as follows in terms of relational image:

$$abs[\{c\_TAA, c\_TAB, c\_TAC\}] = \{a\_TAA\}$$
$$abs[\{c\_TBA, c\_TBB, c\_TBC, c\_TBD\}] = \{a\_TBA\}$$
$$abs[\{c\_TAD, c\_TAE, c\_TAF, c\_TAG\}] = \{a\_TAB\}$$
$$abs[\{c\_TAH\}] = \{a\_TAC\}$$
$$abs[\{c\_TAI, c\_TAJ\}] = \{a\_TAD\}$$

There are a number of necessary conditions on the abstraction function *abs*. These include prominently:

– Points are preserved under abstraction, i.e., a track circuit belonging to a point in the concrete topology is mapped to a point in the abstract topology.
– Routes are preserved under abstraction, e.g.,
  $abs[\{c\_TAD, c\_TAE, c\_TAF, c\_TAG, c\_TAH\}]$ cannot be $\{a\_TBA\}$ since the set of concrete track circuits is not within one route.
– Any concrete *c_next* pair of track circuits should either both be related to the same abstract track circuit, or should reflect the relation between an abstract *a_next* pair, i.e.,

$$\forall c\_t1, c\_t2 \bullet (c\_t1 \mapsto c\_t2) \in c\_next) \Rightarrow$$
$$abs(c\_t1) = abs(c\_t2) \vee (abs(c\_t1) \mapsto abs(c\_t2)) \in a\_next$$

For example, a move within the same abstract track circuit is given by $(c\_TAB \mapsto c\_TAC) \in c\_next \Rightarrow abs(c\_TAB) = abs(c\_TAC)$.

Beside the *abs* function, there are further functions needed in order to describe the full abstraction between track plans. They allow to formulate further conditions upon the relations defined in a track plan also on the tables, e.g.,

$$a\_clearTable \, {}_9 \, abs^{-1} = c\_clearTable$$

Our modelling approach works generically for all scheme plans. Thus, given a concrete and an abstract one, we have two formal models to compare. This comparison is performed using B refinement and CSP trace refinement. In the following, we focus on the B refinement.

We establish the refinement relationship between the *Interlocking* B machines by relating states with a linking invariant. To this end, we prove that each operation preserves the linking invariant. The linking invariant consists of three parts: the relationship between the positions of the trains $a\_pos = c\_pos \, {}_9 \, abs$, the relationship between the current positions of the points (which follows directly due to the static relationships), and the relationship between the track equipment which remains unchanged.

We illustrate the proof by comparing abstract and concrete versions of the *move* operation. For example, the concrete *move.c_TAC.c_TAD* corresponds to the abstract *move.a.a_TAA.a_TAB*; here, both have an effect on the B state.

In contrast to this, the concrete $move.a.c\_TAB.c\_TAC$ corresponds to the abstract $move.a.a\_TAA.a\_TAA$; the latter has no effect on the B state. Therefore, we can consider the abstract event $move.a.a\_TAA.a\_TAA$ as the B operation $skip$. In a B refinement, a new concrete event can refine $skip$. This can be expressed in the following two lemmas:

Lemma 1 (Renamed move). *If* $(abs(c\_t1) \mapsto abs(c\_t2)) \in a\_next$ *then*

$$abs(c\_t1), abs(c\_t2) \longleftarrow a\_move(t) \sqsubseteq c\_t1, c\_t2 \longleftarrow c\_move(t)$$

Lemma 2 (New move). *If* $abs(c\_t1) = abs(c\_t2)$ *then*

$$c\_t1, c\_t2 \longleftarrow skip(t) \sqsubseteq c\_t1, c\_t2 \longleftarrow c\_move(t)$$

As a consequence of the above lemmas (and similar lemmas for all other operations) the relationship between the abstract machine M_A and the concrete one M_C is given by $M_A \sqsubseteq_T f(M_C \setminus N)$, where f and N are defined by:

$$f(move.a.currp.newp) = move.a.abs(currp).abs(newp)$$

$$N = \{move.a.currp.newp \mid abs(currp) = abs(newp)\}$$

for all trains a in the abstract and the concrete model.

Hence we can now consider the combination of the B machines M_A and CSP processes P_A to obtain:

Theorem 4. *Let abs be an abstraction function from a concrete topology to an abstract topology. Let* $P_A \parallel M_A$ *be the* $CSP\|B$ *model wrt the abstract topology, let* $P_C \parallel M_C$ *be the* $CSP\|B$ *model wrt the concrete topology, such that both models are defined over the same set of trains. Let*

1. $M_A \sqsubseteq_T f(M_C \setminus N)$ *and*
2. $P_A \sqsubseteq_T f(P_C \setminus N)$.

Then collision (derailment) freedom of $P_A \parallel M_A$ *implies collision (derailment) freedom of* $P_C \parallel M_C$.

Proof. We compute:

$$P_A \parallel M_A \sqsubseteq_T f(P_C \setminus N) \parallel f(M_C \setminus N) \quad \text{(by conditions 1 and 2)}$$
$$\sqsubseteq_T f(P_C \setminus N \parallel M_C \setminus N) \quad \text{(by distributivity of renaming)}$$
$$\sqsubseteq_T f((P_C \parallel M_C) \setminus N) \quad \text{(by distributivity of hiding)}$$

With regards to collision freedom, we obtain:

$$P_A \parallel M_A \text{ is collision free} \Rightarrow f((P_C \parallel M_C) \setminus N) \text{ is collision free}$$
$$\text{(by trace refinement)}$$
$$\Leftrightarrow P_C \parallel M_C \setminus N \text{ is collision free}$$
$$\text{(as } f(collision) = collision)$$
$$\Leftrightarrow P_C \parallel M_C \text{ is collision free} \quad \text{(as } collision \notin N)$$

Similarly for derailment freedom. □

Note that Theorem 4 decomposes the proof obligation into a B proof and a CSP proof respectively. In order to establish condition 1, we sketched above a general construction based upon techniques related to B refinement. Condition 2 can be verified using the model checker FDR on CSP processes only.

6 Example Scenarios of CSP||B Railway Models

In order to demonstrate the effectiveness of our techniques outlined in Section 4 and Section 5 we conducted experiments on five scenarios. The experiments were carried out using ProB 1.3.5 beta 15 [3] to verify the collision and derailment freedom of the abstract and concrete track plans using CTL model checking over the CSP||B models. The number of trains involved is chosen according to the results of Section 4: collision freedom is checked with number of routes plus one train, derailment freedom is checked with one train. If the verification is successful then we conclude that the model is right and has the right properties. The CSP||B models were also required to be divergence- and deadlock-free. Figure 4 summarises that all our scenarios are collision- and derailment-free.

To give an indication of the size of the track plans: scenario 1 has 6 tracks, 0 points, 2 signals and 2 routes; scenario 2 has 10 tracks, 0 points, 2 signals and 2 routes; scenario 3 has 16 tracks, 2 points, 3 signals and 4 routes; scenario 4 has 15 tracks, 1 point, 5 signals and 6 routes, and finally scenario 5 has 22 tracks, 2 points, 9 signals and 10 routes.

Notice that in all scenarios there is a significant reduction in the number of states being explored, comparing the abstract scenarios with the concrete scenarios. In order to achieve the desired verification results, however, abstraction is necessary only in scenario 4(b).

We gain full verification for the first four scenarios thanks to our two reduction techniques. Scenario 5 can be checked for derailment freedom, however, it cannot be checked for collision freedom. Thus, verification is only partial. However, we make the conjecture that it is possible to strengthen Theorem 1: rather than establishing collision freedom for number of routes plus one trains, it is sufficient to verify collision-freedom with two trains only. Figure 4 shows that verification of the double junction with two trains is possible. The double junction scenario is one which we have referred to in our previous work [13], it provides an interesting example of abstraction since the abstraction surrounding one of the points is a biased one, i.e., the normal position of one of the points remains unchanged in the abstraction, whereas the reverse position of the point is an abstraction of its track circuit and another track circuit. We will revisit the topic of abstractions when, in future work, we come to models which deal with bi-directional track circuits.

7 Related Work

Several industrial studies have been done on using model checking to verify railway applications, e.g., for example SNCF [2], and it is clear that their formal

Scenario	Model	# Trains	Abstract States Checked	Concrete States Checked
1(a) derailment	Linear with 2 tracks per route	1	27	31
1(b) collisions	Linear with 2 tracks per route	3	596	806
2(a) derailment	Linear with 4 tracks per route	1	27	39
2(b) collisions	Linear with 4 tracks per route	3	596	1472
3(a) derailment	Station	1	70	203
3(b) collisions	Station	5	151,508	968,700
4(a) derailment	Single Junction	1	600	756
4(b) collisions	Single Junction	7	326,405	Not completed
5(a) derailment	Double Junction	1	103,598	158,190
5(b) collisions	Double Junction	2	173,846	379,404
5(c) collisions	Double Junction	3	Not completed	Not completed

Fig. 4. Variations of Five Example Scenarios checked

analysis is industrially important. To put our work into context we must first clarify that railway verification falls into two categories: the verification of railway designs prior to their implementation and the verification of the implementation descriptions themselves. Our work is in the first area. A comparison using different model checkers in the analysis of control tables has been conducted by Ferrari *et al.* [6] and falls into the first category. Winter in a recent paper [16] considers different optimising strategies for model checking using NuSMV and demonstrates the efficiency of their approach on very large models. These analyses also fall into the first category but the models are flat in structure compared to our models as they are defined in terms of boolean equations and do not focus on providing behavioural models. The analysis of interlocking tables (cf. control tables) by Haxthausen [7] also falls into the first category and is supported by automated tools that generate the models. The results achieved are comparable in size to our Single Junction scenario. Cimatti *et al.* [5] also have had considerable success using NuSMV but their analysis is focussed on the implementation descriptions.

Others have applied theorem proving in the verification of railway interlocking systems, for example, the Advance FP7 project [1] is developing Event-B models of such systems and verifying comparable safety properties. Indeed it would be interesting for us to investigate further the relationship between the combination of generic proofs and model cecking. In this paper, we have demonstrated that the data abstraction on the B part of the CSP||B models is generic but more work will be needed on this when we enrich the models to contain trains which extend over more than one track circuit and can move in more than one direction.

The research most closely related to ours is Winter [17]. The way in which the ASM models are defined closely relates to ours since they have the same concept of routes, which contain tracks and points, between two signals, and contain a static and a behavioural definition. Their models are more advanced than ours since we currently restrict ourselves to have signals in one direction and we do not include shunting. The simplifications to the Winter models includes combining multiple track circuits into one provided they are always grouped together in the control table; this again resonates with the data abstraction we defined in Section 5, but we formalise the abstraction more explicitly.

8   Conclusion

We have successfully complemented our faithful modelling approach of railway interlockings as presented in [13,12] by defining abstraction techniques that yield effective and efficient verification process based on model checking. We illustrated this process in terms of various scenarios. The correctness arguments in Sections 4 provides a new proof technique for event- and state-based reasoning. Section 5 demonstrates an interesting data abstraction using decomposition.

Heitmeyer in [8] discusses the importance of complete abstractions. Our abstractions are sound. It is future work to investigate if completeness can be established. In Section 6 we identified that the reduction of Theorem 1 is not sufficient for complex scheme plans. Here we hope to prove our conjecture that two trains are sufficient to verify collision freedom. Our current models lack certain details as discussed in Section 7. Adding these features will allow us to study more fine grained data abstractions. Following recent discussions with Winter, we also agree that another obvious optimisation to consider is the decomposition of track schemes.

Acknowledgement. The authors would like to thank S. Chadwick and D. Taylor from the company Invensys Rail for their support and encouraging feedback.

References

1. Advance FP7 project, http://www.advance-ict.eu/ (accessed: July 23, 2012)
2. Practical formal validation method for interlocking or automated systems,   http://www.dcds11.uni-saarland.de/plenaries/practical-formal-validation-method-for-interlocking-or-automated-systems.html (accessed: July 23, 2012)
3. ProB 1.3.5 beta15, http://www.stups.uni-duesseldorf.de/ProB (accessed: July 23, 2012)
4. Abrial, J.-R.: The B-Book: Assigning Programs to Meanings. CUP (1996)
5. Cimatti, A., Corvino, R., Lazzaro, A., Narasamdya, I., Rizzo, T., Roveri, M., Sanseviero, A., Tchaltsev, A.: Formal verification and validation of ERTMS industrial railway train spacing system. In: Madhusudan, P., Seshia, S.A. (eds.) CAV 2012. LNCS, vol. 7358, pp. 378–393. Springer, Heidelberg (2012)

6. Ferrari, A., Magnani, G., Grasso, D., Fantechi, A.: Model checking interlocking control tables. In: FORMS/FORMAT, pp. 107–115 (2010)
7. Haxthausen, A.E.: Automated generation of safety requirements from railway interlocking tables. In: Margaria, T., Steffen, B. (eds.) ISoLA 2012, Part II. LNCS, vol. 7610, pp. 261–275. Springer, Heidelberg (2012)
8. Heitmeyer, C.L., Kirby, J., Labaw, B.G., Archer, M., Bharadwaj, R.: Using abstraction and model checking to detect safety violations in requirements specifications. IEEE Trans. Software Eng. 24(11), 927–948 (1998)
9. Hoare, C.A.R.: Communicating Sequential Processes. Prentice-Hall (1985)
10. Isobe, Y., Moller, F., Nguyen, H.N., Roggenbach, M.: Safety and line capacity in railways – an approach in Timed CSP. In: Derrick, J., Gnesi, S., Latella, D., Treharne, H. (eds.) IFM 2012. LNCS, vol. 7321, pp. 54–68. Springer, Heidelberg (2012)
11. Bjørner, D.: TRain: The Railway domain - A "Grand Challenge" for Computing Science & Transportation Engineering. In: Jacquart, R. (ed.) Building the Information Society, IFIP 18th World Computer Congress, Topical Sessions, Toulouse, France, August 22-27, pp. 604–612. Kluwer (2004)
12. Moller, F., Nguyen, H.N., Roggenbach, M., Schneider, S., Treharne, H.: Combining event-based and state-based modelling for railway verification. Technical Report CS-12-02, University of Surrey (2012)
13. Moller, F., Nguyen, H.N., Roggenbach, M., Schneider, S., Treharne, H.: Railway modelling in CSP‖B: the double junction case study. In: AVOCS (2012)
14. Morgan, C.C.: Of wp and CSP. In: Beauty Is Our Business: A Birthday Salute to Edsger J. Dijkstra. Springer (1990)
15. Schneider, S., Treharne, H.: CSP theorems for communicating B machines. Formal Asp. Comput. 17(4), 390–422 (2005)
16. Winter, K.: Optimising ordering strategies for symbolic model checking of railway interlockings. In: Margaria, T., Steffen, B. (eds.) ISoLA 2012, Part II. LNCS, vol. 7610, pp. 246–260. Springer, Heidelberg (2012)
17. Winter, K., Robinson, N.J.: Modelling large railway interlockings and model checking small ones. In: ACSC, pp. 309–316 (2003)

Word Equations with Length Constraints: What's Decidable?

Vijay Ganesh[1], Mia Minnes[2], Armando Solar-Lezama[1] and Martin Rinard[1]

[1] Massachusetts Institute of Technology
{vganesh,asolar,rinard}@csail.mit.edu
[2] University of California, San Diego
minnes@math.ucsd.edu

Abstract. We prove several decidability and undecidability results for the satisfiability and validity problems for languages that can express solutions to word equations with length constraints. The atomic formulas over this language are equality over string terms (word equations), linear inequality over the length function (length constraints), and membership in regular sets. These questions are important in logic, program analysis, and formal verification. Variants of these questions have been studied for many decades by mathematicians. More recently, practical satisfiability procedures (aka SMT solvers) for these formulas have become increasingly important in the context of security analysis for string-manipulating programs such as web applications.

We prove three main theorems. First, we give a new proof of undecidability for the validity problem for the set of sentences written as a ∀∃ quantifier alternation applied to positive word equations. A corollary of this undecidability result is that this set is undecidable even with sentences with at most two occurrences of a string variable. Second, we consider Boolean combinations of quantifier-free formulas constructed out of word equations and length constraints. We show that if word equations can be converted to a *solved form*, a form relevant in practice, then the satisfiability problem for Boolean combinations of word equations and length constraints is decidable. Third, we show that the satisfiability problem for quantifier-free formulas over word equations in *regular solved form*, length constraints, and the membership predicate over regular expressions is also decidable.

1 Introduction

The complexity of the satisfiability problem for formulas over finite-length strings (theories of strings) has long been studied, including by Quine [23], Post, Markov and Matiyasevich [17], Makanin [15], and Plandowski [12, 20, 21]. While much progress has been made, many questions remain open especially when the language is enriched with new predicates.

Formulas over strings have become important in the context of automated bugfinding [8,25], and analysis of database/web applications [7,14,27]. These program analysis and bugfinding tools read string-manipulation programs and generate formulas expressing their results. These formulas contain equations over string constants and variables, membership queries over regular expressions, and inequalities between string lengths.

A. Biere, A. Nahir, and T. Vos (Eds.): HVC 2012, LNCS 7857, pp. 209–226, 2013.
© Springer-Verlag Berlin Heidelberg 2013

In practice, formulas of this form have been solved by off-the-shelf satisfiability procedures such as HAMPI [8, 13] or Kaluza [25]. In this context, a deeper understanding of the theoretical aspects of the satisfiability problem for this class of formulas may be useful in practice.

Problem Statement: We address three problems. First, what is a boundary for decidability for fragments of the theory of word equations? Namely, is the ∀∃-fragment of the theory of word equations decidable? Second, is the satisfiability problem for quantifier-free formulas over word equations and the length function decidable under some minimal practical conditions? Third, is the satisfiability problem for quantifier-free formulas over word equations, the length function, and regular expressions decidable under some minimal practical conditions?

The question of whether the satisfiability problem for the quantifier-free theory of word equations and length constraints is decidable has remained open for several decades. Our decidability results are a partial and conditional solution. Matiyasevich [18] observed the relevance of this question to a novel resolution of Hilbert's Tenth Problem. In particular, he showed that if the satisfiability problem for the quantifier-free theory of word equations and length constraints is undecidable, then it gives us a new way to prove Matiyasevich's Theorem (which resolved the famous problem) [17, 18].

Summary of Contributions

1. We show that the validity problem (decision problem) for the set of sentences written as a ∀∃ quantifier alternation applied to positive word equations (i.e., AND-OR combination of word equations without any negation) is undecidable. (Section 3)
2. We show that if word equations can be converted to a *solved form* then the satisfiability problem for Boolean combinations of word equations and length constraints is decidable. (Section 4)
3. The above-mentioned decidability result has immediate practical impact for applications such as bug-finding in JavaScript and PHP programs. We empirically studied the word equations in the formulas generated by the Kudzu JavaScript bugfinding tool [25] and verified that most word equations in such formulas are either already in solved form or can be automatically and easily converted into one. (Section 4)
4. We further show that the satisfiability problem for quantifier-free formulas constructed out of Boolean combinations of word equations in *regular solved form* with length constraints and the membership predicate for regular sets is also decidable. This is the first such decidability result for this set of formulas. (Section 5)

We now outline the layout of the rest of the paper. In Section 2 we define a theory of word equations, length constraints, and regular expressions. In Section 3 we prove the undecidability of the theory of ∀∃ sentences over positive word equations. In Section 4 (resp. Section 5) we give a conditional decidability result for the satisfiability problem for the quantifier-free theory of word equations and length constraints (resp. word equations, length constraints, and regular expressions). Finally, in Section 6 we provide a comprehensive overview of the decidability/undecidability results for theories of strings over the last several decades.

2   Preliminaries

2.1   Syntax

Variables: We fix a disjoint two-sorted set of variables $var = var_{str} \cup var_{int}$; var_{str} consists of string variables, denoted $X, Y, S, \ldots$ and var_{int} consists of integer variables, denoted $m, n, \ldots$.

Constants: We also fix a two-sorted set of constants $Con = Con_{str} \cup Con_{int}$. Moreover, $Con_{str} \subset \Sigma^*$ for some finite alphabet, Σ, whose elements are denoted $f, g, \ldots$. Elements of Con_{str} will be referred to as *string constants* or *strings*. Elements of Con_{int} are nonnegative integers. The empty string is represented by ϵ.

Terms: Terms may be string terms or length terms. A string term (t_{str} in Figure 1) is either an element of var_{str}, an element of Con_{str}, or a concatenation of string terms (denoted by the function *concat* or interchangeably by $\cdot$). A length term (t_{len} in Figure 1) is an element of var_{int}, an element of Con_{int}, the length function applied to a string term, a constant integer multiple of a length term, or a sum of length terms.

Atomic Formulas: There are three types of atomic formulas: (1) word equations ($A_{wordeqn}$), (2) length constraints (A_{length}), or (3) membership in a set defined by a regular expression (A_{regexp}). Regular expressions are defined inductively, where constants and the empty string form the base case, and the operations of concatenation, alternation, and Kleene star are used to build up more complicated expressions (see details in [10]). Regular expressions may not contain variables.

Formulas: Formulas are defined inductively over atomic formulas (see Figure 1). We include quantifiers of two kinds: over string variables and over integer variables.

Formula Nomenclature: We now establish notation for the classes of formulas we will analyze. Define $\mathcal{L}^1_{e,l,r}$ to be the first-order two-sorted language over which the formulas described above (Figure 1) are constructed. This language contains word equations, length constraints, and membership in given regular sets. The superscript 1 in $\mathcal{L}^1_{e,l,r}$ denotes that this language allows quantifiers, and the subscripts l, e, r stand for "length", "equation", and "regular expressions" (respectively). Let $\mathcal{L}^1_{e,l}$ be the analogous set of first-order formulas restricted to word equations and length constraints as the only atomic formulas, and let $\mathcal{L}^1_e$ be the collection of formulas whose only atomic formulas are word equations. Define $\mathcal{L}^0_{e,l,r}$ to be the set of quantifier-free $\mathcal{L}^1_{e,l,r}$ formulas. Similarly, $\mathcal{L}^0_{e,l}$ and $\mathcal{L}^0_e$ are the quantifier-free versions of $\mathcal{L}^1_{e,l}$ and $\mathcal{L}^1_e$, respectively.

Recall that a formula is in *prenex normal form* if all quantifiers appear at the front of the expression: that is, the formula has a string of quantifiers and then a Boolean combination of atomic formulas. It is a standard result (see, for example [6]) that any first-order formula can be translated into prenex normal form. We therefore assume that all formulas are given in this form. Intuitively, a variable is *free* in a formula if it is not quantified. For example, in the formula $\forall y \phi(y, x)$, the variable y is *bound* while x is *free*. For a full inductive definition, see [6]. A formula with no free variables is called a *sentence*.

$$
\begin{array}{llll}
F & ::= Atomic & | \ F \wedge F \ | \ F \vee F \ | \ \neg F \\
& | \ \exists x.F(x) \ | \ \forall x.F(x) \\
Atomic & ::= A_{wordeqn} \ | \ A_{length} \ | \ A_{regexp} \\
A_{wordeqn} & ::= t_{str} = t_{str} \\
A_{length} & ::= t_{len} \leq c & & \text{where } c \in Con_{int} \\
A_{regexp} & ::= t_{str} \in RE & & \text{where RE is a regular expression} \\
t_{str} & ::= a \ | \ X \ | \ concat(t_{str}, ..., t_{str}) & & \text{where } a \in Con_{str} \ \& \ X \in var_{str} \\
t_{len} & ::= m \ | \ v \ | \ len(t_{str}) \ | \ \Sigma_{i=1}^{n} c_i * t_{len}^{i} & & \text{where } m, n, c_i \in Con_{int} \ \& \ v \in var_{int}
\end{array}
$$

Fig. 1. The syntax of $\mathcal{L}_{e,l,r}^{1}$-formulas

2.2 Semantics and Definitions

For a word, w, $len(w)$ denotes the length of w. For a word equation of the form $t_1 = t_2$, we refer to t_1 as the left hand side (LHS), and t_2 as the right hand side (RHS).

We fix a string alphabet, Σ. Given an $\mathcal{L}_{e,l,r}^{1}$ formula θ, an *assignment* for θ (with respect to Σ) is a map from the set of free variables in θ to $\Sigma^* \cup \mathbb{N}$ (where string variables are mapped to strings and integer variables are mapped to numbers). Given such an assignment, θ can be interpreted as an assertion about Σ^* and $\mathbb{N}$. If this assertion is true, then we say that θ itself is *true* under the assignment. If there is some assignment which makes θ true, then θ is called *satisfiable*. An $\mathcal{L}_{e,l,r}^{1}$-formula with no satisfying assignment is called an *unsatisfiable* formula. We say two formulas θ, ϕ are *equisatisfiable* if θ is satisfiable iff ϕ is satisfiable. Note that this is a broad definition: equisatisfiable formulas may have different numbers of assignments and, in fact, need not even be from the same language.

The *satisfiability problem* for a set S of formulas is the problem of deciding whether any given formula in S is satisfiable or not. We say that the satisfiability problem for a set S of formulas is decidable if there exists an algorithm (or *satisfiability procedure*) that solves its satisfiability problem. Satisfiability procedures must have three properties: soundness, completeness, and termination. Soundness and completeness guarantee that the procedure returns "satisfiable" if and only if the input formula is indeed satisfiable. Termination means that the procedure halts on all inputs. In a practical implementation, some of these requirements may be relaxed for the sake of improved typical performance.

Analogous to the definition of the satisfiability problem for formulas, we can define the notion of the *validity problem* (aka decision problem) for a set Q of sentences in a language L. The validity problem for a set Q of sentences is the problem of determining whether a given sentence in Q is true under all assignments.

2.3 Representation of Solutions to String Formulas

It will be useful to have compact representations of sets of solutions to string formulas. For this, we use Plandowski's terminology of *unfixed parts* [21]. Namely, fix a set of new variables V disjoint from all of Σ, Con, and var. For θ an $\mathcal{L}_{e,l,r}^{1}$ formula, an *assignment with unfixed parts* is a mapping from the free variables of θ to string elements of the domain or V. Such an assignment represents the family of solutions to θ where each element of V is consistently replaced by a string element in the domain. (See example 1 below.)

Another tool for compactly encoding many solutions to a formula is the use of *integer parameters*. If i is a non-negative integer, we write u^i to denote the i-fold concatenation of the string u with itself. An *assignment with integer parameters* to the formula θ is a map from the free variables of θ to string elements of the domain, perhaps with integer parameters occurring in the exponents. (See example 2 below.)

Combining these two representations, we also consider assignments with unfixed parts and integer parameters. These assignments will provide the general framework for representing solution sets to $\mathcal{L}^1_{e,l,r}$ formulas compactly.

2.4 Examples

We consider some sample formulas and their solution sets. The string alphabet is $\Sigma = \{a, b\}$. (Many of the examples in this paper are from existing literature by Plandowski et al. [21].)

Example 1. *Consider the $\mathcal{L}^0_e$ formula which is a word equation $X = aYbZa$ with three variables (X, Y, Z) and two string constants (a, b). The set of all solutions to this equation is described by the assignment $X \mapsto aybza, Y \mapsto y, Z \mapsto z$, where $V = \{y, z\}$ is the set of unfixed parts. Any choice of $y, z \in \Sigma^*$ yields a solution to the equation.*

Example 2. *Consider the equation $abX = Xba$ with one variable X. This is a formula in $\mathcal{L}^0_e$. The map $X \mapsto aba$ is a solution. The map $X \mapsto (ab)^i a$ with $i \geq 0$ is also an assignment which gives a solution. In fact, this assignment (with integer parameters) exactly describes all possible solutions of the word equation.*

Example 3. *Consider the $\mathcal{L}^0_{e,l,r}$ formula*

$$abX = Xba \wedge X \in (ab \mid ba)(ab)^* a \wedge len(X) \leq 5.$$

The two solutions to this formula are $X = aba$ and $X = ababa$.

3 The Undecidability Theorem

In this section we prove that the validity problem for the set of $\mathcal{L}^1_e$ sentences over positive word equations (AND-OR combinations of word equations) whose prenex normal form has $\forall\exists$ as its quantifier prefix is undecidable.

3.1 Proof Idea

We do a reduction from the halting problem for two-counter machines, which is known to be undecidable [10], to the problem in question. To do so, we encode computation histories as strings. The choice of two-counter machine makes this proof cleaner than other undecidability proofs for this set of formulas (see Section 6 for a comparison with earlier work). The basic proof strategy is as follows: given a two-counter machine M and a finite string w, we construct an $\mathcal{L}_e^1$ sentence $\forall S\, \exists S_1, \ldots, S_4 \theta(S, S_1, \ldots, S_4)$ such that M does not halt on w iff this $\mathcal{L}_e^1$ sentence is valid. By the construction of θ, this will happen exactly when all assignments to the string variable S are not codes for halting computation histories of M over w. The variables $S_1, \ldots, S_4$ are used to refer to substrings of S and the quantifier-free formula θ expresses the property of S not coding a halting computation history.

3.2   Recalling Two-Counter Machines

A *two-counter machine* is a deterministic machine which has a finite-state control, two semi-infinite storage tapes, and a separate read-only semi-infinite input tape. All tapes have a left endpoint and no right endpoint. All tapes are composed of cells, each of which may store a symbol from the appropriate alphabet (the alphabet of the storage tapes is {Z, blank}; the alphabet of the input alphabet is some fixed finite set). The input to the machine is a finite string written on the input tape, starting at the leftmost cell. A special character follows the input string on the tape to mark the end of the input. Each tape has a corresponding tape-head that may move left, move right, or stay put. The input tape-head cannot move past the right end of the input string. The initial position of all the tape-heads is the leftmost cell of their respective tapes. At each point in the computation, the cell being scanned by each tape-head is called that tape's *current cell*.

The symbol Z serves as a *bottom of stack* marker on the storage tapes. Hence, it appears initially on the cell scanned by the tape head and may never appear on any other cells. A non-negative integer i can be represented on the storage tape by moving the tape head i cells to the right of Z. A number stored on the storage tape can be incremented or decremented by moving the tape-head to the right or to the left. We can test whether the number stored in one of the storage tapes is zero by checking if the contents of the current cell of that tape is Z. But, the equality of two numbers stored on the storage tapes cannot be directly tested. It is well known that the two-counter machine can simulate an arbitrary Turing machine. Consequently, the halting problem for two-counter machines is undecidable [10].

More formally, a two-counter machine M is a tuple $\langle Q, \Delta, \{Z, b, c\}, \delta, q_0, F \rangle$ where,

- Q is the finite set of control states of M, $q_0 \in Q$ is the initial control state, and $F \subseteq Q$ is the set of final control states.
- Δ is the finite alphabet of the input tape, $\{Z, b\}$ and $\{Z, c\}$ are the storage tape alphabets for the first and second tapes, respectively. (The distinct blank symbols for the two tapes are a notational convenience.)
- δ is the transition function for the control of M. This function maps the domain, $Q \times \Delta \times \{Z, b\} \times \{Z, c\}$ into $Q \times \{in, stor1, stor2\} \times \{L, R\}$. In words, given a control state and the contents of the current cell of each tape, the transition function specifies the next state of the machine, a tape-head (input or one of the storage tapes) to move, and whether this tape-head moves left (L) or right (R).

3.3   Instantaneous Description of Two-counter Machines as Strings

We define *instantaneous descriptions* (ID) of two-counter machines in terms of strings. Informally, the ID of a machine represents its *entire configuration* at any instant in terms of machine parameters such as the current control state, current input-tape letter being read by the machine, and current storage-tape contents. The set of IDs will be determined both by the machine and the given input to the machine.

Definition of ID: An instantaneous description (ID) of a computation step of a two-counter machine M running on input w is the concatenation of the following components.

- Current control state of M: represented by a character over the finite alphabet Q.
- The input w and an encoding of the current input tape cell. The encoding uses string constants to represent the integers between 0 and $|w| - 1$; let N_i denote the string constant encoding the number i.
- The finite distances of the two storage heads from the symbol Z, represented as a string of blanks (i.e., in unary representation). For convenience, we will use the symbol b to denote the blanks on storage tape 1, and c on storage tape 2.

Each component of an ID is separated from the others by an appropriate special character. In what follows, we will suppress discussion of this separator and we will assume that it is appropriately located inside each ID. A lengthy but technically trivial modification of our reduction formula could be used to allow for the case where this separator is missing.

Definition of Initial ID: For any two-counter machine M and each input w, there is exactly one initial ID, denoted $Init_{M,w}$. This ID is the result of concatenating the string representations of the following data: Initial state q_0 of M, w, 0, ϵ, ϵ. The "0" says that the current cell of the input tape contains the 0th letter of w. The two "ϵ"s represent the contents of the two storage tape: both are empty at this point.

Definition of Final ID: We use the standard convention that a two-counter machine halts only after the storage tapes contain the unary representation of the number 0 and the input tape-head has moved to the leftmost position of its tape. The ID of the machine at the end of a computation is therefore the concatenation of representations of $q_f, w, 0, \epsilon, \epsilon$, where q_f is one of the finitely many final control states $q_f \in F$ of M. Observe that there are only finitely many Final IDs.

3.4   Computation History of a Two-Counter Machine as a String

A *well-formed computation history* of a two-counter machine M as it processes a given input w is the concatenation of a sequence of IDs separated by the special symbol #. The first ID in the sequence is the initial ID of M on w, and for each i, ID_{i+1} is the result of transforming ID_i according to the transition function of M. A well-formed computation history of the machine M on the string w is called *accepting* if it is a finite string whose last ID is a Final ID of M on w. The last ID of a string is defined to be the rightmost substring following a separator #. If a finite computation history is not accepting, it is either not well-formed or rejecting.

3.5   Alphabet for String Formulas and the Universe of Strings

Given a two-counter machine M and an input string w, we define the associated finite alphabet

$$\Sigma_0 = \{\#q_i N_j w : q_i \in Q, 0 \le j < |w|\}.$$

This alphabet includes all possible *initial segments* of IDs, not including the data about the contents of the storage tapes. We also define $\Sigma_1 = b$ and $\Sigma_2 = c$. We define the alphabet of strings as $\Sigma \equiv \{\Sigma_0 \cup \Sigma_1 \cup \Sigma_2\}$, and the universe of strings as Σ^*. Thus, each valid ID will be in the regular set $\Sigma_0 \Sigma_1^* \Sigma_2^*$.

3.6   The Undecidability Theorem

Theorem 4. *The validity problem for the set of $\mathcal{L}_e^1$ sentences over positive word equations with $\forall\exists$ quantifier alternation is undecidable.*

Proof. **By Reduction:** We reduce the halting problem for two-counter machines to the decision problem in question. Given a pair $\langle M, w \rangle$ of a two-counter machine M and an arbitrary input w to M, we construct an $\mathcal{L}_e^1$-formula $\theta_{M,w}(S, S_1, \ldots, S_4, U, V)$ which describes the conditions for $S_1, \ldots, S_4$ to be substrings of S and S to fail to code an accepting computation history of M over w. Thus,

$$\forall S \, \exists S_1, S_2, S_3, S_4, U, V \ (\theta_{M,w}(S, S_1, \cdots, S_4, U, V))$$

is valid if and only if it is not the case that M halts and accepts on w. For brevity, we write θ for $\theta_{M,w}$.

Structure of θ: We will define θ as the disjunction of ways in which S could fail to encode an accepting computation history: either S does not start with the Initial ID, or S does not end with any of the Final IDs, or S is not a well-formed sequence of IDs, or it does not follow the transition function of M over w.

$$\theta = (\bigvee_{E \in \text{NotInit}} S = E \cdot S_1) \vee (\bigvee_{E \in \text{NotFinal}} S = S_1 \cdot E) \vee$$

$$\text{NotWellFormedSequence}(S, S_1, \cdots, S_4) \vee$$

$$((S = S_1 \cdot S_2 \cdot S_3 \cdot S_4) \wedge (Ub = bU) \wedge (Vc = cV) \wedge \neg \text{Next}(S, S_1, S_2, S_3, S_4, U, V))$$

Note that the variables S_i $(i = 1, \ldots, 4)$ represent substrings of S.

- **NotInit and NotFinal:** The set NotInit is a finite set of string constants for strings with length at most that of the Initial ID $Init_{M,w}$ which are not equal to $Init_{M,w}$. Similarly, NotFinal is a set of string constants for strings that that are not equal to any of the Final IDs, but have the same or smaller length.
- **NotWellFormedSequence**: This subformula asserts that S is not a sequence of IDs. Recall that, by definition, the set of well-formed IDs is described by the regular expression $\Sigma_0 \Sigma_1^* \Sigma_2^* = \Sigma_0 b^* c^*$, where strings in Σ_0 (as defined above) include the ID separator # as well as codes for the control state, w, and letter of w being scanned.

A well-formed sequence of IDs is a string of the form $(\Sigma_0 b^* c^*)^* - \epsilon$. Thus, the set described by **NotWellFormedSequence** should be $\Sigma^* - (\Sigma_0 b^* c^*)^*$. In fact, we can characterize this regular set entirely in terms of word equations: a string over $\Sigma = \Sigma_0 \cup \{b, c\}$ is not a well-formed sequence of IDs if and only if it starts with b or c, or contains cb. The fact that a non well-formed sequence may start with b or c is already captured by the NotInit formula above. The fact that a non well-formed sequence contains cb or is an ϵ is guaranteed by the following formula NotWellFormedSequence():

$$(S = \epsilon) \vee (S = S_1 \cdot c \cdot b \cdot S_4).$$

– **Next**:

$Next()$ asserts that the pair of variables S_2, S_3 form a legal transition. It is a disjunction over all (finitely many) possible pairs of IDs defined by the transition function:

$$\bigvee_{(q_2,d,g_1,g_2,q_3,t,m)\in\delta;0\le n_2,n_3<|w|} S_2 = \#q_2 N_{n_2} wUV \wedge S_3 = \#q_3 N_{n_3} wf(U)g(V)$$

where $d = w(n_2)$; $g_1 = Z$ if $U = \epsilon$ and $g_1 = b$ otherwise; $g_2 = Z$ if $V = \epsilon$ and $g_2 = c$ otherwise; and $f(U), g(V), N_{n_3}$ are the results of modifying the stack contents represented by U, V and input tape-head position according to whether the value of t is *in*, *stor1*, or *stor2* and whether m is L or R. Note that the disjunction is finite and is determined by the transition function and w. Also note that each of $\#q_2 N_{n_2} w$ and $\#q_3 N_{n_3} w$ is a single letter in Σ_0.

Simplifying the Formula: The formula θ contains negated equalities in the subformula $\neg Next$. However, each of these may be replaced by a disjunction of equalities because $Q, |w|, \delta$ are each finite. Hence, we can translate θ to a formula containing only conjunctions and disjunctions of positive word equations. We also observe that the formula we constructed in the proof can be easily converted to a formula which has at most two occurrences of any variable [1]. Thus, we get the final theorem.

Theorem 5. *The validity problem for the set of $\mathcal{L}_e^1$ sentences with $\forall\exists$ quantifier alternation over positive word equations, and with at most two occurrences of any variable, is undecidable.*

Bounding the Inner Existential Quantifiers: Observe that in θ all the inner quantifiers $S_1, \cdots, S_4, U, V$ are bounded since they are substrings of S. The length function, $len(S_i) \le len(S)$, can be used to bound these quantifiers.

Corollary 6. *The set of $\mathcal{L}_{e,l}^1$ sentences with a single universal quantifier followed by a block of inner bounded existential quantifiers is undecidable.*

4 Decidability Theorem

In this section we demonstrate the existence of an algorithm deciding whether any $\mathcal{L}_{e,l}^0$ formula has a satisfying assignment, under a minimal and practical condition.

---

[1] We thank Professor Rupak Majumdar for observing this and other improvements.

4.1   Word Equations and Length Constraints

Word equations by themselves are decidable [21]. Also, systems of inequalities over integer variables are decidable because these are expressible as quantifier-free formulas in the language of Presburger arithmetic and Presburger arithmetic is known to be decidable [22]. In this section, we show that if word equations can be converted into *solved form*, the satisfiability problem for quantifier-free formulas over word equations and length constraints (i.e., $\mathcal{L}^0_{e,l}$ formulas) is decidable. Furthermore, we describe our observations of word equations in formulas generated by the Kudzu JavaScript bugfinding tool [25]. In particular, we saw that these equations either already appeared in solved form or could be algorithmically converted into one.

4.2   What Is Hard about Deciding Word Equations and Length Constraints?

The crux of the difficulty in establishing an unconditional decidability result is that it is not known whether the length constraints implied by a set of word equations have a finite representation [21]. In the case when the implied constraints do have a finite representation, we look for a satisfying assignment to both the implied and explicit constraints. Such a solution can be translated into a satisfying assignment of the word equations when the implied constraints of the system of equations is equisatisfiable with the system itself.

4.3   Definition of Solved Form

A word equation w has a *solved form* if there is a finite set S of formulas (possibly with integer parameters) that is logically equivalent to w and satisfies the following conditions.[2]

- Every formula in S is of the form $X = t$, where X is a variable occurring in w and t is the result of finitely many concatenations of constants in w (with possible integer parameters) and possible unfixed parts. (Recall the definitions for integer parameters and unfixed parts from Section 2.) All integer parameters i in S are linear, of the form ci where c is an integer constant.
- Every variable in w occurs exactly once on the LHS of an equation in S and never on the RHS of an equation in S.

The solved form corresponding to w is the conjunction of all the formulas in S, denoted $\wedge S$. If there is an algorithm which converts any given word equation to solved form (if one exists, and halts in finite time otherwise), and if $\wedge S$ is the output of this algorithm when given w, we say that the *effective solved form* of w is $\wedge S$. Solved form equations can have integer parameters, whereas $\mathcal{L}^0_{e,l}$ formulas cannot. The solved form is used to extract all necessary and sufficient length information *implied by* w.

---

[2] The idea of solved form is well known in equational reasoning, theorem proving, and satisfiability procedures for rich logics (aka SMT solvers).

Example 7. Satisfiable Solved Form Example: *Consider the system of word equations*

$$Xa = aY \wedge Ya = Xa.$$

This formula can be converted into solved form as follows:

$$X = a^i \wedge Y = a^i \qquad (i \geq 0).$$

Example 8. Unsatisfiable Solved Form Example: *Consider the formula*

$$abX = Xba \wedge X = abY \wedge len(X) < 2$$

with variables X, Y. The set of solutions to the equation $abX = Xba$ is described by the map $X \mapsto (ab)^i a$ with $i \geq 0$ (recall Example 2). Hence the solved form for the system of two equations is:

$$X = (ab)^i a \wedge Y = (ab)^{i-1} a \qquad (i > 0)$$

The length constraints implied by this system are

$$len(X) = 2c + 1 \wedge len(Y) = 2c - 1 \wedge len(X) < 2 \qquad (c > 0).$$

This is unsatisfiable. Hence, the original formula is also unsatisfiable.

Example 9. Word Equations Without a Solved Form: *Not all word equations can be written in solved form. Consider the equation*

$$XabY = YbaX.$$

The map $X \mapsto a, Y \mapsto aa$ is a solution, as is $X \mapsto bb, Y \mapsto b$. However, it is known that the solutions to this equation cannot be expressed using linear integer parameters [21]. Thus, not all satisfiable systems of equations can be expressed in solved form.

4.4   Why Solved Form?

For word equations with an equivalent solved form, all length information implied by the word equations can be represented in a finite and *complete* (defined below) manner. The completeness property enables a satisfiability procedure to decouple the word equations from the (implied and given) length constraints, because it guarantees that the word equation is equisatisfiable with the implied length constraints. Furthermore, solved form guarantees that the implied length constraints are linear inequalities, and hence their satisfiability problem is decidable [22]. This insight forms the basis of our decidability results. It is noteworthy that most word equations that we have encountered in practice [25] are either in solved form or can be automatically converted into one.

4.5   Proof Idea for Decidability

Without loss of generality, we consider formulas that are the conjunction of word equations and length constraints. (The result can be easily extended to arbitrary Boolean combination of such formulas.) Let $\phi \wedge \theta$ be an $\mathcal{L}^0_{e,l}$-formula, where ϕ is a conjunction of word equations and θ is a conjunction of length constraints. Observe that ϕ implies a certain set of length constraints.

Example 10. *Consider the equation $X = abY$. We have the following set $\mathcal{R}$ of implied length constraints:*

$$\{len(X) = 2 + len(Y), len(Y) \geq 0\}.$$

The set $\mathcal{R}$ is finite but exhaustive. That is, any other length constraint implied by the equation $X = abY$ is either in $\mathcal{R}$ or is implied by $\mathcal{R}$. Consider the $\mathcal{L}_{e,l}^0$ formula

$$X = abY \wedge len(Y) > 1,$$

Note that $X = abY$ is satisfiable, say by the assignment with unfixed parts $X \mapsto aby, Y \mapsto y$. It remains to check whether there is a solution (represented by some choice of the unfixed part) which satisfies the length constraints $\mathcal{R} \cup \{len(Y) > 1\}$. A solution to the set of integer inequalities is $len(X) = 4, len(Y) = 2$. Translating this to a solution of the original formulas amount to "back-solving" for the exponent of unfixed parts in the solution to the word equation. That is, since $X \mapsto aby, Y \mapsto y$ is a satisfying assignment, we can pick any string of length 2 for y: say, $X \mapsto abab, Y \mapsto ab$.

Taking this example further, consider the $\mathcal{L}_{e,l}^0$ formula

$$X = abY \wedge len(Y) > 1 \wedge len(X) \leq 2.$$

The set of length constraints is now: $\{len(X) = 2 + len(Y), len(Y) \geq 0, len(Y) > 1, len(X) \leq 2\}$. This is not satisfiable, so neither is the original formula.

The set of implied length constraints for word equations that have a solved form is also finite and exhaustive. We prove this fact below, and use it to prove that a sound, complete and terminating satisfiability procedure exists for $\mathcal{L}_{e,l}^0$ formulas with word equations in solved form.

Definitions: We say that a set $\mathcal{R}$ of length constraints is *implied by a word equation ϕ* if the lengths of the strings in any solution of ϕ satisfy all constraints in $\mathcal{R}$. And, $\mathcal{R}$ is *complete* for ϕ if any length constraint implied by ϕ is either in $\mathcal{R}$ or is implied by a subset of $\mathcal{R}$. These definitions can be suitably extended to a Boolean combination of word equations.

4.6 Decidability Theorem

We prove a set of lemmas culminating in the decidability theorem.

Lemma 1. *If a word equation w has a solved form $\mathcal{S}$, then there exists a set $\mathcal{R}$ of linear length constraints implied by w that is finite and complete. Moreover, there is an algorithm which, given w, computes this set $\mathcal{R}$ of constraints.*

Proof. Since a word equation w is logically equivalent to its solved form $\mathcal{S}$, every solution to w is a solution to $\mathcal{S}$ and vice-versa. Hence, the set of length constraints implied by w is equivalent to the set of length constraints implied by $\mathcal{S}$. In $\mathcal{R}$, we will have integer variables associated with each string variable in w, integer variables associated with each unfixed part appearing in the RHS of an equation in $\mathcal{S}$, and integer variables associated with each integer parameter appearing in the RHS of an equation in $\mathcal{S}$. For each X appearing in w, consider the equation in S whose LHS is X: $X = t_1 \cdots t_n$, where each t_i is either (1) a constant from w, (2) a constant from w raised to some integer parameter, or (3) an unfixed part. This equation implies a length equation of the form: $len(X) = C + i_1 c_1 + \cdots + i_k c_k + len(y_1) + \cdots len(y_j)$, where C is the sum of the lengths of constants in w that appear on the RHS without an integer parameter; the c_i terms are the lengths of constants with integer parameters; and there are terms for each unfixed part appearing in the equation. The only other length constraints associated with this equation say that the unfixed parts and the integer parameters may be arbitrarily chosen: $i_r \geq 0$, $len(y_s) \geq 0$ for each $1 \leq r \leq k$ and $1 \leq 1 \leq s \leq j$. Note that the minimum length of X is the expression above where we choose each $i_r = 0$ and each $len(y_s) = 0$. Let $\mathcal{R}$ be the union over X in w of the (finitely many) length constraints associated with X discussed above. Since S is finite, so is $\mathcal{R}$.

It remains to prove that $\mathcal{R}$ is complete. By definition of solved form, all length constraints implied by S are of the form included in $\mathcal{R}$. Thus, $\mathcal{R}$ is complete for S. Since S is logically equivalent with w, they imply the same length constraints. Hence, $\mathcal{R}$ is complete for w as well.

Lemma 2. *If a word equation w has a solved form S, then w is equi-satisfiable with the length constraints $\mathcal{R}$ derived from S.*

Proof. Since $\mathcal{R}$ is finite, the conjunction of all its elements is a formula of $\mathcal{L}_{e,l}^0$.

($\Rightarrow$) If w is satisfiable, then so is $\mathcal{R}$: Suppose w is satisfiable and consider some satisfying assignment w. Then since $\mathcal{R}$ is implied by w, the lengths of the strings in this assignment satisfy all the constraints in $\mathcal{R}$. Thus, this set of lengths witnesses the satisfiability of $\mathcal{R}$.

($\Leftarrow$) If $\mathcal{R}$ is satisfiable, then so is w: Suppose $\mathcal{R}$ is satisfiable. Any solution of $\mathcal{R}$ gives a collection of lengths for the variables in w. An assignment that satisfies w is given by choosing arbitrary strings of the prescribed length for the unfixed parts and choosing values of the integer parameters prescribed by the solution of $\mathcal{R}$.

Theorem 11. *The satisifiability problem for $\mathcal{L}_{e,l}^0$ formulas is decidable, provided that there is an algorithm to obtain the solved forms of word equations for which they exist.*

Proof. We assume without loss of generality that the given $\mathcal{L}_{e,l}^0$ formula is the conjunction of a single word equation with some number of length constraints. (Generalizing to arbitrary $\mathcal{L}_{e,l}^0$ formulas is straightforward.) Let the input to the algorithm be a formula $\phi \wedge \theta$, where ϕ is the word equation and θ is a conjunction of length constraints. The output of the algorithm is *satisfiable* (SAT) or *unsatisfiable* (UNSAT).

Plandowski's algorithm [21] decides satisfiability of word equations; known algorithms for formulas of Presburger arithmetic can decide the satisfiability of systems of linear length constraints. Thus, begin by running these algorithms (in parallel) to decide if (separately) ϕ and θ are satisfiable. If either of these return UNSAT, we return UNSAT.

Using the assumption that the word equation ϕ has an effective solved form, compute this form S and the associated (complete and finite) implied set $\mathcal{R}$ of linear length constraints (as in Lemma 1). By Lemma 2, it is now sufficient to check the satisfiability of $(\wedge \mathcal{R}) \wedge \theta$. This can be done by a second application of an algorithm for formulas in

Presburger arithmetic, because the length constraints implied by ϕ are all linear. If this system of linear inequalities is satisfiable, return SAT, otherwise, we return UNSAT.

This procedure is a sound, complete and terminating procedure for $\mathcal{L}_{e,l}^0$-formulas whose word equations have effective solved forms.

4.7 Practical Value of Solved Form and the Decidability Result

JavaScript programs often process strings. These strings are entered into input forms on web-pages or are substrings used by JavaScript programs to dynamically generate web-pages or SQL queries. During the processing of these strings, JavaScript programs often concatenate these strings to form larger strings, use strings in assignments, compare string lengths, construct equalities between strings as part of if-conditionals or use regular expressions as basic "sanity-checks" of the strings being processed. Hence, any program analysis of such JavaScript programs results in formulas that contain string constants and variables, the concatenation operation, regular expressions, word equations, and uses of the length function.

In their paper on an automatic JavaScript testing program (Kudzu) and a practical satisfiability procedure for strings [25], Saxena et al. mention generating more than 50,000 $\mathcal{L}_{e,l,r}^0$ formulas where the length of the string variables is bounded (i.e., the string variables range over a finite universe of strings). Kudzu takes as input a JavaScript program and (implicit) specification, and does some automatic analysis (a form of concrete and symbolic execution [2, 9]) on the input program. The result of the analysis is a string formula that captures the behavior of the program-under-test in terms of the symbolic input to this program. A solution of such a formula is a test input to the program-under-test. Kudzu uses the Kaluza string solver to solve these formulas and generate program inputs for program testing.

We obtained more than 50,000 string constraints (word equations + length constraints) from the Kaluza team (http://webblaze.cs.berkeley.edu/2010/kaluza/). Kaluza is a solver for string constraints, where these constraints are obtained from bug-finding and string analysis of web applications. The constraints are divided into satisfiable and unsatisfiable constraints. We wrote a simple Perl script to count the number of equations per file and the number of equations already in solved form (identifier = expression). We then computed the ratio to see how many examples from this actual data set are already in solved form.

Experimental Results. The results are divided into groups based on whether the constraints were satisfiable or not. For satisfiable small equations (approximately 30-50 constraints per file), about 80% were already in solved form. For satisfiable large equations (around 200 constraints per file), this number rose to approximately 87%. Among the unsatisfiable and small equations (less than 20 constraints per file), again about 80% were already in solved form. Large (greater than 4000 constraints) unsatisfiable equations were in solved form a slightly smaller percentage of the time: 75%.

5 Word Equations, Length, and Regular Expressions

We now consider whether the previous result can be extended to show that the satisfiability problem for $\mathcal{L}_{e,l,r}^0$ formulas is decidable, provided that there is an algorithm to obtain the solved forms of given word equations. A generalization of the proof strategy from above looks promising. That is, given a membership test in a regular set $X \in RE$, we can extract from the structure of the regular expression a constraint on the length of X that is expressible as a linear inequality. Thus, it may seem that the same machinery as in the $\mathcal{L}^0_{e,l}$ theorem may be applied to the broader context of $\mathcal{L}^0_{e,l,r}$. However, there remain some subtleties to resolve.

Example 12. *Consider the $\mathcal{L}^0_{e,l,r}$ formula*

$$abX = Xba \ \wedge \ X \in (ab)^*b \ \wedge \ len(X) \le 3.$$

A naïve translation of each component into length constraints gives us the following:

$$\begin{cases} len(X) = 2i + 1, i \ge 0 & \text{implied by the word equation and regular expression} \\ len(X) \le 3. \end{cases}$$

*This system of length constraints is easily seen to be simultaneously satisfiable: let $i = 0$ or 1 and hence $len(X) = 1$ or 3. However, the formula is **not** satisfiable since solutions of the word equation are $X \in (ab)^*a$ and the regular expression requires any solution to end in a b.*

Thus, in order to address $\mathcal{L}^0_{e,l,r}$ formulas, we must take into account more information than is encapsulated by the length constraints imposed by regular expressions. In particular, if we impose the additional restriction that the word equations must have solved form (without unfixed parts) that are also regular expressions, then we can get a decidability result for $\mathcal{L}^0_{e,l,r}$ formulas.

Lemma 3. *If a word equation has a solved form without unfixed parts that is also a regular expression, then there is a finite set of linear length constraints that can be effectively computed from this solved form and which are equisatisfiable with the equation.*

Proof. It is sufficient to recall the fact, from [1], that given a regular set R, the set of lengths of strings in R is a finite union of arithmetic progressions. Moreover, there is an algorithm to extract the parameters of these arithmetic progressions from the regular expression defining R.

Using the above Lemma, the set of length constraints implied by an arbitrary regular expression can be expressed as a finite system of linear inequalities.

Theorem 13. *The satisifiability problem for $\mathcal{L}^0_{e,l,r}$ formulas is decidable, provided that there is an algorithm to obtain the solved forms of the given word equations, and the solved form equations do not contain unfixed parts and are regular expressions.*

Proof. Let $\theta(X) \wedge \phi \wedge (X \in RE)$ be a $\mathcal{L}^0_{e,l,r}$ formula, where $\theta(X)$ is a word equation, ϕ is a conjunction of length constraints, and $X \in RE$ asserts membership in a specified regular set. The proof can be easily extended to a Boolean combination of atomic formulas. Consider the following satisfiability procedure:

- If any of $\theta(X)$, ϕ, or $X \in RE$ is UNSAT, return UNSAT.
- Convert $\theta(X)$ into a solved form where it is a regular expression. That is, write it as $X \in RE_1$. Compute the intersection of the two regular expressions, $X \in RE \cap RE_1$. If $RE \cap RE_1$ is empty, return UNSAT.
- Extract equisatisfiable length constraints ψ from $X \in RE \cap RE_1$ using Lemma 3. If $\psi \wedge \phi$ is UNSAT, return UNSAT. Else return SAT.

The first step is effective by the same arguments as in Theorem 11 and the observation that membership in regular sets is decidable. The second step is effective since all Boolean operations may be performed effectively on regular sets. Using Lemma 3, it is easy to establish that this satisfiability procedure is sound, complete and terminating.

6   Related Work

In his original 1946 paper, Quine [23] showed that the first-order theory of string equations (i.e., quantified sentences over Boolean combination of word equations) is undecidable. Due to the expressibility of many key reliability and verification questions within this theory, this work has been extended in many ways.

One line of research studies fragments and modifications of this base theory which are decidable. Notably, in 1977, Makanin proved that the satisfiability problem for the quantifier-free theory of word equations is decidable [15]. In a sequence of papers, Plandowski and co-authors showed that the complexity of this problem is in PSPACE [21]. Stronger results have been found where equations are restricted to those where each variable occurs at most twice [24] or in which there are at most two variables [3, 4, 11]. In the first case, satisfiability is shown to be NP-hard; in the second, polynomial (which was improved further in the case of single variable word equations).

Concurrently, many researchers have looked for the exact boundary between decidability and undecidability. Durnev [5] and Marchenkov [16] both showed that the $\forall\exists$ sentences over word equations is undecidable. Note that Durnev's result is closest to our undecidability result. The main difference is that our proof is considerably simpler because of the use of two-counter machines, as opposed to certain non-standard machines used by Durnev. We also note corollaries regarding number of occurences of a variable, and $\mathcal{L}^1_{e,l}$ sentences with a single universal followed by bounded existentials. On the other hand, Durnev uses only 4 string variables to prove his result, while we use 7. We believe that we can reduce the number of variables, at the expense of a more complicated proof.

Word equations augmented with additional predicates yield richer structures which are relevant to many applications. In the 1970s, Matiyasevich formulated a connection between string equations augmented with integer coefficients whose integers are taken from the Fibonacci sequence and Diophantine equations [17]. In particular, he showed that proving undecidability for the satisfiability problem of this theory would suffice to solve Hilbert's 10th Problem in a novel way. Schulz [26] extended Makanin's satisfiability algorithm to the class of formulas where each variable in the equations is specified to lie in a given regular set. This is a strict generalization of the solution sets of word equations. [12] shows that the class of sets expressible through word equations is incomparable to that of regular sets.

Möller [19] studies word equations and related theories as motivated by questions from hardware verification. More specifically, Möller proves the undecidability of the existential fragment of a theory of fixed-length bit-vectors, with a special finite but possibly arbitrary concatenation operation, the extraction of substrings and the equality predicate. Although this theory is related to the word equations that we study, it is more powerful because of the finite but possibly arbitrary concatenation.

References

1. Blumensath, A.: Automatic structures. Diploma thesis, RWTH-Aachen (1999)
2. Cadar, C., Ganesh, V., Pawlowski, P., Dill, D., Engler, D.: EXE: automatically generating inputs of death. In: Juels, A., Wright, R.N., De Capitani di Vimercati, S. (eds.) ACM Conference on Computer and Communications Security, pp. 322–335. ACM (2006)
3. Charatonik, W., Pacholski, L.: Word equations with two variables. In: Abdulrab, H., Pécuchet, J.-P. (eds.) IWWERT 1991. LNCS, vol. 677, pp. 43–56. Springer, Heidelberg (1993)
4. Dabrowski, R., Plandowski, W.: On word equations in one variable. Algorithmica 60(4), 819–828 (2011)
5. Durnev, V.: Undecidability of the positive $\forall\exists^3$-theory of a free semigroup. Siberian Mathematical Journal 36(5), 1067–1080 (1995)
6. Ebbinghaus, H.-D., Flum, J., Thomas, W.: Mathematical Logic. Undergraduate Texts in Mathematics. Springer (1994)
7. Emmi, M., Majumdar, R., Sen, K.: Dynamic test input generation for database applications. In: Rosenblum, D., Elbaum, S. (eds.) ISSTA, pp. 151–162. ACM (2007)
8. Ganesh, V., Kieżun, A., Artzi, S., Guo, P.J., Hooimeijer, P., Ernst, M.: HAMPI: A string solver for testing, analysis and vulnerability detection. In: Gopalakrishnan, G., Qadeer, S. (eds.) CAV 2011. LNCS, vol. 6806, pp. 1–19. Springer, Heidelberg (2011)
9. Godefroid, P., Klarlund, N., Sen, K.: DART: directed automated random testing. In: Sarkar, V., Hall, M. (eds.) PLDI, pp. 213–223. ACM (2005)
10. Hopcroft, J., Motwani, R., Ullman, J.: Introduction to automata theory, languages, and computation. Pearson/Addison Wesley (2007)
11. Ilie, L., Plandowski, W.: Two-variable word equations. ITA 34(6), 467–501 (2000)
12. Karhumäki, J., Mignosi, F., Plandowski, W.: The expressibility of languages and relations by word equations. J. ACM 47(3), 483–505 (2000)
13. Kiezun, A., Ganesh, V., Guo, P., Hooimeijer, P., Ernst, M.: HAMPI: a solver for string constraints. In: Rothermel, G., Dillon, L. (eds.) ISSTA, pp. 105–116. ACM (2009)
14. Majumdar, R.: Private correspondence. SWS, MPI, Kaiserslautern, Germany (2010)
15. Makanin, G.: The problem of solvability of equations in a free semigroup. Math. Sbornik 103, 147–236 (1977); English transl. in Math USSR Sbornik 32 (1977)
16. Marchenkov, S.S.: Unsolvability of positive $\forall\exists$-theory of free semi-group. Sibirsky Mathmatichesky Jurnal 23(1), 196–198 (1982)
17. Matiyasevich, Y.: Word equations, Fibonacci numbers, and Hilbert's tenth problem (2006) (unpublished), http://logic.pdmi.ras.ru/?yumat/Journal/jcontord.htm
18. Matiyasevich, Y.: Computation paradigms in light of Hilbert's Tenth Problem. In: Cooper, S., Löwe, B., Sorbi, A. (eds.) New Computational Paradigms, pp. 59–85. Springer, New York (2008)
19. Möller, O.: $\exists BV_{[n]}solvability$. SRI International, Menlo Park, CA, USA (October 1996) (unpublished manuscript)

20. Plandowski, W.: Satisfiability of word equations with constants is in PSPACE. In: FOCS, pp. 495–500. IEEE Computer Society (1999)
21. Plandowski, W.: An efficient algorithm for solving word equations. In: Kleinberg, J. (ed.) STOC, pp. 467–476. ACM (2006)
22. Presburger, M.: Über de vollständigkeit eines gewissen systems der arithmetik ganzer zahlen, in welchen, die addition als einzige operation hervortritt. In: Comptes Rendus du Premier Congrès des Mathématicienes des Pays Slaves, Warsaw, pp. 92–101, 395 (1927)
23. Quine, W.V.: Concatenation as a basis for arithmetic. The Journal of Symbolic Logic 11(4), 105–114 (1946)
24. Robson, J.M., Diekert, V.: On quadratic word equations. In: Meinel, C., Tison, S. (eds.) STACS 1999. LNCS, vol. 1563, pp. 217–226. Springer, Heidelberg (1999)
25. Saxena, P., Akhawe, D., Hanna, S., Mao, F., McCamant, S., Song, D.: A symbolic execution framework for JavaScript. In: IEEE Symposium on Security and Privacy, pp. 513–528. IEEE Computer Society (2010)
26. Schulz, K.U.: Makanin's algorithm for word equations-two improvements and a generalization. In: Schulz, K.U. (ed.) IWWERT 1990. LNCS, vol. 572, pp. 85–150. Springer, Heidelberg (1992)
27. Wassermann, G., Su, Z.: Sound and precise analysis of web applications for injection vulnerabilities. In: Ferrante, J., McKinley, K. (eds.) PLDI, pp. 32–41. ACM (2007)

Environment-Friendly Safety

Orna Kupferman and Sigal Weiner

School of Computer Science and Engineering, Hebrew University, Israel

Abstract. Of special interest in verification are safety properties, which assert that the system always stays within some allowed region. For closed systems, the theoretical properties of safety properties as well as their practical advantages with respect to general properties are well understood. For open (a.k.a. reactive) systems, whose behavior depends on their on-going interaction with the environment, the common practice is to use the definition and algorithms of safety for closed systems, ignoring the distinction between input and output signals. In a recent work, Ehlers and Finkbeiner introduced *reactive safety* – a definition of safety for the setting of open systems. Essentially, reactive safety properties require the system to stay in a region of states that is both allowed and from which the environment cannot force it out. In this paper we continue their study and extend it to other families of properties. In the setting of closed systems, each safety property induces a set of finite bad prefixes – ones after which the property must be violated. The notion of bad prefixes enables a reduction of reasoning about safety properties to reasoning about properties of finite computations. We study reactive bad prefixes, their detection in theory and in practice, and their approximation by either a non-reactive safety property or by reasoning about the syntax of the formula. We study the dual notion, of reactive co-safety properties, and the corresponding theory of reactive good prefixes. For both safety and co-safety properties, we relate the definitions in the closed and open settings, and argue that our approach strictly extends the range of properties for which we can apply algorithms that are based on finite computations. Since the reactive setting is particularly challenging for general properties, such an application is significant in practice.

1 Introduction

In formal verification, we verify that a system meets a desired property by checking that a mathematical model of the system meets a formal specification that describes the property. Of special interest are properties asserting that the observed behavior of the system always stays within some allowed set of finite behaviors, in which nothing "bad" happens. For example, we may want to assert that every message received was previously sent. Such properties of systems are called *safety properties*. Intuitively, a property ψ is a safety property if every violation of ψ occurs after a finite execution of the system. In our example, if in a computation of the system a message is received without previously being sent, this occurs after some finite execution of the system.[1]

---

[1] Note that the adjective safety describes the properties and not the system. One may say that a system is safe if it satisfies safety specifications, but our use here refers to the specifications.

A. Biere, A. Nahir, and T. Vos (Eds.): HVC 2012, LNCS 7857, pp. 227–242, 2013.
© Springer-Verlag Berlin Heidelberg 2013

In order to formally define what safety properties are, we refer to computations of a nonterminating system as infinite words over an alphabet Σ. Typically, $\Sigma = 2^{AP}$, where AP is the set of the system's atomic propositions. Consider a language L of infinite words over Σ. A finite word u over Σ is a *bad prefix* for L iff for all infinite words v over Σ, the concatenation $u \cdot v$ of u and v is not in L. Thus, a bad prefix for L is a finite word that cannot be extended to an infinite word in L. A language L is a *safety language* if every word not in L has a finite bad prefix.

Safety has been widely studied in the formal-verification community; c.f., [1,8,14]. The theoretical properties of safety properties as well as their practical advantages with respect to general properties are well understood. The definition and studies of safety, however, treat all the atomic propositions as equal. Thus, they do not distinguish between input and output signals and are suited for closed systems – ones that do not maintain an interaction with their environment. In open (also called *reactive*) systems [6,12], the system interacts with the environment, and a correct system should satisfy the specification with respect to all environments. A good way to think about the open setting is to consider the situation as a game between the system and the environment. The interaction between the players in this game generates a computation, and the goal of the system is that only computations that satisfy the specification will be generated.

Technically, one has to partition the set AP of atomic propositions to a set I of input signals, which the environment controls, and a set O of output signals, which the system controls. An open system is then an *I/O-transducer* – a deterministic automaton over the alphabet 2^I in which each state is labeled by an output in 2^O. Given a sequence of assignments to the input signals (each assignment is a letter in 2^I), the run of the transducer on it induces a sequence of assignments to the output signals (that is, letters in 2^O). Together these sequences form a computation, and the transducer *realizes* a specification ψ if all its computations satisfy ψ [12].

The transition from the closed to the open setting modifies the questions we typically ask about systems. Most notably, the *synthesis* challenge, of generating a system that satisfies the specification, corresponds to the satisfiability problem in the closed setting and to the realizability problem in the open setting. As another example, the equivalence problem between LTL specifications is different in the closed and open settings [5]. That is, two specifications may not be equivalent when compared with respect to arbitrary systems on $I \cup O$, but be *open equivalent*; that is, equivalent when compared with respect to I/O-transducers. To see this, note for example that a satisfiable yet non-realizable specification is equivalent to false in the open but not in the closed setting.

As mentioned above, the classical definition of safety does not distinguish between input and output signals. The definition can still be applied to open systems, as a special case of closed systems with $\Sigma = 2^{I \cup O}$. In [2], the authors introduced *reactive safety* – a definition of safety for the setting of open systems. The definition in [2] is by means of sets of trees with directions in 2^I and labels in 2^O. The use of trees naturally locate reactive safety between linear and branching safety. Here, we suggest an equivalent yet differently presented definition, which explicitly use realizability. In our definition, a prefix $u \in (2^{I \cup O})^*$ is bad with respect to a property ψ if the system cannot realize ψ after the generation of u. Thus, reactive safety properties require the system to stay in a region of states that is both allowed and from which the environment cannot force it out.

In order to indicate that in the open setting we take the environment into an account, we use the term *green safety* to refer to safety in the open setting, and refer to classical safety as *black safety*, or, when clear from the context, safety. To see the difference between the green and black definitions, consider the specification $\psi = G(err \rightarrow F\mathit{fix})$, with $I = \{\mathit{fix}\}$ and $O = \{err\}$. Thus, the system controls the generation of errors, the environment controls the fixes, and the specification is satisfied if every error is eventually fixed. Note that ψ is realizable using the system strategy "never err". Also, ψ is clearly not a safety property, as every prefix can be extended to one that satisfies ψ. On the other hand, ψ is green safe. Indeed, every computation that violates ψ has a green bad prefix – a prefix that ends when the system errs. Once this prefix has been generated, the system has no way to realize the specification, as it is the environment that controls the fixes.

We continue the study of green safety in [2]. We first give further examples to specifications that are green safe but not safe and study their properties. We study green bad prefixes and show that, unlike the closed setting, they are not closed under extensions, and we relate their closure under extension to black safety. We show how one can take advantage of green safety when the specification is not safe (but is green safe) and lift the algorithmic advantages of safety properties to green safety properties. We do so by mapping green safety properties to open-equivalent black safety properties. The mapping is the same as a mapping suggested in [2] by means of nodes in the tree in which a violation starts. In addition to the fact that our definition uses realizability explicitly, which we find simpler, our definition and results apply to general languages, and not only to green or black safety languages. We further formalize the connection between green and black safety by showing that a property is green safe iff it is open equivalent to a black safe property.

We extend the green approach to other families of properties. In the setting of closed systems, the fragment of *co-safety* properties dualizes the one of safety properties: a property is co-safe if its complement is safe. Equivalently, a property is co-safe if every computation that satisfies it has a good prefix – one after which the property aught to hold. In the open setting, dualization is more involved, as one has not only to complement the property but to also to dualize the roles of the system and the environment. Since the game between the system and the environment is determined [4], in the sense that either there is an I/O-transducer that realizes ψ (that is, the system wins) or there is an O/I-transducer that realizes $\neg\psi$ (that is, the environment wins), such a dualization is possible, and we actually have four fragments of languages that are induced by dualization of the green safety definition. The different fragments correspond to whether we talk about safety or co-safety, and whether it is the system or the environment that we consider. We study the theoretical properties of the fragments and the connections among them.

In the closed setting, the intersection of safe and co-safe properties induces the fragment of *bounded* properties – there is an integer $k \geq 0$ such that every word of length k is either a good or a bad prefix [9]. We study boundedness in the open setting and show that the fact green bad and good prefixes are not closed under extension makes the boundedness issue more complicated, as a computation may have both infinitely many good and infinitely many bad prefixes.

In the closed setting, detection of special (bad or good) prefixes has the flavor of validity checking. Accordingly, the problem of deciding whether an LTL specification is safe or co-safe is PSPACE-complete [14]. In the setting of open systems, detection of special prefixes has the flavor of realizability. Thus, reasoning about special prefixes is more complicated. In particular, it is shown in [2] that the problem of deciding whether an LTL formula is reactive safe is 2EXPTIME-complete. Similar bounds hold for the problem of detecting special prefixes. Thus, especially in the open setting, it is interesting to find efficient ways to approximate the language of special prefixes and their detection. We suggest such an approximation by means of *informative green prefixes*. The notion of informative prefixes was introduced for the closed setting in [8]. Essentially, a prefix is informative for a safety property ψ if the syntax of ψ explains why it is a bad prefix. Lifting the notion to open systems involves an approximation that is based both on examining the syntax, rather than the semantics of the property, and an approximation of realizability by satisfiability. We argue that for natural specifications, the approximations are accurate.

Finally, our ability to replace green safe properties by simpler safe properties as well as the fact that our syntactic-based approximation is accurate for natural specifications are useful not only for easier reasoning about but also in order to assess the quality of specifications. This later point is very important in the context of property-based design [13]. The setting of open systems is particularly challenging for property assurance: solving the synthesis problem, decomposition of specifications is not always possible, making the detection of dependencies among different components of the specification much more difficult.

Due to the lack of space, some proofs are omitted from this version and can be found in the full version, in the authors' URLs.

2 Preliminaries

2.1 Linear Temporal Logic

The logic *LTL* is a linear temporal logic. Formulas of LTL are constructed from a set AP of atomic proposition using the usual Boolean operators and the temporal operators G ("always"), F ("eventually"), X ("next time"), and U ("until"). We define the semantics of LTL with respect to a *computation* $\pi = \sigma_0, \sigma_1, \sigma_2, \ldots$, where for every $j \geq 0$, we have that σ_j is a subset of AP, denoting the set of atomic propositions that hold in the j-th position of π. We use $\pi \models \psi$ to indicate that an LTL formula ψ holds in the computation π. We use $\|\psi\|$ to denote the set of computations in $(2^{AP})^{\omega}$ that satisfy ψ. A full definition of the syntax and semantics of LTL can be found in [11].

2.2 Safety Languages and Formulas

Consider a language $L \subseteq \Sigma^{\omega}$ of infinite words over the alphabet Σ. A finite word $u \in \Sigma^*$ is a *bad prefix* for L if for all $v \in \Sigma^{\omega}$, we have $u \cdot v \notin L$. Thus, a bad prefix is a finite word that cannot be extended to an infinite word in L. Note that if u is a bad prefix, then all the finite extensions of u are also bad prefixes. A language L is a *safety* language if every word not in L has a finite bad prefix [1,8,14]. For a language L, we denote by $bp(L)$ the set of all bad prefixes for L. We say that an LTL formula ψ is a safety formula iff $\|\psi\|$ is a safety language.

2.3 Open Systems

We model open systems by *transducers*. Let I and O be finite sets of input and output signals, respectively. Given $x = i_0 \cdot i_1 \cdot i_2 \cdots \in (2^I)^\omega$ and $y = o_0 \cdot o_1 \cdot o_2 \cdots \in (2^O)^\omega$, we denote their composition by $x \oplus y = (i_0, o_0) \cdot (i_1, o_1) \cdot (i_2, o_2) \cdots \in (2^{I \cup O})^\omega$. An I/O-transducer is a tuple $\mathcal{T} = \langle I, O, S, s_0, \eta, L \rangle$, where S is a set of states, $s_0 \in S$ is an initial state, $\eta : S \times 2^I \to S$ is a transition function, and $L : S \to 2^O$ is a labeling function. The *run* of $\mathcal{T}$ on a (finite or infinite) input sequence $x = i_0 \cdot i_1 \cdot i_2 \cdots$, with $i_j \in 2^I$, is the sequence $s_0, s_1, s_2, \ldots$ of states such that $s_{j+1} = \eta(s_j, i_{j+1})$ for all $j \geq 0$. The *computation* of $\mathcal{T}$ on x is then $x \oplus y$, for $y = L(s_0) \cdot L(s_1) \cdot L(s_2) \cdots$ Note that $\mathcal{T}$ is responsive and deterministic (that is, it suggests exactly one successor state for each input letter), and thus $\mathcal{T}$ has a single run, generating a single computation, on each input sequence. We extend η to finite words over 2^I in the expected way. In particular, $\eta(s_0, x)$, for $x \in (2^I)^*$ is the $|x|$-th state in the run on x. A transducer $\mathcal{T}$ induces a strategy $f : (2^I)^* \to 2^O$ such that for all $x \in (2^I)^*$, we have that $f(x) = L(\eta(s_0, x))$. Given an LTL formula ψ over $I \cup O$, we say that ψ is I/O-*realizable* if there is a finite-state I/O-transducer $\mathcal{T}$ such that all the computations of $\mathcal{T}$ satisfy ψ [12]. We then say that $\mathcal{T}$ realizes ψ. When it is clear from the context, we refer to I/O-realizability as *realizability*, or talk about realizability of languages over the alphabet $2^{I \cup O}$.

Since the realizability problem corresponds to deciding a game between the system and the environment, and the game is determined [4], realizability is determined too, in the sense that either there is an I/O-transducer that realizes ψ (that is, the system wins) or there is an O/I-transducer that realizes $\neg\psi$ (that is, the environment wins). Note that in an O/I-transducer the system and the environment "switch roles" and the system is the one that provides the inputs to the transducer. A technical detail is that in order for the setting of O/I-realizability to be dual to the one in I/O-realizability we need, in addition to switching the roles and negating the specification, to switch the player that moves first and consider transducers in which the environment initiates the interaction and moves first. Since we are not going to delve into constructions, we ignore this point, which is easy to handle.

3 Green Safety

Let I and O be sets of input and output signals, respectively. Consider a language $L \subseteq (2^{I \cup O})^\omega$. For a finite word $u \in (2^{I \cup O})^*$, let $L^u = \{s : u \cdot s \in L\}$ be the set of all infinite words s such that $u \cdot s \in L$. Thus, if L describes a set of allowed computations, then L^u describes the set of allowed suffixes of computations starting with u.

We say that a finite word $u \in (2^{I \cup O})^*$ is a *system bad prefix* for L iff L^u is not realizable. Thus, a system bad prefix is a finite word u such that after traversing u, the system does not have a strategy to ensure that the interaction with the environment would generate a computation in L. We use $sbp(L)$ to denote the set of system bad prefixes for L. Note that by determinacy of games, whenever L^u is not realizable by the system, then its complement is realizable by the environment. Thus, once a bad prefix has been generated, the environment has a strategy to ensure that the entire generated behavior is not in L.

A language $L \subseteq (2^{I \cup O})^\omega$ is a *green safety language* if every word not in L has a system bad prefix.

Example 1. Let $I = \{q\}$, $O = \{p\}$, $\psi = Gp \vee FGq$, and $L = \|\psi\|$. Note that ψ is realizable using the system strategy "always output p". We show L is green safe. Consider a word $w \notin L$. Since w does not satisfy Gp, there must be a prefix u of w such that u contains a position satisfying $\neg p$. Since words with prefix u do not satisfy Gp, we have that $L^u = \|FGq\|$. Since $q \in I$, the specification FGq is not realizable. Thus, u is a system bad prefix and L is green safe.

On the other hand, L is not safe. Consider for example the word $w = \emptyset^\omega$. While w is not in L, for every finite computation u of w, the suffix $s = \{q\}^\omega$ is such that $u \cdot s \models FGq$, implying that $u \cdot s \in L$. Thus, w has no bad prefix, implying that L is not safe.

Example 2. Let $I = \{q\}$, $O = \{p\}$, $\psi = G(p \rightarrow Fq)$, and $L = \|\psi\|$. Note that ψ is realizable using the system strategy "never output p". Also, ψ is clearly not a safety property, as every prefix can be extended to one that satisfies it. On the other hand, L is green safe. Indeed, every word not in L must have a prefix u that ends with $\{p\}$. Since $L^u = \|Fq\|$ and $q \in I$, so the specification Fq is not realizable, we have that u is a system bad prefix and L is green safe.

Note that when $I = \emptyset$, which corresponds to the case of closed systems, we have that L^u is not realizable iff L^u is empty. Thus, when $I = \emptyset$, safety coincides with green safety.

Explaining the intuition behind green safety, we are going to use the following terminology. We say that the system *errs* when it generates a system bad prefix. The environment, however, may *forgive* these errors and not follow a winning strategy after it. In Example 1, the system errs whenever it outputs $\neg p$. In Example 2, the system errs whenever it outputs p. In both cases, when this happens, the environment may follow a strategy with which the generated computations do not satisfy ψ, say by always inputting $\emptyset$, but it may also forgive the errors by following a strategy with which ψ still holds, say by always inputting $\{q\}$.

Remark 1. While presented differently, our definition of green safety is equivalent to the definition of reactive safety in [2]. The definition there is by means of sets of trees with directions in 2^I and labels in 2^O. The use of trees naturally locate reactive safety between linear and branching safety. On the other hand, we find the explicit use of realizability in our definition much simpler and easier to work with, as it naturally conveys the intuition of safety in the open setting.

3.1 Properties of Green Safety

We start by checking some theoretical properties of green safety.

Proposition 1. *Every non-realizable language is green safe, with ϵ being a system bad prefix.*

Proof: Since $L^\epsilon = L$, we have that L is not realizable iff L^ϵ is not realizable, which holds iff ϵ is a system bad prefix. Therefore, if L is not realizable, every word not in L has ϵ as a system bad prefix, and so L is green safe. ☐

As pointed out in [2], green safety is strictly weaker than safety. We present here the proof using our alternative definition of green safety.

Proposition 2. *Every safe language is green safe, but the other direction is not necessarily true.*

Proof: Let L be a safe language. Consider a word $w \notin L$ and a bad prefix $u \in (2^{I \cup O})^*$ of w. Since u is a bad prefix, the set L^u is empty, and is therefore unrealizable, so u is also a system bad prefix. Thus, every word not in L has a system bad prefix, implying that L is green safe. Strictness is demonstrated in Example 1. ☐

In the closed settings, the set $bp(L)$ is closed under finite extensions for all languages $L \subseteq \Sigma^\omega$. That is, for every finite word $u \in bp(L)$ and finite extension $v \in \Sigma^*$, we have that $u \cdot v \in bp(L)$. As we shall see now, the set of system bad prefixes is not closed under finite extensions. The reason is that the environment need not take advantage of errors made by the system, possibly giving the system another chance to win. Below we give two such examples.

Example 3. Let $I = \{fix\}$, $O = \{err\}$, and $\psi = G(err \to X fix) \wedge FG\neg err$. Thus, ψ states that every error the system makes is fixed by the environment in the following step, and that there is a finite number of errors. Let $L = \|\psi\|$. Clearly, L is realizable, as the strategy "make no errors" is a winning strategy for the system.

We first show that L is green safe. Consider a word $w \notin L$. Since $w \not\models \psi$, there must be a prefix u of w such that u ends in a position satisfying err. We claim that u is a system bad prefix. Indeed, an environment strategy starting with $\neg fix$ guarantees that the condition $G(err \to X fix)$ is not satisfied, and hence is a winning strategy for the environment after u was generated. Hence, L^u is not realizable, implying that L is green safe.

We now show that $sbp(L)$ is not closed under finite extensions. Consider the word $w = (\{err, fix\} \cdot \{fix\})^\omega$. That is, the system makes an error on every odd position, and the environment always fixes errors. Since there are infinitely many errors in w, it does not satisfy ψ. The prefix $u = \{err, fix\}$ of w is a system bad prefix. Indeed, an environment strategy that starts with $\neg fix$ is a winning strategy. On the other hand, u's extension $v = \{err, fix\} \cdot \{fix\}$ is not a system bad prefix. Indeed, L^v is realizable using the winning system strategy "make no errors".

Note that w has infinitely many system bad prefixes and infinitely many undetermined prefixes. For the same language, we can also point to a word with only one system bad prefix. Consider the word $w' = \{err, fix\} \cdot \{fix\}^\omega$. Note that w' is in L. Here, the system makes only one error, which is fixed, and then makes no more errors. While $\{err, fix\}$ is a system bad prefix, every longer prefix of w' contains the fix for the first error, and does not contain further errors by the system, Therefore, it is not a system bad prefix.

Example 4. In the previous example, we saw a word w' with only one system bad prefix, but w' was in L. Let $I = \{fix\}$, $O = \{err, ack\}$, and $\psi = G(err \rightarrow X(fix \wedge Fack))$. Thus, ψ states that after the system makes an error, the environment must fix it, and the system must also eventually acknowledge the error. Let $L = \|\psi\|$. In the full version we show that L is green safe and not safe and that here is a word not in L that has only one system bad prefix.

We can conclude with the following:

Proposition 3. *The set of system bad prefixes is not closed under extension.*

3.2 From Green to Black Safety

As studied in [8], reasoning about safety properties is easier than reasoning about general properties. In particular, rather than working with automata on infinite words, one can model check safety properties using automata (on finite words) for bad prefixes. In the open setting, when the specification we reason about is safe, we can use algorithms developed for safety languages. The question is whether and how we can take advantage of green safety when the specification is not safe (but is green safe). In this section we answer this question positively and lift the algorithmic advantages of safety properties to green safety properties. We do so by mapping green safety properties to open-equivalent black safety properties.

For a language $L \subseteq (2^{I \cup O})^{\omega}$, we define $black(L) = L \cap \{w : w$ has no system bad prefix for $L\}$. Equivalently, $black(L) = L \setminus \{w : w$ has a system bad prefix for $L\}$. Intuitively, we obtain $black(L)$ by defining all the finite extensions of $sbp(L)$ as bad prefixes. Accordingly, it is easy to see that $sbp(L) \subseteq bp(black(L))$. We sometimes apply $black$ on LTL formulas, mapping formulas to formulas.

Example 5. Consider the specification $\psi = G(err \rightarrow Xfix) \wedge FG\neg err$, with $I = \{fix\}$, $O = \{err\}$. In Example 3 we saw that ψ is green safe. Moreover, an infinite word contains a system bad prefix for ψ iff it has a position that satisfies err. Accordingly, $black(\psi) = G\neg err$. The specification ψ is a basis to similar specifications. For example, in a thread-management context, if we replace err by $Zero\_x$ and fix by $Interrupt$, where interrupt stands for the operating system interrupting the system thread, then the formula $\psi = G(Zero\_x \rightarrow XInterrupt) \wedge FG\neg Zero\_x$ states that the value of x, which the system controls, can be 0 only finitely often and that whenever it is 0, the environment must not interrupt the system in the next transition. For this formula, we get that $black(\psi) = G\neg Zero\_x$. This matches our intuition: If an interrupt can occur at any time, and we want to avoid an interrupt when x is 0, we must never set x to 0.

Example 6. Consider the specification $\psi = G(err \rightarrow X(fix \wedge Fack))$, with $I = \{fix\}$, $O = \{err, ack\}$. In Example 4 we saw that ψ is green safe. Moreover, an infinite word contains a system bad prefix for ψ iff it has a position that satisfies err. Accordingly,

$black(\psi) = G\neg err$. Here too, the structure of ψ is a basis to similar specifications. For example, in a network with packet loss, replacing err with $\neg legal$ (for sending an illegal packet), fix with $drop$ (for packet dropped by the network), and ack with $resend$, we get the specification "illegal packets are eventually resent, and no illegal packet reaches its destination". For this formula, we get that $black(\psi) = Glegal$. This matches our intuition: the only way to avoid an arrival of an illegal packet to its destination is to never send one.

Remark 2. A similar transition from green to black safety is described in [2], by means of nodes in the tree in which a violation starts, which are analogous to our system bad prefixes. In addition to the fact that our definition uses realizability explicitly, which we find simpler, our definition and results apply to general languages, and not only to green or black safety languages.

Theorem 1. *Consider a language $L \subseteq (2^{I \cup O})^\omega$. The following are equivalent:*

1. *L is green safe.*
2. *$\{w : w$ has no system bad prefix$\} \subseteq L$; that is, $black(L) = \{w : w$ has no system bad prefix$\}$.*
3. *$black(L)$ is black safe.*

Proof: We first prove if L is green safe then $\{w : w$ has no system bad prefix$\} \subseteq L$. Assume that L is green safe. Consider a word $w \in \{w : w$ has no system bad prefix$\}$, and assume by way of contradiction that $w \notin L$. Since L is green safe and $w \notin L$, we have that w has a system bad prefix for L, contradicting the fact that $w \in \{w : w$ has no system bad prefix$\}$.

We now prove that if $\{w : w$ has no system bad prefix$\} \subseteq L$ then $black(L)$ is black safe. Consider a word $w \notin black(L)$. By definition, $black(L) = L \cap \{w : w$ has no system bad prefix$\}$, and since $\{w : w$ has no system bad prefix$\} \subseteq L$, we have that $black(L) = \{w : w$ has no system bad prefix$\}$. Therefore, w has a system bad prefix u. For every suffix $s \in (2^{I \cup O})^\omega$, the word $w' = u \cdot s$ contains the system bad prefix u and therefore $w' \notin black(L)$. Thus, u is a bad prefix in $black(L)$, implying that $black(L)$ is black safe.

Finally, we prove that if $black(L)$ is black safe then L is green safe. Assume that $black(L)$ is black safe, and consider a word $w \notin L$. Since $black(L) \subseteq L$, we have that $w \notin black(L)$. Therefore, w has a bad prefix u in $black(L)$. If $u \in sbp(L)$, we are done since w indeed has a system bad prefix. Otherwise, we claim that u has a prefix v such that $v \in sbp(L)$. Since u is not a system bad prefix, the system has a winning strategy from u, and that strategy generates a suffix $s \in (2^{I \cup O})^\omega$ such that $w' = u \cdot s \in L$. Since $u \in bp(black(L))$, we have that $w' \notin black(L)$, so w' has a prefix $v \in sbp(L)$. We claim that $|v| \leq |u|$. Indeed, every prefix of w' that is not a prefix of u was generated by a winning strategy for the system. Therefore, it cannot be a system bad prefix. Now, if $|v| \leq |u|$ then v is also a prefix of w, so w has a system bad prefix. Therefore, L is green safe. $\square$

While L and $black(L)$ are not equivalent, they are *open equivalent*, in the sense of [5]. Formally, we have the following.

Theorem 2. *For every language $L \subseteq (2^{I \cup O})^\omega$ and I/O-transducer $\mathcal{T}$, we have that $\mathcal{T}$ realizes L iff $\mathcal{T}$ realizes $black(L)$.*

Proof: Since $black(L) \subseteq L$, then clearly every transducer that realizes $black(L)$ also realizes L. For the other direction, let L be some language and consider an I/O-transducer $\mathcal{T}$ that realizes L. Assume by contradiction that $\mathcal{T}$ does not realize $black(L)$. Then, there is a computation w of $\mathcal{T}$ such that $w \in L \setminus black(L)$. Since $black(L) = L \cap \{w : w$ has a system bad prefix for $L\}$ and $w \in L \setminus black(L)$, it must be that $w \notin \{w : w$ has a system bad prefix for $L\}$. Thus, w has a system bad prefix u. Since u is a system bad prefix, we have that L^u is not realizable, which means that after u was generated, the environment has a winning strategy. Since L is ω-regular, there is also an O/I-transducer that implements such a winning strategy. Let $\mathcal{T}'$ be such an O/I-transducer. Consider the word $w' = u \cdot (x \oplus y)$, where $x \in (2^I)^\omega$ and $y \in (2^O)^\omega$ are the input and output sequences generated when the environment follows $\mathcal{T}'$, and the system follows $\mathcal{T}^u$ (that is, $\mathcal{T}$ after u has been generated). So, $x = \mathcal{T}'(y)$ and $y = \mathcal{T}^u(x)$. Since $y = \mathcal{T}^u(x)$, we have that $w' = u \cdot (x \oplus \mathcal{T}^u(x))$ is a computation of $\mathcal{T}$. Since $\mathcal{T}'$ is a winning strategy for the environment, we have that $w' = u \cdot (\mathcal{T}'(y) \oplus y) \notin L$. On the one hand, since $\mathcal{T}$ realizes L, all the traces of $\mathcal{T}$ are in L. On the other hand, w' is a trace of $\mathcal{T}$, so we have reached a contradiction. Therefore, T also realizes $black(L)$. $\square$

Note that Theorem 2 applies to arbitrary languages and not only for green safe ones.

Theorem 2 suggests that we can reason about ψ, and in particular solve its model-checking (with respect to transducers) and synthesis problems by reasoning about $black(\psi)$. Consider for example the green safety property $\psi = G(p \rightarrow Fq)$, where $black(\psi) = G \neg p$ (recall that p is an output signal, see Example 2). Our ability to replace ψ by the much simpler formula $black(\psi)$ is similar to our ability to simplify specifications with *inherent vacuity* [3]. Indeed, green-but-not-black safety typically indicates that the specifier is not fully aware of the many aspects of the specification. Thus, green safety is useful not only for reasoning about simpler specifications but also in order to assess the quality of specifications, which is very important in the context of property-based design [13], especially in the setting of open systems. The setting of open systems is indeed particularly challenging for property assurance: solving the synthesis problem, decomposing of specifications is not always possible, making the detection of dependencies among different components of the specification much more difficult.

It is shown in [2], that given an LTL formula ψ, it is possible to construct a deterministic looping word automaton for $black(\psi)$ with doubly-exponential number of states.[2] In fact, as suggested in [8], it is then possible to generate also a deterministic automaton for the bad prefixes of $black(\psi)$. Note that when L is not realizable, we have that $\epsilon \in sbp(L)$, implying that $black(L) = \emptyset$. It follows that we cannot expect to construct small automata for $black(L)$, even nondeterministic ones, as the realizability problem for LTL can be reduced to easy questions about them.

Theorem 2 implies that a green safety language L is open equivalent to a safe language, namely $black(L)$. We complete the picture by showing that open equivalence to a safe language implies green safety.

---

[2] A looping automaton is a Büchi automaton in which all states are accepting. It is known [8,14] that safety properties can be translated to looping automata.

Theorem 3. *A language L is green safe iff L is open equivalent to a safe language.*

Proof: First, if L is green safe, then, by Theorem 1, we have that $black(L)$, which is open equivalent to L, is safe.

For the other direction, assume that L is open equivalent to a safe language L'. We show that L is green safe. Assume by way of contradiction that L is not green safe. Then, there is a word $w \notin L$ with no system bad prefix. In the full version we show that the above implies that the word w also has no system bad prefix in L', which implies, as L' is a safe language, that $w \in L'$. Consider the following (infinite) transducer T: As long as T gets inputs that agree with w, it generates outputs that agree with w and continues. Once the input does not agree with w, the prefix generated so far is a prefix of w. Since w has no system bad prefix in L', there is a system winning strategy in L' from this prefix, and T plays that strategy. Since T either generates $w \in L'$, or reaches a position from which it plays a system winning strategy in L', it follows that T realizes L'. Since, however, T generates w, which is not in L, it does not realize L, contradicting the fact that L and L' are open equivalent. We note that, by [5], the existence of an infinite transducer that distinguishes between L and L' implies the existence of such a finite transducer. □

4   Green Co-safety

For a language $L \subseteq \Sigma^\omega$, we use $comp(L)$ to denote the complement of L; i.e., $comp(L) = \Sigma^\omega \setminus L$. In the closed setting, we say that a language $L \subseteq \Sigma^\omega$ is a *co-safety* language if $comp(L)$ is a safety language. (The term used in [10] is *guarantee* language.) Equivalently, L is co-safety iff every $w \in L$ has a *good prefix* $x \in \Sigma^*$ such that for all $y \in \Sigma^\omega$, we have $x \cdot y \in L$. For a co-safety language L, we denote by $gp(L)$ the set of good prefixes for L. Note that $gp(L) = bp(comp(L))$ [8]. Finally, an LTL formula ψ is a co-safety formula iff $\|\psi\|$ is a co-safety language or, equivalently, $\|\neg\psi\|$ is a safety language.

In the setting of open systems, dualization of specifications is more involved, as one has not only to complement the language but to also dualizes the roles of the system and the environment. Accordingly, we actually have four fragments of languages that are induced by dualization of the green safety definition. We define them by means of bad and good prefixes.

Consider a language $L \subseteq (2^{I \cup O})^\omega$ and a prefix $u \in (2^{I \cup O})^*$. We say that

- u is a *system bad prefix* if L^u is not I/O-realizable.
- u is a *system good prefix* if L^u is I/O-realizable.
- u is an *environment bad prefix* if L^u is not O/I-realizable.
- u is an *environment good prefix* if L^u is O/I-realizable.

Now, a language $L \subseteq (2^{I \cup O})^\omega$ is a *system (environment) safety language* if every word not in L has a system (environment, respectively) bad prefix. The language L is a *system (environment) co-safety language* if every word in L has a system (environment, respectively) good prefix. Note that system safety coincides with green safety. Here, that we parametrize safety with either a system or an environment, we simplify the notation and omit "green".

Since each language L^u is either I/O-realizable or not I/O-realizable, and the same for O/I-realizability, all finite words are determined, in the following sense.

Proposition 4. *Consider a language $L \subseteq (2^{I \cup O})^\omega$. All finite words in $(2^{I \cup O})^*$ are determined with respect to L. That is, every prefix is either system good or system bad, and either environment good or environment bad, with respect to L.*

Note that while every prefix is determined, a word may have both system bad and system good prefixes, and similarly for the environment, which is not the case in the setting of closed systems. For example, recall the language $L = \|G(err \to X\mathit{fix}) \wedge FG\neg err\|$, for $I = \{\mathit{fix}\}$ and $O = \{err\}$. In Example 3 we saw that the word $(\{err, \mathit{fix}\} \cdot \{\mathit{fix}\})^\omega$ has both a system bad prefix $\{err, \mathit{fix}\}$, and a system good prefix $\{err, \mathit{fix}\} \cdot \{\mathit{fix}\}$.

In a dual manner to Proposition 1, every realizable language is system co-safe with ϵ being a system good prefix for every word in L. Accordingly, our goal in studying co-safety is two fold. First, since a system good prefix u is such that L^u is I/O-realizable, then the set of system good prefixes describe the "hopeful scenarios" for the system – ones after which it would be able to realize a non-realizable specification. Second, the story of safety and co-safety is told about both the system and the environment. As we shall now see, system safety and environment co-safety dualize each other.

Proposition 5. *For every language $L \subseteq (2^{I \cup O})^\omega$, we have that L is system safe iff $comp(L)$ is environment co-safe.*

By switching the roles of the system and the environment, we get that L is system co-safe iff $comp(L)$ is environment safe.

It is interesting to consider the special case when $I = \emptyset$. There, O/I-realizability coincides with validity. Therefore, given a language $L \subseteq (2^O)^\omega$, a prefix u is an environment good prefix iff $L^u = \Sigma^\omega$, which coincides with the definition of a good prefix in the closed settings. Therefore, when $I = \emptyset$, environment co-safety coincides with co-safety.

4.1 Boundness

We say a property ψ is *bounded* if there is an integer $k \geq 0$ such that every word of length k is either a good or a bad prefix for ψ. In the closed settings, a language that is both safe and co-safe is bounded [9]. In the open setting, we can talk about two relevant intersections. The first is languages that are both system safe and system co-safe (or dually, both environment safe and environment co-safe). The second is languages that are both system safe and environment co-safe (or dually, both environment safe and system co-safe). In this section we consider the fragments corresponding to both types of intersection.

We start with the first fragment. We denote by $[\![P]\!]$ the set of languages that have the property P. As we have previously seen, every unrealizable language is system safe, and every realizable language is system co-safe. Therefore, $[\![\text{system safe}]\!] \cap [\![\text{system co-safe}]\!] = ([\![\text{realizable}]\!] \cap [\![\text{system safe}]\!]) \cup ([\![\text{unrealizable}]\!] \cap [\![\text{system co-safe}]\!])$. As we have seen in Section 3, system safety is of interest in the case of realizable languages, and the realizable languages that are system safe are not bounded. Likewise, unrelizability does not impose boundedness on specifications that are system co-safe. Thus, there is no reason to expect a language that is both system safe and system co-safe to be bounded. We are going to confirm this intuition in Example 7 below. Thus, interestingly, the intersection system safe and system co-safe properties is not related to boundedness and instead suggests a characterization of realizable and non-realizable specifications.

We continue to the second fragment. Let L be a language that is both system safe and environment co-safe. Consider a word $w \in (2^{I \cup O})^\omega$. If $w \in L$, then, as L is environment co-safe, w has a good environment prefix. If $w \notin L$, then, as L is system safe, w has a bad system prefix. As in the closed setting, it follows that w must have a "special" – either environment co-safe or system safe prefix. In the closed setting, it was possible to use this information in order to bound the length of the shortest such prefix. As we shall see now, this strongly depends on the fact the bad and good prefixes in the closed setting are closed under extensions, and is no longer valid in the open setting.

Example 7. Consider the formula $\psi = G(err \to Gfix)$, for $I = \{fix\}$ and $O = \{err\}$. Let $L = \|\psi\|$. It is easy to see that L is I/O-realizable with the system strategy "make no errors". Thus, L is system co-safe. For every word $w \notin L$, we have that $w \models F(err \wedge F\neg fix)$. Therefore, every word $w \notin L$ has a prefix that contains a position satisfying err, and ends in a position satisfying $\neg fix$. Such a prefix is a black bad prefix, and is thus both a system bad and an environment bad prefix. Therefore, L is both environment safe and system safe. Finally, L is also O/I-realizable, with the environment environment strategy "always fix". It follows that L is also co-safe.

Hence, L belongs to the four green safety and co-safety fragments. On the other hand, L is not bounded. To see this, consider the word $w = \emptyset^\omega$. For every prefix u of w, the suffix $s = \{err\}^\omega$ is such that $u \cdot s \notin L$, and the suffix $s' = \emptyset^\omega$ is such that $u \cdot s' \in L$. Thus, w has undetermined prefixes of unbounded length, and so L is not bounded.

Since in this example we show a language that has all four green safety properties, but is not bounded, we can conclude with the following.

Proposition 6. *A language in an intersection of system safety, system co-safety, environment safety, and environment co-safety, need not be bounded.*

In the full version, we consider a dualization of $black(L)$, namely the set $white(L)$ obtained by adding all the infinite extensions of environment good prefixes to L. An environment good prefix in L is thus a good prefix in $white(L)$.

We show that for every language $L \subseteq (2^{I \cup O})^\omega$, we have $comp(white(L)) = black(comp(L))$. By dualizing our results on green and black safety, we thus have that L is environment co-safe iff $white(L)$ is co-safe, and that L and $white(L)$ are co-open-equivalent.

5   Green Informative Prefixes

In the closed setting, detection of special (bad or good) prefixes has the flavor of validity checking. Accordingly, the problem of deciding whether an LTL specification is safe or co-safe is PSPACE-complete [14], and the size of an automaton for the special prefixes is doubly-exponential in the LTL formula that describes the specification

[8]. The doubly-exponential blow up is present even when the automaton is nondeterministic. Intuitively, the need to accept all the special prefixes requires the construction to have the flavor of determinization, as one has to relate different components of the specification. In the setting of open systems, detection of special prefixes has the flavor of realizability. Thus, reasoning about special prefixes is more complicated. In particular, it is shown in [2] that the problem of deciding whether an LTL formula is reactive safe is 2EXPTIME-complete. In fact, as we show in the full version, the problem is 2EXPTIME-hard even for specifications that are known to be realizable. Similarly, as showed in [2], automata that recognize the system bad prefixes of a reactive safety property are of size doubly-exponential in the LTL formula.

In [8], the authors introduced the notion of *informative prefixes* in the context of closed systems. Given an LTL formula ψ, the set of informative prefixes for ψ is a subset of $bp(\psi)$ that is easier to detect. Essentially, a prefix is informative for ψ if the syntax of ψ explains why it is a bad prefix. In this section we lift the notation of informative prefixes and their applications to the open setting. We first need the following definition and notations. We assume that LTL formulas are written in a positive normal form, where negation is pushed inward and is applied only to atomic propositions. For this, we have to introduce the dual R ("release") of U ("until"). We use $cl(\psi)$ to denote the set of subformulas of ψ (after transferring ψ to a positive normal form).

For an LTL formula ψ over $AP = I \cup O$ and a finite computation $\pi = \sigma_1 \cdot \sigma_2 \cdots \sigma_n$, with $\sigma_i \in 2^{I \cup O}$, we say that π is *green informative* for ψ if there exists a mapping $L : \{1, \ldots, n+1\} \to 2^{cl(\neg\psi)}$ such that the following hold.

1. $\neg\psi \in L(1)$.
2. $L(n+1)$ contains only formulas over I, and the formula $\bigwedge_{\varphi \in L(n+1)} \varphi$ is satisfiable.
3. For all $1 \leq j \leq n$ and $\varphi \in L(j)$, the following hold:
   - If φ is a propositional assertion, it is satisfied by σ_j.
   - If $\varphi = \varphi_1 \vee \varphi_2$ then $\varphi_1 \in L(j)$ or $\varphi_2 \in L(j)$.
   - If $\varphi = \varphi_1 \wedge \varphi_2$ then $\varphi_1 \in L(j)$ and $\varphi_2 \in L(j)$.
   - If $\varphi = X\varphi_1$, then $\varphi_1 \in L(i+1)$.
   - If $\varphi = \varphi_1 U \varphi_2$, then $\varphi_2 \in L(j)$ or $[\varphi_1 \in L(i)$ and $\varphi_1 U \varphi_2 \in L(j+1)]$.
   - If $\varphi = \varphi_1 R \varphi_2$, then $\varphi_2 \in L(j)$ and $[\varphi_1 \in L(i)$ or $\varphi_1 V \varphi_2 \in L(j+1)]$.

If π is informative for ψ, then the mapping L is called the *green witness* for $\neg\psi$ in π. Intuitively, $L(j)$, for $j \geq 0$, is the set of subformulas in $cl(\neg\psi)$ that are yet to be satisfied in order for $\neg\psi$ to be satisfied in a computation that has $\sigma_1 \cdot \sigma_2 \cdots \sigma_{j-1}$ as a prefix. In the closed setting, the requirement on $L(n+1)$ is to be empty, corresponding to the requirement that no more obligations have to be satisfied in order for $\neg\psi$ to hold in all possible suffixes. In the open setting, the corresponding requirement would have been that $L(n+1)$ is such that the conjunction of the formulas in it is O/I-realizable. We refer to prefixes that satisfy the above as *strong green informative prefixes*. As we shall see below, while such prefixes are more precise, they are harder to detect. In the other extreme, we could have require the formulas in $L(n+1)$ to only refer to I and give up the satisfiability checking. We call such prefixes *weak informative green prefixes*. While checking for weak prefixes is easier, they do not guarantee that the prefix is system bad.

In the definition above, the requirements left to be checked in $L(n+1)$ are on I and their conjunction has to be satisfiable. Since all the requirements are on I, satisfiability and realizability coincide, which guarantees that a green informative prefix is indeed a system bad prefix.

Note that when $I = \emptyset$, the requirement above for $L(n+1)$ is equivalent to the requirement $L(n+1) = \emptyset$, thus the definition of a green informative prefix coincides with the definition of informative prefix.

Example 8. Let $I = \{q\}$, $O = \{p\}$ and let $\psi_1 = G(p \rightarrow Fq)$. Using the positive normal form, we have that $\neg\psi_1 = F(p \wedge G\neg q)$, where we use $F\varphi$ as an abbreviation for $true\, U\varphi$, and $G\varphi$ as an abbreviation for $false\, R\varphi$. The finite computation $\pi = \emptyset \cdot \{p\}$ is a green informative prefix for ψ_1, as witnessed by the mapping L with $L(1) = \{F(p \wedge G\neg q)\}$, $L(2) = \{F(p \wedge G\neg q), p \wedge G\neg q, p, G\neg q, \neg q\}$, $L(3) = \{G\neg q\}$. Indeed, $|\pi| = 2$ and $L(2+1)$ contains a satisfiable formula over I.

We now consider two variants of the previous example. The first is $\psi_2 = G(p \rightarrow (Fq \vee (Xr \wedge X\neg r)))$, where $I = \{q\}$, $O = \{p, r\}$. Note that since $Xr \wedge X\neg r$ is not satisfiable, the specifications ψ_1 and ψ_2 are equivalent. Still, informative prefixes consider the syntax of the formula. To see that the syntax may be crucial, let us examine π again, now with respect to $\neg\psi_2 = F(p \wedge (G\neg q \wedge ((X\neg r) \vee Xr)))$. We can see π is not a green informative prefix for ψ_2, as such a prefix must contain at least one state after the first state in which p holds, to syntactically verify that $(X\neg r) \vee Xr$ holds. Note that if r had been an input, then π would have been a green informative prefix.

The second variant is $\psi_3 = G(p \rightarrow ((X\neg q) \wedge Xq))$, where $I = \{q\}$ and $O = \{p\}$. Now, $\neg\psi_3 = F(p \wedge (Xq \vee X\neg q))$. We can see that π is a green informative prefix, as $((X\neg q) \vee Xq)$ is over I and is satisfiable. Formally, the mapping L with $L(1) = \{\neg\psi_3\}$, $L(2) = \{\neg\psi_3, p \wedge (Xq \vee X\neg q), p, Xq \vee X\neg q, Xq\}$, and $L(3) = \{q\}$ is a green witness for $\neg\psi_3$. On the other hand, in the closed setting π is not an informative prefix for ψ_3, as such a prefix must contain at least one state after the first state in which p holds, to syntactically verify that $((X\neg q) \vee Xq)$ holds.

The fact that the requirement about $L(n+1)$ is easier to satisfy in the open rather than in the closed setting, together with the example of ψ_3 above, imply the following.

Theorem 4. *Green information is weaker than black information. That is, every informative prefix is also a green informative prefix, but the other direction is not necessarily true.*

The syntax-based definition leads to an easier detection of bad prefixes:

Theorem 5. *Given an LTL formula ψ and a finite computation π, the problem of deciding whether π is green informative for ψ is PSPACE-complete.*

Proof: We start with the upper bound. Consider a prefix $\pi = \sigma_1, \ldots, \sigma_n$ and an LTL formula ψ. As shown in [8], it is possible to construct in time $O(n \cdot |\psi|)$ a mapping $L_{max} : \{1, \ldots, n+1\} \rightarrow 2^{cl(\neg\psi)}$ such that $L_{max}(j)$ contains exactly all the formulas $\neg\varphi$ such that the suffix $\sigma_j, \ldots, \sigma_n$ is informative for φ. Extending this construction to the open setting requires a guess of the formulas in $L(n+1)$, making the guess and the check that the conjunction of the formulas is satisfiable the computational bottleneck.

Since satisfiability, as well as going over all possible guesses, can be done in PSPACE, we are done.

For the lower bound, we show a reduction from LTL satisfiability problem, which is PSPACE-complete. Given an LTL formula ψ over AP, we consider the specification $\theta = \neg\psi$, with $I = AP$ and $O = \emptyset$. It is easy to see ϵ is a green informative prefix for θ iff ψ is satisfiable. $\square$

Remark 3. Since the generation of $L(n + 1)$ is the computational bottleneck, working with the strong and weak green informative prefix definition results in detection problems that are 2EXPTIME-complete and linear-time, respectively.

Finally, as in the closed setting, it is possible to define an automaton that recognizes exactly all the informative green prefixes of a given safety formula. It is also possible to use the notion of informative green prefixes in order to classify green safety formulas according to the level in which informative prefixes approximate the set of all bad prefixes. The technical details are similar to these in [8], with the different conditions on $L(n + 1)$ imposing the expected changes, in both the algorithms and the complexity. We describe the full details in the full version.

References

1. Alpern, B., Schneider, F.B.: Recognizing safety and liveness. Distributed Computing 2, 117–126 (1987)
2. Ehlers, R., Finkbeiner, B.: Reactive safety. In: Proc. 2nd GANDALF. EPTCS, vol. 54, pp. 178–191 (2011)
3. Fisman, D., Kupferman, O., Sheinvald-Faragy, S., Vardi, M.Y.: A framework for inherent vacuity. In: Chockler, H., Hu, A.J. (eds.) HVC 2008. LNCS, vol. 5394, pp. 7–22. Springer, Heidelberg (2009)
4. Gale, D., Stewart, F.M.: Infinite games of perfect information. Ann. Math. Studies 28, 245–266 (1953)
5. Greimel, K., Bloem, R., Jobstmann, B., Vardi, M.: Open implication. In: Aceto, L., Damgård, I., Goldberg, L.A., Halldórsson, M.M., Ingólfsdóttir, A., Walukiewicz, I. (eds.) ICALP 2008, Part II. LNCS, vol. 5126, pp. 361–372. Springer, Heidelberg (2008)
6. Harel, D., Pnueli, A.: On the development of reactive systems. In: Logics and Models of Concurrent Systems, NATO Advanced Summer Institutes, vol. F-13, pp. 477–498 (1985)
7. Kress-Gazit, H., Fainekos, G.E., Pappa, G.J.: Temporal-logic-based reactive mission and motion planning. IEEE Trans. on Robotics 25(6), 1370–1381 (2009)
8. Kupferman, O., Vardi, M.Y.: Model checking of safety properties. Formal Methods in System Design 19(3), 291–314 (2001)
9. Kupferman, O., Vardi, M.Y.: On bounded specifications. In: Nieuwenhuis, R., Voronkov, A. (eds.) LPAR 2001. LNCS (LNAI), vol. 2250, pp. 24–38. Springer, Heidelberg (2001)
10. Manna, Z., Pnueli, A.: The Temporal Logic of Reactive and Concurrent Systems: Specification. Springer (1992)
11. Pnueli, A.: The temporal logic of programs. In: Proc. 18th FOCS, pp. 46–57 (1977)
12. Pnueli, A., Rosner, R.: On the synthesis of a reactive module. In: Proc. 16th POPL, pp. 179–190 (1989)
13. PROSYD. The Prosyd project on property-based system design (2007), http://www.prosyd.org
14. Sistla, A.P.: Safety, liveness and fairness in temporal logic. Formal Aspects of Computing 6, 495–511 (1994)

Deterministic Compilation of Temporal Safety Properties in Explicit State Model Checking

Kristin Yvonne Rozier and Moshe Y. Vardi[*,**]

Rice University, Houston, Texas 77005
{kyrozier,vardi}@cs.rice.edu

Abstract. The translation of temporal logic specifications constitutes an essential step in model checking and a major influence on the efficiency of formal verification via model checking. We devise a new explicit-state translation of Linear Temporal Logic to automata for the class of LTL specifications that describe *safety properties*, arguably the most used formal specifications in real-world systems. By exploiting the inherent determinism in safety specifications, we can build deterministic Promela never claims that accept only the bad prefixes of the safety specification. In contrast to previous works, we focus on compilation to never claims rather than simply automata and measure Spin model-checking time separately from compilation time and automata size. An extensive experimental evaluation over a space of configurations demonstrates that our new translation consistently results in better model-checking performance, for a large array of benchmarks, over the best current translation.

1 Introduction

In linear-time model checking, the negation of the temporal specification is translated into a nondeterministic Büchi automaton, combined with the system model, and then checked for nonemptiness [33]. The model checker searches for a *lasso-shaped counterexample trace* in this combined model, a trace that starts at an initial system state and reaches a cycle that contains an accepting state. The explicit-state translation of Linear Temporal Logic (LTL) formulas to Büchi automata constitutes an essential step in explicit-state linear-time model checking and has a major influence on the efficiency of model checking [10]. Consequently, this topic has received a significant level of attention over the past two decades and there are many available tools; see [27] for an extensive survey. Most of that research has focused on minimizing the size of the generated automata. The rationale was that minimizing the size of the automaton would minimize the size of the space in the product of the system model and the automaton

---

[*] A version of this paper with appendices included is available at http://ti.arc.nasa.gov/m/profile/kyrozier/papers/RozierVardiHVC2012.pdf, but the paper can be read without appendices.

[**] This research was supported in part by NSF grants CNS 1049862 and CCF-1139011, by NSF Expeditions in Computing project "ExCAPE: Expeditions in Computer Augmented Program Engineering", by BSF grant 9800096, by a gift from Intel, and by the Shared University Grid at Rice funded by NSF under Grant EIA-0216467 and a partnership between Rice, Sun Microsystems, and Sigma Solutions, Inc.

A. Biere, A. Nahir, and T. Vos (Eds.): HVC 2012, LNCS 7857, pp. 243–259, 2013.
© Springer-Verlag Berlin Heidelberg 2013

that the model checker must search. Yet this heuristic approach has no experimental evidence that would demonstrate its efficacy [32]. In fact, the extensive experimental investigation reported on in [27], which focused on *satisfiability checking*, a special case of model checking, shows little correlation between automaton size and model-checking time. It is argued in [9] that larger automata may result in less work for LTL model checking. In this paper we revisit the translation of LTL formulas to automata, which we call *LTL compilation*, specifically focusing on model-checking performance.

We concentrate on model checking *safety properties*, which assert "something bad never happens" [1]. Safety properties are the most often used formal properties in practice, capturing the desired behaviors of a wide variety of real-world systems, such as of fault tolerance [11] and hardware resets [7]. Safety properties can also describe most intended properties of real-time systems, since responses are usually required within bounded intervals [15].

Intuitively, "something bad" only needs to happen once in a computation for the property to be violated. Thus, a violation of a safety property can always be witnessed by a finite prefix of a violating infinite trace. Rather than search the system model for a violating infinite trace, we can search the system model for this *bad prefix*. This insight forms the basis for an alternative automata-theoretic approach for model checking safety properties, proposed in [20]: construct a *deterministic* automaton for the language of bad prefixes, take its product with the system model, and then search for an accepting finite trace. A disadvantage of this approach is that while the translation from LTL to nondeterministic Büchi automata is, in the worst case, exponential [34], the translation from safety LTL formulas to deterministic automata for bad prefixes is, in the worst case, doubly exponential [20]. Perhaps because of this additional blow-up, this approach, which we refer to as *deterministic compilation*, has yet to be seriously explored.

There has been recent evidence that deterministic compilation may be a viable approach in spite of the possible additional exponential blow-up. Deterministic compilation proved to be effective for SAT-based model checking [2] and explicit-state hybrid-systems analysis [26]. Determinizing finite automata representing safety formulas has been correlated with smaller system model/automaton products even without minimizing the formula automaton [21]. Intuitively the product–system model times automaton–is simpler when the automaton is deterministic, as nondeterminism in the product stems solely from nondeterminism in the system. In the standard approach the search algorithm has to find both a counterexample trace in the system and an accepting run of the specification automaton. This second search is not needed when the specification automaton is deterministic, as it has a unique run on a given input word. (It has been argued in [30], though without evidence, that "more deterministic" compilation may be an advantageous approach.) Recent work on deterministic compilation in the context of run-time verification demonstrated both that the doubly exponential blow-up rarely appears in practice, and that the resulting deterministic automata are often actually *smaller* than their nondeterministic counterparts since we can minimize deterministic automata efficiently [31,11].

The main result of this paper is that deterministic compilation is indeed an effective approach to explicit-state model checking of safety properties. To demonstrate this, we build on the theoretical foundations developed in [4,20]. We show how to use SPOT [6], the best LTL-to-automaton translator (see [27]), and BRICS Automaton [23], a tool for determinizing and minimizing finite-word automata, in order to go from a nondeterministic Büchi automaton $\mathcal{A}_\varphi$ representing a safety property φ to a deterministic automaton $\mathcal{A}^d$ that accepts the bad prefixes of φ. This construction uses the fact that determinization of finite-word automata is much simpler than determinization of ω-automata; while nondeterministic finite automata can be determinized with a simple subset construction [14], determinization of nondeterministic ω-automata requires a complex subset-tree-based construction [28].

To use $\mathcal{A}^d$ for model checking, we apply Spin, the canonical explicit-state model checker [12]. We introduce 26 novel encodings of LTL safety properties as deterministic automata in the form of Promela (PROcess MEta LAnguage) never claims, describing behaviors that should *not* occur in the system model. We implement these encodings as an extension of the open-source CHIMP tool[1] [31] that creates SystemC monitors for LTL formulas; our extension, CHIMP-Spin,[2] creates Spin never claims. Our systematic empirical investigation of the effectiveness of these automata as never claims also constitutes a novel contribution since earlier works focused on translation to automata without considering their encodings as never claims. We show over a large array of benchmarks that our deterministic encodings for model checking of safety properties consistently result in significantly reduced model-checking times over the SPOT encoding. We also demonstrate that the encoding used to represent deterministic automata as never claims has a significant impact on performance and we identify a single encoding that dominates all other encodings.

A key point of our approach is that we concentrate on reducing *model-checking time*, while typical experimental work in LTL model checking measures total time–compile plus model-checking time, e.g., [9]. Since in real-world applications of model checking, properties are written once and then checked against a changing system design multiple times, we find it worthwhile to reduce model-checking time even at the cost of increased property-compilation time. This choice is particularly pertinent for regression testing: when the system is changed to fix a bug or add a new feature it is necessary to re-check all properties checked earlier to ensure that previous checks produce the same results. To streamline regression testing future versions of Spin should not require a recompilation of never claims for each run of the model checker, even when they have not changed. Such an adjustment would more accurately reflect industrial applications of model checking and, combined with our reduced model-checking times, reduce the amortized cost of model checking.

The structure of this paper is as follows. We detail the theory underlying our construction of deterministic encodings of LTL safety specifications in Section 2 and describe our 26 novel constructions of Promela never claims in Section 3. We then describe our experimental methodology in Section 4, and present our experimental results, which demonstrate that we can consistently outperform SPOT, the current best LTL-compilation tool, in Section 5. We conclude with a discussion in Section 6.

---

[1] http://sourceforge.net/projects/chimp-rice/

[2] Our tool extension is released under an open-source license; contact us for a copy.

2   Theoretical Background

We interpret LTL formulas over infinite computations of the form $\pi : \omega \to 2^{Prop}$, where ω is the set non-negative integers and *Prop* is a set of atomic propositions. We define $\pi, i \vDash \varphi$ (computation π at time instant $i \in \omega$ satisfies LTL formula φ) as follows [8]:

- $\pi, i \vDash p$ for $p \in Prop$ if $p \in \pi(i)$,
- $\pi, i \vDash g_1 \wedge g_2$ if $\pi, i \vDash g_1$ and $\pi, i \vDash g_2$,
- $\pi, i \vDash \neg g$ if $\pi, i \nvDash g$,
- $\pi, i \vDash Xg$ if $\pi, i+1 \vDash g$,
- $\pi, i \vDash g_1 \mathcal{U} g_2$ if $\exists j \geq i$, such that $\pi, j \vDash g_2$ and $\forall k, i \leq k < j$, we have $\pi, k \vDash g_1$,
- $\pi, i \vDash g_1 \mathcal{R} g_2$ if $\forall j \geq i$, if $\pi, j \nvDash g_2$, then $\exists k, i \leq k < j$, such that $\pi, k \vDash g_1$,
- $\pi, i \vDash \Diamond g$ if $\exists j \geq i$, such that $\pi, j \vDash g$,
- $\pi, i \vDash \Box g$ if $\forall j \geq i, \pi, j \vDash g$.

We take *models*(φ) to be the set of computations that satisfy φ at time 0: $\{\pi : \pi, 0 \vDash \varphi\}$.

In automata-theoretic model checking, we represent LTL formulas using Büchi automata. A *Nondeterministic Büchi Word Automaton* (NBW) is a quintuple $\mathcal{A} = (Q, \Sigma, \delta, Q^0, F)$, where Q is a finite set of states, Σ is a finite alphabet, $\delta : Q \times \Sigma \to 2^Q$ is a transition function, $Q^0 \subseteq Q$ is a set of initial states, and $F \subseteq Q$ is a set of accepting states. If $q' \in \delta(q, \sigma)$ then we say that we have a transition from q to q' labeled by σ. A run of a Büchi automaton $\mathcal{A}$ over an infinite computation $\pi = \pi_0, \pi_1, \pi_2, \ldots \in \Sigma$ is a sequence $q_0, q_1, q_2, \ldots$ of states such that $q_0 \in Q_0$, and $\langle q_i, \pi_i, q_{i+1} \rangle \in \delta$ for all $i \geq 0$. $\mathcal{A}$ accepts π if the run over π visits states in F infinitely often. We denote the set of infinite words accepted by $\mathcal{A}$ by $\mathscr{L}_\omega(\mathcal{A})$. Computations are infinite words over the alphabet $\Sigma = 2^{Prop}$.

Theorem 1. [34] *Given an LTL formula φ, we can construct an NBW $\mathcal{A}_\varphi = (Q, \Sigma, \delta, q_0, F)$ such that $|Q|$ is in $2^{O(|\varphi|)}$, $\Sigma = 2^{Prop}$, and $L_\omega(\mathcal{A}_\varphi)$ is exactly models(φ).*

In the automata-theoretic approach to model checking [33], to check that a model M under verification satisfies an LTL formula φ, we translate $\neg\varphi$ into the automaton $\mathcal{A}_{\neg\varphi}$ and compose $\mathcal{A}_{\neg\varphi}$ with M, forming the automaton $\mathcal{A}_{M, \neg\varphi}$, which the model checker checks for emptiness. If there is no accepting run of $\mathcal{A}_{M, \neg\varphi}$ (i.e. the language $\mathscr{L}(\mathcal{A}_{M, \neg\varphi}) = \emptyset$), we have proven that $M \models \varphi$.

The automata-theoretic approach can be refined when dealing with *safety properties*. A formula φ is a safety formula if its failure can always be witnessed by a finite prefix [1]; that is, if $\pi \nvDash \varphi$ then there there is a finite word $w \in \Sigma^*$ such that $w \cdot \pi \nvDash \varphi$ for every infinite computation $\pi \in \Sigma^\omega$. Here w is called a *bad prefix* for φ. The set of bad prefixes for φ is *pref*(φ). It is argued in [19] that *pref*(φ) is a regular language; consequently, we can use automata on finite words for model checking safety properties.

A *Nondeterministic Finite Word Automaton* (NFW) is a quintuple $\mathcal{A} = (Q, \Sigma, \delta, Q_0, F)$, where Q is a finite set of states, Σ is a finite alphabet, $\delta : Q \times \Sigma \to 2^Q$ is a transition function, $Q_0 \subseteq Q$ is the set of initial states, and $F \subseteq Q$ is a set of accepting states. If Q_0 is a singleton, and $\delta(q, a)$ contains at most one state for every state q and letter a, then we say that $\mathcal{A}$ is a *Deterministic Finite Word Automaton* (DFW). A run of $\mathcal{A}$ over a finite word $w \in \Sigma^*$ is accepting if it terminates in an accepting state.

Theorem 2. [19] *Given a safety LTL formula φ, we can construct a DFW $\mathcal{A}^d = (Q, \Sigma, \delta, q_0, F)$ such that $|Q|$ is in $2^{2^{O(|\varphi|)}}$, $\Sigma = 2^{Prop}$, and $\mathscr{L}(\mathcal{A}^d)$ is exactly pref(φ).*

Therefore, when φ is a safety property, we can opt to form an NFW or a DFW corresponding to $\neg\varphi$ instead of an NBW, since we only need to construct an automaton that accepts the set of finite prefixes that witness violations of φ.

A concrete algorithm to construct automata for bad prefixes was given in [4]. Given a safety formula φ, we first form the NBW $\mathcal{A}_\varphi$. Here we use SPOT [6] for this translation; we showed earlier that SPOT is the best LTL-to-automata translator [27]. Let $empty(\mathcal{A}_\varphi)$ be the set of states in $\mathcal{A}_\varphi$ that cannot appear on an accepting run. SPOT can compute this set of states and remove them from $\mathcal{A}_\varphi$. We now turn this NBW into an NFW $\mathcal{A}_\varphi^f$ by re-labeling all remaining states to be accepting. We now have the NFW $\mathcal{A}_\varphi^f$ defined by the quintuple $(Q', \Sigma, \delta', q_0 \cap Q', F \cap Q')$, where $Q' = Q - empty(\mathcal{A}_\varphi)$ and δ' is restricted to $Q' \times \Sigma$. Note that this approach is not sound for liveness formulas.

Theorem 3. [4] $\mathcal{A}_\varphi^f$ *rejects precisely* $pref(\varphi)$.

To model check a safety formula, we need an automaton that accepts $pref(\varphi)$ [31]. If we apply the subset construction to $\mathcal{A}_\varphi^f$ we obtain a DFW $\mathcal{A}_\varphi^d$, where all nonempty sets of states of $\mathcal{A}_\varphi^f$ are accepting states, that rejects $pref(\varphi)$. Its complement $\mathcal{A}_{\neg\varphi}^d$, where only the empty set of states is accepting, accepts $pref(\varphi)$.

3 Never Claim Generation

A never claim is a Promela code sequence that defines a system behavior that should never happen. Since we use never claims to specify properties that should *never* happen, that is, bad properties we wish to assert the system does not have, we create a never claim corresponding to the negation of the property we wish to hold. In other words, when we create a never claim that accepts exactly $\mathscr{L}(\neg\varphi)$ we are stating that it would be a correctness violation of the system if there exists an execution sequence in which $\neg\varphi$ holds. For the system to be considered correct, φ must always hold.

To generate a Promela never claim for LTL formula φ, Spin translates $\neg\varphi$ into the NBW $\mathcal{A}_{\neg\varphi} = (Q, \Sigma, \delta, q_0, F)$, enumerates and creates labels for the states in Q, labels q_0 with 'init' to designate the state in which the never claim starts, labels accepting states with 'accept,' and implements δ by a nondeterministic choice: for each state, nondeterministically choose from among enabled transitions given the set of propositions true in the current state. Currently, all LTL-to-Promela translators follow this high-level construction. (They vary widely in the details of the formation of $\mathcal{A}_{\neg\varphi}$ as described in [27].)

In this paper, we construct Promela never claims corresponding to the DFW $\mathcal{A}_\varphi^d$ for bad prefixes of safety formulas. We now describe several novel alternatives for constructing never claims for safety properties.

To prove that a system model M satisfies the LTL property $\varphi = (\Box good)$, we create a never claim that accepts the negation of this property. Spin can do this automatically using the command spin -f '![] good'. Intuitively, the never claim generated by the formula would restrict system behavior to those states where $(\Diamond !good)$ holds. If any such execution of the system is found, Spin reports a violation.

In addition to the infinite-behavior never claims produced by Spin, SPOT, and other tools, never claims can be also be used to specify finite automata; the distinction is implicit in the structure of the claim rather than explicitly stated. Finite behavior is matched if the claim can reach its closing curly brace while executing in lockstep with the system model [13]. Spin automatically checks for this type of never claim termination. A never claim corresponding to the NFW that accepts $pref(\varphi)$ simply needs to reach its closing curly brace, for example, when the formula is $\Box good$, if $!good$ is ever true, thus accepting the finite prefix indicating a correctness violation of the system. Note that we check the finite-behavior never claim using different Spin commands than the infinite-behavior version, where the run-time flag -a explicitly tells Spin to check for acceptance cycles. Specifically, we check for finite acceptance using the following commands:

```
cat Model > pan_in
cat finite_never_claim >> pan_in
spin -a pan_in
gcc -w -o pan -D_POSIX_SOURCE -DMEMLIM=1550 -DSAFETY -DXUSAFE -DNOFAIR
            -DNXT pan.c
./pan -v -X -m10000 -w19  -A -E -c1
```

3.1 Determinization and Minimization

As in [31], there are two approaches to constructing the DFW $\mathcal{A}_\varphi^d$. First, we can explicitly determinize the NFW $\mathcal{A}_\varphi^f$ using an NFW-to-DFW translator (BRICS Automaton[23]), which we refer to as the det construction. Second, we can construct a never claim directly from $\mathcal{A}_\varphi^f$, essentially performing the subset construction on-the-fly. For consistancy with previous work [31], we refer to this as the nondet construction, because determinism is delayed. The advantage of pre-compilation determinization is the ability to minimize $\mathcal{A}_\varphi^d$ before constructing the never claim; we use BRICS Automaton to produce a minimal equivalent DFW. We refer to this as the min construction. The additional steps of determinization and minimization may incur a nontrivial computational cost during the construction of the never claim. The trade-off between property-compilation time and model-checking time is a key issue in this paper.

To use BRICS Automaton, we have to find a way to represent the alphabet of the automata [31]. SPOT labels transitions with Boolean formulas over the set $Prop$ of atomic propositions, while BRICS Automaton represents the alphabet of the automaton as Unicode characters. Therefore, we adapt the techniques of [31] for describing the alphabet in terms of 16-bit integers. We have two alphabet representations: OBDD-based and assignment-based.

We can represent Boolean formulas using *Ordered Binary Decision Diagrams (OBDDs)* [3]. We implement this approach as follows. First, we obtain references to all Boolean formulas that appear as transition labels in the automaton using SPOT's spot:: tgba_reachable_iterator_breadth_first::process_link() function. Second, we assign a unique integer label to the OBDD representation of each Boolean formula (up to $2^{|\varphi|}$ in the worst case) using SPOT's spot::tgba_succ_iterator::current_cond ition() function. The formulas labeling automaton transitions can now be replaced by the corresponding integers.

Alternatively, we can represent Boolean formulas in terms of their satisfying truth *assignments*. By selecting an order for $Prop = \{p_1, \ldots, p_n\}$, we can represent an assignment as an n-bit vector $\mathbf{a} = [a_1, a_2, \ldots, a_n]$. Every such bit vector corresponds to an integer $I(\mathbf{a})$ in the domain $\{0, \ldots, 2^n - 1\}$; $I(\mathbf{a}) = a_1 2^{n-1} + a_2 2^{n-2} + \ldots + a_n 2^0$. We can use this domain as a new alphabet, replacing a transition labeled by a Boolean formula α by several transitions labeled by the integers corresponding to truth assignments satisfying α. Once we have used BRICS Automaton to form a DFW, we convert transition labels back to Boolean formulas that we use to construct Promela never claims.

The assignment-based approach sometimes creates a large number of transitions. For example, the Boolean formula **true** corresponds to 2^n assignments. We introduce an *edge-abbreviation* technique to merge separate transitions. When we have several transitions with the same source and destination states, we can remove these transitions and replace them by a single transition labeled by the disjunction of the labels of the removed transitions. For each such disjunction, we utilize SPOT's built-in formula_to_bdd() function to create a BDD representing the disjunction, extract a simplified formula from the BDD via the reverse bdd_to_formula() function, and then label the associated transition by this new formula. A related optimization is to replace all else branches in the Promela never claims by explicit Boolean formulas corresponding to the negation of the conjunction of the labels of all of the other transitions (reduced using SPOT's built-in BDD functions). This enables us to eliminate redundant trap states and reduce never claim code size.

3.2 Never Claim Encodings

Inspired by the work in [31], we introduce 26 ways of encoding automata for safety properties as Promela never claims. We form these encodings by combining our never claim adaptations of the constructions for transition direction (front vs back), determinism (det vs nondet), state minimization (min vs nomin), and alphabet representation (bdd vs abr) from [31] with the options to encode never claim states either using Promela state labels or integer state numbers (state vs number), to employ either finite or infinite acceptance conditions (fin vs inf), and to reduce the size of the generated never claim via edge abbreviation and trap-state elimination (ea). We illustrate our encodings in Appendix A for benchmark safety formula 4 from Table 2.

Nondeterministic Encodings. We introduce 12 novel Promela encodings that perform determinization on-the-fly. In nondet never claims we maintain an array used to describe sets of states of $\mathcal{A}_\varphi^f$. An array that corresponds to an empty set indicates that $\mathcal{A}_\varphi^f$ got stuck, which means that we have discovered a violation of φ. We can encode the transition relations either in a front fashion, where for any state q we enumerate the outgoing transitions from q, or in a back fashion, where for any state q we enumerate the incoming transitions that lead to q.

The front_nondet encoding uses an if statement to check each outgoing transition from each possible current state and marks all possible next states in the next_state array. If there is no possible next state, the automaton fails. For never claims with finite acceptance conditions, this is accomplished by breaking from the do loop and coming to the end } of the claim. The back_nondet encoding works similarly, but the branching is over incoming transitions rather than over outgoing transitions. See Appendix A.2 for examples.

Deterministic Encodings. In contrast to nondet encodings, where we determinize on the fly, in det encodings we already have the states of $\mathcal{A}_\varphi^d$ and we can encode them directly. We introduce 14 novel deterministic Promela encodings that presume $\mathcal{A}^d$ has been minimized and determinized using assignment-based encoding. We use two ways to encode the states. First, we can encode states by using a Promela variable, whose value refers to the current state (number). Second, we can use Spin's standard state-label format coupled with goto statements to transition between states. We illustrate each of these two state representations in turn.

The back_det encoding uses state numbers. The never claim first calculates the system_state_index, the integer corresponding to the current valuation of the system variables. Like its back_nondet counterpart, it transitions by checking for an enabled incoming transition to the current state. The front_det_switch_number_fin encoding uses a series of if statements, the closest Promela construction to a C-like switch statement, to check for enabled outgoing transitions from the current state. See Appendix A.3 for examples.

Alternatively, we can encode the never claim without using any state numbers, by taking advantage of Promela's constructs for representing automata states. The front_det_switch_state_inf encoding transitions to program labels corresponding to the names of the states in $\mathcal{A}_\varphi^d$. The initial state is labeled "init" and appears first, the accepting state is labeled "accept," and all other states are assigned unique names. See Appendix A.3 for examples.

Table 1. The configuration space for generating never claims. Each row in the table represents an encoding configuration. Components of the winning encoding are bolded.

State Minimization	Alphabet Representation	Automaton Acceptance	Never Claim Encoding	State Representation
no	BDDs		front_nondet	
			back_nondet	
	assignments	finite	front_nondet	number
			back_nondet	
			back_det	
yes			front_det_memory_table	
		infinite	**front_det_switch**	**state** number
	assignments with edge abbreviation		back_det	number

Look-Up Tables. The above encodings represent automaton transition functions as if statements. Alternatively, we can declare a state look-up table in memory storing the next state as a function of the current state and the system_state_index. This forms very compact never claims and the next state can be found in one operation. The front_det_memory_table encoding declares the table directly as a one-dimensional, row-major array. See Appendix A.3 for an example.

Configuration Space. The different options allow 26 possible combinations for generating never claims, summarized in Table 1.

4 Experimental Method

Platform We ran all tests on the Shared University Grid at Rice (SUG@R), an Intel Xeon compute cluster.[3] SUG@R is comprised of 134 SunFire x4150 nodes, each with two quad-core Intel Xeon processors running at 2.83GHz and 16GB of RAM per processor. The OS is Red Hat Enterprise 5 Linux, 2.6.18 kernel. Each test was run with exclusive access to one node. Times were measured using the Unix time command.

Table 2. Industrial safety formulas used in model-scaling benchmarks

0 $\Box\neg bad$	"Something bad never happens."
1 $\Box(request \to X grant)$	"Every request is immediately followed by a grant"
2 $\Box(\neg(p \land q))$	Mutual Exclusion: "p and q can never happen at the same time."
3 $\Box(p \to (XXXq))$	"Always, p implies q will happen 3 time steps from now."
4* $X((p \land q)\mathcal{R}r)$	"Condition r must stay on until buttons p and q are pressed at the same time."
5* $X(\Box(p))$	slightly modified *intentionally safe* formula from [19]
6* $X(\Box(q \lor X\Box p) \land \Box(r \lor X\Box\neg p))$	slightly modified *accidentally safe* formula from [19]
7* $X([\Box(q \lor \Diamond\Box p) \land \Box(r \lor \Diamond\Box\neg p)] \lor \Box q \lor \Box r)$	slightly modified *pathologically safe* formula from [19]
8 $\Box(p \to (q \land Xq \land XXq))$	safety specification from [31]
9 $(((((p0\mathcal{R}(\neg p1))\mathcal{R}(\neg p2))\mathcal{R}(\neg p3))\mathcal{R}(\neg p4))\mathcal{R}(\neg p5))$	Sieve of Erathostenes [13,21]
10 $(\Box((p0 \land \neg p1) \to (\Box\neg p1 \lor (\neg p1\,\mathcal{U}(p10 \land \neg p1)))))$	G.L. Peterson's algorithm for mutual exclusion algorithm [25,22,13,24,21]
11 $(\Box(\neg p0 \to ((\neg p1\,\mathcal{U}p0) \lor \Box\neg p1)))$	CORBA General Inter-Orb Protocol [17,21]
12 $((\Box(p1 \to \Box(\neg p1 \to (\neg p0 \land \neg p1)))) \land (\Box(p2 \to \Box(\neg p2 \to (\neg p0 \land \neg p1)))) \land (\Box\neg p2 \lor (\neg p2\,\mathcal{U}p1)))$	GNU i-protocol, also called iprot [5,24,21]
13 $((\Box(p1 \to \Box(\neg p1 \to (\neg p0 \land \neg p1)))) \land (\Box(p2 \to \Box(\neg p2 \to (\neg p0 \land \neg p1)))) \land (\Box\neg p2 \lor (\neg p2\,\mathcal{U}p1)))$	Sliding Window protocol [16,21]

---

[3] http://rcsg.rice.edu/sugar/

4.1   Model-Scaling Benchmarks

We chose a set of 14 typical safety formulas, taken from related literature, listed in Table 2. We model checked them against scaled linearly-sized Universal Models (UM) from [27]. (See also Appendix B.) By scaling up the size of these UMs to dwarf the sizes of the safety formulas, we create difficult model-checking benchmarks.

For each of the formulas in Table 2, we model checked against a series of linearly-sized UMs, described in [27], starting with the 10-variable UM and scaling up the number of variables in the model, thereby exponentially increasing its state space. We used two configurations of UMs; starred formulas are checked against UMs that set all variables to *true* first; see Appendix B.

4.2   Formula-Scaling Benchmarks

For our formula-scaling benchmarks, we model checked each formula against a universal model with 30 variables and 1,073,741,824 states. We employed two types of formula-scaling benchmarks: random and syntactically safe random. We scaled each of the formulas until model checking became unachievable within machine bounds of timeout/spaceout.

We generated two sets each of 500 m-length safety specifications over n atomic propositions, for m in $\{5, 10, 15, 20, 25\}$ and n in $\{2..6\}$ (25,000 random formulas in these two benchmark sets, combined). The probability of each temporal operator was $P = 0.5$. For the first set, we generated syntactic safety formulas, allowing negation only directly before atomic propositions and limiting the temporal operators to $\{X, G, R\}$. For the second set, we generated each specification randomly over the full syntax of LTL. We then checked if the generated specification represented a safety property using the SPOT command ltl2tgba -O, adding the specification to our test set if so and rejecting it if not.

Test Method. We encoded every benchmark LTL formula as a set of Promela never claims using SPOT and our novel encodings. We experimented with scheck [21] encodings; that tool produced too many bugs to be included. However, it is reasonable to assume that the results would not be comparable to our best encoding since the algorithm implemented by scheck constructs a nondeterministic finite automaton from the restricted closure of the formula that accepts precisely the informative prefixes of the formula and then determinizes as a last step without employing optimizations that we found particularly influential, such as minimization or edge abbreviation. Each never claim, was model checked by Spin.[4]

We measured model-checking time separately from the times for various compilation stages. This is important for two reasons. It is relevant for regression testing and system debugging applications where the system is repeatedly changed but model checked against the same specifications. It is also essential for demonstrating our claim that deterministic encoding of LTL safety formulas can reduce model-checking time; it is clear

---

[4] We also investigated using the SPOT back-end; SPOT is unable to analyze Promela never claims at the time of this writing.

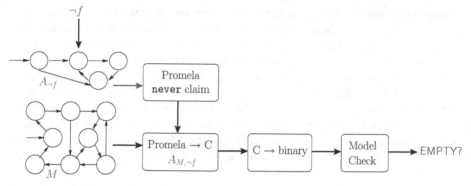

Fig. 1. System Diagram illustrating the Spin model checking process. We present an improved encoding for the LTL formula $\neg f$ to the Promela never claim $A_{\neg f}$.

that we are not, for example, encoding LTL formulas in a manner that compiles more quickly but requires the same or more time to model check than the equivalent SPOT-encoding.

Figure 1 depicts the Spin model checking process. Unlike previous works, which report only the total time required for analysis via Spin, we measure the time required for compilation of LTL-to-never claim (by either SPOT or CHIMP-Spin), never claim-to-C (via the spin command), and C-to-binary (via gcc) separately. In the following plots, we refer to the sum of these three times as *compile time* and separate this sum from from *model-checking time*, or the time required to run the pan executable produced by Spin. Because we ran SPOT as a step in the creation of each of our new encodings, the specification automaton generation times incurred by our algorithm will always be greater than running SPOT alone. (It is important to note that our automaton generation times are consistently dwarfed by the corresponding model-checking times.) To streamline regression testing, we argue that future versions of Spin should not require us to recompile never claims for each run of the model checker, even when they have not changed. Such an adjustment would more accurately reflect industrial applications of model checking and, combined with our reduced model-checking times, reduce the amortized cost of model checking.

5 Experimental Results

Our experiments demonstrate that the new Promela never claims we have introduced significantly improve the translation of LTL safety formulas into explicit automata, as measured by model-checking time. We found that one of our encodings is always best: front_det_switch_min_abr_ea_state_fin. Using this encoding, we can consistently improve on the model-checking time required for SPOT encodings. We recommend using our front_det_switch_min_abr_ea_state_fin encoding for safety formulas and the standard SPOT encoding for non-safety formulas. (Recall that SPOT can test for safety formulas.)

We found certain encoding aspects to be always better. This helps explain why the front_det_switch_min_abr_ea_state_fin encoding is always the fastest: it is the encoding that combines all of the fastest never claim components. We found the following trends to hold: deterministic (det) never claims are faster than determinized-on-the-fly (nondet) never claims; finite acceptance (fin) is faster than infinite acceptance (inf); state labels (state) are faster than state numbers (number); minimized automata (min) are faster than not (nomin); edge abbreviation (ea) always equates to better performance. Note that deterministic encoding (det) enables faster features such as state minimization and edge abbreviation and that, all other encoding aspects being equal, there seems to be a positive correlation between the code size of a given never claim and the required model-checking time, explaining the efficiency of this encoding. Also note that the (front_det_switch) encoding enables the faster state labels representation (state).

5.1 Model-Scaling Experimental Results

Figure 2 demonstrates empirically that our deterministic automata require less time to model check than SPOT's nondeterministic automata. For some benchmarks, we found that all of our encodings, whether they determinized $\mathcal{A}^d$ up front or on the fly, required less model-checking time than the equivalent nondeterministic SPOT never claims.[5] For example, for the iprot and sliding window benchmarks (formulas 12 and 13) pictured in Figures 2(a) and 2(b), all of our new encodings performed better than SPOT, though our front_det_switch_min_abr_ea_state_fin encoding was best. In these figures, the SPOT encoding is shown in red, our best encoding is shown in purple, and our 25 other encodings are shown in magenta. Note also that these plots demonstrate the orthogonality of automata size and model-checking time: all of our encodings represent the same automaton so the differences in model-checking times in these graphs stem entirely from the type of encoding and not the number of states in the automaton. Deterministic encodings can result in significant improvements in model-checking performance by reducing calls to the internal nested depth-first search algorithm in the model checker; see Appendix A.1.

Figure 3 shows a speedup of a factor of two when using our best CHIMP-Spin encoding to model check our 14-formula workload against a 34-variable UM. Since we terminated the plot when the first benchmark formula exceeded machine bounds, this plot does not show instances where our encoding was able to scale to larger model-checking benchmarks than the equivalent SPOT encoding. For example, Figure 2 demonstrates that our encoding was more scalable than SPOT's when model checking formulas 12 and 13.

Out of all of our benchmarks, the formula 4 benchmark displayed the smallest difference between our encoding and SPOT. For the 36-variable universal model, the SPOT never claim took 4606.94 seconds, or roughly 77 minutes whereas our never claim took 4281.22 seconds, or roughly 71 minutes Still, our front_det_switch_min_abr_ea_state_fin encoding encoding enabled Spin to scale to model check a 40-variable model whereas model checking the SPOT never claim timed out at 39 variables.

Since we call SPOT as a step in our encoding, our automaton generation times must always be higher than SPOT but compile times were consistently dwarfed by

---

[5] Note that not all SPOT never claims are nondeterministic; for other benchmarks SPOT produced deterministic never claims.

model-checking times. Our total compile times were comparable to SPOT for our model-scaling benchmarks. For the set of 14 safety formulas in our workload, when model checking against a 34-variable UM as shown in Figure 3, the sum of our compile times was 6.01 seconds (that breaks down into a sum of LTL-to-never claim times of 1.74 seconds, a sum of Promela-to-C times of 0.05 seconds, and a sum of C-to-binary times of 4.22 seconds), while the sum of our model-checking times was 122662.78 seconds. For SPOT encodings, the sum of compile times was 4.53 seconds (including a sum of LTL-to-never claim times of 0.14 seconds, a sum of Promela-to-C times of 0.06 seconds, and a sum of C-to-binary times of 4.33 seconds) with a sum of model-checking times of 225132.7 seconds. Note that the unix time command is not accurate to hundredths of a second so there is a potential for some error contributions in these sums.

5.2 Formula-Scaling Experimental Results

Figures 4(a) and 4(b) show the sums of the model checking times of randomly-generated safety formulas: completely randomly generated in Figure 4(a) and syntactically safe in Figure 4(b). Model-checking times summed over all non-trivial randomly-generated formulas for our best encoding were significantly lower than for SPOT encodings.

Since we call SPOT as a step in our encoding, our automaton generation times were always higher than SPOT but were consistently dwarfed by model-checking times. This trend holds for syntactically safe random formulas as well. See Figure 5.2.

BRICS Automaton experienced some errors when encoding some randomly-generated formulas. These were rare enough as to not significantly impact our timing results, i.e. for the set of 500 5-variable, 15-length random formulas in Figure 4(a), BRICS Automaton experienced nine errors. We summed data only for formulas where both the SPOT and CHIMP-Spin model-checking runs completed without an error or timeout.

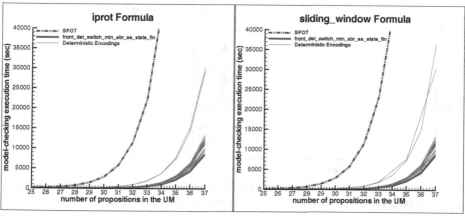

(a) Benchmarks for the iprot specification (for-mula 12).

(b) Benchmarks for the sliding window specification (formula 13).

Fig. 2. Model-scaling benchmarks, showing the model-checking times based on the number of propositions in the UM

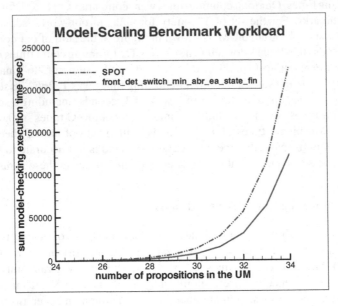

Fig. 3. Sums of the model-checking times for all model-scaling benchmark instances, based on the number of propositions in the UM

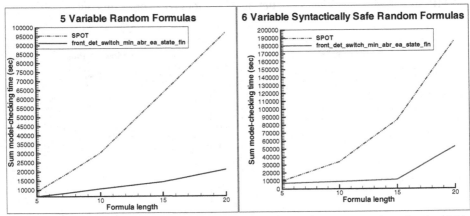

(a) Sum of model-checking times for 5 variable random formula benchmark.

(b) Sum of model-checking times for 6 variable syntactically safe benchmark.

Fig. 4. Graphs of sums of model-checking times for both categories of randomly-generated formulas, showing that our model-checking times were consistently lower than SPOT

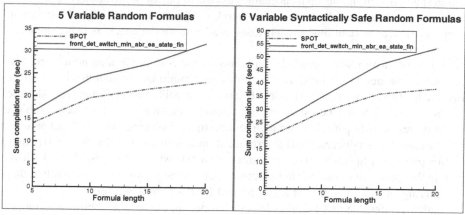

(a) Sum of compilation times for 5 variable ran-(b) Sum of compilation times for 6 variable syn-
dom formula benchmark.   tactically safe benchmark.

Fig. 5. Sums of compilation times for both categories of randomly-generated formulas, showing that compilation times were dwarfed by model-checking times. Note that the unix `time` command is not accurate to hundredths of a second; the times presented here may contain substantial error contributions. These graphs simply show that the sum of compile times over all formulas in a test set was always under a minute, for both SPOT and the best CHIMP-Spin encoding.

The difference in model-checking time is not directly correlated with other statistics we measured, such as the length of counterexamples returned for formula violations. Across all of the randomly-generated formulas, we found that the number of states and the lengths of counterexamples associated with our `front_det_switch_min_abr_ea_state_fin` never claims and with SPOT's were usually very close, within a few states of each other. In general, the number of transitions had a higher variance between these two encodings; in the median cases, we ended up with less than or equal to the number of transitions in the equivalent SPOT never claim.

6   Discussion

In this paper we brought attention to the benefit of deterministic compilation for safety LTL properties. We defined novel encodings of safety LTL properties as deterministic never claims and showed that one encoding consistently leads to faster model-checking times than the state-of-the-art SPOT encoding or any of our other new encodings. Therefore, we recommend a multiple-pronged property-compilation approach to the Spin model checker: use SPOT for the compilation of non-safety properties and use deterministic compilation with our new `front_det_switch_min_abr_ea_state_fin` encoding for safety properties. This approach is *extensible*; different encodings of never claims may be appropriate for different types of LTL formulas, see [29].

Determinizing never claims for safety properties up front, rather than on-the-fly, seems to have a major effect on model-checking performance. While either method of determinizing yields better performance due to the simpler structure of the product search space, determinizing up front enables the use of other optimizations that improve performance: state labels (rather than numbers), state minimization, edge abbreviation. There is also a consistent time savings associated with model checking using finite acceptance conditions.

In general, deterministic compilation is more time consuming than nondeterministic compilation due to the need to determinize and minimize, though this overhead is dwarfed by the improvements in model-checking time. Still, our experiment revealed the BRICS Automaton tool to be a slow link in our tool chain; improving this link is a subject for future research. In particular, we plan to investigate replacing the BRICS Automaton tool by (currently undocumented) determinization functions provided by SPOT. Also, for this paper we implemented our encoding as an extension of the CHIMP tool. However, in the future we would like to implement our best encoding more efficiently rather than relying on a modification of a tool created for a different purpose.

Finally, Kupferman and Lampert [18] developed an alternative approach to model checking of safety properties, which involves the construction of a nondeterministic finite-word automaton for bad prefixes. That approach may yield longer counterexamples, but it does not involve the theoretical additional exponential blow-up that is involved in the approached pursued here. A comparison with that approach is another subject for future research.

References

1. Alpern, B., Schneider, F.B.: Recognizing safety and liveness. Dist. Comp. 2, 117–126 (1987)
2. Armoni, R., Egorov, S., Fraer, R., Korchemny, D., Vardi, M.Y.: Efficient LTL compilation for SAT-based model checking. In: ICCAD, pp. 877–884. IEEE (2005)
3. Bryant, R.E.: Symbolic Boolean manipulation with Ordered Binary-Decision Diagrams. ACM Computing Surveys 24(3), 293–318 (1992)
4. d'Amorim, M., Roşu, G.: Efficient monitoring of ω-languages. In: Etessami, K., Rajamani, S.K. (eds.) CAV 2005. LNCS, vol. 3576, pp. 364–378. Springer, Heidelberg (2005)
5. Dong, Y., Du, X., Holzmann, G.J., Smolka, S.A.: Fighting livelock in the GNU i-protocol: a case study in explicit-state model checking. STTT 4(4), 505–528 (2003)
6. Duret-Lutz, A., Poitrenaud, D.: SPOT: An extensible model checking library using transition-based generalized Büchi automata. In: MASCOTS, pp. 76–83. IEEE (2004)
7. Eisner, C., Fisman, D., Havlicek, J., Lustig, Y., McIsaac, A., Van Campenhout, D.: Reasoning with temporal logic on truncated paths. In: Hunt Jr., W.A., Somenzi, F. (eds.) CAV 2003. LNCS, vol. 2725, pp. 27–39. Springer, Heidelberg (2003)
8. Emerson, E.A.: Temporal and modal logic. In: Handbook of Theoretical Computer Science, vol. B, ch. 16, pp. 997–1072. Elsevier, MIT Press (1990)
9. Geldenhuys, J., Hansen, H.: Larger automata and less work for LTL model checking. In: Valmari, A. (ed.) SPIN 2006. LNCS, vol. 3925, pp. 53–70. Springer, Heidelberg (2006)
10. Gerth, R., Peled, D., Vardi, M.Y., Wolper, P.: Simple on-the-fly automatic verification of Linear Temporal Logic. In: PSTV, pp. 3–18. Chapman & Hall (1995)
11. Havelund, K., Roşu, G.: Synthesizing monitors for safety properties. In: Katoen, J.-P., Stevens, P. (eds.) TACAS 2002. LNCS, vol. 2280, pp. 342–356. Springer, Heidelberg (2002)
12. Holzmann, G.J.: The model checker Spin. IEEE TSE 23(5), 279–295 (1997)
13. Holzmann, G.J.: The SPIN Model Checker: Primer and Reference Manual. Addison-Wesley (2003)

14. Hopcroft, J.E., Ullman, J.D.: Introduction to Automata Theory, Languages, and Computation. Addison-Wesley (1979)
15. Jategaonkar Jagadeesan, L., Puchol, C., Von Olnhausen, J.E.: Safety property verification of ESTEREL programs and applications to telecommunications software. In: Wolper, P. (ed.) CAV 1995. LNCS, vol. 939, pp. 127–140. Springer, Heidelberg (1995)
16. Kaivola, R.: Using compositional preorders in the verification of sliding window protocol. In: Grumberg, O. (ed.) CAV 1997. LNCS, vol. 1254, pp. 48–59. Springer, Heidelberg (1997)
17. Kamel, M., Leue, S.: Validation of a remote object invocation and object migration in CORBA GIOP using Promela/Spin. In: SPIN (1998)
18. Kupferman, O., Lampert, R.: On the construction of fine automata for safety properties. In: Graf, S., Zhang, W. (eds.) ATVA 2006. LNCS, vol. 4218, pp. 110–124. Springer, Heidelberg (2006)
19. Kupferman, O., Vardi, M.Y.: Model checking of safety properties. FMSD 19(3), 291–314 (2001)
20. Kupferman, O., Vardi, M.Y.: Weak alternating automata are not that weak. ACM TOCL 2(2), 408–429 (2001)
21. Latvala, T.: Efficient model checking of safety properties. In: Ball, T., Rajamani, S.K. (eds.) SPIN 2003. LNCS, vol. 2648, pp. 74–88. Springer, Heidelberg (2003)
22. Lynch, N.A.: Distributed Algorithms. Morgan Kaufmann Publishers Inc. (1996)
23. Møller, A.: dk.brics.automaton (2004), http://www.brics.dk/automaton/
24. Pelánek, R.: BEEM: Benchmarks for explicit model checkers. In: Bošnački, D., Edelkamp, S. (eds.) SPIN 2007. LNCS, vol. 4595, pp. 263–267. Springer, Heidelberg (2007)
25. Peterson, G.L.: Myths about the mutual exclusion problem. Inf. Process. Lett. 12(3), 115–116 (1981)
26. Plaku, E., Kavraki, L.E., Vardi, M.Y.: Falsification of LTL safety properties in hybrid systems. In: Kowalewski, S., Philippou, A. (eds.) TACAS 2009. LNCS, vol. 5505, pp. 368–382. Springer, Heidelberg (2009)
27. Rozier, K.Y., Vardi, M.Y.: LTL satisfiability checking. International Journal on Software Tools for Technology Transfer (STTT) 12(2), 123–137 (2010)
28. Safra, S.: On the complexity of ω-automata. In: FOCS, pp. 319–327 (1988)
29. Schneider, K.: Improving automata generation for linear temporal logic by considering the automaton hierarchy. In: Nieuwenhuis, R., Voronkov, A. (eds.) LPAR 2001. LNCS (LNAI), vol. 2250, pp. 39–54. Springer, Heidelberg (2001)
30. Sebastiani, R., Tonetta, S.: "More deterministic" vs. "Smaller" Büchi automata for efficient LTL model checking. In: Geist, D., Tronci, E. (eds.) CHARME 2003. LNCS, vol. 2860, pp. 126–140. Springer, Heidelberg (2003)
31. Tabakov, D., Rozier, K.Y., Vardi, M.Y.: Optimized temporal monitors for SystemC. Formal Methods in System Design 41(3), 236–268 (2012)
32. Vardi, M.Y.: From monadic logic to PSL. In: Avron, A., Dershowitz, N., Rabinovich, A. (eds.) Pillars of Computer Science. LNCS, vol. 4800, pp. 656–681. Springer, Heidelberg (2008)
33. Vardi, M.Y., Wolper, P.: An automata-theoretic approach to automatic program verification. In: Proc. 1st Symp. on Logic in Comp. Sci., Cambridge, pp. 332–344 (June 1986)
34. Vardi, M.Y., Wolper, P.: Reasoning about infinite computations. Information and Computation 115(1), 1–37 (1994)

FoREnSiC – An Automatic Debugging Environment for C Programs*

Roderick Bloem[1], Rolf Drechsler[2], Görschwin Fey[2], Alexander Finder[2],
Georg Hofferek[1], Robert Könighofer[1], Jaan Raik[3],
Urmas Repinski[3], and André Sülflow[2]

[1] Graz University of Technology, Austria
[2] University of Bremen, Germany
[3] Tallinn University of Technology, Estonia

Abstract. We present FoREnSiC, an open source environment for automatic error detection, localization and correction in C programs. The framework implements different automated debugging methods in a unified way covering the whole design flow from ESL to RTL. Currently, a scalable simulation-based back-end, a back-end based on symbolic execution, and a formal back-end exploiting functional equivalences between a C program and a hardware design are available. FoREnSiC is designed as an extensible framework. Its infrastructure, including a powerful front-end and interfaces to logic problem solvers, can be reused for implementing new program analysis or debugging methods. In addition to the infrastructure, the back-ends, and a few experimental results, we present an illustrative application scenario that shows FoREnSiC in use.

1 Introduction

Debugging incorrect programs is labor-intensive, frustrating, and costly, yet unavoidable in modern software and hardware development. Errors have to be detected, located and corrected. Many methods and tools exist to automate error detection, e.g., automatic test case generation or model checking. Error localization and correction are mostly done manually. At the same time, these are the most challenging steps. Understanding the program and tracking down errors is time-consuming. Bug fixes often do not consider special cases, have side-effects, or create new bugs. The need for further automation and tool support is obvious.

Existing tools and methods automate error localization and correction in different settings. An extension of the Tarantula fault localizer [10] with mutation-based repair is presented in [8]. Model-based diagnosis [13] has been applied in various settings already. A counterexample-based repair method is presented in [5]. Sketch [15] uses similar techniques for program sketching. Also, several approaches have been proposed to check equivalence between system-level specifications and

---

* This work was supported in part by the European Commission through project DIAMOND (FP7-2009-IST-4-248613), and by the Austrian Science Fund (FWF) through the national research network RiSE (S11406-N23).

A. Biere, A. Nahir, and T. Vos (Eds.): HVC 2012, LNCS 7857, pp. 260–265, 2013.

designs in *Hardware Description Language* (HDL), e.g. [6,16]. In contrast to our framework, these existing tools implement only one specific method in isolation. Refer to [11,12] for a more elaborate discussion of related work.

We present FoREnSiC, an automatic debugging environment for C programs. FoREnSiC is short for "**Fo**rmal **Re**pair **En**vironment for **Si**mple **C**", but it has already outgrown its name: it also detects and locates errors, and it applies also semi-formal and dynamic methods. FoREnSiC makes two main contributions.

First, it implements various debugging methods in different back-ends. They can be accessed in a unified way and provide different trade-offs between scalability and reasoning power. Currently, there are three back-ends. The *simulation-based back-end* [12] locates and repairs errors by executing the program on given test vectors, featuring good scalability. It is similar to [8], but uses techniques like program slicing to obtain better results. The *symbolic back-end* is based on symbolic execution and SMT-solving [11]. It uses model-based diagnosis [13] and a repair method similar to [15] and [5] (but with templates [7]) to synthesize repairing expressions. The *cut-based back-end* exploits functional equivalences between a C program and any HDL design for error localization and correction.

Second, FoREnSiC also serves as a framework for implementing new program analysis, verification, and debugging techniques. The infrastructure includes a GCC-based front-end to transform C programs into a graph-based representation. Moreover, FoREnSiC provides data structures to represent logic formulas and interfaces to logic solvers for solving them. FoREnSiC is available as open-source tool at http://www.informatik.uni-bremen.de/agra/eng/forensic.php.

This paper is organized as follows. Section 2 illustrates FoREnSiC on an example. Section 3 explains FoREnSiC's architecture, the internal model, the front-end, and the back-ends. Section 4 shows experimental results and Section 5 concludes.

2   Application Scenario

We demonstrate the features of FoREnSiC on the following scenario. Assume we want to implement an algorithm to compute the *Greatest Common Divisor* (GCD) of two integers. We start with the following draft program in C.

```
 1  unsigned gcd(unsigned u,        16      while((v & 1) == 0)
 2               unsigned v) {       17        v >>= 1;
 3    unsigned sh = 0, res;          18      if(u <= v) {
 4    if(u == 0 || v == 0) {         19        v += u;
 5      res = 0;                     20      } else {
 6      return res;                  21        unsigned diff = u - v;
 7    }                              22        u = v;
 8    while(((u | v) & 1) == 0) {    23        v = diff;
 9      u >>= 1;                     24      }
10      v >>= 1;                     25      v >>= 1;
11      ++sh;                        26    } while(v != 0);
12    }                              27    res = u << sh;
13    while((u & 1) == 0)            28    return res;
14      u >>= 1;                     29  }
15    do {
```

Now we want to verify the correctness of our program. We use FoREnSiC's symbolic back-end to compare it to the Euclidean algorithm, which serves as a reference. The back-end detects an error and automated debugging commences. First, error localization reports the "0" in line 5 as potentially faulty. Next, the back-end synthesizes the following expressions to substitute "0" with: u + v and 4294967295 & u | 4294967295 & v. The reason is clear: our program computes gcd(0,x) = gcd(x,0) = 0 for any x, but the result should be x instead. Replacing "0" with "u + v" fixes this bug. Since 4294967295 is 0xFFFFFFFF, the second suggestion is actually "u | v", which is correct as well. We can now decide which fix we prefer. The symbolic back-end took only 6 seconds to locate and fix this bug. When analyzing the revised program in more detail, the back-end detects another error but is unable to locate or fix it within reasonable time. Therefore, we now switch to the simulation-based back-end.

The simulation-based back-end performs simulation-based verification, diagnosis, and mutation-based repair. For our example, verification fails if enough test cases are provided. Thus, diagnosis starts by ranking statements according to their suspiciousness. In case of a single fault assumption (see Section 3.1), the fault candidates are those statements which occur in all failing test cases. Next, mutation-based repair is applied to one fault candidate after the other. Each mutated design is verified by simulation to check whether the mutation constitutes a repair. For our example, the back-end finds a fix after 149 mutations. The mutation that fixes the fault is the replacement of the assignment operator += in line 19 by -=. The two back-ends complement each other: while the simulation-based back-end had no difficulties debugging the second bug, it could not come up with the suggestions produced by the symbolic back-end for the first bug. The reason is that a mutation from 0 to u | v would be too far-fetched.

Assume that we now want to implement this algorithm in hardware. We use the cut-based back-end to verify equivalence between the HDL implementation and the C program serving as specification. The cut-based back-end implements a new verification, localization and repair method based on functional equivalences, so-called cutpoints, between two designs. For the equivalence check, the cut-based back-end determines corresponding output values in the two design descriptions automatically. Mismatches lead to counterexamples which are used to debug the HDL description or the C program respectively. The cut-based back-end localizes components in the design under debug to be replaced by corresponding ones from the reference to fix a bug. Alternatively, the counterexamples may be used as inputs for the simulation-based back-end for further debugging of the C program. The equivalence proof for the GCD example took 15 minutes, unrolling the hardware design for up to 78 time cycles.

3   Description of **FoREnSiC**

FoREnSiC consists of three functional parts: the front-end, the model, and the back-ends. Fig. 1 illustrates the architecture in a simplified form. A C program is the main input. The front-end parses it and builds an internal model in form of a flow graph representing the program in *Static Single Assignment* (SSA) form [1]. Each graph node represents a statement and is linked with its abstract syntax

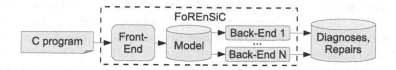

Fig. 1. The architecture of FoREnSiC

tree. All parts of the model have references to the original source code in terms of line and column numbers for communicating results to the user. The front-end is based on the GCC plug-in API, so that complete C/C++ is supported and upward compatibility is ensured. FoREnSiC also includes classes to represent logic formulas and interfaces to SMT-solvers. This yields an infrastructure such that FoREnSiC can be easily extended with new back-ends and features.

FoREnSiC currently contains three back-ends operating on the model. They implement different advanced debugging methods. The back-ends require different supplementary inputs such as test vectors or a reference model. Not all back-ends fully support all language features. For instance, the symbolic back-end cannot accurately reason about pointer arithmetic. However, our main focus are programs modeling hardware designs, where these advanced features do not play such an important role. Details can be found in the manual [3].

3.1 Simulation-Based Debugging

The simulation-based back-end [12] simulates the design to detect and fix faults. The specification can be given as input vectors together with either expected output responses or a reference program in C. In the latter case, both programs are simulated on the same inputs while comparing the outputs.

The back-end performs three steps. First, simulation-based verification is performed. Second, if an error is detected, statistical methods are used to determine fault candidates. In case of a single fault assumption, nodes in the model of the design are associated with the number of failing simulation runs in which they occurred. The nodes with the maximum numbers are reported as fault candidates. In case of a multiple fault assumption, candidates are selected using the method presented in [8]. Dynamic slicing is applied to discard candidates that do not influence the simulation result. Finally, mutation-based repair is applied to fix the error by mutating (i.e., modifying) operators and numbers, and checking if this renders the program correct. The types of mutations can be configured.

3.2 Symbolic Debugging

The symbolic back-end implements the debugging method of [11]. It uses `assert` statements as specification. Assertions also allow flexible comparisons with reference implementations. Debugging is performed in three steps. First, symbolic or concolic execution is used to compute a formula defining when the program satisfies the specification. The symbolic execution engine has been implemented from scratch, the concolic engine is based on CREST [4]. Both provide many options for configuring the thoroughness of the analysis. In the second step, the diagnosis engine computes potentially faulty components using model-based diagnosis [13]. Finally, the repair engine synthesizes new implementations of the faulty components using templates for expressions and iterative refinements which are guided by counterexamples [11]. Diagnosis and repair rely on SMT-solving. Currently, the solvers Yices and Z3 can be used with linear integer arithmetic and bit-vector arithmetic, either via their C-APIs or via SMT-LIBv2 [2].

3.3   Cut-Based Debugging

This back-end formally verifies the equivalence between a C program, taken as reference specification, and an implementation in HDL. In case of a mismatch, a counterexample is returned, and input stimuli similar to the counterexample are generated for simulation of both designs. After simulation, a frontier of functional equivalences within both designs is computed, i.e. parts of implementation and specification which are found to be equivalent. Starting at the frontier, components within the implementation are replaced by components from the specification. Each replacement is checked whether it leads to further functional equivalences between implementation and specification. If this is the case, the repair is verified formally. In case of inequivalence, the repair engine suggests which parts of the implementation may be replaced by which parts of the specification in order to achieve functionally equivalent designs. Diagnosis and repair rely on SAT-solving using MiniSat2 [9].

4   Experimental Results

We briefly compare our back-ends on the tcas benchmarks of the Siemens suite [14]. tcas implements a collision avoidance system for aircrafts, has 12 integer inputs, around 180 lines of code, and comes in 41 faulty variants. The simulation-based back-end fixes 26 versions, including 5 that cannot be solved with the symbolic back-end and 6 that cannot be solved with the cut-based back-end. The symbolic back-end fixes 23 versions, including 2 that cannot be solved with the simulation-based method and 5 that cannot be solved with the cutpoint-based back-end. The cutpoint-based back-end solves 29 versions, including 9 that cannot be solved with the simulation-based back-end and 11 that cannot be solved with the symbolic back-end. This demonstrates that the back-end complement each other. Due to space constraints, we refer to [11] and [12] for more experimental data. The FoREnSiC archive contains additional data.

5   Summary and Conclusion

FoREnSiC is a novel environment for automating error detection, location, and correction in C programs. The back-ends can be accessed in a unified way, and complement each other in features and characteristics. This makes FoREnSiC a powerful tool for reducing manual debugging effort. FoREnSiC is also interesting for developers as an open-source framework for new program analysis and debugging techniques. Using the existing infrastructure, the developer can focus on the new methods rather than parsing or interfacing solvers. By this, FoREnSiC can alleviate and stimulate further research and development in the challenging fields of automated hardware and software verification and debugging.

Future work includes improving the back-ends regarding performance, the subset of C that can be handled, and their fault models. Integrating back-ends more tightly, or combining their methods in a hybrid back-end is also planned.

References

1. Alpern, B., Wegman, M.N., Zadeck, F.K.: Detecting equality of variables in programs. In: POPL, pp. 1–11. ACM (1988)
2. Barrett, C., Stump, A., Tinelli, C.: The Satisfiability Modulo Theories Library, SMT-LIB (2010), http://www.SMT-LIB.org
3. Bloem, R., Drechsler, R., Fey, G., Finder, A., Hofferek, G., Könighofer, R., Raik, J., Repinski, U., Sülflow, A.: FoREnSiC - A Formal Repair Environment for Simple C (2011), http://www.informatik.uni-bremen.de/agra/eng/forensic.php
4. Burnim, J., Sen, K.: Heuristics for scalable dynamic test generation. In: ASE, pp. 443–446. IEEE (2008)
5. Chang, K.-H., Markov, I.L., Bertacco, V.: Fixing design error with counterexamples and resynthesis. In: ASP-DAC, pp. 944–949. IEEE (2007)
6. Clarke, E., Kroening, D., Yorav, K.: Behavioral consistency of C and Verilog programs using bounded model checking. In: DAC, pp. 368–371. ACM (2003)
7. Colón, M.A., Sankaranarayanan, S., Sipma, H.B.: Linear invariant generation using non-linear constraint solving. In: Hunt Jr., W.A., Somenzi, F. (eds.) CAV 2003. LNCS, vol. 2725, pp. 420–432. Springer, Heidelberg (2003)
8. Debroy, V., Wong, W.E.: Using mutation to automatically suggest fixes for faulty programs. In: ICST, pp. 65–74. IEEE (2010)
9. Eén, N., Sörensson, N.: An extensible SAT-solver. In: Giunchiglia, E., Tacchella, A. (eds.) SAT 2003. LNCS, vol. 2919, pp. 502–518. Springer, Heidelberg (2004)
10. Jones, J.A., Harrold, M.J.: Empirical evaluation of the Tarantula automatic fault-localization technique. In: ASE, pp. 273–282. ACM (2005)
11. Könighofer, R., Bloem, R.: Automated error localization and correction for imperative programs. In: FMCAD, pp. 91–100. FMCAD Inc. (2011)
12. Raik, J., Repinski, U., Hantson, H., Jenihhin, M., Di Guglielmo, G., Pravadelli, G., Fummi, F.: Combining dynamic slicing and mutation operators for ESL correction. In: ETS, pp. 1–6. IEEE (2012)
13. Reiter, R.: A theory of diagnosis from first principles. Artif. Intell. 32(1), 57–95 (1987)
14. Siemens Corporate Research. Siemens benchmark suite, http://pleuma.cc.gatech.edu/aristotle/Tools/subjects
15. Solar-Lezama, A., Tancau, L., Bodik, R., Saraswat, V., Seshia, S.A.: Combinatorial sketching for finite programs. In: ASPLOS, pp. 404–415. ACM (2006)
16. Vasudevan, S., Abraham, J.A., Viswanath, V., Tu, J.: Automatic decomposition for sequential equivalence checking of system level and RTL descriptions. In: MEMOCODE, pp. 71–80. IEEE (2006)

Towards Beneficial Hardware Acceleration in HAVEN: Evaluation of Testbed Architectures*

Marcela Šimková and Ondřej Lengál

Faculty of Information Technology, Brno University of Technology, Czech Republic
{isimkova,ilengal}@fit.vutbr.cz

Abstract. Functional verification is a widespread technique to check whether a hardware system satisfies a given correctness specification. As the complexity of modern hardware systems rises rapidly, it is a challenging task to find appropriate techniques for acceleration of this process. In our previous work, we developed HAVEN, an open verification framework that enables hardware acceleration of functional verification runs by moving the design under test (DUT) into a verification environment in a field-programmable gate array (FPGA). In the original version of HAVEN, the generator of input stimuli, the scoreboard and the transfer function still resided in a software simulator, and the peak acceleration ratio achieved was over 1,000. In the currently presented paper, we further extend HAVEN with hardware acceleration of the remaining parts of the verification environment. This enables the user to choose from several different testbed architectures which are evaluated and compared. We show that each architecture provides a different trade-off between the comfort of verification and the degree of acceleration. Using the highest degree of acceleration, we were able to achieve the speed-up in the order of hundreds of thousands while still being able to employ assertion and coverage analysis.

1 Introduction

Functional verification is a simulation-based technique which is typically used in the pre-silicon phase of the development cycle to verify not only functional aspects but also reliability and safety properties of hardware systems. Due to its ability to uncover the vast majority of design errors in a reasonable time and thus decrease the *time to market* of the developed product, functional verification has become the verification method of choice for many successful projects.

The main idea of functional verification is to *generate* a set of constrained-random test vectors and apply them to the verified system (called the *design under test*, or DUT) in a simulator. The observed response is then compared to the expected one as specified by a provided *transfer function*. In order to have a strong confidence in the correctness of the verified system, a high level of coverage of the system's state space needs to be achieved. This issue can be addressed in the following two ways: (*i*) to find a method how to generate test vectors that cover critical parts of the state space, and (*ii*)

---

* This work was supported by the Czech Science Foundation (project 102/09/H042), the Czech Ministry of Education (projects LD12036 and MSM 0021630528) and the BUT FIT projects FIT-S-11-1 and FIT-S-12-1. An extended version of this paper is available as the technical report [1].

A. Biere, A. Nahir, and T. Vos (Eds.): HVC 2012, LNCS 7857, pp. 266–273, 2013.

to maximise the number of the vectors tested. Simulation-based pre-silicon verification approaches including functional verification provide verifiers and designers with great comfort while debugging a failing component, checking formal assertions or performing coverage analysis.

Because of the limitation in the speed of software simulation, even with a high effort devoted to the pre-silicon verification, some previously uncovered functional errors are recognised only after the system is manufactured. In order to eliminate as many remaining bugs as possible before the target device is fabricated, verification is currently applied even in the post-silicon phase of the development cycle when a prototype running at the frequency close to that of the target device is available [3].

In recent years, several approaches that addressed the issue of performance of pre-silicon verification appeared. The first approach discussed in [4,5,6] translates VHDL or Verilog testbenches, which contain not directly synthesisable behavioural constructs, using advanced synthesis techniques into the synthesisable subset of the corresponding language. Note that these techniques are limited since some of the non-synthesisable constructs, such as reading from a file or evaluation of recursive functions, still cannot be synthesised. With the advent of higher-level *hardware verification languages* (HVLs) for writing testbenches, with SystemVerilog being the most prominent, automatic synthesis of testbenches that use advanced features, such as *constrained-random stimulus generation*, *coverage-driven* and *assertion-based* verification, has become even more infeasible.

However, soon after the introduction of HVLs, several *transaction-based* methodologies emerged, e.g. SystemVerilog-based VMM, OVM, and UVM. These methodologies use higher-level of abstraction and group sequences of stimuli applied to the DUT into *transactions* that are delivered to drivers of the DUT. Then it is possible to accelerate the performance of a testbench by dividing the testbench into the synthesised part (including the drivers) that is placed in a hardware emulator, and the behavioural part that runs on a CPU, such that the two parts communicate using simple channels. Solutions that use emulators to accelerate functional verification has been provided by major companies that focus on tools for hardware verification. Examples of these emulator-based solutions are Mentor Graphics' Veloce2 technology [7] and Cadence's TBA [8] that use emulators running on frequencies in the order of MHz. Synopsys [11] provide solution for prototyping of ASICs based on *field-programmable gate arrays* (FPGAs). A similar approach is taken by Huang *et al* [9]; their proposal is also to place the DUT with necessary components in an FPGA, and in addition provide limited observability of the DUT's signals. Nevertheless, to the best of our knowledge, there is currently still no available working implementation based on their proposal. Unfortunately, we could not perform a detailed comparison of these solutions as they are not available to us.

The authors of [3] relate pre-silicon and post-silicon verification in terms of achieving *coverage closure*. Instead of observing values of internal signals, the approach presented for post-silicon verification observes the behaviour of a post-silicon exerciser (which is not given by a set of test vectors but rather by a test template) in the pre-silicon simulation environment and determines the probability of the exerciser hitting certain cover points in a given number of clock cycles.

We focus our research on bridging the gap between pre- and post-silicon verification using hardware acceleration with functional verification features. In [2], we introduced **HAVEN** (**H**ardware-**A**ccelerated **V**erification **EN**vironment), an open framework[1] for hardware-accelerated functional verification of hardware that tackles the bottleneck of the simulation speed of a DUT by moving the DUT into a verification environment in an FPGA. Using this solution, we were able to achieve the speed-up of over 1,000.

In the currently presented paper, we describe the new features added to HAVEN in order to support seamless transition from pre- to post-silicon verification using several architectures of the verification testbed. The user can start with the pure software version of the functional verification environment to debug base system functions and discover the main bulk of errors. Later, when the simulation cannot find any new bugs in a reasonable time, the user can start to incrementally move some parts of the verification environment from software to hardware, with each step obtaining a different trade-off between the acceleration ratio and the debugging comfort.

The rest of the paper is structured as follows. In Section 2, we give a detailed description of the main features of HAVEN. In Section 3 we propose several architectures of the HAVEN testbed and in Section 4 we evaluate them using a set of experiments. Section 5 concludes the paper and gives directions for future work.

2   The HAVEN Verification Framework

HAVEN [2] is a SystemVerilog verification framework that allows to speed up functional verification runs using an FPGA-based accelerator. The DUT that is being verified is synthesised and placed into a testbed in the FPGA, and generated transactions are passed to the accelerator instead of the model of the DUT in the software simulator. The cycle accuracy is maintained in the accelerator so that a failed accelerated verification run can be easily reproduced in the perfect debug environment of the simulator. In order to be able to detect a violation of expected internal behaviour, protocols' specifications, etc., and debug a failing component directly in hardware, HAVEN enables to connect *assertion checkers* and *signal observers* that check validity of assertions and observe values of internal signals and display them as waveforms.

Using the solution presented in [2], we were able to achieve the acceleration ratio of over 140 when we included the time for generation of test vectors in software and over 1,000 when we did not include it (for pre-generated test vectors). During the evaluation, we observed that the main performance bottlenecks were generation of constrained-random transactions, maintaining transactions in the scoreboard and comparing them to the outputs of the DUT. In this paper, we address these issues and extend HAVEN with even better support for hardware acceleration by providing hardware implementations of the following components of the verification environment:

Hardware Generator. The Hardware Generator consists of a random number generator (we used the fast hardware implementation of the Mersenne Twister from [10] which provides a random vector in each clock cycle) and an adapter to the desired format with a constraint solver. The generator seed as well as parameters of transactions can be set from the simulator using a configuration interface.

---

[1] http://www.fit.vutbr.cz/~isimkova/haven/

Hardware Scoreboard. Compares data from the DUT and the Transfer Function unit.

Transfer Function. Hardware implementation of a transfer function depends on the verified component and can be performed in several ways. For components with an already existing reference hardware implementation, we can use this as the transfer function. If only a software implementation of the transfer function is available, it is possible to use a soft processor core and run the function on the processor.

Coverage Monitor. In order to be able to guarantee reaching coverage closure in larger designs, the Coverage Monitor may be used to check whether given points of the DUT's state space have been covered. The component is connected to the wires which are to be checked and periodically sends the information about triggered cover points to the simulator. Since this component uses a register for every cover point, it is recommended for monitoring coverage of so far not covered points only.

3 Architectures of HAVEN

In this section we show how the components presented in the previous section may be (together with the components from [2]) assembled to create several different testbed architectures, each suitable for a different use case and a different phase of the overall verification process. We start our description with the non-accelerated version running solely in the simulator and proceed by moving components of the verification environment into hardware in several steps.

Software Version (SW-FULL). All components of the verification environment are in the software simulator (Fig. 1). The Software Generator produces input transactions which are propagated to the Software Driver and further supplied on the input interface of the DUT. Copies of transactions are sent to the Software Scoreboard where the expected output is computed using a reference transfer function. The Software Monitor drives the output interface of the DUT and sends received output transactions also to the Software Scoreboard to be compared to the expected ones.

Hardware Generator Version (HW-GEN). The architecture is similar to the **SW-FULL** version with the exception of the Hardware Generator and the Constraint Solver, which are placed in the FPGA and send generated transactions to the simulator.

Hardware DUT Version (HW-DUT). In this architecture (Fig. 2), the Software Generator sends input transactions to the verification environment in hardware. In addition, a copy of every transaction is passed to the Software Scoreboard for further comparison. The Hardware Driver and the Hardware Monitor fulfill the same functions as their counterparts in the **SW-FULL** version, but they drive the input and output interfaces of the DUT running in the FPGA. The output transactions produced by the DUT are directed from the Hardware Monitor to the Software Scoreboard.

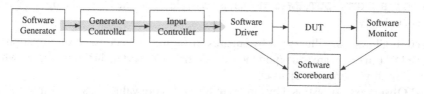

Fig. 1. Software version (**SW-FULL**)

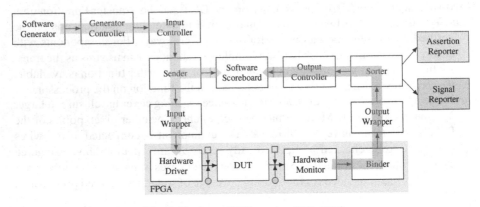

Fig. 2. Hardware DUT version (**HW-DUT**)

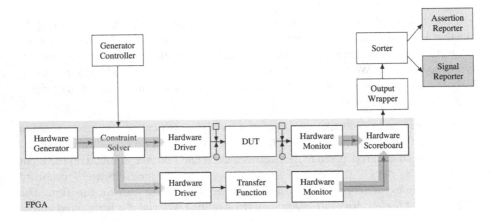

Fig. 3. Hardware version (**HW-FULL**)

Hardware Generator and DUT Version (HW-GEN-DUT). This architecture is similar to the **HW-DUT** version but the generator is in hardware, as in **HW-GEN**.

Hardware Version (HW-FULL). All core components of the verification environment in this architecture (Fig. 3) reside in the FPGA. The components in the software only set constraints for the Constraint Solver and report assertion failures, coverage statistics, or display waveforms of signals from hardware components.

For those architectures of the HAVEN testbed that place the DUT into the FPGA (**HW-DUT, HW-GEN-DUT, HW-FULL**), it is possible to use the following optional components in hardware:

Assertion Checkers. (illustrated by squares in figures) detect assertion violations of the DUT in hardware and report them to Assertion Reporters in the simulator, which in turn display them to the user.

Signal Observers. (illustrated by circles in figures) store values of signals in hardware and send them to Signal Reporters in the simulator to be displayed as waveforms.

Coverage Monitors. check coverage as described in Section 2.

Table 1. Results of experiments: times for verifying 100,000 transactions (in seconds)

Component	FIFO	HGEN	HGEN×2	HGEN×4	HGEN×8	HGEN×16
SW-FULL	199.	319.	1,126.	1,617.	2,539.	5,650.
HW-GEN	268.	308.	1,101.	1,984.	3,274.	7,534.
HW-DUT	65.	45.	48.	48.	48.	48.
HW-GEN-DUT	74.	22.	12.	12.	13.	13.
HW-FULL	0.0148	0.0205	0.0205	0.0239	0.0341	0.0410

Table 2. Results of experiments: acceleration ratios

Component	FIFO	HGEN	HGEN×2	HGEN×4	HGEN×8	HGEN×16
HW-GEN	0.743	1.036	1.023	0.815	0.776	0.750
HW-DUT	3.062	7.089	23.458	33.688	52.896	117.708
HW-GEN-DUT	2.689	14.500	93.833	134.750	195.308	434.615
HW-FULL	13,429.	15,564.	54,925.	67,626.	74,347.	137,875.

4 Evaluation

We performed a set of experiments using an acceleration card with the Xilinx Virtex-5 FPGA supporting fast communication through the PCIe bus in a PC with two quad-core Intel Xeon E5620@2.40 GHz processors and 24 GiB of RAM, and Mentor Graphics' ModelSim SE-64 10.0c as the simulator. We evaluated the performance of the architectures of HAVEN presented in the previous section on several hardware components: a simple FIFO buffer and several versions of a hash generator (HGEN) which computes the hash value of input data, each version with a different level of parallelism (2, 4, 8, and 16 units connected in parallel)[2].

For each of the components, Table 1 gives the wall-clock time it took to verify the component for 100,000 input transactions for each architecture of the HAVEN testbed (because of issues with precise measurements of the time for the **HW-FULL** architecture, for this case we measured the time it took to verify the component for 1,000,000,000 input transactions and computed the average time for 100,000 transactions). Table 2 in turn shows the acceleration ratio of each of the architectures of the HAVEN testbed against the **SW-FULL** architecture.

We can observe several facts from the experiments. First, they confirm that the time of simulation (**SW-FULL**) increases with the complexity of the verified DUT, so it is not feasible to simulate complex designs for large numbers of transactions. Second, we can observe that it is not reasonable to use the simulator with hardware acceleration of the transaction generator only (**HW-GEN**), at least for simple input protocols, which is the case of our protocol. In this case, the overhead of communication with the accelerator is too high. However, for the case when the DUT is also in hardware (**HW-GEN-DUT**),

---

[2] Further details about the components and the experiments can be found in [1].

hardware generation of transactions is (with the exception of the FIFO unit) advantageous compared to software generation (**HW-DUT**). Lastly, we can observe that the major speed-up of the hardware version (**HW-FULL**) makes this version preferable to use for very large amounts of transactions, e.g. when trying to reach coverage closure. Running verification of HGEN×16 for a billion transactions, which took less than 7 minutes in this version, would take more than 21 months in the **SW-FULL** version.

5 Conclusions and Future Research

In this paper, several extensions of the HAVEN verification framework were presented. These extensions allow the user to incrementally move parts of a verification environment into an FPGA-based accelerator and thus accelerate the verification process. Several architectures of the HAVEN testbed allow the user to choose the most suitable version for the preferred trade-off between acceleration ratio and debugging capabilities. The best speed-up achieved in our experiments for the case that used the **HW-FULL** testbed was over 100,000 while still performing assertion and coverage analysis.

In the future, we wish to extend HAVEN with a technique to automatically drive generation of test vectors to target coverage holes given by continuously measured coverage information. As a result, we expect to obtain a set of input test vectors or settings of the software generator which would achieve a high level of coverage in regression testing. These could also be used in the hardware generator, thus improving its ability of reaching coverage closure. Such generators might also be useful in post-silicon validation as they are closer to the speed of real hardware. A challenging direction is to develop a technique for representation of triggered cover points that would be feasible to be used in hardware Coverage Monitors for a large amount of cover points, as the currently used technique does not scale well. In addition, our future effort will lead also to the integration of HAVEN into various research areas, especially into diagnostics, where we wish to explore the capability of functional verification to improve the quality of fault-tolerant systems. Collaboration on any of these issues is welcome.

References

1. Šimková, M., Lengál, O.: Towards Beneficial Hardware Acceleration in HAVEN: Evaluation of Testbed Architectures. Technical Report FIT-TR-2012-03, FIT BUT (2012), http://www.fit.vutbr.cz/~ilengal/pub/FIT-TR-2012-03.pdf
2. Šimková, M., Lengál, O., Kajan, M.: HAVEN: An Open Framework for FPGA-Accelerated Functional Verification of Hardware. In: Eder, K., Lourenço, J., Shehory, O. (eds.) HVC 2011. LNCS, vol. 7261, pp. 247–253. Springer, Heidelberg (2012)
3. Adir, A., Nahir, A., Ziv, A., Meissner, C., Schumann, J.: Reaching Coverage Closure in Post-silicon Validation. In: Barner, S., Kroening, D., Raz, O. (eds.) HVC 2010. LNCS, vol. 6504, pp. 60–75. Springer, Heidelberg (2011)
4. Henftling, R., Zinn, A., Bauer, M., Zambaldi, M., Ecker, W.: Re-Use-Centric Architecture for a Fully Accelerated Testbench Environment. In: Proc. of DAC 2003, pp. 372–375. ACM (2003)
5. Kakoee, M.R., Riazati, M., Mohammadi, S.: Generating RTL Synthesizable Code from Behavioral Testbenches for Hardware-Accelerated Verification. In: Proc. of DSD 2008, pp. 714–720. IEEE (2008)

6. Kim, Y.-I., Kyung, C.-M.: Automatic Translation of Behavioral Testbench for Fully Accelerated Simulation. In: Proc. of ICCAD 2004, pp. 218–221. IEEE (2004)
7. Mentor Graphics. Veloce2 (2012),
   http://www.mentor.com/products/fv/emulation-systems/veloce/
8. Cadence. Transaction-based Acceleration, TBA (2012),
   http://www.cadence.com/products/sd/pages/transactionacc.aspx
9. Huang, C.-Y., Yin, Y.-F., Hsu, C.-J., Huang, T.B., Chang, T.M.: SoC HW/SW Verification and Validation. In: Proc. of ASPDAC 2011. IEEE (2011)
10. HT-LAB. Mersenne Twister, MT32: Pseudo Random Number Generator for Xilinx FPGA (2007), http://www.ht-lab.com/freecores/mt32/mersenne.html
11. Synopsys. FPGA-Based Prototyping (2012),
    http://www.synopsys.com/Systems/FPGABasedPrototyping/Pages/default.aspx

Using Domain Specific Languages
to Support Verification in the Railway Domain

Phillip James, Arnold Beckmann, and Markus Roggenbach

Swansea University, UK

Abstract. We explore the support of automatic verification via careful design of a domain specific language (DSL) in the context of algebraic specification. Formally a DSL is a loose specification the logical closure of which we regard as implicitly encoded "domain knowledge". We systematically exploit this "domain knowledge" for automatic verification. We illustrate these ideas within the Railway Domain using the algebraic specification language CASL and an existing DSL, designed by Bjørner, for modelling railways. Empirical evidence to the benefit of our approach is given in the form of the successful automatic verification of four railway track plans of real world complexity.

1 Introduction

For many years, verification based on techniques such as model checking or interactive theorem proving has been successful in various industrial case studies, e.g., see [10,4,6]. However, the use of formal methods within industry is still limited as it often requires verification experts. Domain specific languages [3] aim to abstract away technical details from the user. Classically, DSLs allow non-experts to create programs or specifications. In the context of *programming*, additional motivation for using DSLs includes *improved tool support*, improved ease of use, and increased productivity. Here we demonstrate, for algebraic *specification*, an approach where DSLs within the railway domain aid *verification*.

We suggest the following approach: Given a DSL for a particular class of systems and a set of decidable properties one is interested in, the DSL can be systematically extended to allow for automatic verification. We claim that the principles underlying this extension are universal, i.e., can be applied whenever one designs or adapts a DSL for verification. The overall aim of our approach is to develop a "push button" verification process for critical systems.

To illustrate this approach, we take an established DSL from Bjørner [1] and formalize it in the algebraic specification language CASL [9]. This allows connections with modern theorem proving technology via the Heterogeneous Toolset (HeTS) [8]. We then extend the DSL for automatic proof support. Finally, we give strong empirical evidence that our approach works by modelling and verifying four track plans provided by our industrial partner Invensys Rail.

Concretely, we demonstrate that we can exploit features of Bjørner's DSL to allow automatic verification of safety properties, e.g., routes that share railway components can not be open at the same time. To gain these results, we

A. Biere, A. Nahir, and T. Vos (Eds.): HVC 2012, LNCS 7857, pp. 274–275, 2013.

show that Bjørner's DSL (1) contains inherent structure allowing property specific abstraction and lifting of domain models and (2) is rich enough to prove suitable domain specific lemmas over such property specific abstractions. This demonstrates that domain specific languages can be designed to support automatic verification. To the best of our knowledge, we are the first to consider and formulate such a methodology for designing DSLs aimed at verification [7]. The underlying general principles we present include domain specific abstraction, domain specific property lifting and systematic property support. The result of this work is a step towards a platform for creating domain specific languages with effective automatic verification support for domain engineers.

1.1 Related Work

Various formal methods have been applied to railway verification. These include approaches using process algebraic modelling and verification in CSP [10], algebraic specification with ASF+SDF [4] and model-oriented specification using the B method, where, for example in [2] several lines of the Paris Metro system were verified. Finally, of close relevance to this work is the development environment for verification of railway control systems created by Haxthausen and Peleska [5]. This environment includes a DSL allowing modelling of control systems, and an automatic translation from models described in this DSL to executable control programs. At each level of production, various safety checking steps are taken.

References

1. Bjørner, D.: Dynamics of Railway Nets: On an Interface between Automatic Control and Software Engineering. In: CTS 2003 (2003)
2. Boulanger, J., Gallardo, M.: Validation and verification of METEOR safety software. In: Allen, J., Hill, R.J., Brebbia, C.A., Sciutto, G., Sone, S. (eds.) Computers in Railways VII, vol. 7, pp. 189–200. WIT Press (2000)
3. Fowler, M.: Domain Specific Languages. Addison-Wesley (2010)
4. Groote, J.F., van Vlijmen, S., Koorn, J.: The Safety Guaranteeing System at Station Hoorn-Kersenboogerd. Technical report. Utrecht University (1995)
5. Haxthausen, A., Peleska, J.: A domain-oriented, model-based approach for construction and verification of railway control systems. In: Jones, C.B., Liu, Z., Woodcock, J. (eds.) Formal Methods and Hybrid Real-Time Systems. LNCS, vol. 4700, pp. 320–348. Springer, Heidelberg (2007)
6. James, P., Roggenbach, M.: Automatically verifying railway interlockings using SAT-based model checking. In: Bendisposto, J., Leuschel, M., Roggenbach, M. (eds.) AVoCS 2010, vol. 35. ECEASST (2010)
7. James, P., Roggenbach, M.: Designing domain specific languages for verification: First steps. In: Hofner, P., McIver, A., Struth, G. (eds.) ATE 2011, vol. 760. CEUR (2011)
8. Mossakowski, T., Maeder, C., Lüttich, K.: The Heterogeneous Tool Set, HETS. In: Grumberg, O., Huth, M. (eds.) TACAS 2007. LNCS, vol. 4424, pp. 519–522. Springer, Heidelberg (2007)
9. Mosses, P.D. (ed.): CASL Reference Manual. LNCS, vol. 2960. Springer, Heidelberg (2004)
10. Winter, K.: Model checking railway interlocking systems. Australian Computer Science Communications 24, 303–310 (2002)

From Fault Injection to Mutant Injection: The Next Step for Safety Analysis?

Guillermo Rodriguez-Navas[1], Patrick Graydon[1], and Iain Bate[1,2]

[1] Dept. of Engineering, Design and Technology. Mälardalen University, Sweden
guillermo.rodriguez-navas@mdh.se, patrick.graydon@mdh.se
[2] Dept. of Computer Science. University of York, UK
iain.bate@cs.york.ac.uk

Abstract. Mutation testing has been used to assess test suite coverage, and researchers have proposed adapting the idea for other uses. Safety kernels allow the use of untrusted software components in safety-critical applications: a trusted software safety kernel detects undesired behavior and takes remedial action. We propose to use specification mutation, model checking, and model-based testing to verify safety kernels for component-based, safety-critical computer systems.

Keywords: Safety-critical systems, safety analysis, mutation testing, component based design.

1 Introduction

Mutation testing has been used to assess test suites [1]. Test software applies *mutation operators* to the software, creating mutant versions with known forms of implementation faults. The more mutants a given test suite detects, the more confidence we can have in the tested software. Researchers have applied mutation to specifications, interfaces, and contracts to assess coverage of faults introduced in the specification and design phases. Safety researchers have even suggested mutations based on Hazard and Operability studies (HAZOP) [2].

Software components are frequently used out of context. However, it is not possible to verify a component for adequately safe use in all possible contexts and applications [3]. Thus, safety-critical, component-based software systems must tolerate unexpected behavior from components re-used out of context.

Safety kernels permit using untrusted software components—such as COTS or SOUP—in safety-critical applications [4]. The trusted safety kernel wraps the untrusted component, detects undesired behavior, and takes remedial action as appropriate. For example, a safety kernel might detect a postcondition violation, restart the offending component, and flag its output as potentially erroneous.

Model checking allows the exploration of whether certain key properties of the system hold, e.g. those enforced by the safety kernel. When combined with mutation testing, we can ascertain whether the key safety properties hold in the presence of failures which is important when assuring the safety and dependability of critical systems. Despite the model being used being an abstract form

A. Biere, A. Nahir, and T. Vos (Eds.): HVC 2012, LNCS 7857, pp. 276–277, 2013.

of the final system, it allows the subsequent development steps to be de-risked and provide invaluable evidence as to the ability of the safety kernel to prevent hazards. Finally, model-based testing will validate the implementation.

2   Our Approach

Verifying the safety kernel specification. We assume: (a) a specification of each component and its functional and temporal behavior, e.g. in EAST-ADL with suitable extensions; (b) a specification of the safety kernel's behavior; and (c) a specification at the system level of the hazardous conditions to avoid. Our challenge is to verify that *if* the safety kernel behaves as specified, no plausible single failure of a wrapped component will put the system into a hazardous state.

Validating the safety kernel implementation. It is possible that the safety kernel will be faulty. This is true even if it is automatically generated from a correct specification: compilers and other tools might be buggy. Our challenge here is to automatically generate test cases to validate the implemented safety kernel. We have identified three test mechanisms: (1) mutating the wrapped components' code (if available); (2) modifying values passing through framework communication channels (where applicable); and (3) generating stub components.

Research challenges. First challenge is extending the nominal behavior of the components with both a set of plausible failures and their corresponding repair mechanisms. Second challenge is to automatically link these new potential behaviors with the specified safety kernel. Third challenge is introducing some kind of behavioral propagation of failures into the models, not based on transformation rules but on the real evolution of the components. Our ambition is to be able to introduce all these features directly into the timed automata models with as little user intervention as possible. The challenges associated to the validation of the implementation will be studied during a second phase of this work.

Acknowledgment. This work was partially supported by the Swedish Foundation for Strategic Research (SSF), under grant number RIT10-0070 (SYNOPSIS).

References

1. Jia, Y., Harman, M.: An analysis and survey of the development of mutation testing. IEEE Transactions on Software Engineering 37(5), 649–678 (2011)
2. Araujo, R., Maldonado, J., Delamaro, M., Vincenzi, A., Delebecque, F.: Devising mutant operators for dynamic systems models by applying the HAZOP study. In: Proc. of the 6th Int'l Conference on Software Engineering Advances (2011)
3. Rushby, J.: Modular certification. Technical Report CR-2002-212130, National Aeronautics and Space Administration, Hampton, VA, USA (December 2002)
4. Wika, K.G., Knight, J.C.: On the enforcement of software safety policies. In: Systems Integrity, Software Safety and Process Security: Proceedings of the 10th Annual Conference on Computer Assurance (COMPASS), pp. 83–93 (June 1995)

Test Case Generation by Grammar-Based Fuzzing for Model-Driven Engineering*

Magdalena Widl

Knowledge-based Systems Group, Vienna University of Technology, Austria
widl@kr.tuwien.ac.at

1 Introduction

Software models, traditionally used mainly for documentation and informal specification purposes, are becoming first-class development artifacts in the area of Model-driven Engineering (MDE). In MDE, code is generated automatically from multi-view models described in languages like the Unified Modeling Language (UML).[1] Maintaining consistency between the different views of a model is crucial for the generation of correct code. As software models undergo evolution, particularly in cooperative development environments, tool support for evolution tasks like versioning and merging is indispensable. It is important to thoroughly test such tools in order to avoid the introduction of inconsistent models. However, real-life test cases that cover sufficient evolution scenarios are difficult to obtain. We therefore suggest a method to generate artificial scenarios to facilitate fuzz testing of model evolution tools. In previous work [2] we presented an approach to merge concurrently evolved sequence diagrams with respect to the behavior modeled in their corresponding state machines view. We described the *sequence diagram merging* (SDM) problem formally, suggested a method to solve this problem, and implemented a prototype based on the EMF framework.[2] As there were no benchmarks available, we manually created a set of test cases. However, this is a very cumbersome testing method particularly when a good coverage is needed. A set of randomly generated instances solves this problem, as we show in the following.

2 Grammar-Based Fuzzing of Model Evolution Scenarios

Fuzz testing is a black-box software testing technique based on large amounts of randomized input data and has been successfully applied in many areas, e.g. in error detection for UNIX applications [1]. We propose to create randomly generated sequence diagrams and state machines based on a language definition given as metamodel and on a formal specification of the dependencies between the two views. Sequence diagrams model possible communication scenarios between different instances of state machines. A sequence diagram is *correct* if the messages are totally ordered and the sequence of

---

* This work was supported by by the Vienna Science and Technology Fund (WWTF) through project ICT10-018.
[1] http://www.omg.org/spec/UML/
[2] http://www.eclipse.org/modeling/emf/

A. Biere, A. Nahir, and T. Vos (Eds.): HVC 2012, LNCS 7857, pp. 278–279, 2013.

received message symbols on each lifeline occurs as path of triggers in the state machine that models its behavior (cf. definitions given in [2]). Based on the Ecore implementation of the multi-view metamodel presented in [2], we first create a state machine view as a set of state machines. Using this view, we create a correct sequence diagram that instantiates the state machines with its lifelines. The number of state machines, upper and lower bounds for the number of both states and transitions, the number of messages, and the number of lifelines are defined as input parameters. The generation of states, transitions, transition labels and the assignment of state machines to lifelines is done at random. When generating the message sequence of a sequence diagram, the following restriction is required to ensure its correctness: the symbol of each message must continue a path of triggers in the state machine modeling the behavior of the lifeline that receives the message. Hence only symbols can be considered that occur on outgoing transitions of states to which the previous message symbol has led. Out of these symbols, one is chosen randomly. We can also generate evolutionary changes to the models: a versioning scenario of a sequence diagram is created by copying the diagram and adding messages.

Using this approach, we generated 100 instances of the SDM problem with different parameter settings to find errors in and to assess the scalability of our approach presented in [2]. These tests helped us to find some minor implementation errors and one error in the algorithm solving the SDM problem. With the random instances being much larger than the manual ones, we could also easily identify a performance bottleneck in the first version of the implementation. The errors were not found by using the handcrafted instances because their detection required a certain combination of lifelines and message sequences that does not occur often and is not naturally thought of by a human. The detected errors resulted in merged sequence diagrams that were inconsistent with the set of state machines.

3   Conclusion and Future Work

We proposed to use a grammar-based fuzzing approach for testing and evaluating MDE tools. This has shown to be very effective in detecting errors in our implementation of an algorithm for the SDM problem. While being specific to a metamodel in our implementation, our approach can be easily adapted to a different Ecore metamodel and thus serve to test different MDE tools. Depending on particular test cases some adaptations may be useful. For instance, to test the SDM problem, instances that actually have a solution (a correctly merged sequence diagram) are desirable. This could be done by first generating a sequence diagram that represents the solution, and then infer an instance (an original and two modified diagrams) from it.

References

1. Miller, B., Koski, D., Pheow, C., Maganty, L.V., Murthy, R., Natarajan, A., Steidl, J.: Fuzz revisited: A re-examination of the reliability of unix utilities and services. Technical Report CS-TR-1995-1268, University of Wisconsin (1995)
2. Widl, M., Biere, A., Brosch, P., Egly, U., Heule, M., Kappel, G., Seidl, M., Tompits, H.: Guided merging of sequence diagrams. In: Czarnecki, K., Hedin, G. (eds.) SLE 2012. LNCS, vol. 7745, pp. 164–183. Springer, Heidelberg (2013), http://modelevolution.org/publications/sle12.pdf

Author Index